MODALITY

# Modality

*Metaphysics, Logic, and Epistemology*

Edited by
BOB HALE AND AVIV HOFFMANN

OXFORD
UNIVERSITY PRESS

# OXFORD

UNIVERSITY PRESS

Great Clarendon Street, Oxford OX2 6DP

Oxford University Press is a department of the University of Oxford.
It furthers the University's objective of excellence in research, scholarship,
and education by publishing worldwide. Oxford is a registered trade mark of
Oxford University Press in the UK and in certain other countries

British Library Cataloguing in Publication Data
Data available

Library of Congress Cataloging in Publication Data
Library of Congress Control Number: 2009942574

ISBN 978–0–19–956581–8 (Hbk.)
ISBN 978–0–19–967150–2 (Pbk.)

# Contents

## II. EPISTEMOLOGY

# Introduction

## Bob Hale and Aviv Hoffmann

This introduction has two sections—the first sets the papers collected together here in the research context in which they were originally presented, and the second provides a brief overview of the papers themselves.

1

In addition to their various thematic interconnections, the papers collected together in this volume share a common historical origin: all of them were contributions to a research project—*The Metaphysics and Epistemology of Modality*[1]—funded by the Arts and Humanities Research Council, and based in the Arché Centre for Logic, Language, Metaphysics and Epistemology in St Andrews. Over its three-year lifetime (2003–5), with the help of Leverhulme Trust network funding, the project ran five two-day workshops at which versions of Chapters 3–9 were presented; earlier versions of the remaining papers, and of the comments on them reproduced here, were presented at a post-project conference held in St Andrews in June 2006, again with generous support from the Leverhulme Trust. It is, therefore, appropriate to recall, by way of introduction, the research programme to which these papers made so substantial a contribution.

Modal notions—notions of necessity and possibility—are implicit in our understanding of a wide class of fundamental concepts: for instance, the notion of one proposition following logically from others, the idea of what would be true if such and such were the case, the idea of a law of nature (as opposed to a mere regularity), the notion of causation (that is, of the occurrence of certain events and conditions necessitating that of others), and the idea that one kind of property or state of affairs may supervene on others (i.e. that things can never differ in the former kind of way without differing, somehow, in the latter kind of way)—each of these, explicitly or implicitly, involves modal notions of one sort or another.

---

[1] For further information, go to <http://www.st-andrews.ac.uk/~arche/projects/modality/index.shtml>.

This breadth of implication in ordinary and philosophical thought makes it philosophically especially important to try to achieve a satisfactory analytic understanding of the content of modal claims; and the extensive attention given to modality by analytical philosophers, particularly in the latter half of the twentieth century, is testimony to this sense of their importance. Yet the key issues—concerning the nature of modal facts, and the ways they might be known—seem to remain as perplexing as ever, with almost no view of them apparently too extreme to be adopted and defended with ingenuity by leading theorists in the field. Thus the contemporary literature offers accounts of so innocent-seeming a claim as that Margaret Thatcher might never have become Prime Minister ranging from the proposal that it is made true by the existence of a flesh-and-blood counterpart of Margaret Thatcher inhabiting a concrete, natural world very much like that in which we live but spatially unrelated to it, who fails to become Prime Minister of the counterpart of Britain in that world, to the suggestions that it is made true by linguistic convention, or that it is merely an expression of our abilities of imagination. The broad aims of our project were to clarify the pressures which have generated such extreme proposals, to review what should be demanded of a satisfactory account of modality, to re-assess existing proposals in the light of that clarification, and to pave the way for—and indeed to make—progress on this difficult range of issues.

Our project largely concentrated (as much recent work in the area has done) on what are sometimes called *absolute*, as opposed to merely relative, notions of necessity and possibility—notions of what is unconditionally, or unrestrictedly, necessary or possible. In terms of the standard world semantics, the contrast, in the case of necessity, is roughly that between what holds true at all worlds without restriction[2] and what holds true at all worlds within some restricted range (e.g. all worlds at which the actual laws of nature hold); similarly, what is absolutely possible is what holds true at *any* one or more worlds as contrasted with what holds true at one or more worlds within a restricted range. Alternatively, without invoking worlds we may, to a first approximation, characterize absolute necessities as those whose opposites are in no sense 'possible'. However, it is clear on very little reflection that these explanations will not do as they stand. For the words 'may' and 'might' are commonly employed to express what is often called *epistemic* possibility. We say, for example, 'The car keys may still be in the ignition', meaning that for all we know, that is where they are (or something along those lines)—we are not asserting that the key's being in the ignition is consistent with the laws of nature, much less that there is some metaphysically possible world in which that is where they are. On any plausible view, there are (unknown) absolute necessities whose opposite is epistemically possible—that is, true substitution-instances of

---

[2] If, as some practitioners of world semantics advocate, we admit so-called impossible worlds, the absolutely necessary will be what holds true at all *possible* worlds without restriction, and the absolutely possible what holds at some *possible* world.

'it may (or might) be that not-*p*', expressing epistemic possibility, where it is absolutely necessary that *p*. Thus absolute necessities may be more accurately characterized as those whose opposites are in no non-epistemic sense possible—in terms of worlds, those which hold true in all worlds save, perhaps, those which are merely epistemically possible. It is plausible—but certainly neither obvious nor incontestable—that other, more specific modalities can, for the most part, be characterized in terms of these absolute notions.[3]

Prescinding from its questionable, and perhaps not seriously intended, suggestion of uniqueness, Michael Dummett's well-known statement[4] that 'the philosophical problem of necessity is twofold: what is its source, and how do we recognise it?' provides a vivid and forceful formulation of what may certainly be regarded as two of the central questions any satisfying philosophy of absolute modality needs to tackle. It is, perhaps, less clear than one might wish what precisely Dummett's first question is after. It could be understood as assuming that facts about necessity, and modal facts quite generally, must either be reducible to, or at least have their basis in, facts of some other, non-modal, kind. It is true enough that philosophers of otherwise quite different persuasions have felt themselves pulled in that general direction—towards an account of modality which avoids admitting brute facts about what must or might be (or have been). But it is not a datum of the problem that some such reductive or quasi-reductive explanation of modal facts must be provided, if such facts are to be acknowledged at all, much less that it must be possible to provide one. So Dummett's formulation is best heard as innocent of any such implication. His questions do, however, clearly carry two other presuppositions of which we should take note, since both can be, and have been, seriously challenged. His first question plainly presupposes that there *is* such a thing as necessity; and his second equally plainly presupposes that it is a possible object of *knowledge*—that at least sometimes, we can and do recognize not just that something is so, but that it could not have been otherwise.

The middle decades of twentieth-century analytical philosophy exhibited a strong current of scepticism towards the absolute modal notions, nowhere more forceful than in Quine's contributions, which both challenged the intelligibility of modal idioms (and especially, of course, that of modal sentential operators)

---

[3] One familiar model for characterizing other, more specific modalities, such as physical, biological, etc., necessity and possibility, sees them as relative—the result of restricting attention to those absolute possibilities (or possible worlds) in which certain actual truths (the laws of physics, biology, etc.) are held constant. What is physically possible is then simply what is consistent with the laws of physics, and what is physically necessary is what follows from them. A standard approach to epistemic uses of modal idioms sees them as expressing relative possibilities and necessities in this sense: what may (epistemically) be is what is consistent—or perhaps not obviously inconsistent—with some assumed body of knowledge or state of information. Stephen Yablo's contribution to this volume (Ch. 11) presents a powerful challenge to this kind of account of epistemic modalities, and develops a radically different alternative treatment.

[4] Dummett (1959), p. 169.

and questioned the very existence of any absolute necessities (statements 'true come what may', in Quine's phrase). That current has lost much of its force, at least partly as a result of Kripke's convincing separation of notions which Quine scrambled together—in particular, his separation of (metaphysical) necessity from analyticity and apriority. But while, swept along on the tide of the Kripkean counter-revolution, many of us are now much less inclined to be moved by Quinean doubts, and much readier to deploy modal idioms when engaged in serious philosophy without nagging consciences than we (or our recent philosophical ancestors) used to be, there is not much evidence that this happy re-instatement of modal notions is based upon any clear and agreed story about where and why modal scepticism goes wrong, and how it is to be answered.[5] It is, accordingly, arguable that the most basic question which any thoroughgoing discussion of modality must confront is how, if it can be, the case for abstaining altogether from modal discourse, at least when engaged in serious philosophy, is to be answered. A broadly Quinean case for abstention may draw upon the alleged unclarity of modal notions, the difficulties in explaining them without circularity or ineptitude, the obscurity of modal epistemology, and the suspicion that modal notions have no important work to do—that they are, for instance, eliminable without serious loss from the vocabulary of successful empirical science. Against that needs to be set the consideration already stressed, that modal notions are implicated in very many other, fundamental ways of thinking. There are, in addition, certain arguments of a 'transcendental' nature which, if sustained, show that modal thought is unavoidable—arguments broadly to the effect that recognition, a priori, of the necessarily truth-preserving character of some forms of inference is a precondition for rational thought in general, and scientific theorizing in particular.[6] Two questions calling for attention are, then:

(1) Are there compelling arguments for supposing that modal thought (embedding the absolute modal notions) is essential?

and if so:

(2) Are there good reasons to think that at least some modal judgements must be a priori?

The presupposition of Dummett's first question—that there is such a thing as necessity at all—is naturally understood as the claim that there are facts about

---

[5] To some extent, this shows in the variety of ways in which philosophers who have, at least ostensibly, gone past Quine's scepticism have sought to accommodate modality—and, in particular, in the opposition between those who have felt the need for a *reductive* explanation of modal notions (such as David Lewis) or at least an account which does without any residual modal facts (various forms of non-cognitivism—see below), and on the other side, those willing to accept modal notions as primitive, and modal facts as neither reducible to, nor supervenient upon, facts of some other sort. One may see Quine's scepticism as still—from beyond the grave, as it were—exerting a pull on the former.

[6] Such as those developed in Wright (1986), McFetridge (1990b), and in Hale (1999).

what must be so, as distinct from what simply is so. Whilst it would be at best somewhat eccentric to agree that there are facts about necessity and possibility—at least if 'fact' is understood in any substantial, non-deflationary, way—and yet deny that such facts are ever known, or even knowable, it is certainly not obviously incoherent, or otherwise indefensible, to accept that there is such a thing as necessity, at least in the sense that talk of what must, or can't, be so is perfectly intelligible, and plays a useful and perhaps indispensable role in our intellectual economy, but to deny that necessity is, properly speaking, a possible object of knowledge (that is, to reject the presupposition of his second question). Perhaps the simplest and most obvious way to implement this pattern of acceptance and rejection would be to adopt an analogue of expressivist views about the character of ethical judgements, or evaluative and normative talk and thought in general. Just as, on some well-known views, talk of what is right or wrong, good or bad, obligatory or permissible, etc., should be understood as expressive of attitudes of one sort or another—approval, disapproval, etc.—rather than as descriptive of a distinctive species of non-natural fact, so talk of what must or can't be the case is best construed, on this view, not as answerable to some additional layer of external, irrefragable fact, but as airing some characteristic kind of internal state—an irresistible habit of thought (Hume on causation) or imaginative block encountered when trying to see how summing 2 and 3 might result in anything other than 5.[7] More generally, a *non-cognitivist* approach to modality accepts that there is a respectable use for talk of necessities and possibilities, whilst rejecting the idea that statements of the forms 'Necessarily p', 'Possibly q', etc., are to be understood as true or false in virtue of a distinctive modal fact—a special kind of fact over and above those recorded by the non-modal statements to which modal operators are applied. On the face of it, the non-cognitivist can return an affirmative answer to question (1) above, and even one, perhaps, to question (2) as well—of course, he won't view necessitated judgements as *known* a priori, but he may still treat them as exempt from empirical revision. Among the apparent attractions of the non-cognitivist approach are its easy consistency with a broadly philosophical naturalism, its promise of an explanation of the basis of necessity (or at least of our talk of it) which makes no extra demands on ontology, and its apparent avoidance of the troublesome epistemological issues that go with accepting Dummett's questions, and their presuppositions, at face-value. To be weighed against these attractions there are, of course, various more or less well-known difficulties and objections. These include some of an internal and structural kind: at least one—that any non-descriptive construal of modal statements looks bound to run up against a version of the notorious Frege–Geach problem, widely discussed in relation to expressivist and more sophisticated quasi-realist treatments of ethical statements—afflicts any species of non-cognitivism; others, such as an apparent incapacity to accommodate, or

---

[7] Cf. Blackburn (1984), p. 216, and (1986).

even make sense of, iterated modalities, are peculiar to a non-cognitivist approach to modality. Thus two further questions here are:

> (3) What constraints should be imposed on a satisfactory non-cognitivist conception of modality?

and

> (4) What are the prospects for a workable non-cognitivist account of modality?

and unless—somewhat implausibly in view of its ostensibly revisionary character—one takes non-cognitivism to be the default-acceptable position, we should also ask:

> (5) Are there any compelling arguments in favour of a non-cognitivist approach to modality?

Of special interest and importance here is a dilemma formulated by Simon Blackburn:[8] whatever considerations a theorist proposes as underlying the necessity of a proposition, the question must arise whether they themselves are conceived as obtaining of necessity or merely contingently. If the former, then we have merely explained one necessity in terms of another, and have not attained the desired general account of how necessity originates—there is, as Blackburn puts it, a 'bad residual 'must' '. If instead we seek to ground necessity in a mere contingency, then we escape circularity only at the cost of undermining what we sought to explain—for if the explanans is something which could have been otherwise, then the same must go, surely, for the explanandum. Blackburn himself sees the dilemma as motivating a shift away from what he labels 'the truth-conditional approach' to modality, and towards the quasi-realist form of non-cognitivism he recommends across the board. Others have questioned its capacity to do so.[9] But his seemingly straightforward challenge illustrates a more general concern about the mutual coherence of the constraints on explanation which might individually seem compulsory for a satisfactory 'account' of metaphysical necessity and possibility. Even if it does not enforce the precise shift its author intends, Blackburn's dilemma might seem to push in the direction of a kind of quietism about modality, or at least towards supposing that there are significant and topic-specific a priori limits on what can be accomplished by a philosophical account of it.

Accepting Dummett's questions, together with their presuppositions, at face-value amounts to a kind of realism about modality—not, of course, realism about worlds, in either the extreme form famously advocated by David Lewis or the more moderate form defended by Robert Stalnaker[10] and others, but a

---

[8] See Blackburn (1986), pp. 120–1.

[9] See Ross Cameron's contribution to this volume (Ch. 7), also Hale (2002).

[10] See Stalnaker (1976).

realism that consists in accepting modal propositions as objectively true or false and at least sometimes within our ken. Realism in this sense has, obviously, no inbuilt commitment to any sort of reductionist programme, such as Lewis's—but neither is it necessarily opposed to such a programme: whether modal notions can be explained in other terms, and whether modal facts are reducible to or supervene upon facts of some other kind (e.g. facts of about Lewisian worlds) are further questions. But while it is perhaps less clear how a realist who has no reductive aspirations may set about answering Dummett's first question than one who does, he owes some sort of account of the nature and basis of modal facts, as well as an account of our epistemic access to them. For modal realists, then, two pressing questions are:

> (6) What is the nature and basis of facts about what is necessary and (counterfactually) possible, and of modal facts more generally?

and

> (7) How may we acquire knowledge, or at least warranted beliefs, about such facts?

In answering these questions about the metaphysics and epistemology of modality, realists of any sort have to face up to a number of constraints. Prominent among them is what Christopher Peacocke termed 'the integration challenge'—the challenge of squaring a proposed account of the character of modal fact with the possibility of our knowledge of such facts (and indeed, with the possibility of knowledge of them by what we pre-theoretically regard as satisfactory ways of achieving it). Peacocke explicitly presented this challenge as a generalization of one laid down for accounts of mathematical truth by Paul Benacerraf.[11] There are indeed parallels in the modal case with the tensions Benacerraf emphasized thirty years ago between straightforward construals of the semantics of mathematical discourse and a generally naturalistic conception of human knowledge and its limitations—would-be accounts of the basis of modal fact have not always seemed to leave room for a credible explanation of modal knowledge.[12] More generally, it is plausible that a satisfactory realist account should be responsive to at least the following four constraints:

(a) The account should be based on a principled rejection of abstentionism and quietism, and its detail should respect the grounds for that rejection. (If, for example, abstentionism falls to a compelling argument that modalizing is indispensable for certain theoretical purposes, then a realist account must respect whatever bearing on the content of modal statements is carried by that argument.)

---

[11] For Peacocke's challenge, see Peacocke (1999), ch. 1, and for its Benacerrafic ancestor, Benacerraf (1973).

[12] Lewis's account is an obvious case—see Peacocke (1999), and for Lewis's own response to Benacerraf's dilemma, Lewis (1986b), pp. 108–15.

(b) The account should be properly 'integrated': the conception it provides of the truth-conditions of modal statements should put no obstacles in the way of our knowledge of them, by procedures on which we actually rely.

(c) Relatedly, the account should allow for a satisfying connection between the content it ascribes to modal judgements and, in the broadest sense, our interests and purposes in making such judgements—their role in our intellectual lives.

(d) At least ideally, the account should contribute towards making conspicuous the logical relationships among modal statements (and here, of course, possible-worlds semantics is a great success).

2

Although those who contributed to the conference, workshops and seminars which constituted the major part of the collaborative activity in the Arché research project were under no constraint in planning their contributions, save the very broad one that they should deal with questions bearing on the metaphysics, logic, or epistemology of modality, many of the papers collected together here can be seen as directly addressing various aspects of the questions highlighted in the foregoing summary of the project's objectives, and those that do not have a pretty clear, if indirect, bearing upon them.

With two exceptions, the papers are concerned with the absolute notions of necessity and possibility roughly circumscribed above. One exception is Stephen Yablo's 'Permission and (So-Called Epistemic) Possibility' (Chapter 11); but even this exception has an important connexion with our central concern—if only because, as we saw, a satisfactory characterization of the absolute notions is likely to appeal to the notion of epistemic possibility, and so presupposes an independent grasp of that notion. On a more or less standard account, when 'it may (or might) be that $p$' is used to express epistemic possibility, it says something like: '$p$'s truth is not ruled out by what we know' (or not obviously ruled out by what we know, or some such). Yablo raises a generous handful of objections to this kind of account, which lead him to explore an alternative 'dynamic' treatment exploiting a parallel he finds between epistemic ('descriptive') and permissive ('prescriptive') uses of modal words. Roughly, just as 'You may take Friday off' can be seen as expanding what David Lewis called the 'sphere of permissibility' (adds to the set of possible worlds in which agents behave as they are required to do), so, on Yablo's proposal, 'He may (might) be in his office' can be seen as expanding our 'sphere of believability' (adds to the set of possible worlds which model our information state). In both cases, the big money question is: which worlds get added? Lewis struggled with this question as regards permissions—clearly allowing you to take Friday off doesn't let in *all* worlds in which you do that, else you could take a permanent holiday! Yablo proposes a novel answer to it, which can be carried over—or so he contends—to the epistemic case. David Efird's comment raises an interesting difficulty.

The other exception is Kit Fine's paper 'Semantic Necessity' (Chapter 3). The overall aim of Fine's paper is to argue that the notion of semantic necessity has a role to play in understanding the nature and content of semantics comparable to that which the notion of metaphysical necessity is now generally recognized as possessing in relation to metaphysics. Fine distinguishes two senses—one broader, the other narrower—in which a fact may be said to be semantic. In the broader sense, a semantic fact is one which 'pertains to the exemplification of semantic properties or relations', such as truth, designation, and synonymy. In a narrower sense, there are semantic facts which are 'part of the semantics of a given language'. These include facts about synonymy, for example, but not, in general, facts about what particular expressions designate (e.g. the fact that 'The author of Waverley' designates Scott) or about which sentences are true (e.g. the fact that 'Snow is white' is true). It is semantic facts of this narrower sort that Fine calls 'semantic necessities' or 'semantic requirements'. His central thesis is that the semantics of a language is best understood as a body of such semantic requirements. The notion of a semantic requirement is elaborated in various ways. In particular, readers familiar with Fine's earlier work on essence and modality will find interesting and illuminating parallels with his development of the idea that facts about the essences (or natures or identities) of things—so far from being reducible to, or explicable in terms of, facts about necessity and possibility expressible using standard modal operators—should be seen as more basic and as underpinning facts of the latter sort. Much as Fine argued, in the earlier work, that the standard treatment of modality by means of sentential operators is too blunt an instrument to do justice to the facts about essence and essential properties and relations, so now, he argues that the standard approaches to semantics are likewise insufficiently discriminating adequately to capture the semantic facts. Accordingly, much of his paper is devoted to pointing up what he sees as the deficiencies of the main rivals to his requirement-based conception of semantics—the approach on which, following Frege's lead, semantics is taken to consist in an assignment of values to the expressions of the language under study, and the truth-theoretical approach deriving from Tarski and continued in Davidson's work.

The remaining papers can be grouped in various ways going beyond the broad division of our contents page between those belonging to Metaphysics and Logic and those belonging to Epistemology.

If one views the logic of modality from the perspective of world semantics, then, although a dyadic counterfactual operator is not plausibly definable in terms of the usual monadic modal operators for necessity and possibility, the logic of counterfactuals is apt to appear as a special case which results from restricting the strict conditional by focusing on a limited but variable range of worlds—the 'closest' worlds at which the counterfactual's antecedent is true. But—as several writers have observed—another perspective is possible, in terms of which the priorities are reversed. If the counterfactual is taken as understood, the standard necessity and possibility operators can be defined in terms of it. This can be done in more than one way, as Timothy Williamson reminds us in his contribution to the volume (Chapter 4). Perhaps the most illuminating, philosophically, is to interpret necessity in terms of a generalized counterfactual: $\Box p$ may be defined as $\forall q(q \,\Box\!\!\rightarrow p)$—what is necessary is what would be so, no matter what (else) were true (and so what is true absolutely unconditionally). Alternatively, $\Box p$ may be defined $\neg p \,\Box\!\!\rightarrow p$, or as $\neg p \,\Box\!\!\rightarrow \bot$. These are perhaps a little less natural, but may be more convenient for working purposes, and more economical on background resources, since the generalized counterfactual definition calls for propositional quantification and thus requires an underlying higher-order logic (with propositional variables as zero-place predicate variables). The interest of such an approach is both philosophical and logical. Philosophically, it invites us to see the notions of absolute or unrestricted (metaphysical) necessity and possibility, which are not much employed outside philosophy, as special cases of a kind of thinking—counterfactual thinking—in which we engage much more widely. We may hope thereby both to throw welcome light on the truth-conditions of unrestricted claims about necessity and possibility, and perhaps also a better understanding of their epistemology. We may also hope that this approach would help clarify some disputed questions in the logic of metaphysical modality, by connecting them with more tractable questions about counterfactuals and plausible principles governing them. Williamson's paper shows how the logic of metaphysical $\Box$ and $\Diamond$ can be developed within counterfactual logic. It also offers to help clarify some disputed questions in the logic of metaphysical modality, by connecting them with more tractable questions about counterfactuals and plausible principles governing them.

While perhaps only Williamson's paper directly dealing with modal logic as such, it goes together with three other papers concerned with logical questions about modality.

The leading questions of Ian Rumfitt's paper (Chapter 2) concern logical necessity: Is there a coherent notion of logical necessity, and if there is, how is it related to other modal notions, such as those of metaphysical necessity and being knowable *a priori*? Rumfitt presents a novel argument for the view that there is a distinctive notion of necessity implicated in the notion of logical consequence. The view itself accords well with our tendency to employ modal idioms both in expressing claims about what follows from what, and in explaining the notion of consequence itself; and while certainly not universally accepted, it has been endorsed in some relatively recent work, including, notably, Ian McFetridge's posthumously published essay on this topic.[13] In that essay, McFetridge offered no explicit account of what logical necessity is—his proposal was, roughly, that to believe an inference logically necessarily truth-preserving is to believe that it would preserve truth, no matter what else we suppose to be the case—but Rumfitt claims that this fits well with his own proposal, according to which it is logically necessary that A if and only if A's negation is (broadly) logically contradictory. McFetridge argued that logical necessity, understood in essentially this way, is the strongest kind of non-epistemic necessity. The central argument of Rumfitt's paper is a new defence of this thesis, and McFetridge's argument for it, against an initially powerful-looking objection presented by Dorothy Edgington, turning on the claim that while Leverrier could have validly argued from the supposition that Neptune exists to the conclusion that it is causally responsible for the observed perturbations in the orbit of Uranus, it is (metaphysically) possible that Neptune should have been knocked off course a million years earlier, and so not been their cause. This and similar examples appear to show that a conditional—one corresponding to a valid inference—may be logically but not metaphysically necessary, contrary to McFetridge's thesis. Rumfitt argues, to the contrary, that we can avoid this conclusion by invoking a needed distinction, similar to one suggested by Gareth Evans, between 'deep' and 'superficial' necessities. In addition to providing a new clarification of this distinction, Rumfitt further argues that it can be used to defuse an argument of Michael Dummett's which purports to show that S5 cannot be the logic of metaphysical necessity.

The key distinction between deep and superficial necessity, as Rumfitt explains it, depends upon another, between—in his terminology—a statement's being *true with respect to* a possibility,[14] and its being *true in* a possibility. A statement A, expressing the proposition that p, is true with respect to the possibility x if, were x to obtain, it would be the case that p; but A is true in the possibility x if, were x to obtain, A would be true, meaning what it actually means. A statement is true with respect to every possibility if and only if it has a true necessitation; such a statement is superficially necessary. By contrast, a deeply necessary statement is one that is true in every possibility, meaning what it actually means. In essence, Rumfitt's answer to the difficulty raised against McFetridge's argument is that once the distinction is made, we can see that Leverrier's premise merely superficially necessitates its conclusion—we have no counterexample to the thesis that every deep logical necessity is metaphysically necessary.

A superficially similar—but certainly different—distinction lies at the heart of Robert Stalnaker's paper (Chapter 1), and is put to a somewhat similar dialectical use. Stalnaker's distinction is, as he observes, a version of one drawn

---

[13] McFetridge (1990b).

[14] Possibilities, for Rumfitt, are ways things might be, or might have been. In contrast with possible worlds, possibilities need not be fully determinate.

by Kit Fine, between what he called inner and outer truth:[15] in Stalnaker's terms, between a proposition's being *true of,* or *true with respect to* a possible world, and a proposition's being *true in* a possible world. The distinctions—Rumfitt's and Stalnaker's—are differently drawn, however. For one thing, Rumfitt's is drawn at the level of statements, rather than propositions—where a statement is an ordered pair of meaningful declarative sentence and a possible context of utterance in which it expresses a determinate proposition—and makes explicit reference to a statement's meaning in explaining his notion of truth in a possibility. But Stalnaker's distinction is drawn for what he calls 'coarse-grained propositions'—propositions differentiated no more finely than sets of worlds, so that necessarily equivalent propositions are identical—and in drawing it, he makes no appeal (or at least, no overt appeal) to sentence meaning or any similar notion. In his terms, a proposition is true *in* a world if it has, in that world, the property of truth. By contrast, if we think of a world *w* as a fully determinate way things could be, then a proposition *p* is *true of w* if and only if *w* (more precisely, the maximal proposition that corresponds to *w*) entails *p*. It is only by upholding such a distinction, Stalnaker argues, that we can acknowledge, as he thinks we should, that some propositions exist only as a matter of contingency. The obvious (but in his view, not the only) examples of plausible candidates are what are often called singular propositions—propositions which depend for their existence on that of the individuals they are about, that being itself taken to be a contingent matter. The existence of singular propositions in this sense has been denied, for example by Alvin Plantinga, who takes it for granted that some individuals exist only contingently but argues that propositions about them are not object-dependent. Moving in the opposite direction, Timothy Williamson has argued that since singular propositions about him depend for their existence on his, the proposition that he does not exist must be necessarily false and his existence must be necessary. Stalnaker shows how his distinction enables one to convict both arguments of equivocation, and argues against Williamson's reasons for rejecting the distinction. In his response, Aviv Hoffmann argues that Stalnaker's theory does *not* support the thesis that singular propositions are ontologically dependent on the individuals they are directly about. According to Hoffmann, in Stalnaker's theory, propositions (and possible worlds) are *necessary* existents. The theory is *accidentalist* in the sense that it allows that some propositions may not be essentially propositions.

Williamson's purported proof of his necessary existence takes centre stage again in David Efird's paper (Chapter 5). Efird considers, but rejects as too costly, a response to it based on Fine's inner–outer truth distinction, and finds fault too with a somewhat different way of avoiding Williamson's seemingly unpalatable conclusion, based on the claim that the truth-operator is non-redundant in

---

[15] Fine's distinction is discussed in section 2 of David Efird's paper in this volume (Ch. 5).

modal contexts.[16] Instead, he recommends an ostensibly novel and quite radical remedy. Crudely, this consists in denying that there are any necessary truths about contingently existing objects. As Efird develops it, this involves rejecting the standard treatment of $\Box$ and $\Diamond$ as interdefinable with the aid of negation. Following an old suggestion of Arthur Prior's, this is to be done by taking $\Box P(a)$ to be true if and only if $a$ exists in every possible world and $P(a)$ is true with respect to every world, while $\Diamond P(a)$ is to be true if and only $P(a)$ is true with respect to some possible world in which $a$ exists. Adopting this non-standard, Priorian, semantics has, Efird claims, at least two advantages—first, it allows us to deny Williamson's necessary existence, whilst acknowledging that his non-existence is not possible; second, it enables us to give a simple semantic account of the *de dicto/de re distinction*, by equating '$a$ is essentially $F$' (contrast 'Necessarily, $a$ is $F$') as $\neg\Diamond\neg Fa$.

Four papers—those by Rosen, Cameron, Sherratt, and Shalkowksi—are primarily concerned with metaphysical, rather than epistemological, matters. The first three all bear directly on the nature and basis of modal facts—the source of necessity and possibility, to borrow and extend Dummett's phrase.

Gideon Rosen (Chapter 6) construes metaphysical dependence (or grounding) as a relation between facts, conceived as structured entities individuated by their constituents and composition. The relation, he argues, is irreflexive and asymmetric, but not connected, so that it induces 'at best a partial order on the domain of facts'. Since he also takes it to be transitive, his grounding relation *is* a partial ordering. The overall aim of his paper is to clarify this important and frequently used, but not well-understood, notion by mapping out the general principles governing it. One central question concerns the relation between grounding and reduction, where (the proposition that) $p$ reduces to $q$ if $q$ says what it is for $p$ to be the case. Rosen proposes the Ground–Reduction Link: if $p$ is true and $p$ reduces to $q$, then the fact that $q$ grounds the fact that $p$. An immediate worry is that the link will generate violations of the irreflexivity of grounding—for surely if what it is, for example, for a figure to be a square is for it to be an equilateral rectangle, the fact that it is a square just *is* the fact that it is an equilateral rectangle, so that a single fact grounds itself! To answer this, Rosen argues that we must take reduction to be a relation between distinct propositions (so that grounding facts can always be distinct from the facts grounded). This rich and wide-ranging paper discusses, inter alia, the relation between grounding and metaphysical necessity, grounds for various types of fact, including modal facts, and the important question whether grounding principles themselves may always be explained in terms of facts about essences or natures or whether, instead, some grounding principles have to be recognized as an additional source of absolute necessity.

---

[16] See Rumfitt (2003).

Ross Cameron (Chapter 7) focuses on Blackburn's dilemma (vide supra) and argues that neither horn is effective. In particular, he endorses the suggestion that the necessity horn—which claims that any explanation of a necessity in which the explanans is itself necessary is either viciously circular or regressive—can be blunted by appeal to a distinction between transmissive and non-transmissive explanations of necessity. A transmissive explanation is one in which the necessity of one truth is explained by appeal to the necessity of others—often, if not always, such explanations can be cast in the form: 'Necessarily *q* because necessarily *p* and necessarily if *p* then *q*'. The thought is that an explanation: 'Necessarily *q* because *p*' may be such that it is necessary that *p*, but that the explanation appeals only to the *truth*, not the necessity, of the explanans. Thus far, Cameron agrees with Hale (2002). But from this point on, his argument diverges sharply from Hale's. Cameron observes that a Lewisian realist can give a non-transmissive explanation of necessities in terms of there being propositions which are true at all possible worlds (at least provided that worlds can be characterized in non-modal terms). But his own proposal invokes both possible and impossible worlds (understood, respectively, as 'abstract entities which represent ways things could have been and abstract entities which represent ways things couldn't have been') and sees the problem of the source of modal truth as one of explaining what it is about the possible worlds that makes them possible. We should not, in Cameron's view, take the distinction between possible and impossible worlds as 'tracking some prior modal truths'—instead, we should, he claims, embrace a form of 'neo-conventionalism' according to which the distinction simply reflects 'our perspective—we simply call certain worlds 'impossible' because they deviate from the actual world in matters we consider important'.

Whether this neo-conventionalism should be classified as an anti-realist position depends, obviously, on how we understand that classification. Cameron claims to answer Dummett's first question, and nothing he says appears to rule out a straight answer to Dummett's second question, about how modal knowledge may be acquired. To that extent, his view may count as realist. But a view which, while accepting that there are modal facts, holds such facts to be, in some way or other, mind-dependent is naturally viewed as a kind of anti-realism, and on the face of it, neo-conventionalism (together, surely, with older and more familiar versions of conventionalism about necessity) does see modal facts as mind-dependent, and so should be seen as a form of anti-realism. Anna Sherratt's paper (Chapter 8) focuses on anti-realism in this sense, and presents a simple, novel, and potentially decisive objection to it. She develops the objection initially against an 'ideal conceiver' theory of possibility advocated by Peter Menzies, according to which what makes it possible that *p* is that a suitably idealized conceiver can conceive of its being the case that *p*. If this is to be an anti-realist theory, she argues, it must be claimed that the biconditional between possibility and ideal conceivability can be known a priori. But given that we know a priori that whatever is true is possible, it follows that we can know a priori that whatever is true is ideally conceivable. But the transparency of truth to ideal conception is not, Sherratt argues, something we should think we can know a priori. If the argument of the second half of her paper is right, this simple objection can be generalized to dispose of any form of anti-realism which postulates a biconditional and a priori connection between modality and the mental, while weaker forms of anti-realism fall—or so she argues—to other objections.

Scott Shalkowski's paper (Chapter 9) also bears, albeit indirectly, on questions about the basis of modality; its primary focus, however, is a somewhat more general issue in the methodology of metaphysics, and the metaphysics of modality in particular. His leading question is whether metaphysical theses in general may be justified by appeal to their alleged explanatory advantages, and in particular, whether Lewisian realism about possible worlds (Genuine Modal Realism, as it has been called) can be justified, as Lewis himself claimed, by an inference to the best explanation. If such an inference is to avoid simply begging the question, the criteria by which a theory is judged to provide the best explanation must not include truth (or greater likelihood of truth). Which theory is best, it seems, needs to be assessed by reference to criteria such as economy of explanatory primitives, simplicity, generality of application, and so on. But then we face a serious question, with any inference to the best explanation, why the fact that a theory does better than its rivals affords any good reason to think it true. Where the theories among which we are choosing are susceptible of empirical check, there may be independent reasons to think that inference to the best explanation can be relied upon to lead us to a theory that is at least more likely to be true than its rivals. But matters are more problematic—or so Shalkowski argues—when we are concerned, as we are with Lewis's would-be inference to the best explanation, with a theory that is evidently not subject to any comparable independent ratification.

A different, but equally important, methodological issue—one which links with constraints (a) and (c) above—is central to John Divers's paper (Chapter 10). Although he does not express himself in quite these terms, Divers can be seen as proposing a new kind of application of Ockham's Razor to modal theorizing. He argues that we need, but lack, an account of the distinctive function or purposes served by modalizing—engaging in modal thought and talk. Assuming that we are neither abstainers or quietists (vide supra), we shall expect a good theory of modality to provide an analysis or account of modal talk and thought which, inter alia, brings out its ontological commitments and clarifies its epistemology. But just how much of ordinary, or philosophical, modalizing must a good theory seek to accommodate? More controversially, Divers argues that, given an adequate inventory of the functions served by modalizing, a constraint on modal theory should be that it commit itself to no more than is required to accommodate that part of modal talk and thought necessary to discharge those functions. More controversially still, he suggests, this constraint is likely to favour a philosophy of modality which avoids substantial ontological commitments (e.g. to merely possible worlds). Daniel Nolan, in his comment on Divers's paper, asks whether investigating the function of modal judgement is philosopher's business at all, and whether Divers's proposed functional constraint may be too strong, and comes up with an answer to the first that is congenial to Divers's approach, and one to the second that is considerably less so—very roughly, on a reading which gives it real teeth, a functional constraint of the type proposed would very likely result, in other areas, in scrapping some perfectly respectable theories, and there is no evident reason to think that isn't true of modality. But while Nolan is critical of the functional constraint, he thinks the question about the function of modal judgement is a good one, and sketches an interesting answer to it which links modal judgements to desires with modal content.

The papers by Jackson, Sturgeon, and Gregory, together with the associated comments, focus on various aspects of modal epistemology.

Frank Jackson (Chapter 12) argues that one reading of Quine's most widely discussed objection to essentialism can be seen as posing an important epistemological problem for the necessary *a posteriori*—as he puts it '[r]oughly, the problem is that if *S* is . . . a candidate necessary *a posteriori* truth, how could we *show* that it is necessary, in the face of the fact that it takes investigation to show that *S* is true, and so, in some sense, *S* might have turned out to be false?' In the first section of his paper, Jackson defends his view that this problem can be solved by appeal to the two-dimensionalist account of necessary *a posteriori* truth. In the second, he tackles what he sees as a descendant of Quine's objection, which can be understood as posing a problem about what can possibly make *a posteriori* truths true, and argues that two-dimensionalism provides a good answer to this problem too. Jackson's paper can thus be seen as aimed at buttressing the case for two-dimensionalism. Penelope Mackie's central purpose in her comment is to question whether any appeal to the two-dimensionalist apparatus is actually needed to deal with either problem.

The remaining two papers are both concerned, in one way or another, with the relations between conceivability and possibility, but they approach the question in very different and opposed ways.

In a fresh assault on the question whether conceivability can ground beliefs about possibility, Dominic Gregory (Chapter 14) argues that we should understand conceiving as a matter of being presented in imagination with an appearance of how things could be, in parallel to the way in which, in perception, we are presented with an appearance of how things are. Then, provided that we can rely upon a suitable general principle licensing us, in the absence of specific reasons to the contrary, to take appearances as a guide to reality, it may seem that we are well placed to explain how conceivings can issue in justified beliefs about what's possible. Given some such principle, there are, he claims, some basic cases in which we are presented with an appearance which clearly entitles us to a belief in possibility. Thus in his main example, we can imagine having an auditory experience as of a tune being played on a trombone—here, Gregory claims, we are presented with the appearance that a certain auditory experience is possible, and on that basis, we are justified in thinking that such an experience really is possible. But seeing how to extend the account beyond such basic cases, in which the appearance of possibility relies on sensory imagining, is—or so Gregory argues—anything but plain sailing. The difficulty, as he presents it, is that when we move from *sensory* imaginings to *perceptual* imaginings—from imagining having certain sensory experiences to imagining perceiving objects in the external world—the distinction between veridical and non-veridical perceptual experience is not marked by any appearance with which we may be presented in imagination. It then becomes hard to see how, when we move beyond purely sensory imagining, conceivability can serve as a guide to possibility. Gregory's paper thus promises a negative result—if conceiving has to be understood as he proposes, then it can serve at best as a very limited guide to possibility—and challenges those who would claim more for it to provide an alternative account of how the link between conception and possibility is to be forged which avoids the problems he raises. In his comment, Ross Cameron raises a worry about whether conceivability can serve as a guide at all, unless backed by an appeal to modal intuition (so that it is the latter which really justifies modal belief, not the former), but argues that Gregory has the resources to answer it. But there are, he claims, two more serious difficulties. First, there are (as Gregory would certainly acknowledge) certainly cases in which a possibility has no distinctive appearance—but if, for such cases, we need to appeal to some other source of modal knowledge, why do we need conceivability at all? Second, he doubts, that even in the cases where Gregory would hold that we do enjoy a distinctive appearance of possibility, that it is that—rather than an appeal to some principle of recombination—which gives rise to modal knowledge.

For Scott Sturgeon (Chapter 13), the leading question is whether what he calls *a priori* coherence can be an *infallible* guide to genuine metaphysical possibility, where a proposition counts as *a priori* coherent if it cannot be ruled out by *a priori* reflection.[17] Clearly it can't, if ordinary *a priori* reflection is what is in question—but what Sturgeon has in mind is rather an idealized, or 'limit', notion, and then his question admits no such quick answer. As we might expect, Sturgeon sees Kripkean *a posteriori* necessities as undercutting any simple or naïve form of *a priori* infallibilism, but then proceeds to argue that any attempt to re-instate a 'less naïve' infallibilism which seeks to avoid the problem by factoring Kripkean *a posteriori* necessities into the conditions for a more refined concept of *a priori* coherence must fall to essentially the same objection. In particular, he argues, no version of infallibilism can be rescued by recourse to two-dimensionalist semantics. The moral he draws is that we

---

[17] Sturgeon does not put his question in terms of conceivability being a guide, but his notion of *a priori* coherence is one reasonable way to interpret conceivability.

must cleanly separate metaphysics and epistemology—the expectation that *a priori* reflection, at least if sufficiently refined, should 'infallibly depict genuine possibility . . . springs from our disposition to blur epistemic and metaphysical fact'. But the *ep-&-met tendency*, as he dubs it, should be resisted; and resisting it leads us, he argues, to a quite radical kind of fallibilism—whether *a priori* reflection is even a *reliable* guide to possibility is a theoretical issue: it will be a trustworthy guide, if, but only if, there is a good alignment between *a priori* detectable conceptual possibility and genuine metaphysical possibility, and that in turn is a matter of whether the supposition that there is such an alignment leads to the best systematization of 'total theory'. C. S. Jenkins, in her comments on Sturgeon's paper, takes issue with what she sees as a misplaced preoccupation on his part with infallibilism. The real issue here, she claims, is whether conceivability can serve even as a reliable guide.

# PART I
# METAPHYSICS AND LOGIC

# 1

# Merely Possible Propositions

*Robert Stalnaker*

E. J. Lowe, in a general discussion of ontology, makes the following remark, in passing:

Many abstract objects—such as numbers, propositions and some sets—appear to be necessary beings in the sense that they exist 'in every possible world' . . . . Indeed, possible worlds themselves, conceived of as abstracta—for instance as maximal consistent sets of propositions—surely exist 'in every possible world'. (Lowe 1998, p. 248)

I think this is false. Possible worlds, in the sense in which it is reasonable to believe that there are many of them—the sense in which they are 'conceived of as abstracta'—are contingent objects. My aim in this paper is to sketch one way of making sense of this claim, and to draw some consequences from it. And I want to respond to two closely related arguments (by Alvin Plantinga and Timothy Williamson) with the help of a conception of possible worlds that allows for their contingency.

According to the actualist about possible worlds (as many people have observed), the kind of entity we are committed to by a theory of possible worlds would be more accurately labelled a possible *state* of the world, or a *way that a world might be*. It is something like a property that a total universe might have, and it is a maximal property in the sense that saying that a world has a particular property of this kind is enough to determine the truth or falsity of every proposition. That is, for each possible world-state $w$, the assumption that the world is in world-state $w$ either entails the proposition $x$, or it entails its contradictory, for every proposition $x$. I, and many others, have suggested that one might define propositions as sets of possible worlds, or at least to model propositions as sets of possible worlds, or equivalently, functions from possible worlds to truth values. But I don't think that there is any kind of conceptual priority here, and there are some limitations to this order of analysis that will emerge. Even if one is operating with a coarse-grained conception of proposition,

Thanks to Aviv Hoffmann for his incisive comments on my paper at the St Andrews conference, as well as for discussion about these issues over the years. Thanks also to Tim Williamson for correspondence that helped me to understand and appreciate his position.

according to which propositions *x* and *y* are identical if and only if they are necessarily equivalent, it may be better, for some purposes, to think of possible worlds as maximal consistent propositions. Whichever direction the analysis goes, each coarse-grained proposition will determine a unique set of maximal propositions: those that entail it. And each such set will determine a unique proposition that is true if and only if one member of the set is true (at least on the assumption that for any set of propositions, there is a proposition that is true if and only if one of the members of the set is true).[1]

Suppose we identify possible worlds with maximal consistent propositions and we also allow that some propositions exist only contingently (and that there might exist propositions that do not in fact exist). Then we will face the following prima facie problem: suppose there is a proposition *x* that would not exist if a certain maximal proposition *w* were true. Presumably, the contradictory of *x* would not exist either (since we may assume that every proposition has a contradictory, and that the contradictory relation is symmetric). Since the maximality of *w* implies that for each proposition *y*, *w* entails either *y* or the contradictory of *y*, we can conclude that *w* will entail either *x* or its contradictory, even though neither *x* nor its contradictory would exist if *w* were true. One will have to say that either the proposition *x* or its contradictory will be *true* with respect to the possible world *w*, even though neither of those propositions would exist if *w* were actual. And what may seem even worse, if we allow that there might exist propositions that do not in fact exist, then we will be committed to saying that there might have been propositions that would have been true with respect to the actual world, even though there in fact are no such propositions.

These are puzzling and surprising consequences that require some explanation. Why should one accept a thesis that saddles us with this problem? One reason is that the thesis that there are contingently existing propositions is entailed by a pair of assumptions that each has considerable intuitive support: first, a thesis that Alvin Plantinga calls '*existentialism*': the thesis that 'a singular proposition is ontologically dependent on the individuals it is directly about'.[2] Second is the assumption that there are some things that exist only contingently. The second of these assumptions seems to require little explanation or defence, although some philosophers have denied it, as we will see. It seems at least prima facie reasonable to take it to be a Moorean fact that people and ordinary physical objects are things that might not have existed. But what about the first assumption? There are different accounts of what propositions are that might motivate this thesis. If you think of a singular proposition as a kind of Russellian proposition, an ordered sequence containing the individual, along with properties and relations,

---

[1] In Stalnaker (1976), I compare the two orders of analysis, and note that given certain independently plausible assumptions, a minimal theory of propositions will yield the conclusion that there is a 1-1 correspondence between propositions and sets of maximal propositions.

[2] Plantinga (1983), p. 160.

as constituents, then it is natural to think that the existentialist thesis must be true, since it is natural to believe that sets and sequences are ontologically dependent on their elements. But even if one is presupposing, as I am, a coarse-grained conception according to which propositions are individuated by their truth conditions, it seems prima facie reasonable to think that propositions about particular individuals are ontologically dependent on the individuals they are about. A singular proposition, on this conception of proposition, is a proposition that is true if and only if some particular individual or individuals exist and satisfy some condition. The case for the conclusion that such propositions are ontologically dependent on the individuals they are about is clearest if we consider the possibility of singular propositions about individuals that do not in fact exist. Consider the possibility — surely a metaphysical possibility — that Saul Kripke had seven sons. If he had had seven sons, then there would be a particular person who was his seventh son, and there would be singular propositions about that person; for example, there would be a true singular proposition of the form '$x$ is Saul Kripke's seventh son', where the value of $x$ is that person. Given the assumption that nothing actually exists which is that person (or that would be that person), it seems reasonable to think that there is no such proposition, no determinate truth condition that might individuate it. Suppose, in a world in which Saul Kripke had seven sons, he says to his seventh son: 'you might never have existed; my seventh son might have been someone else'. How do we (in the actual world) distinguish the condition that it is this $x$ who was the seventh son from the corresponding condition that would be satisfied if the possibility to which Kripke would be alluding were satisfied?

I think singular propositions about contingent concrete particulars are only the clearest case of contingently existing propositions, since I see no reason to assume that even contingent general propositions, such as universal and existential generalizations involving purely qualitative properties, might not be contingently existing propositions as well. Consider, for example, colour properties — paradigms of purely qualitative properties. If there are metaphysically possible worlds with radically different physical laws, perhaps worlds without light or other kinds of electromagnetic radiation, then there will be worlds in which nothing is or could be coloured, and I think it would also be reasonable to conclude that the colour properties would not exist in such a world. But suppose we assume, for the moment, that the only contingency in the existence of propositions arises from the contingent existence of individuals. Then we can give a more specific account of the kind of structure that will model the situation. A completely orthodox Kripke model for a quantified modal language, supplemented with a theory of propositions, will be an account of the kind we want.

So suppose we have a first order modal language with names as well as predicates and quantifiers. The orthodox model will be a structure, $<W, @, \{D_w : w \in W\}>$. $W$ is the set of possible worlds, where here the 'worlds' consist of the points in logical space, and not the maximal propositions, which will vary from point to point. $@$ is a designated member of $W$, representing the actual world. (I will refer to the members of $W$ as points, rather than worlds, just to distinguish them from maximal propositions.[3]) $D_w$ is the domain of point $w$, and we allow that these domains may vary from point to point. The members of the domain of the actual world @ may be in some other domains as well, and more generally, possible individuals may be members of the domains of more than one world. This is the kind of model we want, but we need to take the intuitive account of what is being modelled by this structure with a grain of salt. The theory of propositions that we add to it is intended to give a little substance to the explanation of what part of the orthodox story we want to take back.

Now we can define, in terms of the standard model, an equivalence relation on points, relative to each point. The rough idea is this: for all $x, y$, and $z \in W$, $y \approx_x z$ if and only if every proposition that is entirely about members of the domain of $x$ has the same truth value in $y$ as it has in $z$. Propositions entirely about the members of the domain of $x$ are those expressible in a language with (rigid) names only for the members of the domain of $x$. These equivalence relations determine a set of equivalence classes with respect to each member of $W$, and these will model the maximal propositions that would exist if that point were realized. The differences between points that are equivalent with respect to the actual world have no representational significance. Any permutation of the 'possible individuals' that preserved identity and difference, as well as the qualitative character of the individuals, and that mapped all *actual* individuals onto themselves would be an equivalent representation—a representation of the same facts, including the modal facts. The domains of other possible worlds (or those members of the domains that are not actually existing individuals) represent the generic possibility of there being individuals of a certain kind, though if individuals of the kinds that might exist did exist, they would be individuals with modal properties, and whatever concrete individuality that actual individuals have.

That is the general picture. Now I want to make one remark about a feature of any account of propositions and possible worlds, this one or any alternative to it, that allows for contingently existing propositions. Any such account will require a distinction between what Kit Fine has called inner and outer truth: there will be propositions that are true *of*, or *with respect to*, a possible world, while not being true *in* that possible world. For a proposition to be true *in* a possible world is for it to have, in that world, the property of truth. For a proposition to be true *of* a possible world is for it to stand (in the actual world) in a certain relation to

---

[3] The actualist who wants to talk of possible worlds is already committed to a distinction between two senses of 'possible world' that might be confused: a 'world' as a way a world might be, and a world or universe in the literal sense of a world that *is* the way that a world might be. According to the actualist, there are many things of the former kind, but only one of the latter kind. The actualist who accepts the further thesis that I am defending, and who develops it in the way I am proposing, must admit a third distinct way of understanding the notion of a possible world. The 'worlds' of the model are the points, which are different both from maximal propositions, or maximal ways a world might be, and from things that instantiate those ways.

that possible world. If we think of possible world-states as maximal propositions (or at least as corresponding to maximal propositions), then a proposition $x$ is *true of* a possible world-state $w$ if and only if $w$ entails $x$ (or the maximal proposition corresponding to world-state $w$ entails $x$). That these two notions will come apart follows from the following assumptions: (1) some propositions exist only contingently; (2) every proposition has a contradictory—a proposition that necessarily is true if and only if the given proposition is false; (3) necessarily, only existing things have properties, and in particular, only existing propositions have the property of truth. Here is the argument: By (1), there is a proposition $x$ that exists only contingently, which means that there will be a possible world-state $w$ that does not include $x$ in its domain. But then, by (2) its contradictory will also not be in the domain of $w$, and so by (3) neither $x$ nor its contradictory will, in $w$, have the property of truth. But world-states are, by definition, maximal, and so for any proposition, $w$ will entail either the proposition or its contradictory. So since $w$ will entail either $x$ or the contradictory of $x$, there will be a proposition that is true of that world-state, but not true in it.

This distinction is either ignored or rejected in the arguments by Plantinga and Williamson against contingently existing propositions, arguments that I want now to examine.

The two arguments I will consider draw different conclusions, since they stand in a modus ponens/modus tollens relation to each other. Plantinga takes it as given and uncontroversial that there are things that exist contingently, and argues that singular propositions about such individuals are not object-dependent. Williamson takes it as given that singular propositions are object-dependent, and argues that there are no things that exist contingently. But the route from premise to conclusion (or from negation of conclusion to negation of premise) is essentially the same. The arguments yield the common conclusion that there are no contingently existing propositions, and both arguments force their proponents to make ontological commitments that some may find unpalatable: in Plantinga's case, to individual essences, or 'thisnesses' for each possibility of an entity. So for Plantinga, while there may be no actually existing thing that would be Saul Kripke's seventh son if he had seven sons, there do exist properties, probably infinitely many of them, that would suffice to individuate each of the possible individuals who, in each of the possible worlds in which Saul Kripke had seven sons, would have been his seventh son. For Williamson, the individuals themselves, and not just their individual essences, actually exist, though they do not, in the actual world, have the properties of being human beings, or even concrete objects that are located in space and time. Some who find both of these metaphysical pictures implausible see little difference between them, but it is often hard to see the relationship between different metaphysical views that one rejects. If forced to choose, I suppose I would find Plantinga's metaphysics more palatable, but I don't think one has to choose.

Let me start with Plantinga's version of the argument, and then look at Williamson's similar but simpler argument, and at his reasons for rejecting the criticism of it that relies on the distinction between the two notions of truth.

Plantinga's argument[4] has five premises:

P1. Possibly, Socrates does not exist.

P2. If P1, then the proposition *Socrates does not exist* is possible.

P3. If the proposition *Socrates does not exist* is possible, then the proposition *Socrates does not exist* is possibly true.

P4. Necessarily, if *Socrates does not exist* had been true, then *Socrates does not exist* would have existed.

P5. Necessarily, if *Socrates does not exist* had been true, then Socrates would not have existed.

The conclusion drawn from these premises is as follows:

C. It is possible that both Socrates does not exist, and the proposition *Socrates does not exist* exists.

The argument goes as follows: the first three premises obviously entail that *Socrates does not exist* is possibly true, and this, together with P4 and P5, entails C. The latter inference has the form:

$$\Diamond P, \Box(P \to Q), \Box(P \to R), \text{ therefore}, \Diamond(Q\&R).$$

This is an inference that is valid in any normal modal logic.

Plantinga takes premise P1 to be uncontroversial, not anticipating Williamson's reason for rejecting his conclusion, and everyone will accept P5. But Plantinga notes that each of the other premises has been denied (by Larry Powers, Arthur Prior, and John Pollock respectively), and he considers three different defences of object-dependence that choose one of these premises to reject. This way of setting up the problem exaggerates the differences between the three responses to the argument that he considers, since (I will argue) there is an equivocation in the consequent of P2 (and the antecedent of P3), and the choice of which premise to reject depends on how that equivocation is resolved. The responses that Plantinga calls 'Priorian existentialism', which rejects P2 and 'Powersian existentialism', which rejects P3, are different only in that they resolve the equivocation in different ways. The third response that Plantinga considers, 'Pollockian existentialism', which rejects P4, also turns on the distinction between the two ways of understanding truth, though since I don't think one can get to the second stage of the argument in any case, the rejection of P4, on one (less natural) interpretation, is not necessary to defeat the argument.

[4] Plantinga (1983).

To bring out the different interpretations of the clause that is the consequent of P2 and the antecedent of P3, let me introduce some notation: First, I will use '$\pi$' as a term-forming operator on sentences. For any sentence $\phi$, '$\pi\phi$' will denote the proposition expressed by $\phi$. So if S abbreviates the sentence 'Socrates does not exist', then '$\pi$S' will abbreviate 'the proposition *Socrates does not exist*'. Second, I will use the letter 'T' to be a monadic truth predicate, applied to propositions. Third, I will use a binary predicate, 'E' relating propositions, for 'entails'. So '$Exy$' says that proposition $x$ entails proposition $y$. Fourth, I will use a variable-binding abstraction operator to form complex predicates. '$\lambda x(Fx \lor Gx)$' will be a monadic predicate that will have, as its extension, the individuals that are in the extension of either F or G.

I will be assuming that the propositions that are the values of variables ranging over propositions, and the referents of expressions of the form '$\pi\phi$' are coarse-grained propositions: mutually entailing propositions are identical. Possible worlds will be identified with maximal propositions. To say that a proposition is true *of* a given possible world is just to say that the "world" (which is a maximal proposition) entails the proposition: '$Ewx$' says that proposition $x$ is true *of* world $w$. To say that a proposition is true *in* a given possible world is just to say that the truth predicate applies to it in that possible world: '$Ew\pi Tx$' says that proposition $x$ is true *in* world $w$. As we have seen, these two notions inevitably come apart if there are contingent objects, and object-dependent propositions, so it would beg the question just to assume that they coincide.

I will use the symbol '@' for the actual world (or world-state), which is the maximal true proposition. A proposition will be true if and only if it is entailed by the actual world: $(x)(Tx \leftrightarrow E@x)$. For present purposes, the variables '$x$' and '$y$' will range over propositions generally, but the variable '$w$' will be restricted to possible worlds, or maximal propositions.

Plantinga's premises P2 and P3 are stated in terms of a predicate of propositions, 'is possible', which might be defined in terms of truth or entailment in several different ways. Here are two definitions, which are not equivalent:

'possible$_1$' $=_{df} \lambda x \Diamond Tx$
'possible$_2$' $=_{df} \lambda x(\exists w)Ewx$.

The first predicate applies to those propositions that are true *in* some possible world, while the second applies to those propositions that are true *of*, or *entailed by*, some possible world. The two definitions will be equivalent if all propositions exist necessarily, but not if some do not.

If one understands the predicate of possibility, as it occurs in the premises of Plantinga's argument in the first way, then one should reject P2, but accept P3 (opting for the Powers response). On the other hand, if one understands the predicate in the second way, then one should accept P2, but reject P3 (opting for the Prior response). The singular proposition *Socrates does not exist* is a proposition that will be true *of*, or entailed by, only possible worlds in which that

.proposition does not exist. Since we are agreeing with Plantinga that nothing can be truly predicated of something that does not exist, the truth predicate will not apply to any proposition in a possible world in which that proposition does not exist.

The Pollock response rejects P4. The most natural way to take P4 is to take the antecedent of the conditional at face value as an application of the predicate of truth to the proposition. But there may be some uses of the word 'true' that should be understood as treating it like a redundant operator, its role being either rhetorical, or to help mark a scope distinction. But given that there is a way to understand P4 so that it is true, it does not really help to find an interpretation according to which it is false. So I think it is the diagnosis in terms of the equivocation in P2 and P3 that shows where the argument fails.

Now Plantinga does not explain how his possibility predicate is to be understood, or address the distinction between the two ways of understanding truth, but Williamson does respond to a diagnosis of his argument that attempts to avoid the conclusion by appealing to this distinction. The distinction between true-in and true-of cannot, he argues, be sustained. Let me sketch Williamson's simpler version of the argument, which bypasses the possibility predicate, and then consider the criticism and response.

Williamson's argument[5] uses himself, rather than Socrates, as his exemplar (or perhaps he is inviting us each to give the argument about him or herself).

> W1 Necessarily, if I don't exist, then the proposition that I don't exist is true.
>
> W2 Necessarily, if the proposition that I don't exist is true, then it exists.
>
> W3 Necessarily, if the proposition that I don't exist exists, then I exist.
>
> Therefore, necessarily, I exist.

The true-in/true-of distinction comes into play because 'true' in these premises occurs within the scope of a modal operator. A proposition might be true *of* a counterfactual possible world while not being true *in* it because it does not exist there. We can bring out the difference between the alternative interpretations of W1 and W2 by paraphrasing the necessity claims in terms of their possible worlds analyses:

> W1a For any world $w$, if I don't exist in $w$, then in $w$, the proposition that I don't exist is true.
>
> W1b For any world $w$, if I don't exist in $w$, then the proposition that I don't exist is true of $w$.
>
> W2a For any world $w$, if, in $w$, the proposition that I don't exist is true, then, in $w$, the proposition that I don't exist exists.

---

[5] Williamson (2002).

W2b  For any world $w$, if the proposition that I don't exist is true of $w$, then, in $w$, the proposition that I don't exist exists.

The proponent of contingently existing propositions accepts W1b and W2a, while rejecting W1a and W2b, and the conclusion.

The main role of the distinction, in diagnosing Williamson's argument, is to help explain the temptation to accept the first premise. The critic grants that there is a way to understand that premise so that it is true, but argues that there is no way of understanding the premises so that both are true, and the argument is valid.

Williamson rejects the distinction, as applied to propositions, though acknowledging that it can be made for sentences and other objects that express propositions. He claims that the only way to understand 'true-of' is as 'true-in', and he would also reject the possible-worlds paraphrases of the premises of his argument. I find his reasons for rejecting the distinction unpersuasive. One of his reasons is a worry about circularity. The second reason, which Williamson takes to be more decisive, is an argument that relies on what I think is a bad analogy between the true-of concept and the Tarskian notion of satisfaction.

First, here is Williamson's circularity worry: Suppose we define a possible world as a consistent and complete set of propositions, where a set $X$ of propositions is consistent if and only if for any proposition $y$, if there is a valid argument from $X$ to $y$, then there is not a valid argument from $X$ to the contradictory of $y$, and $X$ is complete if and only if for any $y$, there is a valid argument either from $X$ to $y$ or from $X$ to the contradictory of $y$. Suppose further that the notion of validity is explained as *necessary* truth preservation. Possible worlds are thus explained in terms of the notion of validity, which is explained in terms of truth and necessity. But necessity is explained in terms of truth at (or with respect to) all possible worlds.

It should certainly be acknowledged that one cannot combine a definition of validity (or entailment) in terms of truth and necessity with an analysis of necessity in terms of a notion defined in terms of validity, but the circularity of such a combination of analyses seems to be problematic independently of the true-in/true-of distinction. It is not obvious which of these fundamental notions (truth, propositional validity, possible world, etc.) should be taken as more basic and used to explain the others, but wherever we start, I don't think this argument threatens the intelligibility of the distinction. Suppose we take propositions as primitive, as Williamson suggests. We must also help ourselves to some primitive relations and operations on propositions: propositions are essentially objects that exemplify a certain structure. Williamson's notion of propositional validity, or entailment, is one relation determined by the minimal structure that propositions must have, and it cannot be defined or explained in terms of the property of truth alone. Suppose we assume, in our theory of propositions, that propositions are bearers of truth (that some of them are true, and others false) and that there is a primitive relation of entailment holding between certain sets of propositions and propositions. We must also assume that the entailment relation has the appropriate structure, and that entailment and truth are related in the appropriate way (specifically, that all the entailments of a set of truths are true). The resources necessary for a minimal theory of propositions will give us the material to define the *true-of* relation (in a theory in which possible worlds are defined in the way Williamson suggests, as maximal consistent sets of propositions): a proposition is *true-of* a possible world if and only if it is entailed by it. A proposition $x$ will be true *in* a world if and only if $x$ has the monadic property *true* with respect to that world, which will be true if and only if the proposition that $x$ is true is entailed by, or is a member of, that world. There is no circularity here. 'True-of' is defined independently of the monadic property of truth, though if we define the actual world as the set of all truths, then it will be a consequence of this little theory of propositions that a proposition is true *in* the actual world if and only if it is true *of* the actual world, as one would expect. It will not follow that a proposition $x$ is true-*in* an arbitrary world $w$ if and only if $x$ is true-*of* $w$.

One might think that if one took *necessity* as primitive, not trying to analyse it in terms of possible worlds, then one could define propositional validity or entailment, in terms of necessity and truth in a way that was not circular: $x$ entails $y$ if and only if necessarily, if $x$ is true, then $y$ is true. But this equivalence will fail if we allow that a proposition might be true-*of* a possible world, while not existing, and so not being true-*in* that world. And as Williamson has observed (in correspondence), there is also no other way to analyse entailment in terms of truth and necessity, on the account I am defending. This is right, and it must be acknowledged that the equivalence (entailment = necessary truth preservation) has considerable intuitive plausibility. But I don't think it could count as a *definition* of entailment in any case, since we cannot understand the notions of truth and necessity without some account of the objects that have these properties (being true, or being necessary)—propositions—and I don't think we can have an account of propositions without assuming that they have at least the minimal structure that gives rise to relations of entailment, compatibility, exclusion, etc.

Williamson grants that the circularity objection is not decisive; the second objection he takes to have more force, but I think its target is not the distinction in question. As I understand this objection, it assumes that the true-of notion is modelled on the Tarskian notion of satisfaction. Open sentences that are satisfied by, or true of, some things in the domain but not others are not true or false simpliciter, and express propositions only relative to a specification of the values of the free variables. The analogy suggests that contingent propositions, which are true-of some possible worlds but false-of others, will also express determinate propositions, with absolute truth values, only relative to the specification of the value of a tacit reference to a possible world. But truth is a monadic property, and propositions, including contingent ones, have their truth values absolutely. Here is the relevant part of his argument:

Consider the contingently true proposition that Blair was Prime Minister in 2000. It is supposed to be true of the actual world @ and false of some other possible world $w$. On the model, the sentence contains a tacit variable; if @ is assigned to the variable, a truth results, if $w$ is assigned, a falsehood. But. . . it is not contingent that Blair was Prime Minister in 2000 in @ and that he was not Prime Minister in 2000 in $w$.　(Williamson 2002, p. 239)

I think this objection misconstrues the true-of notion, which is not similar, in relevant respects, to the notion of satisfaction (perhaps the true-of terminology is misleading). True-of, in the relevant sense, is just entailment: a proposition is true with respect to a given possible state of the world if and only if that proposition is entailed by the maximal proposition that is that possible state of the world. That a proposition is entailed by various maximal propositions, and not by others, does not prevent it from having the monadic property of truth. It is certainly right that the proposition *that Blair was Prime Minister in 2000 in @, and not Prime Minister in 2000 in w* is not a contingent proposition, and it is clear and not at issue that this necessarily true proposition is different from the proposition that Blair was Prime Minister in 2000, which is contingent. This latter proposition does not have a tacit world variable—it is true, just as it stands. The defender of the view being criticized has no reason to suppose that this sentence really expresses, not the contingent proposition that it seems to express, but instead the necessary proposition that the contingent proposition is entailed by @.

We can distinguish these (possibly) different propositions:

(1) That Blair was Prime Minister in 2000.

(2) That proposition (1) is true.

(3) That (1) is true of @ and false of $w$.

On our coarse-grained account of propositions, (1) = (2); since they are mutually entailing (though it is not true of every proposition $x$ that $x$ is necessarily equivalent to the proposition that $x$ is true). But everyone will agree that both (1) and (2) are different from (3). I don't see why the distinction between truth in a world and truth of a world should require one to say otherwise.

I don't have an argument against the existence of the kind of individual essences for non-existent things that Plantinga believes in, nor do I have an argument against the existence of a vast population of actual things that could have been living people, and other material beings, but that actually are not, and that reside in some realm outside of space and time. The famous incredulous stare that David Lewis took to be the strongest argument against his modal realism is good enough for me, not only for Lewis's modal realism, but also for the metaphysical commitments of Plantinga and Williamson, which seem to me to have about the same degree of prima facie plausibility. My aim has been just to show that one can at least give a coherent account of modality that allows for an expansive view of what is possible—one that accords with our pre-theoretic modal beliefs—without committing oneself to an excessively extravagant view of what actually exists. The modal framework is supposed to be neutral, allowing for the kinds of ontologies that Williamson and Plantinga endorse, as well as for those that accord more closely with common opinion. But if we succeed in rebutting some unsound arguments in support of such ontologies, I think the temptation to believe in them should go away.

# Response to Robert Stalnaker

*Aviv Hoffmann*

Robert Stalnaker intends his theory to be a theory in which possible worlds and propositions exist contingently. I will argue that it is not such a theory.

Stalnaker's theory builds on a standard Kripke model structure $<W, @, \{D_w: w \in W\}>$, where $W$ is the set of points in logical space (not to be confused with possible worlds in the sense to be explained shortly), $@$ (a member of $W$) is the realized (i.e., actual) point, and, for each member $w$ of $W$, $D_w$ is the domain of $w$ (the set of objects that *exist* in the point $w$ in the sense that they would exist if $w$ were realized). Possible worlds (maximal ways a universe might be) enter the picture as follows. The theory requires that each member of $W$ have an equivalence relation associated with it. Stalnaker explains: 'These equivalence relations determine a set of equivalence classes with respect to each member of $W$, and these will model the maximal propositions that would exist if that point were realized.' Possible worlds are thought of as maximal (and consistent) propositions so, by Stalnaker's explanation, the equivalence classes with respect to each member of $W$ model the possible worlds that would exist if that point were realized.

To show that, in Stalnaker's theory, possible worlds are necessary existents, I will argue first that, in the theory, each point in logical space exists in each point. As we saw, an equivalence class with respect to a point models a possible world that exists in the point (a world that would exist if the point were realized) so, in the *intended* model (logical space), the class itself exists in the point. A class (a set-like object) exists in a point only if its members exist in the point: the set existence axiom of modal set theory states that 'a set exists in a possible world if and only if all of its members exist in that possible world' (Fine 1981, p. 180). (Stalnaker associates the domains $D_w$ with points, rather than with possible worlds, so the set existence axiom must be reworded so that it speaks of existence in a point rather than a possible world.) Thus, (i) the members of the equivalence classes with respect to each point exist in the point. Moreover, (ii) the equivalence classes with respect to each point *exhaust* logical space: for each member $w$ of $W$, each member $v$ of $W$ is a member of some (at most one) equivalence class with respect to $w$. This is so because Stalnaker defines the equivalence relations *universally* on $W$: 'for all $x, y$, and $z \in W, y \approx_x z$ if

Thanks to Robert Stalnaker and Peter Vranas for their comments on this Response.

and only if. . .' (my emphasis). By (i) and (ii), each point in logical space exists in each point. Again, by the set existence axiom, it follows that each class of points—hence each equivalence class (each possible world) with respect to each point—exists in each point. Thus, possible worlds are necessary existents. Note that a possible world may be a *possible world* contingently: a class of points may be an equivalence class with respect to one member of $W$ but not with respect to another.

Modal set-theoretic considerations also show that, in Stalnaker's theory, propositions are necessary existents. As I argued, the equivalence classes with respect to each point exist in each point. Modal set theory entails that sets exist in a point only if their union exists in the point. It follows that the unions of the equivalence classes with respect to each point exist in each point. The unions of the equivalence classes with respect to each member of $W$ model the propositions that would exist if that point were realized. So, for each member $w$ of $W$, the propositions that exist in $w$ exist in each point: (necessarily) propositions are necessary existents. Note that a proposition may be a *proposition* contingently: a class of points may be a union of equivalence classes with respect to one member of $W$ but not with respect to another.

To motivate his theory, Stalnaker invokes the thesis that Plantinga has labelled *existentialism*, namely that 'a singular proposition is ontologically dependent on the individuals it is directly about'. When we attribute wisdom to Socrates directly—when we say that *he* (rather than, say, *the philosopher who drank hemlock*) is wise—we assert a singular proposition about Socrates, call it *Socratwise*. Existentialism entails that, had Socrates not existed, Socratwise would not have existed. A thesis weaker than existentialism is that, had Socrates not existed, there would have been no such *proposition* as Socratwise. Let *accidentalism* (about propositions) be the thesis that propositions are not essentially propositions. Accidentalism allows that, had Socrates not existed, Socratwise *would* have existed but it would not have been a proposition. My objection then is that Stalnaker's theory is accidentalist rather than existentialist.

# 2

# Logical Necessity*

*Ian Rumfitt*

Is there a coherent notion of logical necessity? If so, how is it related to other modal notions, notably those of metaphysical necessity, and of being knowable *a priori*? This essay addresses these questions in turn.

What does it mean to say that there is a notion of logical necessity? I mean this: there is a sense of 'necessary' for which ⌜It is necessary that $A$⌝ implies and is implied by ⌜It is logically contradictory that not $A$⌝. If we assume a classical logic, as I shall throughout this essay, we immediately have the following meta-theorem: whenever $B$ follows logically from $A_1, \ldots, A_n$, the statement ⌜It is logically necessary that if $A_1$ and . . . and $A_n$ then $B$⌝ is true (where the conditional is understood to be material).[1] So logical necessity is implicated in logical consequence. However, the meta-theorem does not by itself characterize logical necessity. An analogue of the meta-theorem will hold for any species of necessity which validates the 'rule of necessitation',[2] a rule which is widely assumed to be valid for physical and metaphysical necessity, among other modalities. Our characterization of logical necessity is far more exacting: it is physically impossible that a particle should have travelled from the Sun to the Earth in less than a minute, but it is not logically contradictory that it should have done so.

---

* This essay differs markedly from the paper I read at the St Andrews conference. The paper proposed a formal treatment of logical necessity, applicable even when the underlying non-modal logic was as weak as minimal logic. In the discussion at the conference, however, I realized that the conceptual issues surrounding logical necessity needed a more thorough airing than I had given them: this essay confines itself to those conceptual issues, and leaves the formal matters for a future paper. It condenses three lectures I have delivered on a number of occasions during the past five years at the Universities of Oxford and London. For comments on a draft, I am much indebted to Jonathan Barnes, Dorothy Edgington, Crispin Wright (my commentator at St Andrews), and (especially) Bob Hale.

[1] For suppose $B$ follows logically from $A_1, \ldots, A_n$. Then the statement ⌜It is logically contradictory that $A_1$ and . . . and $A_n$ and not $B$⌝ is true. So, if 'if . . . then' is read as a material conditional, the statement ⌜It is logically contradictory that not (if $A_1$ and . . . and $A_n$ then $B$)⌝ is true. So, on the recommended conception of logical necessity, the statement ⌜It is logically necessary that if $A_1$ and . . . and $A_n$ then $B$⌝ is true.

[2] This is the rule of proof that licenses the inference from the theoremhood of $A$ to the theoremhood of ⌜It is necessary that $A$⌝.

What does it mean to say ⌜It is logically contradictory that $A$⌝? I mean that some overt contradiction follows logically from the supposition $A$. Overt contradictions include formal contradictions of the form ⌜$B$ and not $B$⌝, but I also take them to include 'This is red all over and green all over' and 'This is red and not coloured'. The criterion for being an overt contradiction relates to our practice of deducing consequences from hypotheses. Sometimes, in making such deductions, we reach a point from which no forward inferential step can be taken: all we can do is to retrace our steps and ask which of our hypotheses led us to the impasse. An overt contradiction marks an impasse of this kind. Thus, if a hypothesis yields the consequence 'This is red and not coloured', we know that the hypothesis must be wrong; deduction can proceed only by discharging it, and exploring the consequences of its negation.

'Consequence' here is to be taken in the broad sense that Moore gestured towards when he appropriated the word 'entails' from the lawyers: we shall 'be able to say truly that "$p$ entails $q$" when and only when we are able to say truly that "$q$ follows from $p$",. . . in the sense in which the conclusion of a syllogism in Barbara follows from the two premises. . .; or in which the proposition "This is coloured" follows from "This is red"' (Moore 1922, p. 291). As it stands, this is little more than a gesture, and one of my aims is to fill out Moore's explanation. Some elaboration of it is surely needed. There is of course a close relationship between consequence and argumentative soundness—when an argument is sound its conclusion follows from its premises—but by itself this is of little help in glossing the notion of broadly logical consequence, for our ordinary standards for deeming arguments to be sound vary greatly from context to context. In some contexts of evaluation, even the package tourist's syllogism—'It's Tuesday; so this is Belgium'—may meet the operative standards for soundness, and its conclusion may then be said to stand to its premiss in a relation of consequence that sets those standards.[3] A philosopher may seek marks which distinguish broadly logical consequence from other consequence relations such as these. But to seek such marks is in part to ask whether there is any theoretically interesting grouping that includes Moore's two cases while excluding the tourist's syllogism and, if so, what the most fruitful criterion for membership in that group might be. So the discussion will need to transcend the trading of 'intuitions' about which arguments are broadly logically valid and at least glance towards wider issues about the scope of logic, and about the value of our capacity for deductive argument.

In advance of that discussion, some terminological remarks are in order. I take the primary *relata* of consequence relations, and the premisses and conclusions of arguments, to be what I call *statements*. To see what I mean

---

[3] For this example, and for others that convey a lively sense of the plethora of consequence relations implicated in everyday deductive reasoning, see Smiley (1995). For a theory of logic that takes account of this plethora of consequence relations, see Rumfitt (2009).

by this term, consider those ordered pairs whose first element is a meaningful, indeed disambiguated, declarative type sentence and whose second element is a possible context of utterance; by a possible context of utterance, I mean a determination of all the contextual features which can bear upon the truth or falsity of a declarative utterance. Some of these ordered pairs are such that, were the declarative type sentence that is the pair's first element uttered in the context that is the second element, a determinate proposition, or complete thought, would then be expressed. As I use the term, a *statement* is an ordered pair that meets this condition. Not every ordered pair of declarative type sentence and possible context of utterance will qualify as a statement in this sense. For example, an ordered pair of sentence and context whose first member is the English sentence 'You are ill' will not count as a statement unless the context supplies an addressee. On this understanding of the matter, each statement belongs to a language, namely, the language of the sentence that is its first element. Furthermore, each statement possesses a sense or propositional content: this will be the thought that would be expressed by uttering the statement's first element (the declarative sentence) in the context that comprises its second element. It then makes sense to classify a statement as true or false *simpliciter*, according as that thought is true or false. Both assertions and utterances made within the scope of suppositions may be instances of statements: utterances of either kind will instantiate a given statement when the utterance is of the declarative sentence that is the statement's first member and is made in the context that is the statement's second member. It is, I admit, somewhat infelicitous to have unasserted statements, for 'states' often means 'asserts'; however, alternative terms are more likely to mislead. The term 'proposition', for instance, would have done better (one may propound without asserting) had not philosophers already appropriated it to stand for what a declarative utterance expresses.

Statements in this sense serve well as the *relata* of consequence relations. The obscurities that attend questions of propositional identity are bracketed: whatever may be said about the thoughts they express, the statements 'There is a choice function for every set of non-empty sets' and 'Every set can be well ordered' are evidently distinct, for their first members are distinct sentences. Furthermore, the quantification over all possible contexts of utterance ensures that statements are not confined to actual utterances or inscriptions, so laws concerning all statements can exhibit the sort of generality we expect of logical laws. The premisses and conclusion of a single argument may be understood to be statements with a common second element. We assume, in other words, that the context is held constant throughout an argument. This seems to be a presupposition of the logical appraisal of arguments. In assessing the argument 'I am taller than you. So you are shorter than me', a logician is not expected to take account of the possibility that our relative heights may have changed in the course of my propounding it. Nor is that argument an enthymeme because it takes for granted that there has been no shift in reference between the two occurrences of the pronoun 'you'.[4] If we assume that consequence correlates with argumentative soundness, this means we need only consider consequence as it relates statements that share a context of utterance.

## 1. RUSSELL'S PHILONIANISM, AND WHY IT FAILS

The claim that there is a modality related in this way to logical consequence goes back to Aristotle: 'a deduction is a discourse in which, certain things being stated, something other than what is stated follows of necessity from their being so'—that is, from their being true (*Analytica Priora*, 24$^b$18–19). The claim is supported by our tendency to use modal locutions in glossing the concept of consequence. If 'Thomas is material' follows from 'Everything is material', then it *must* be the case that Thomas is material if everything is; 'Most dogs bark' and 'Fido is a dog' do not jointly entail 'Fido barks', because it is *possible* for Fido to be a dog and for most dogs to bark without Fido's barking. (I shall follow Moore in using 'entails' as the converse of 'follows from'.) All the same, some philosophers have denied that consequence has a modal aspect. Their arguments deserve scrutiny, and are not to be silenced by a mere linguistic tendency.

Perhaps the most prominent recent sceptic about logical necessity was Bertrand Russell, who argued as follows in his *Introduction to Mathematical Philosophy*:

> In order that it be *valid* to infer $q$ from $p$, it is only necessary that $p$ should be true and that the proposition 'not-$p$ or $q$' should be true. Whenever this is the case, it is clear that $q$ must [*sic*] be true. But inference will only in fact take place when the proposition 'not-$p$ or $q$' is *known* otherwise than through knowledge of not-$p$ or knowledge of $q$. Whenever $p$ is false, 'not-$p$ or $q$' is true, but is useless for inference, which requires that $p$ should be true. Whenever $q$ is already known to be true, 'not-$p$ or $q$' is of course also known to be true, but is again useless for inference, since $q$ is already known, and therefore does not need to be inferred. In fact, inference only arises when 'not-$p$ or $q$' can be known without our knowing already which of the two alternatives it is that makes the disjunction true. Now, the circumstances under which this occurs are those in which certain relations of form exist between $p$ and $q$ . . . But this formal relation is only required in order that we may be able to *know* that either the premiss is false or the conclusion is true. It is the truth of 'not-$p$ or $q$' that is required for the *validity* of the inference; what is required further is only for the practical feasibility of the inference.   (Russell 1919, p. 153)

---

[4] Contextual factors 'may be expected to influence the interpretation of an ambiguous [*sic*] expression uniformly wherever the expression recurs in the course of the argument. This is why words of ambiguous reference such as 'I', 'you', 'here', 'Smith', and 'Elm Street' are ordinarily allowable in logical arguments without qualification; their interpretation is indifferent to the logical soundness of an argument, provided merely that it stays the same throughout the space of the argument' (Quine 1982, p. 56).

In other words, *material* or *Philonian* consequence[5]—the relation that obtains when either the conclusion is (actually) true or some premiss is (actually) untrue—suffices for an argument's validity or soundness.[6]

What does Russell mean by an inference? An inference from $p$ to $q$, he tells us, requires that $p$ should be true, and that $q$ should not be known. This is scarcely comprehensible unless we take 'inference', as it comes from his pen, to mean 'an instance of reasoning in which a thinker comes to know a conclusion by deducing it from premises that he knows already'. So the argument tacitly presents as the focal cases of logical appraisal those instances of argumentation in which a thinker applies his capacity for deductive reasoning to gain new knowledge from old.

There is, I think, something right about Russell's decision to take these cases as central: much of the value of our capacity for deductive argument lies in the fact that, by exercising it, we can gain knowledge that we could not otherwise obtain. Suppose I am strapped to the chair in my study. From that chair, I cannot see the street below. I do, however, see that it is raining, and thus know that it is raining. Moreover I know, ultimately on inductive grounds, that if it is raining the street is wet. Accordingly, I reason as follows:

1. It is raining

2. If it is raining, the street is wet

So

3. The street is wet.

My reasoning here is a simple example of what Russell calls an inference. And the case brings out how, by exercising a deductive capacity, a thinker can gain knowledge—knowledge that he would not have been able to gain otherwise. In the case described, I know that it is raining by virtue of seeing that it is raining. And I know through induction that if it is raining, the street is wet. By making the deduction, I thereby come to know that the street is wet. *Ex hypothesi*, I cannot see that the street is wet, so I cannot come to know the conclusion by exercising my perceptual capacities, which is how I came to know the first premiss. Similarly, I cannot come to know the conclusion on inductive grounds alone, which is how I came to know the second premiss. Even

---

5 'Philo [of Megara] says that a sound conditional is one that does not begin with a truth and end with a falsehood, e.g. when it is day and I am conversing, the statement "If it is day, I am conversing"' (Sextus, *Pyrrhoneiae Hypotyposes*, ii. 110, as translated in Kneale and Kneale 1962, p. 128). 'Sound conditional' translates the Greek dialecticians' term for what we would now call a correct sequent.

6 By a 'sound' argument, I mean one whose eventual conclusion (along with any intermediate or subsidiary conclusions) stands to its premises in the contextually operative relation of consequence; the truth of the premises is not required for soundness. By a 'valid' argument, I mean one that is sound when the relation of consequence is 'logical'. A purpose of this essay is to explain the sense of 'logical'.

in England, so pessimistic view of the weather (or of the wastefulness of the water companies) would not yield knowledge. But by exercising my deductive capacity on the knowledge that is delivered by perception and induction, I can come to know something that I could not know on either of those bases alone.[7]

All the same, this consideration does not vindicate Russell's Philonianism. In the first place, while our deductive capacities may be valuable because they enable us to extend our knowledge, we also apply them to things we do not know, as when we trace the implications of things we believe but cannot be said to know. Second, and more importantly, Russell has too narrow a conception of how knowledge is attained by deduction: when we widen our gaze as we are in the end forced to widen it, we see that his strict Philonianism cannot be sustained.

Russell tells us that we can infer $Q$ from $P$ when we know that either not $P$ or $Q$ otherwise than through knowing that not $P$ or knowing that $Q$. But *how* might a thinker know that either not $P$ or $Q$ without knowing that not $P$ or knowing that $Q$? In many cases, I claim, there is no convincing explanation that does not at some point advert to our ability to apply our deductive capacities to suppositions—to things we suppose to be true, or take as hypotheses—as well as to things that we know. Fully substantiating this claim would involve a long excursus into the epistemology of logic, but consideration of a few candidate explanations may convince the reader that the claim is plausible. So, for example, let us grant for the sake of argument that the thinker knows that either not $P$ or $P$. How is that to yield knowledge that either not $P$ or $Q$? In general, the answer must be: because the thinker is able to deduce $Q$ from the supposition that $P$ (where the deduction tracks the contextually relevant consequence relation). Only having made that deduction from a supposition or hypothesis can he infer, in Russell's sense, from his knowledge that either not $P$ or $P$ to attain knowledge that either not $P$ or $Q$.

Now there is nothing alien in the idea that we may exercise our deductive capacities in reasoning from suppositions just as much as in reasoning from what we know. Thus someone might exercise the deductive capacity that is the mark of good reasoners about physics by arguing 'Suppose a (resultant) force is acting on the body. Then—sc., in that case, on that supposition—it will be accelerating' as well as by making a Russellian inference from the knowledge that a force is acting. But reasoning from a supposition plainly demands a stronger condition for validity than Philonian consequence: the bare fact that either the conclusion is true or the premiss is untrue is insufficient to underwrite the soundness of arguments from suppositions, for what is supposed to be

---

[7] There remains the problem, which preoccupied J. S. Mill, of explaining *how* our capacity for deductive argument can yield new knowledge. I discuss this problem in Rumfitt (2008).

the case may fail to be true. Let it be that no force is acting on the relevant body. In that case, any statement whatever will be a Philonian consequence of 'A force is acting on the body'. Yet the argument 'Suppose a force is acting. Then the moon is made of iron' is not a sound argument in physics. To explain why it is unsound, moreover, we have to invoke possibilities, or some cognate modal notion: the argument is unsound because it is physically possible for a force to act on the body without the moon's being made of iron.

Following Frege, Russell formalized his logic *more geometrico*, that is, as a system of putatively known axioms and rules of inference by applying which a thinker can come to know theorems on the basis of those already known axioms. And, it might seem, the possibility of formalizing logic in this way shows that one could in principle avoid any reasoning from suppositions, and so rehabilitate Russell's Philonian account of consequence. But the availability of this style of formalization does not save the account. Formalizing logic in the geometric style is possible. But the question pressed on Russell was how the thinker comes by the relevant knowledge. If logic is formalized in the geometric style, the crucial questions become: how does a thinker know that the axioms are true, and how does he know that the rules preserve truth? And there is no plausible answer to these questions which does not appeal at some point to the subject's ability to make deductions from suppositions. Certainly, the 'elucidations' by which Frege originally justified his 'geometrical' axioms and rules rely on that ability. Thus, in justifying *modus ponens*—from $A \to B$ and $A$, infer $B$—Frege reasons as follows: 'if $B$ were not the True, then since $A$ is the True, $A \to B$ would be the False' (Frege 1893, §14, p. 25; I have updated his logical symbolism). In a case where *modus ponens* is applied in a Russellian inference, $B$ will in fact be true. So Frege's reasoning here traces the consequences of the false supposition that $B$ is not true. His argument is none the worse for that, but it shows how even an adherent of a geometrical formalization of logic is driven to rely on our ability to reason from suppositions in grounding one of the formalization's primitive rules. And what goes for the rules goes equally for the axioms. If the geometrical style of formalization is now little more than a quaint anachronism, that is largely because it fails to show logical truths for what they are: simply the by-products of rules of inference that are applicable to suppositions—by-products that arise when all the suppositions on which a conclusion rests have been discharged.[8]

---

[8] Thus Michael Dummett: 'The first to correct this distorted perspective, and to abandon the analogy between a formalization of logic and an axiomatic theory, was Gentzen...In a sequent calculus or natural deduction formalization of logic, the recognition of statements as logically true does not occupy a central place...The generation of logical truths is thus reduced to its proper, subsidiary, role, as a by-product, not the core, of logic' (Dummett 1981, pp. 433–4).

It will pay dividends later to be more precise about the sort of supposing, or hypothesizing, that is relevant here. One pertinent division corresponds—roughly—to the division between indicative and counterfactual conditionals. 'Suppose Shakespeare didn't write *Hamlet*.' That sends us off in one direction: 'In that case, Marlowe did; nobody else at the time could have done it.' Contrast 'Suppose Shakespeare hadn't written *Hamlet*.' That sends us off along a different path, as it may be: 'In that case, Stoppard wouldn't have written *Rosencrantz and Guildenstern are Dead*.' A full account of the difference between these two kinds of supposing would be complicated, but the crux is that in elaborating suppositions of the first kind, but not the second, we are entitled to draw on what we know. We know that someone wrote *Hamlet*, and given that only Shakespeare and Marlowe were capable of writing it, the only consequent elaboration of the supposition that Shakespeare did not write it is that Marlowe did. In elaborating the supposition that Shakespeare had not written it, by contrast, our knowledge that someone did write it, while not lost, is temporarily set aside.

When I say that our capacity to elaborate suppositions will be part of any satisfactory account of a thinker's logical knowledge, it is the first kind of supposition that I have in mind. Frege's justification of *modus ponens* shows why it is this style of hypothesizing that is relevant. Prior to having made a Russellian inference from *A* to *B*, we shall not know whether *B* is true, so in entertaining the hypothesis 'Suppose that *B* were not true', we do not need to set any knowledge aside. What underpins our knowledge of logical truths, then, is our ability to elaborate suppositions or hypotheses as to what *is* the case; it is not essential that we should also be able to elaborate suppositions about what might have been the case.

## 2. McFETRIDGE'S ACCOUNT OF LOGICAL NECESSITY

The argument of the previous section shows that a consequence relation cannot be Philonian if it supports reasoning from a supposition that may be false. Even the consequence relation that underlies the tourist's argument supports such reasoning ('Suppose it's Tuesday; in that case, this must be Belgium'), so even that relation involves some notion of possibility. Further reflection on the objection to Philonianism, moreover, suggests a principled ground for distinguishing a relation of broadly logical consequence. As we have seen, some modal element will be implicit in any relation of consequence that is understood to relate premises that are entertained merely as suppositions to conclusions that are asserted only within the scope of those suppositions, as well as relating premises and conclusions that are asserted outright. All the same, most consequence relations are such that certain suppositions render them inapplicable in tracing consequences of those suppositions. When a classical physicist reasons 'Suppose a force is acting on this body; in that case, it will be accelerating', it may be reasonable to assess his reasoning against a relation of consequence, $R$, that excludes as impossible all circumstances that conflict with Newton's laws of motion. Just for that reason, though, the argument 'Suppose a force is acting on a body; suppose also that Newton's laws of motion are false; in that case, the body will be accelerating' cannot sensibly be assessed against $R$. The introduction of the new suppositional premiss creates a new argumentative context in which the contextually relevant consequence relation cannot be $R$.

The question then arises, whether there is a relation of consequence that is *absolute* in the sense of being applicable no matter what is supposed to be the case. Ian McFetridge proposed that logical consequence is such a relation, and that logical necessity is the correlative kind of necessity. He quotes with approval Mill's dictum that 'that which is necessary, that which *must* be, means that which will be, whatever supposition we make with regard to other things'.[9] And he goes on to suggest

that we treat as the manifestation of the belief that a mode of inference is logically necessarily truth-preserving, the preparedness to employ that mode of inference in reasoning from any set of suppositions whatsoever. Such a preparedness evinces the belief that, no matter what else was the case, the inferences would preserve truth . . . A central point of interest in having such beliefs about logical necessity is to allow us to deploy principles of inference across the whole range of suppositions we might make. (McFetridge 1990b, p. 153)

(By the same token, belief that a truth is logically necessary amounts to belief that it is true, no matter what is supposed to be the case.) There is no suggestion here that the only modes of inference that are logically necessarily truth-preserving are those codified by the formal rules of logic books. For example, we are surely prepared to apply the rule of inference 'From "$x$ is red" infer "$x$ is coloured" ' in reasoning from any set of suppositions whatsoever. Thus we may read McFetridge as discussing the 'broad', Moorean, notion of logical necessity that we are seeking to elucidate.

McFetridge does not advance an account of what logical necessity is: he only undertakes to say what the *belief* that an inference is logically necessary truth-preserving comes to. But what he says about the latter issue is entirely consonant with the account of logical necessity recommended here. According to that account, $\ulcorner$It is logically necessary that $A\urcorner$ is equivalent to $\ulcorner$It is logically contradictory that not $A\urcorner$. Suppose, then, that it is logically contradictory that

---

[9] McFetridge (1990b), p. 153, quoting Mill (1891), bk. III, ch. v, sect. 6 (not ch. iv, as the editors of McFetridge's *Nachlass* claim). Mill was characterizing causal necessity.

not *A*. In that case, the supposition that not *A* yields a contradiction, no matter what else is supposed to be the case. So, given a classical meta-logic, we are indeed committed to the truth of *A*, no matter what we suppose to be the case. Conversely, if we are committed to the truth of *A*, no matter what we suppose to be the case, then the supposition that not *A* must yield a contradiction. We may, then, read McFetridge as spelling out the cash value of beliefs in logical necessity in just the sense recommended here. His account, moreover, coheres nicely with the original ground for recognizing a modal element in consequence—namely, its applicability to assessing reasoning from suppositions.

The idea that logical consequence is distinguished from other consequence relations through its applicability to any suppositions whatever is supported when we reflect on how we trace the consequences of a supposition that is contrary to an accepted logical law. A classical logician who reduces to absurdity that supposition that $\neg(P \vee \neg P)$ need not consider how his logic might change if excluded middle had a false instance. In his *reductio*, he will apply the normal classical inference rules without demur. I do not mean to imply that the rules of classical logic cannot be challenged: they can be. But someone who accepts classical logic will apply its constitutive inference rules to all suppositions whatever, even to suppositions that are contrary to classical logical laws. That is what it means to accept the classical rules as one's logic.

The proposed account of logical necessity has, then, many merits. Apart from one class of apparent exceptions, which I shall analyse in detail below, it delivers the expected classifications when applied to paradigms of arguments that are, and that are not, logically valid in the broad sense. Even more importantly, the relation it identifies as broadly logical consequence is theoretically significant: since any consequence relation has a modal aspect by virtue of being applicable to suppositions, special interest naturally attaches to a relation that is applicable to absolutely any supposition. We need to inquire, though, how the cognate notion of logical necessity relates to other central modal notions.

There seems to be no reason to suppose that any statement that is logically necessary in the present sense is knowable *a priori*. Indeed, there is no general reason to suppose that a logically necessary statement is knowable at all. If a statement is logically necessary, there will be a contradiction among the consequences of its negation. But its having that property does not imply that someone could know it.

In denying that logical necessity entails knowability *a priori*, I am at odds with Dorothy Edgington. Pre-Kripkean discussions of validity, she remarks, made us 'familiar with two thoughts: first, an argument is valid if and only if it is necessary that the conclusion is true if the premisses are true; and second, if an argument is valid, and you accept that the premisses are true, you need no further empirical information to enable you to recognize that the conclusion is true . . . Given Kripke's work, and taking "necessary" in its metaphysical sense, these two thoughts are not equivalent' (Edgington 2004, p. 9). So we have to choose what the criterion for validity is to be. It is, she claims, 'the least departure from traditional, pre-Kripkean thinking, and more consonant with the point of distinguishing valid from invalid arguments, to take validity to be governed by epistemic necessity, i.e., an argument is valid if and only if there is an *a priori* route from premisses to conclusion' (2004, p. 10).

I shall soon return to the relationship between broadly logical validity and metaphysical necessity, but Edgington's positive account of the former notion does not, I think, capture the concept we are trying to explicate. First, there are statements which we can know *a priori* but which we are reluctant to classify as logically true even on the most generous demarcation of the bounds of logic. Some people now know *a priori* that when the index $n$ is greater than two, there are no integral solutions of the equation $x^n + y^n = z^n$. All the same, it is not simple prejudice to resist the claim that Fermat's Last Theorem is *logically* true. The ground for resistance is not the complexity of the proof: there are long and complex logical deductions. Rather, it is the heavy ontological and ideological commitments of the mathematical theories on which the proof depends. There are good reasons for postulating the truth of those theories: if there were not, then we should not have a proof of the theorem. But supposing that they are false does not lead to the sort of impasse that we have taken to be the mark of the logically contradictory. The reason for this is that the postulates lie far beyond anything that it required for the regulation of *reasoning*, as opposed to calculating, and then theorizing about the numbers invoked in making calculations.

Perhaps Edgington would respond to this point by emending her position, and proposing that an argument is broadly logically valid if and only if there is a route from its premisses to its conclusion that a thinker may traverse purely by exercising his ability to reason. But this emended theory faces a second objection. On the emended proposal, the conclusion of a valid argument must be deducible from its premisses, but while this principle may have been part of 'traditional thinking about validity', it is surely too strong. It excludes notions of validity (such as validity in full second-order logic) for which no complete set of deductive rules can be given. A conclusion may be a second-order consequence of some premisses even when it cannot be deduced from those premisses. Inasmuch as old-fashioned thinking about validity overlooked this point, it was wrong. As for Edgington's suggestion that her account comports best with the point of distinguishing valid from invalid arguments, many philosophers have taken broadly logical consequence to be a relation to which our rules of deduction must *answer*: a rule is to be rejected as (logically) unsound if it enables us to deduce from some premises a purported conclusion that does not follow from them in the broad sense. The idea that deductions answer to consequence would become incomprehensible if consequence were taken to consist in deducibility.

For these reasons, we should not equate logical necessity with being knowable *a priori*. How does the present notion of logical necessity relate to Kripkean metaphysical necessity?[10] It is reasonably clear that some metaphysical necessities are not logically necessary. It is metaphysically necessary that, if Hesperus exists, it is identical with Phosphorus. It is tolerably clear, however, that this is not logically necessary. The supposition that Hesperus exists but is distinct from Phosphorus does not yield a logical contradiction. If certain hypotheses had led to the conclusion that the two planets were distinct, we should not thereby have reached an impasse, from which we have to turn back. On the contrary, we should be able to make further deductions: given that Hesperus is bright and that Phosphorus is bright, there are at least two bright objects; etc.[11]

What of the converse, though? Are there logical necessities that are not meta-physically necessary? McFetridge claims not. Indeed, he advances an interesting general argument that purports to show that logical necessity (conceived as he conceives it) is the strongest form of non-epistemic necessity.[12] His argument rests on two assumptions. First, 'that adding extra premises to a [logically] valid argument cannot destroy its validity . . . If the argument "*P*; so *Q*" is valid then so is the argument "*P*, *R*; so *Q*" *for any R*. Second, that there is this connection

[10] I cannot discuss metaphysical modality in any detail here, but I assume that a metaphysical possibility respects the actual identities of things—in a broad sense of 'thing' that encompasses stuffs such as water, and phenomena such as heat, as well as individual objects such as the planet Venus. This, at least, seems to be the gloss that best vindicates Kripke's attributions of metaphysical necessity in *Naming and Necessity* (1980)—notably his claims that 'Water is $H_2O$' and 'Heat is the motion of molecules' express metaphysically necessary propositions (1980, pp. 99 and 128–33), and his crucial thesis that if $x = y$ then it is metaphysically necessary that $x = y$ (1980, pp. 3–5 and 97–105). For an elaboration and defence of this gloss, see Fine (2002).

[11] While it is widely agreed that there are metaphysically necessary truths that are not logically necessary, Kit Fine has suggested that various narrower notions of necessity, including logical necessity, can still be defined in terms of metaphysical necessity by the method of 'restriction'. Thus we may 'define a proposition to be <logically> necessary if it is necessary in the metaphysical sense and if, in addition, it is a <logical> truth—where this latter notion is presumably one that can be defined in non-modal terms' (Fine 2002, p. 237; I have replaced 'mathematical' by 'logical' at the places indicated). No doubt one can define in non-modal terms the notion of being a logical truth of certain specified formal systems. So it may be possible to define by restriction various species of formally logical necessity. (This may be all that Fine meant to claim.) However, it is very far from obvious that there is any non-modal definition of *broadly* logical truth. So the conjecture that broadly logical necessity—which is the notion I am exploring here—may be defined in terms of metaphysical necessity by restriction seems unpromising.

[12] Thus he expressly excludes the notion of necessity that corresponds to 'mere time- and person-relative epistemic possibility—which can be asserted even when logical possibility cannot. I mean the notion expressed by that use of "It may be that *p*" which just comes to "For all I know, not *p*"' (1990b, p. 137). I shall follow him in setting aside epistemic notions of possibility and necessity.

between deducing $Q$ from $P$ and asserting a conditional: that on the basis of a deduction of $Q$ from $P$ one is entitled to assert the conditional, *indicative or subjunctive*, if $P$ then $Q$' (McFetridge 1990b, p. 138; emphasis in the original). The argument then runs as follows. Suppose it is logically necessary that if $P$ then $Q$. Suppose also, for *reductio*, that in some other sense of 'necessary', it is not necessary that if $P$ then $Q$. Then, in the sense of 'possible' that corresponds to this other sense of 'necessary', it is possible that $P$ and not $Q$. But

if that *is* a possibility, we ought to be able to describe the circumstances in which it would be realized: let them be described by $R$. Consider now the argument '$P$ and $R$; so $Q$'. By the first assumption if '$P$; so $Q$' is valid, so is '$P$ and $R$; so $Q$'. But then, by the second assumption, we should be entitled to assert: if $P$ and $R$ were the case then $Q$ would be the case. But how can this be assertible? For $R$ was chosen to describe possible circumstances in which $P$ and not $Q$. I think we should conclude that we cannot allow, where there is such an $R$, that an argument is valid.[13]

When it is logically necessary that if $P$ then $Q$, however, the argument '$P$; so $Q$' will be valid. So in that case there is no such $R$. So it is in no sense possible that $P$ and not $Q$. So it is in every sense necessary that if $P$ then $Q$. Hence McFetridge's conclusion: 'Logical necessity, if there is such a thing, is the highest grade of necessity.'

What should we make of this argument? Given McFetridge's conception of broadly logical consequence, his first assumption is unassailable. If '$P$; so $Q$' is logically valid, then the inference from $P$ to $Q$ preserves truth no matter what is supposed to be the case. In particular, then, it preserves truth if it is also supposed that $R$ is the case. So the argument '$P$, $R$; so $Q$' will also be valid.

As for the second assumption, the part claiming that we may assert the indicative conditional 'If $P$ then $Q$' on the strength of a deduction of $Q$ from $P$ is an application of the rule of conditional proof, a rule that is often held to specify the sense of the indicative conditional. The corresponding claim for subjunctives is less obvious, but is still very plausible.[14] As it concerns subjunctives, the second assumption amounts to this: that we can apply our capacity for broadly logical deduction in elaborating counterfactual suppositions. And the worry about not accepting this assumption is that if we were not able to apply *that* capacity, we should be quite unable to elaborate counterfactual suppositions at all. Of course, in elaborating a given counterfactual supposition, some of our deductive capacities will not be applicable. A capacity for deducing the consequences of suppositions according to the principles of classical physics, for example, is quite inapplicable in elaborating the counterfactual supposition 'Suppose that the gravitational force between two bodies had varied with the inverse cube of

[13] McFetridge (1990b), pp. 138–9. Like McFetridge, I shall not mark use *versus* mention where there is no danger of confusion.

[14] I am indebted to Crispin Wright, my respondent at the St Andrews conference, for pressing this point on me.

the distance between them'. Just for that reason, though, we badly need some
rules which are guaranteed to yield consequent elaborations of our counterfactual
suppositions. Since logic (broadly conceived) is traditionally supposed to apply
to anything that is so much as thinkable, one would expect logical rules (even
rules that are logically valid in the broad sense) to provide what we need. If they
do not, it is wholly unclear what else does.[15]

All the same, the two assumptions have consequences which some have
found unpalatable. In support of her positive account of broadly logical validity,
Edgington elaborates Kripke's example of Leverrier, who postulated a nearby,
hitherto unobserved planet as the cause of certain observed perturbations in the
orbit of Uranus, and who introduced the name 'Neptune' as a term which was
to stand (rigidly) for such a planet, if indeed there was one (Kripke 1980, p. 79).
About this case, she remarks that 'it is epistemically possible that [Leverrier's]
hypothesis was wrong—that there is no such planet. But if his hypothesis is
right—if Neptune exists—it is the planet causing these perturbations. And
this conditional is known *a priori*—at least by Leverrier: it follows from his
stipulation about the use of "Neptune"' (Edgington 2004, p. 7). Thus Leverrier's
'argument from the premiss that Neptune exists to the conclusion that [some
planet] causes these perturbations is trivial'—and hence valid. Although I have
denied that validity follows from the existence of an *a priori* route from premisses
to conclusion, we may still be tempted to accept Edgington's assessment of
this particular argument—call it (*A*)—as valid and correspondingly tempted to
ascribe logical necessity to the conditional 'If Neptune exists, then some planet is
the cause of the observed perturbations'. For although it is not formally valid, the
inference from the premiss to the conclusion of (*A*) is trivial. And it is tempting
to assume that a trivially correct argument must be valid in the broad sense we
are trying to elucidate.

On McFetridge's principles, though, it seems that (*A*) cannot be valid.
Certainly, he took himself to be committed to denying its validity. Discussing
an ancestor of the paper of Edgington's from which I have been quoting, he
writes:

Following Kripke and Evans Edgington claims, and I agree, that [Leverrier] knows *a priori*
that if Neptune exists it is a planet causing such and such perturbations. Thus, on her
account, the argument: 'Neptune exists, so Neptune causes such and such perturbations'
is deductively valid. But there certainly is a 'timeless' metaphysical possibility that the
premiss should have been true and the conclusion false: suppose Neptune had been
knocked off course a million years ago. What then, of the argument: 'Neptune exists and
was knocked off course a million years ago, so Neptune is the cause of these perturbations'?

---

[15] Those concerned to formalize the logic of counterfactual conditionals have, indeed, proposed
rules which subsume the counterfactual part of McFetridge's second assumption. Thus it is a special
case of both David Lewis's rule of Deduction within Conditionals (Lewis 1986a, p. 132) and
Timothy Williamson's rule of Closure (Williamson 2007b, p. 293).

If the original argument is valid so is this one (by the first assumption). But if it is we ought (by the second assumption) to be entitled to assert: if Neptune had existed and been knocked off its course a million years ago then it would have been the cause of these perturbations. But of course we are not entitled to assert that: had the antecedent been true the consequent would have been false.[16]

McFetridge's two assumptions, then, reduce to absurdity the claim that argument (*A*) is broadly logically valid. However, the inference in (*A*) is trivial, and it seems hard to deny that a trivially correct inference is broadly logically valid. Something in the analysis seems to have gone seriously wrong. But what could it be?

The problem is not confined to this one example. As Edgington recognizes, parallel cases may be constructed whenever we have what Gareth Evans called a 'descriptive name'. Evans's own example was 'Julius', which he introduced as a descriptive name that rigidly designates the person (if there was one) who actually invented the zip fastener (see Evans 1979). Thus Edgington invites us to 'consider the argument [*B*]: Julius was a mathematician; the person who invented the zip fastener emigrated to Tahiti; therefore, some mathematician emigrated to Tahiti'. As before, the triviality of the inference here makes it tempting to classify (*B*) as valid in the broad sense. 'Yet there are metaphysically possible situations in which the premisses are true and the conclusion false, namely, ones in which Julius, the actual inventor of the zip fastener, did not do so and someone else, who emigrated to Tahiti, did, and no mathematician emigrated to Tahiti' (Edgington 2004, pp. 9–10). Contrary to McFetridge's master thesis, then, we seem to have a case of a logically necessary statement that is not metaphysically necessary.

Edgington tries to resolve the difficulty by rejecting the subjunctive part of McFetridge's second assumption. 'We are familiar with the fact that an indicative and a subjunctive "If *A*, *B*" can disagree', she says. 'In the indicative, the antecedent presents something as an epistemic possibility, while in the subjunctive the antecedent typically presents something as *not* an epistemic possibility, but as something which *was* a real possibility. Each kind of conditional goes with a different kind of possibility. McFetridge's second assumption, that there is a unitary sense of "possible" that governs both, is not obligatory' (Edgington 2004, 13). But his second assumption does not require a unitary space of possibilities. All it requires is that broadly logical deduction should be applicable in elaborating both epistemic possibilities and the 'once real' possibilities that Edgington takes subjunctives to present. Edgington does not explain why broadly logical deduction should be inapplicable to the latter cases, nor does she tell us what inferential principles we can rely on in elaborating 'once real' possibilities if it is not so applicable. In the absence of such an explanation, we are left with an *aporia*, perhaps even with a paradox.

---

[16] McFetridge (1990b), p. 139. See also McFetridge (1990a) for an interesting explication of *a priori* knowledge that vindicates the claim that Edgington's conditional is knowable *a priori*.

## 3. THE PARADOX RESOLVED

How should we resolve the paradox?

On the conception of logical necessity recommended here, McFetridge is surely right to deny that it is logically necessary that Neptune is the cause of the observed perturbations if it exists. If this were logically necessary, then it would be logically contradictory to suppose that Neptune exists but is not the cause of the observed perturbations. But there is no contradiction in making that supposition: supposing so much does not lead to an impasse. The name 'Neptune' is a rigid designator. So to suppose that Neptune exists but is not the cause of the perturbations is simply to suppose that a certain planet—the planet that in fact caused the perturbations—did not do so, perhaps because it was not in a position to perturb Uranus at the relevant time.

All the same, something remains to be explained. Argument (*A*) is trivially correct; we need to explain how it can be so when it is logically possible for its premiss to be true and its conclusion false. And in order to explain this, we need to attend more closely to some peculiar features of our problem cases.

We are tempted to classify (*A*) as broadly valid because it is trivial. But the argument is trivial only in a context where it is common knowledge that the name 'Neptune' was introduced by Leverrier's stipulation, and where people still understand the name in strict conformity with that stipulation. While the very earliest astronomical uses of the name may have conformed to this requirement, later ones do not: within a few months of Leverrier's having made his conjecture, Neptune had been sighted through telescopes, enabling people to understand the name 'Neptune' in ways that did not depend on knowing how it had originally been introduced. Were the argument (*A*) to come from such a person—for example, from someone who understands the name 'Neptune' as standing for the eighth most distant planet from the Sun—it would not be trivial, and we would have no inclination at all to classify it as valid. In other words, the temptation whose source we are trying to diagnose only arises in contexts where the component occurrence of 'Neptune' is understood to be a descriptive name for the planet (if there is one) that is the cause of certain observed perturbations in the orbit of Uranus. As for the argument (*B*), it is already explicit that 'Julius', as it occurs there, is to be understood as a descriptive name.

Now descriptive names have some rather special semantical features. They are rigid, in the sense that the truth or falsity with respect to a counterfactual situation of a predication involving one of them depends on the properties, in that situation, of the descriptive name's actual referent.[17] Indeed, 'Neptune'

---

[17] For an argument that the concept of rigid designation is best understood along lines such as these, see Cartwright (1997).

must be treated as rigid in this sense if the conditional 'If Neptune exists, then some planet is the cause of these perturbations' is to have a false metaphysical necessitation. On the other hand, they differ from ordinary proper names in that it is not constitutive of a descriptive name's meaning that it should have the reference that it actually has. In saying this, I understand the *meaning* of an expression, in a given use, to be specified by the proposition, common knowledge of which among the relevant speakers sustains that use. What sustains the use of the ordinary proper name 'the Moon' among English speakers is their common knowledge, concerning the Moon, that the name designates it. Accordingly, it is part of the meaning of the English name 'the Moon' that it designates the Moon. By contrast, what sustained the use of name 'Neptune', during the short period when it was a descriptive name, was not speakers' common knowledge, concerning an object that is in fact Neptune, that the name designates it. Rather, it was their common knowledge that 'Neptune' designates whatever planet caused the observed perturbations, if there was one such planet, and otherwise designates nothing. Thus the meaning of 'Neptune' (during that early period of its use within astronomy) consisted in its designating any planet that was the unique planetary cause of the observed perturbations. It was not part of the meaning of the descriptive name 'Neptune' that it should designate the planet Neptune. Similarly, what sustains the current use of the name 'Julius' among philosophical logicians is their common knowledge that the name designates whoever invented the zip, if there was one such person, and otherwise designates nothing. Accordingly, the meaning of the name 'Julius', in its current use among philosophers, will consist in its designating any person who uniquely invented the zip.

This unusual combination of semantic features has some interesting consequences. As we have seen, the rigidity of the descriptive name 'Neptune' means that the conditional (*a*) 'If Neptune exists, then some planet is the cause of these perturbations' has a false necessitation: because 'Neptune' is taken to designate its actual referent, even when we are evaluating statements involving modal operators, the statement 'It is possible that Neptune should have existed while a comet caused the perturbations' is true. On the other hand, our thesis about the meaning of the descriptive name 'Neptune' implies that there is no possible circumstance in which (*a*) is false, meaning what it actually means.[18] For in any possible circumstance in which 'Neptune' and 'exists' mean what they actually mean, the statement 'Neptune exists' will be true only if there is a planet which is the cause of the relevant perturbations, and in any such circumstance the conditional's consequent will be true, assuming that it too means what it

---

[18] Note that it makes sense to say that a statement (in my sense) could have meant something different from what it actually means. For the type sentence 'Neptune exists' (which is the first member of a number of statements) could have meant something different from what it actually means.

actually means. So, despite its having a false necessitation, it is necessary that the conditional statement (*a*) is true, when taken in its actual sense. The same is true of 'If Julius was a mathematician and the person who invented the zip fastener emigrated to Tahiti, then some mathematician emigrated to Tahiti'. For the reason Edgington gives, the necessitation of this conditional is false. But there is no possible circumstance in which the conditional is false, meaning what it actually means.

These observations provide the key, I think, to reconciling the trivial correctness of arguments like (*A*) with their broadly logical invalidity. For why is (*A*) a correct argument? Well, its premiss is the statement 'Neptune exists', where 'Neptune' is understood to be a descriptive name. So the conditions for the truth of its premiss are the conditions for the truth of 'Neptune exists'. These conditions obviously include whatever conditions must obtain for the descriptive name 'Neptune' to designate something. Given the way the name was introduced, these latter conditions obviously include the condition that some planet is the cause of the observed perturbations. This last condition is obviously the condition for the truth of (*A*)'s conclusion. So the truth-conditions of (*A*)'s premiss obviously include the truth-conditions of its conclusion. This is why argument (*A*) is trivially correct; a similar explanation accounts for the trivial correctness of (*B*).

The argument just given shows that there is no logical, or indeed metaphysical, possibility in which (*A*)'s premiss is true—meaning what it actually means—but in which its conclusion is not true. So it is logically (and metaphysically) necessary that (*A*)'s conclusion is true—meaning what it actually means—whenever its premiss is true, meaning what *it* actually means.

Consider now the argument (*A*+) with an added premiss: 'Neptune exists. Neptune was knocked off its course a million years ago. So some planet is the cause of the observed perturbations.' Does it follow, as McFetridge's argument requires that it should follow, that it is logically necessary that the conclusion of (*A*+) is true whenever both its premisses are? I think it does follow. Since it is logically necessary that (*A*)'s conclusion is true whenever its premiss is true, and since (*A*+) differs from (A) only in having an extra premiss, it is logically necessary that the conclusion of (*A*+) is true whenever both its premisses are (assuming that the premisses and conclusion mean what they actually mean).

But are we not then committed to the truth of the counterfactual: 'If the statements "Neptune exists" and "Neptune was knocked off its course a million years ago" had both been true (meaning what they actually mean), then the statement "Neptune is the cause of these perturbations" would have been true'? Again, yes: we are so committed. But if we take a counterfactual conditional with an impossible antecedent to be vacuously true,[19] then the present counterfactual *is* true. For it is impossible for the statements 'Neptune exists' and 'Neptune

---

[19]  For powerful arguments in favour of doing so, see now Williamson (2007b), pp. 171–5.

was knocked off its course a million years ago' both to be true while meaning what they actually mean. As we have already remarked, a condition for the truth of the statement 'Neptune exists' is that the name 'Neptune' should designate something, and (for the duration of the period during which 'Neptune' was a descriptive name) a pre-condition of its doing so is that its *designatum* should have been positioned so as to cause the observed perturbations. It is, then, logically (and metaphysically) impossible that the premisses of (*A*+) should be true together, while meaning what they actually mean, so our counterfactual is vacuously true.

But are we not *then* committed to the truth of the counterfactual: 'Had Neptune existed, but been knocked off its course a million years ago, Neptune would have been the cause of these perturbations'? And is that counterfactual not clearly false? This last counterfactual *is* false, but we are not committed to its truth. In order to infer it from the true counterfactual of the previous paragraph, certain disquotational principles must be necessarily true. In particular, it must be necessary that if 'Neptune exists' is true (meaning what it actually means), then Neptune exists. But this is not necessary. It is not necessary because it is not necessary that the descriptive name 'Neptune' (meaning what it actually means) should designate the planet Neptune. As we have seen, it is no part of the meaning of the descriptive name 'Neptune' that it should designate Neptune. So even if we accept that an object has its constitutive properties as a matter of necessity, there is no ground for deeming it necessary that the name 'Neptune' (meaning what it actually means) should designate the planet Neptune. Moreover, surprising as this may be to those philosophers who are wedded to minimalist accounts of truth, the distinction between the two counterfactuals is perfectly intuitive. The false counterfactual, 'If Neptune had existed and been knocked off its course a million years ago, then it would have been the cause of these perturbations', elaborates an hypothesis about the history of the planet Neptune. The vacuously true counterfactual, 'Had the premisses of (*A*+) been true, meaning what they actually mean, its conclusion would also have been true, meaning what it actually means', elaborates a hypothesis about the truth of certain statements, on the supposition that there is no change in the common knowledge that sustains an understanding of them. There is no reason why these two very different enterprises should invariably converge on the same truth-value.

How do these considerations resolve our paradox? The resolution that I am proposing may be summarized as follows:

(1) We should accept McFetridge's thesis that logical necessity is the strongest form of non-epistemic necessity. Any non-epistemic possibility is a logical possibility. Moreover, McFetridge's argument for his thesis is correct.

(2) The problematic argument (*A*) does not threaten this thesis by providing an example of a statement that is metaphysically possible but logically

impossible. Rather, it shows that when descriptive names are involved, closely related statements can differ in modal status. Edgington and others are quite right to hold that it is metaphysically possible that Neptune should exist without having caused the perturbations. But this is no threat to McFetridge's thesis, for it is also logically possible that Neptune should exist without having caused them. This means that argument (*A*) is not (broadly) logically valid. The temptation to think that it is derives from its being trivially correct, but what follows from its correctness is not the logical impossibility of Neptune's existing without its having caused the perturbations. Rather, what follows is the logical impossibility of a situation in which the statement 'Neptune exists' is true (meaning what it actually means) while the statement 'Some planet is the cause of the perturbations' is not true (meaning what it actually means). Since such a situation is also metaphysically impossible, there is again no threat to McFetridge's thesis.

(3) The distinction invoked in (2) can be made out only if we recognize that certain disquotational principles are not necessarily true. Of course, no one thinks it necessary that the words 'the Moon', identified simply as a linguistic type, should designate the Moon. The words, identified purely typographically, could always have been used to stand for something else. But it is plausible to hold it to be necessary that the words 'the Moon', used as they are actually used in English, should designate the Moon. For it is constitutive of that use of the words that they should designate the Moon. If we think of the English language as constituted by its semantics, as well as by its syntax, phonology, etc., we can put this by saying that it is necessary that the English name 'the Moon' should designate the Moon.[20] But while the like will hold good of other ordinary proper names, it will not hold good of descriptive names. For the period when 'Neptune' functioned as a descriptive name, it was not necessary that that English name should have designated the planet Neptune. 'Neptune' is a rigid designator so, if this had been necessary, it would have followed that Neptune is necessarily such that the English descriptive name 'Neptune' designates *it*. But that descriptive name could have meant what it actually means while standing for something else. As I stressed, the use of the term 'meaning' that yields this result is principled. The underlying principle is that an expression's meaning is given by the proposition, common knowledge of which sustains the expression's use. The relevant proposition in the present case is simply that 'Neptune' designates whichever planet was the cause of the observed perturbations in the orbit of Uranus.

---

[20] In my (2001), I called languages individuated in this way 'Peacockian languages', after Peacocke (1978).

I hope this analysis has dispelled the air of paradox that arguments (*A*) and (*B*) have engendered for McFetridge's claim that logical necessity implies metaphysical necessity. But does the account extend to explain, or explain away, every apparent instance of a statement's being logically necessary but not metaphysically necessary—even when the statement contains no descriptive name? I cannot canvass here all the putative examples that philosophers have discussed, but a rather different sort of case is 'A red object looks red to a normal viewer in optimal viewing conditions', where a 'normal' viewer is understood to be one who is neither blind, nor colour-blind, nor otherwise unable to identify or discriminate between colours by sight. Again, there is some initial temptation to classify this statement as analytically true, and hence as (broadly) logically necessary. But it is equally plausible to deem the statement to be metaphysically contingent, in the sense of having a false metaphysical necessitation. Human beings, it seems, could have been constituted so as to see red things as violet, violet things as red, and so on, in which case red things would not have looked red, even in optimal viewing conditions, to the people who are best able to identify colours by sight.

Even though the present statement contains no descriptive name, our analysis may be applied to head off any threat it may present of a renewed paradox. I shall not here essay a theory of meaning for colour terms. But a plausible constraint on any such theory is that it should entail that, whenever the words 'red', 'looks red', 'normal viewer', and so on, have their actual meanings, 'red' is co-extensive with the expression 'looks red to a normal viewer in optimal viewing conditions'. (That is why it is tempting to deem our statement analytic.) However, all that follows from the constraint is that the statement 'A red object looks red to a normal viewer in optimal viewing conditions' is (logically and metaphysically) necessarily true, meaning what it actually means. And this is entirely consistent with its being (logically and metaphysically) possible that red things should not look red to normal viewers in optimal viewing conditions. The apparent threat to McFetridge's thesis is defused, then, essentially as before.

## 4. DEEP VERSUS SUPERFICIAL NECESSITY

The examples we have been considering show the need to distinguish two alethic relations between statements and possibilities.[21] Suppose that a statement *A* says

[21] By a (logical) possibility, I mean a way things might (logically) be or might (logically) have been, and similarly for the other species of modality. Robert Stalnaker uses the same formula to characterize a possible world, but by a world he really means a *fully determinate* way things might have been. If there are such things, then Stalnakerian possible worlds are examples of possibilities in my sense; but since I am unsure whether there is even a fully determinate way things actually are, I prefer to avoid commitment to possible worlds (see further Humberstone 1981). These scruples, though, do not really affect the present analysis: a reader who does not share them may take my 'possibilities' to be possible worlds.

that $P$. Then we can explain as follows the notion of $A$'s being true *with respect to* a possibility $x$: were $x$ to obtain (or had $x$ obtained), it would be (or would have been) the case that $P$. We should contrast this with the notion of $A$'s being true *in* a possibility $x$: were $x$ to obtain (or had $x$ obtained), $A$ would be true (or would have been true), meaning what it actually means. When a statement contains a descriptive name, the notions are liable to come apart. The zip fastener was in fact invented by an American, who was known to his friends as 'Whitcomb L. Judson'. Let $x$ be a possibility in which the zip was not invented by Judson but by a Russian, but in which Judson retains his actual nationality. Since 'Julius' rigidly designates Judson, it would be wrong to say: 'Had $x$ obtained, it would have been the case that Julius was Russian'. So 'Julius was Russian' is not true with respect to $x$. But we may say: 'Had $x$ obtained, the statement "Julius was Russian" would have been true, meaning what it actually means'. For had $x$ obtained, the name 'Julius' (meaning what it actually means) would have designated a Russian. Thus 'Julius was Russian' is true in $x$.

These two alethic relations between a statement and a possibility correspond to two senses in which a statement might be said to be necessary. Again suppose that the statement $A$ says that $P$. Suppose too that $A$ is true with respect to every possibility. Then, no matter what were to obtain or had obtained, it would be, or would have been, the case that $P$. Thus it will be necessarily the case that $P$. The converse implication also holds, so we may say that the statement $A$ is true with respect to every possibility if, and only if, it is necessarily the case that $P$. In other words, a statement is true with respect to every possibility just in case it *has a true necessitation*. Following Evans (see below), let us call such a statement *superficially* necessary. By contrast, if $A$ is true in every possibility then, no matter what were to obtain or had obtained, $A$ would be or would have been true, meaning what it actually means. Thus a statement is true in every possibility just in case it is *necessarily true*, meaning what it actually means. We may call such a statement *deeply* necessary.

This distinction applies to each underlying species of necessity. Thus a statement is superficially logically (metaphysically, physically) necessary just in case it has a true logical (metaphysical, physical) necessitation, which obtains just in case it is true with respect to every logical (metaphysical, physical) possibility. And a statement is deeply logically (. . .) necessary just in case it is logically (. . .) necessarily true (meaning what it actually means), which obtains just in case it is true in every logical (. . .) possibility. Again, statements involving descriptive names provide examples where these distinctions mark a difference. Because Judson need not have invented the zip, the statement 'If anyone invented the zip, Julius did' is superficially (logically) contingent: its (logical) necessitation is false. But it is (logically) necessarily true, taken in its actual meaning, so it is deeply (logically) necessary. Because the name 'Julius' is rigid, the statement 'Julius is identical with Judson' has a (metaphysically) true necessitation: Julius could not have been anyone other than Judson. Thus it is superficially (metaphysically) necessary. But the statement is not deeply (metaphysically) necessary: it is not (metaphysically) necessary that it is true, meaning what it actually means. The descriptive name 'Julius' could have designated someone other than Judson without any change in its meaning—that is, without any change in the facts, common knowledge of which sustains the relevant use of the name.

There is a corresponding bifurcation in the sense of the phrase 'an argument's premisses necessitate its conclusion'. By this one could mean: the conclusion is true with respect to any possibility with respect to which all the premisses are true. When this obtains, let us say that the premisses *superficially* necessitate the conclusion. Let us define an argument's *validating conditional* to be the indicative conditional whose antecedent is the conjunction of the argument's premisses, and whose consequent is its conclusion; thus $(a)$ above is the validating conditional for the argument $(A)$. Then an argument's premisses will superficially necessitate its conclusion if and only if the argument's validating conditional has a true necessitation. A second thing one might mean by 'The premisses necessitate the conclusion' is that the conclusion is true *in* any possibility in which all the premisses are true. When this second condition obtains, let us say that the premisses *deeply* necessitate the conclusion. An argument's premisses will deeply necessitate its conclusion if and only if it is necessary that the argument's conclusion is true if its premisses are true (meaning what they actually mean). This will obtain if and only if the argument's validating conditional is necessarily true (meaning what it actually means). As before, we can and should make this distinction in respect of each species of necessity.

We can reformulate in these terms our solution to the paradox that argument $(A)$ presented. The premiss of $(A)$ deeply logically necessitates its conclusion. The argument's validating conditional is true *in* every logical possibility. Since every metaphysical possibility is a logical possibility, it follows that $(A)$'s premiss also deeply metaphysically necessitates its conclusion. But the argument's premiss does not superficially metaphysically necessitate its conclusion. There are metaphysical possibilities (and hence logical possibilities) *with respect to* which the validating conditional is false. It is metaphysically possible that Neptune should have existed without its having caused the perturbations. That is why the subjunctive conditional 'If Neptune had existed and been knocked off its course a million years ago then it would have been the cause of these perturbations', which involves no semantic ascent, is false.

I believe that the distinction just drawn between superficial and deep notions of necessity makes more precise a distinction that Gareth Evans drew in the same terms in his 'Reference and Contingency' (1979). Evans's explanation of the superficial modal notions matches mine: 'a [true] sentence (Q) is superficially contingent if and only if $\ulcorner \Diamond \neg (Q) \urcorner$ is true' (Evans 1979, p. 211). The test for ascribing a superficial modality, then, is the simple truth of the appropriate modalized statement. His explanation of the deep notions, however, invokes an undefined notion of a state of affairs' verifying a statement:

A deeply contingent statement is one for which there is no guarantee that there exists a verifying state of affairs. If a deeply contingent statement is true, there will exist some state of affairs of which we can say both that had it not existed the sentence would not have been true, and that it might not have existed.    (1979, p. 212)

Even acute readers have found this explanation somewhat impenetrable,[22] but I hope my account is recognizable as one way of emancipating it from its reliance upon states of affairs. A deeply necessary statement, in Evans's sense, will be one for which a verifying state of affairs is guaranteed to exist. Since a statement is true just in case some verifying state of affairs obtains, a natural gloss on this is that the statement is necessarily true (meaning what it actually means).[23]

I first advanced this gloss in print some years ago,[24] but a very different way of explicating Evans's ideas continues to predominate. Something one might say about 'Julius' is that there are many possible zip-inventors, and whichever possible zip-inventor had been the actual zip-inventor, the name 'Julius' (introduced as Evans introduced it) would have designated him. One might then go on to say that, whichever possible zip-inventor had been the actual zip-inventor, the statement 'If anyone invented the zip, Julius did' would have been true. Thoughts along these lines led Martin Davies and Lloyd Humberstone to explain deep necessity by way of a new modal operator, $\ulcorner$It is deeply necessary that $A\urcorner$, which is understood to say: 'whichever world had been actual, $A$ would have been true at that world considered as actual'.[25] Thus a statement will be deeply necessary if *this* necessitation of it is true, whereas it is superficially necessary if its 'ordinary' necessitation is true. The difference between the two necessity operators is explained within the framework of a 'two-dimensional' modal logic.[26] We are said to be able to make sense of a truth-predicate, '$A$ is true$_{w,v}$', which is doubly

---

[22] Having quoted it, Bostock comments 'I do not myself find Evans's article to be very explicit on how the notion of "deep" necessity is to be understood' (1988, p. 358).

[23] Evans also distinguishes two alethic relations between a statement and a possibility (which he takes to be a possible world). Here too, though, his explanations give out sooner than one might wish. His account of 'true $(s, w)$' (1979, p. 188) matches my explanation of 'Statement $s$ is true in $w$'. But while his use of 'true$_w$ $(s)$' corresponds to my '$s$ is true with respect to $w$', he makes the surprising claim that 'the notion "true$_w$" is purely internal to the semantic theory, and needs no independent explanation' (1979, p. 207). The primitive technical terms of any theory, though, surely do need explanation.

[24] See Rumfitt (2001), pp. 318–19. That paper also shows how rejecting the equivalence between '$A$ has a true necessitation' and '$A$ is necessarily true' does not preclude a 'modalist' semantic theory, in which the meaning of 'necessarily' in the object language is specified by an operator with precisely the same sense in the metalanguage.

[25] Davies and Humberstone (1980), p. 3. In fact, 'it is deeply necessary that' is not a primitive operator in their system, being defined as 'it is fixedly actually the case that'. But nothing turns on this nicety for present purposes.

[26] There are many other ways of interpreting the framework: see Davies (2004) for a comparison of Davies and Humberstone's interpretation with others.

relativized to possible worlds, and means 'Statement $A$ is true as evaluated at $v$, with $w$ considered to be the actual world'. In these terms, $A$ will be deeply necessary if, for any possible world $w$, $A$ is true$_{w,w}$; it will be superficially necessary if, for any world $v$, $A$ is true$_{a,v}$, where $a$ is the world that really is actual (see Davies and Humberstone 1980, p. 26 n. 4).

There is much in this theory, and its consequent elaborations, with which I can agree. 'The truth which matters', Davies and Humberstone say, 'the truth at which sincere asserters in [a world] $w$ aim, is truth$_{w,w}$' (1980, p. 16). So the sort of argumentative validity which matters will be preservation of truth$_{w,w}$ ('real world validity', as they call it), whereby the premises deeply necessitate the conclusion. This would account for our tendency to classify arguments like ($A$) as correct, even though their premises do not superficially necessitate their conclusions. Brian Weatherson (2001) has further suggested that the doubly relativized truth-predicate, interpreted in Davies and Humberstone's style, can capture the difference between indicative and counterfactual or subjunctive conditionals. The indicative 'If $A$, then $B$' is correctly assertible if and only $B$ is true$_{w,w}$ for the nearest world $w$ for which $A$ is true$_{w,w}$. The corresponding subjunctive conditional, by contrast, is assertible if and only $B$ is true$_{a,w}$ for the nearest world $w$ for which $A$ is true$_{a,w}$. I am not committed to the correctness of Weatherson's conjecture but, if it were correct, it would offer a nice explanation of why the indicative conditional ($a$) above is assertible, whilst the corresponding subjunctive conditional is not. All the same, I persist in preferring my metalinguistic gloss on Evans's distinction. The matter deserves fuller discussion than I can give it here, but three points are particularly salient in the present context.

First, my gloss seems more faithful to Evans's intentions. In 2004, Martin Davies published some comments that Evans had sent him on a draft of 'Two Notions of Necessity' (Evans 2004; see also Davies 2004 for discussion). Evans is not enamoured of the attempt to capture deep necessity by way of a new modal operator. He holds that in the explanation of the new operator quoted above, 'actual' can work in the intended way only if the new operator is a 'context-shifter'—akin to the notional operator, 'As for Lloyd', which we imagine to be used in such a way that 'As for Lloyd (I am hot)', as uttered by Martin at time $t$, is true just in case Lloyd is hot at $t$ (Evans 2004, p. 14; Davies 2004, p. 90). Whilst Evans allows that this form of embedding is coherent, he 'should like its distinctness from previously recognized forms to be made explicit' (Evans 2004, p. 11). Part of Evans's worry here seems to be that the introduction of the new operator is concealing the fact that the notion of deep necessity is *au fond* metalinguistic. My account, whereby a statement is deeply necessary if it is necessarily true (when taken in its actual sense), makes this feature explicit.

Second, whilst many philosophers have adopted it, it is not easy to interpret the doubly relativized truth-predicate which Davies and Humberstone use to explain the difference between their two necessity operators. '$A$ is true$_{w,v}$', is said to mean: '$A$ is true as evaluated at $v$, with $w$ considered to be the actual world', but it is unclear quite what is involved in 'considering' a particular world to be actual. A world is usually taken to be a fully determinate way that things could have been; but then one might seriously wonder whether anyone is capable of 'considering' such a thing at all. I can of course consider a particular possibility as actual—as it might be, the possibility that the Earth is getting warmer. But in doing that, I shall be considering as actual the whole swathe of possible worlds in which the Earth is getting warmer, so what I am doing does not help to specify the sense of the three-place predicate '$A$ is true$_{w,v}$' which purports to relate a statement to two particular worlds. Perhaps the explanation would run more easily if possibilities were to replace possible worlds, but then the semantics of Davies and Humberstone's paper would need to be recast. Because possibilities are incomplete, even a classical logician cannot assume that a statement will be either true or false with respect to an arbitrary possibility.

Third, and most importantly, there is something odd about the whole idea of distinguishing between the deep and superficial forms of the various modalities by postulating two modal operators. This would be the natural way to proceed if ordinary modal auxiliaries were ambiguous between deep and superficial readings, but I have been unable to find any examples of English statements where a modal auxiliary *needs* to be construed as expressing 'it is deeply necessary that' (or 'it is deeply contingent that', or 'it is deeply possible that'). There are many statements where a modal auxiliary *cannot* be construed in this way. Bostock (1988, p. 359) gives the example of the unambiguous statement 'There might have existed things other than the things that do actually exist'. That statement seems to be, and is equivalent to 'It is not the case that, necessarily, everything that exists actually exists'. However, it is not equivalent to 'It is not the case that, no matter which world is considered as actual, everything which exists in that world actually exists'. In these circumstances, the natural way to make out the distinction between the deep and superficial forms is to take the modal verbs unambiguously to express the superficial forms, and to render the distinction between the deep and superficial modal properties of statements by way of some interaction between the modal operators and something else. And when the problem is posed in those terms, the obvious partner is a truth-predicate.[27]

## 5. ON UNICORNS

Whilst much more needs to be said about this, the distinction between a statement's having a true necessitation and its being necessarily true (taken in its actual sense) is surely genuine. I conclude by showing how drawing the

---

[27] I hope this paragraph may allay Martin Davies's sense of 'surprise' that deep necessity should not be expressed by any modal operator at all (2004, p. 98).

distinction exposes the flaw in an apparently powerful objection to the widely accepted thesis that the logic of metaphysical necessity is S5.[28]

To understand the objection, it helps to recall one of the 'strange views about unicorns' that Saul Kripke propounded in *Naming and Necessity*—the view, namely, that given that there are in fact no unicorns, it is false that there *might* have been unicorns (Kripke 1980, p. 24): 'no counterfactual situation is properly describable as one in which there would have been unicorns' (1980, p. 156). The 'might' and 'would have been' here express metaphysical modalities. Kripke allows—as anyone surely must allow—that if we were to discover animals conforming to the pictures and stories of the unicorn myth, and also discovered some historical connection between those animals and the genesis of the myth, then we should rightly say that those animals were unicorns (1980, p. 157). But he insists that, given that there are in fact no such animals, it is false that there might be unicorns. For 'regarding the several distinct species, with different internal structures (some reptilic, some mammalian, some amphibious), which would have the external appearances postulated to hold of unicorns in the myth of the unicorn, one cannot say which of these distinct mythical species would have *been* the unicorns. If we suppose, as I do, that the unicorns of the myth were supposed to be a particular species, but that the myth provides insufficient information about their internal structure to determine a unique species, then there is no actual or possible species of which we can say that it would have been the species of unicorns' (1980, pp. 156–7). Kripke surely overstates his case in saying that unicorns may be reptiles: the myth implies that they are warm-blooded. But his argument need not rest on this. As Michael Dummett has pointed out (1993, p. 346), the myth does not tell us whether they are even-toed ungulates like deer, or odd-toed ungulates like horses, and so does not determine to which order of mammals (Artiodactyla or Perissodactyla) they would belong.

Should we accept this argument of Kripke's? Dummett insists that it is 'incoherent. Its proponent would like to assert that, if there were animals in the actual world resembling the unicorns of the pictures, and all or most of the same species [and if these animals were the source of the myth], they would *be* unicorns; but he cannot do so consistently with his maintaining that, if there are no unicorns in the actual world, there are none in any merely possible world either. He cannot do so, because to talk about how things would be in the actual world in hypothetical circumstances just is to talk about how they are in certain possible worlds' (1993, p. 343). Since Dummett thinks (surely rightly) that what the proponent 'would like to assert' is true, he concludes that there *might* be unicorns, even given that in fact there are not. Kripke is right that the myth fails to determine which species of animal unicorns would be. 'They might, for

---

[28] Now that we have gone some way towards specifying the sense of the modal operator 'It is broadly logically necessary that', we can also sensibly ask what *its* modal logic is. But I must leave that question for future work.

instance, be of the order Artiodactyla, like deer, or of the order Perissodactyla, like horses. In the language of possible worlds, there are no unicorns in the actual world $w$, but there is a possible world $u$ in which there are unicorns, which belong to the order Artiodactyla, and another possible world $v$ in which there are also unicorns, which in that world belong to the order Perissodactyla' (1993, p. 346). But Dummett thinks that this can be reconciled with the principle that a species must have a determinate taxonomy:

In world $u$, any animal, to be a unicorn, must have the same anatomical structure as the unicorns in $u$, and hence, in particular, must belong to the order Artiodactyla. It follows that the world $v$ is not possible relatively to $u$, and, conversely, that $u$ is not possible relatively to $v$. How about the actual world $w$—is that possible relatively to either $u$ or $v$? It would at first seem so, since the principal difference we have stipulated is that there are no unicorns at all in $w$. But $u$ is a world in which it holds good that unicorns are necessarily of the order Artiodactyla, whereas in $w$ it is possible for unicorns to be of the order Perissodactyla. Since a proposition necessarily true in $u$ is possibly false in $w$, $w$ cannot be possible relatively to $u$, although $u$ is possible relatively to $w$. The relation of relative possibility (accessibility) is therefore not symmetrical.   (1993, p. 346)

Thus, Dummett concludes, the propositional logic of metaphysical necessity cannot be S5, which it is usually assumed to be. For S5 requires relative possibility to be an equivalence relation. Rather, he suggests, the logic will be S4: relative possibility will be reflexive and transitive, but not symmetrical.[29]

Ingenious as it is, I think that this riposte to Kripke fails, and our analysis enables us to say precisely where it goes wrong. The crux of the riposte is the alleged inconsistency between asserting 'If there were animals that stood in the appropriate relationship to the unicorn myth, they would be unicorns', and denying 'There might be unicorns'. There certainly seems to be an inconsistency here, given what is allowed on all sides, that it is metaphysically possible for there to be animals that stand in the relevant relationship to the myth. But I wish to argue that in the sense in which the conditional assertion is correct, it does not preclude denying that there might be unicorns.

For what exactly is Kripke allowing when he allows that animals suitably related to the myth would be unicorns? The most that Kripke can consistently allow, Dummett thinks, is the truth of the indicative conditional, 'If there are animals, most of them of same species, that resemble the unicorns of the pictures, they are unicorns'. He insists, however, that 'the indicative conditional does not succeed . . . in expressing all that [the proponent of the argument] wishes to say. However sure he feels that there are in fact no animals resembling the

---

[29] See, though, Salmon (1989) for an argument that relative possibility is not even transitive, so that metaphysical necessity fails to validate the characteristic S4 schema, ⌜If it is necessary that $A$, then it is necessary that $A$⌝. If both Dummett and Salmon were right, the logic of metaphysical necessity would be very weak—perhaps no stronger that the system whose characteristic axioms are instances of the schemata K and T.

unicorns of the pictures, he still wishes to declare that, if there *were*, we should be right to call them "unicorns" provided that they were of a single species; but he cannot say this without contradicting his stated view that there are no unicorns in possible worlds if there are none in the actual world' (Dummett 1993, p. 343). Once, however, we take the sort of care over semantic ascent that we have seen to be necessary in analysing some modal arguments, the apparent inconsistency vanishes. The claim that Kripke allows to be true may indeed be expressed by a counterfactual conditional. But, as Dummett implicitly recognizes, the counterfactual should include a semantic notion: 'if there were such-and-such animals, we *should be right to call* them "unicorns"'. In our terms, then, the argument's proponent is claiming:

> (1) Had there been animals suitably related to the myth of the unicorn, the term 'unicorn' (meaning what it actually means) would have been true of them.

However, the claim that entails 'There might have been unicorns', given that there might have been animals suitably related to the myth, is not (1) but

> (2) Had there been animals suitably related to the myth, they would have been unicorns.

In order to move from (1) to (2), we need an additional assumption:

> (3) Necessarily, animals of which the term 'unicorn' (meaning what it actually means) is true are unicorns.

As we have seen, however, there is no general reason to accept claims like (3). Certainly, we should not accept the corresponding claim for 'Julius'. That claim is:

> (4) Necessarily, any man designated by the name 'Julius' (meaning what it actually means) is Julius.

Since the used occurrence of the name 'Julius' in (4) rigidly designates Whitcomb L. Judson, (4) implies

> (5) Judson is necessarily such that the name 'Julius' (meaning what it actually means) designates him

which we have already seen to be false. The name 'Julius' could have stood for other men without changing its actual meaning.

The proponent of the argument that Dummett criticizes, then, can stabilize his position by rejecting (3). This will enable him consistently to accept (1) and reject (2), and rejecting (2) will in turn open up the logical space he needs in order to accept that there could have been a species of animals that was the source of the unicorn myth, while denying that there could be unicorns. In rejecting (3), he is not committed to treating 'unicorn' as a descriptive name. On the contrary: the reason why (3) is false is not the non-rigidity of a meaning-specifying description, but rather the incomplete sense of the term 'unicorn'. As a purported name for a biological species, we expect members of that species to help fix its sense (see Wiggins 1993); in the absence of any exemplars, that sense is left incomplete. Our analysis of descriptive names, however, is still crucial in undermining the natural but incorrect presumption that (3) and claims like it *must* be true. Once that presumption is undermined, the allowance that Kripke rightly makes in (1) is revealed to be consistent with his thesis that there could not have been unicorns.

Dummett's counterexample to the symmetry of relative (metaphysical) possibility collapses, then. There is no metaphysically possible world $u$ in which it holds good that unicorns are necessarily of the order Artiodactyla, for there is no metaphysically possible world in which there are unicorns. So his objection to S5 as the logic of metaphysical necessity collapses with it.

# 3

# Semantic Necessity

*Kit Fine*

In the recent monograph 'Semantic Relationism', I made use of a certain notion of what was semantically necessary, or required, in arguing that it might be a semantic requirement that two names were coreferential even though there were no intrinsic semantic features of the names in virtue of which this was so. In the present paper, I wish to consider the bearing of the notion on the nature and content of semantic enquiry. I shall argue that a semantics for a given language is most perspicuously taken to be a body of semantic requirements and that the notion of a semantic requirement should itself be employed in articulating the content of those requirements. There are two main alternatives to this conception to be found in the literature. According to one, a semantics for a given language is taken to be an assignment of semantic values to its expressions; and according to the other, a semantics for a given language is taken to be a theory of truth for that language. I attempt to show how these alternatives do not provide us with the most perspicuous way of representing the semantic facts and that it is only in terms of our conception that one can properly appreciate what these facts are.

The importance of the notion of metaphysical necessity for metaphysics has long been appreciated, in regard to both explicating the nature of the subject and articulating the content of its claims. If the argument of this paper is correct, then it will help to show that the notion of semantic necessity has a similar and equally important role to play in understanding the nature and content of semantics.

## 1. SEMANTIC NECESSITY

Certain properties and relations are, in a clear sense, semantic; they pertain to the meaning of the expressions to which they apply. *Truth*, for example, is a semantic property of sentences, *designation* a semantic relation between a term and an

I should like to thank the audiences of a modality conference held at St Andrews in 2005 and of a metaphysics conference held at Geneva in 2008 for helpful remarks; and I am grateful to Ernest Lepore for some helpful correspondence on his views.

object, and *synonymy* a semantic relation between two expressions. A fact may be said to be semantic in the *topic-oriented* sense if it pertains to the exemplification of semantic properties or relations. Thus the fact that 'the author of Waverly' designates Scott or the fact that 'bachelor' is synonymous with 'unmarried man' will be semantic in this sense. From within the facts that are semantic as to topic, we may distinguish those that are also semantic *as to status*. These facts are not merely stable in semantic terms; they are also part of the semantics of a given language (or of given languages). Thus the fact that the sentence 'snow is white' is true will not be semantic in this sense, since it is not a fact about the semantics of English, while the synonymy of 'bachelor' and 'unmarried man' presumably will be.[1]

It is the facts that are semantic as to status that will be of interest to us. We might also call them semantic *requirements* or *necessities* since they are naturally regarded as laws which govern—or are imposed upon—the languages to which they are meant to apply.

The fact that something is a semantic requirement holds in unqualified fashion. It may perhaps hold relative to this or that language, but not relative to this or that expression. There is, however, a qualified sense of semantic requirement that holds relative to this or that expression. Suppose that 'he' is used as an anaphor for 'John'. It is then a semantic requirement that the use of 'he' and the use of 'John' should be coreferential. This semantic fact *concerns* both the use of 'he' and the use of 'John'. But whereas it is a semantic requirement *on* the use of 'he' that it be coreferential with 'John', it is not a semantic requirement *on* the use of 'John' that it be coreferential with 'he'. It is in this sense that the reference of 'he' derives from 'John' while the reference of 'John' does not derive from 'he'.

We might therefore talk of a *relative* semantic fact, or of a semantic requirement *on* certain expressions, when the fact or requirement has its source in the semantics of those expressions. I have drawn an analogous distinction between metaphysical necessity and essence in my paper 'Essence and Modality' (1994). Thus whereas it is a metaphysical necessity that the number 2 is a member of singleton 2, it is essential to singleton 2 that it should have the number 2 as a member, though not essential to the number 2 that it should belong to singleton 2. The singleton derives its identity from the member, rather than the other way around, just as the anaphor derives its reference or meaning from the antecedent, not the antecedent from the anaphor. It is curious that there should be such a close parallel between the two cases and I suspect that the distinction in the two cases is, at bottom, the same.

It will be important to distinguish between the notion of semantic fact, on the one hand, and the two related notions of *semantic truth* and *analytic truth*, on the

---

[1] Cf. Fine (2007a), pp. 43–4, 122–3. I am not using the term 'fact' in a heavy-duty sense; and most of what I want to say could be said without appeal to facts or propositions or the like. I distinguished in Fine (2007a), pp. 49–50 between semantic facts and requirements but that distinction, important as it may be to the earlier project, will not be relevant here.

other. Semantic facts are *propositions* while semantic truths are *sentences*. Thus the proposition that 'Cicero' refers to the particular object Cicero is a semantic fact (at least for the referentialist) while the sentence ' 'Cicero' refers to Cicero' is a semantic truth. The semantic fact involves the name 'Cicero', the particular object Cicero, and the relation of referring, while the semantic truth involves the quotation-mark name ' 'Cicero' ' for 'Cicero', the name 'Cicero' itself, and the predicate 'refers to'.

Analytic truths are like semantic truths in being sentences rather than propositions but, in contrast to semantic truths, they occur at a lower semantic level than the semantic facts. Thus whereas a semantic truth will convey some semantic content, such as that this name refers to that object, an analytic truth, such as 'bachelors are unmarried', will generally have no semantic content. It will be about bachelors or the like and not about words.

There is, however, a natural connection between analytic truths and semantic facts. For one may take a sentence to be analytic if it is a semantic fact that it is true. The analyticity of the sentence 'bachelors are unmarried', for example, will consist in its being a semantic fact that it is true. Thus from this point of view, the analytic truths are but one case, or aspect, of the semantic facts.

Although one is able to define the notion of analytic truth in terms of the notion of semantic fact, it is not clear to me that the Quinean need be as troubled by the notion of semantic fact as he is by the notion of analytic truth. We may distinguish between two sources of Quinean scepticism about the distinction between analytic and synthetic truths. There is first of all scepticism as to whether we can meaningfully factor the truth of a sentence into a purely semantic component and a purely factual component. But even if it is granted that one can factor the truth of a sentence into two components in this way, a further form of scepticism may arise over whether the factual component is ever null. Can a sentence ever be true *solely* in virtue of its meaning? The existence of analytic truths requires both that the distinction between the two components be made and that the second component sometimes be null. But just as one might accept the distinction and yet deny that a sentence could ever be true solely in virtue of the *non*-semantic facts, so one might accept the distinction and yet deny that a sentence could ever be true solely in virtue of the semantic facts.

Someone who only embraces the second form of scepticism may be perfectly happy with the idea of a semantic fact. He may take it to be a semantic fact that 'Cicero' refers to Cicero, for example, or that 'snow is white' is true iff snow is white. To be sure, this involves some sort of separation between fact and meaning. For we will want it to be a *purely* semantic fact that 'snow is white' is true iff snow is white. Thus we will want to distinguish between the fact that 'snow is white' is true iff snow is white and the fact that 'snow is white' is true iff grass is green, with the second depending upon a non-semantic fact in a way that the first does not. But our accepting this more limited distinction between the semantic and non-semantic facts does not mean that we should ever take it to be a semantic fact that a given sentence is true. We may grant that it is a semantic fact that 'bachelors are unmarried' is true iff bachelors are unmarried, for example, but deny that it is a semantic fact that 'bachelors are unmarried' is true on the grounds that its truth will partly turn on the non-semantic fact that bachelors are unmarried.[2]

## 2. SEMANTICS AS A BODY OF REQUIREMENTS

Once given, the concept of a semantic requirement or fact naturally gives rise to a conception of semantics as a body of semantic requirements. Thus for any language, there will be requirements that concern the language or the expressions of the language and the semantics for the language will be given by the body of those requirements.

Although this account of semantics may seem rather thin, there are a number of ways in which it can be embellished or applied and which provide it with a great deal more interest. In the first place, the concept of a semantic requirement may be *internalized*, i.e. it may itself be imported into the content of a semantic requirement. Thus given that it is a semantic requirement that $p$, one might take it to be a semantic requirement that it be a semantic requirement that $p$. So the semantic requirements will include not merely $p$, but also its being a semantic requirement that $p$. However, this step, even if correct, does not affect the essential content of a semantics, since the higher order semantic requirements (that $p$ be semantically required, for example) may always be discerned from the lower order semantic requirements (that $p$).

A more significant step in the same direction is to take it to be a semantic requirement that it be a *relative* semantic requirement on an expression that it behave in a certain way. Thus on a referentialist view, we may take it to be a semantic requirement that it be a semantic requirement on 'Cicero' that it refer to Cicero, so that the semantic requirements include not merely that 'Cicero' refer to Cicero but also that it be a semantic requirement on 'Cicero' that it refer to Cicero.

The advantage of this further step is that it enables us to state from within the semantics from whence the semantic requirements derive. Of course, in the case of the semantic requirement that 'Cicero' refer to Cicero, it should be evident that the requirement derives from 'Cicero' since this is the only expression in sight. But other cases may not be so evident. Suppose, for example, that 'Charlie' is a name for the name 'Cicero'. Then it is a semantic requirement that 'Charlie' refer to 'Cicero'. But this requirement could in principle derive from 'Cicero' or from 'Cicero' and 'Charlie' together; and so some genuinely new information

---

[2] And likewise for 'bachelors are bachelors'. Thus on this conception, there will be no basis for thinking of logical truths as a relatively unproblematic species of analytic truth.

is added by taking it to be a semantic requirement on 'Charlie' that it refer to 'Cicero'.

Once we allow relative semantic requirements within the semantics, we then have the means for stating how the semantic requirements on a complex expression may derive from the semantic requirements on its component expressions (cf. Fine 2007a, pp. 125–6). We may take it to be a semantic requirement on 'even prime', for example, that it be true of the objects of which 'even' and 'prime' are true; and we may take it to be a semantic requirement on 'even' that it be true of the even numbers, and of 'prime' that it be true of the prime numbers. Using an obvious 'chaining' principle, it will then follow that it is a semantic requirement on 'even prime' that it be true of the even prime numbers.[3]

A semantics for a given language is not only constituted by semantic requirements on particular expressions but also by more general requirements to which the particular requirements should conform. Thus not only is it a semantic requirement on the name 'Cicero' that it should refer to Cicero and a semantic requirement on the name 'Aristotle' that it should refer to Aristotle, it is also a general semantic requirement that if a name refers to a particular object then it should be a semantic requirement on the name that it refer to that object. This is the generic semantic requirement on names, so to speak; and the particular semantic requirement on any particular name should conform to the template that this more general requirement lays down. But as is evident from this case, it is only through internalizing the concept of semantic necessity that it will be possible to formulate more general requirements of this sort.

These general requirements have a broader significance. For a language is given not only by the expressions it actually contains but also by the expressions it might contain; and likewise, the semantics of a language is given not only by the meanings of the expressions it actually contains but also by the meanings of the expressions that it might contain. In presenting the semantics for a language, it is usual to focus on the language in its actual rather than its potential aspect. But a full account should cover both; and it is only by making use of general requirements, that make no reference to particular expressions, that this can be done.

There are a number of other advantages to be gained by internalizing the concept of semantic necessity, some of which are discussed in Fine (2007a, pp. 23–5, 127–8). But perhaps the most significant benefit of the present conception has nothing to do with internalization and simply arises from its providing a touchstone by which the content of any particular semantics might be assessed. For in specifying a semantics for a language, it should be possible to regard it as a body of semantic requirements; we should be able to state in this way what information the semantics conveys. But as we shall see, it is often not evident from the specification of a particular semantics what its requirements are;

---

[3] An analogous chaining principle is naturally used in developing the logic of essence (as in Fine 2000), thereby providing further support for the parallel between meaning and essence.

and it is through using the present conception of semantics as a touchstone that we can become clear as to what the content of a particular semantics actually is.

## 3. SEMANTICS AS AN ASSIGNMENT OF VALUES

Although the present conception of semantics might seem obvious, and even trivial, it stands in striking contrast to the conceptions of semantics to be found in the literature. There are perhaps two standard models for what it is to specify a semantics within the representational tradition (and perhaps, to some extent, outside of this tradition). According to the first, deriving largely from Frege, a semantics is given by an assignment of semantic values to the expressions of the language in question; and according to the second, deriving from Tarski via Davidson, a semantics is given by a theory of truth. Let us discuss each in turn and see how they relate to the previous requirement-based approach.

A semantics for a language, under the first model, is given by a function which assigns a semantic value to each meaningful expression of the language. Thus it might assign Cicero to 'Cicero' and the set of orators to the predicate 'is an orator'; and it might thereby assign True to the sentence 'Cicero is an orator' on the basis of the individual assigned to 'Cicero' and the set of individuals assigned to 'is an orator'. I have suggested in Fine (2007a) that it might be better to regard the semantics as a function that operates simultaneously on *several* expressions, rather than on a *single* expression, and that yields a semantic *connection* on those expressions, rather than a semantic *value*. However, the core idea of specifying the semantics by means of a function remains the same.

But how is a semantics, on this conception, to be transcribed into a body of semantic requirements? For a function in itself says nothing and so what information, in specifying such a semantics, are we actually conveying?

What is being conveyed, it may be suggested, is that the function is the *right* function. However, it is hard to believe that the semantics should be given in the form of a single semantic requirement. And it is, in any case, plausible that there should be some further account of what it is for the function to be the right one and of what, in particular, the assignment of values to expressions should be taken to correspond.

The most plausible next move is to suppose that we have an independent understanding of a semantic function holding between expressions and entities and that it is the aim of the semantics to characterize this function. So in order to discern the content of the semantics, we will first need to identify the 'target' function. Let us call it 'designation'. Then where $f$ is the assignment function, the semantics will tell us that the designation of $E$ is $v$, whenever $v$ is the value assigned by $f$ to $E$ or, on a more refined conception still, the semantics will tell us that in these circumstances it is a semantic requirement *on* the expression $E$ that its designation be $v$.

But even this may not be adequate. For the intended semantic relation between an expression and its value may vary from case to case. Suppose, for example, that the semantic value of a name is taken to be its bearer and the semantic value of a sentence to be its truth-value. Then it might well be thought, pace Frege, that the semantic relationship between a name and its bearer is different from the semantic relationship between a sentence and its truth-value, that whereas a name *names* its bearer, a sentence does not name but *has* its truth-value. In this case, the semantics would be incorrect if the relation of designation, to which the assignment of values is meant to correspond, were taken to be either of these semantic relations, since it would not be correct to say that the name *has* its bearer or that the sentence *names* its truth-value. Of course, the relation of designation could be taken to be the disjunction of these relations; we could be saying that a name either names or has its bearer and that a sentence either names or has its truth-value. But in that case, the semantics would be incomplete. For we would not be saying that the name *names* its bearer or that the sentence *has* its truth-value. In order to repair this deficiency, we must therefore allow the single assignment function and its corresponding target function to be replaced by a range of assignment functions and a corresponding range of target functions.

There is a further difficulty concerning not the assignment function itself but the manner in which it is given. For the function is not simply given as a *list* of argument-value pairs—it is not that we run through all the expressions of the language in turn and state that this expression goes with this value, that expression with that value, and so on. Rather, the semantic value of a complex expression will be specified *as* a function of the semantic values of its component expressions. In the case of 'not funny', for example, we will not directly declare that 'not funny' should designate *not funny*. We will first declare that 'not funny' should designate the complement of what is designated by 'funny' (or something more general still) and that 'funny' designates *funny*; and from these facts, the fact that 'not funny' designates *not funny* will then be derived.

Presumably the manner in which the values are specified should also be incorporated into the content of the semantic requirements. In the case above, for example, we do not merely want it to be a semantic requirement that 'not funny' should designate *not funny*, we also want it to be a semantic requirement that 'not funny' should designate the complement of what is designated by 'funny'. If we are systematically to incorporate the manner in which the values are specified into the content of the requirements, then perhaps the best we can do is to take each clause $M(f)$ in the specification of the assignment function $f$ and interpret it as a semantic requirement $M(d)$ on the designative function $d$.[4] So our aim in specifying the designative function is not merely to specify the right function but to specify it in the right way.

---

[4] We might in this way also attempt to recover some *general* semantic requirements from the specification of the function.

There is another, potentially more serious, shortcoming in this approach. For it might be thought that the underlying semantic facts in virtue of which an expression is assigned a semantic value do not directly involve the expression standing in some semantic relationship to that value.

Suppose, for example, that one takes the semantic value of a sentence to be a truth-value and that, in defining the assignment function from expressions to semantic values, one takes the truth-value of the sentence 'not-$S$' to be the opposite of the truth-value of $S$. Then on a very natural understanding of such a semantics, one will take there to be a semantic relation of designation between a sentence and a truth-value and one will take it to be a semantic requirement that the truth-value designated by the negation 'not-$S$' should be the opposite of the truth-value designated by the negated sentence $S$. However, on a very different understanding of the semantics, it will be taken to have nothing to do with a sentence *designating* a truth-value or the like but with the conditions under which a sentence is true or false. The semantics will be taken to be concerned with a semantic *feature* of sentences, their being true or false, rather than with a semantic relationship between a sentence and its *value*, True or False. And on such an understanding, the proper form of the semantic requirement on negative sentences will not be that:

The truth-value designated by 'not-$S$' should be the opposite of the truth-value designated by $S$,

but that:

The sentence 'not-$S$' should be true (or false) just in case the sentence $S$ is false (or respectively true).

If we are to see the first formulation of the requirement as giving expression to the second, it must be supposed that the semantic features of sentences are somehow encoded as values. To say that a sentence designates True or False is code, so to speak, for its being true or false; and under such a code or 'translation-scheme', we should then see the requirement that the negation not-$S$ designate True when $S$ designates False as a way of encoding the requirement that not-$S$ be true when $S$ is false.

Another, more interesting, example of the phenomenon concerns the parallelism of sense and reference within the framework of Fregean semantics. It is something of an embarrassment that the Fregean framework provides for the compositional determination of both sense and reference. For surely only one of these can correspond to the compositional determination of meaning and the other must somehow be derived. But then which? And how?

The standard view is that the determination of sense is primary and the determination of reference derived. For what is most directly assigned to an expression is its sense; and the reference of an expression may then be taken to be the object picked out by its sense. The compositional determination of reference is similarly mediated through sense. For the compositional determination of sense will be extensional in that the object picked out by the determined sense will always be the same when the objects picked out by the determining senses are the same; and so from the compositional determination of the sense may be derived a corresponding compositional determination of the reference.

On an alternative view, it is the determination of reference that is primary and the determination of sense that is derived. Now on the face of it, this is impossible since many different senses will correspond to the very same referent. But it may be supposed that the determination of sense is merely a reflection of the manner of determination of the reference. It might be taken to be a semantical requirement on the name 'Cicero', for example, that:

Cicero refers to the most famous Roman orator,

where what is important is that we use this particular description 'the most famous Roman orator' in specifying the referent rather than some alternative description, such as 'the author of 'De Amicitia' '.[5] The assignment of the sense *the most famous Roman orator* to 'Cicero' will then encode the use of this description as opposed to some other in the assignment of reference.

On this view, then, there is no genuine duality of semantic value. At the most basic level of stating the semantic requirements, each expression simply refers; and the assignment of sense serves merely to indicate the manner in which the referent has been specified.

A third example (which first made me vividly aware of the issue) arises from the doctrine of coordination in 'Semantic Relationism'. I there wanted to say that the sentence 'Cicero = Tully' designates the (uncoordinated) singular proposition that Cicero is identical to Cicero while the sentence 'Cicero = Cicero' designates the coordinated singular proposition that Cicero is identical to Cicero (something which we might represent by 'drawing' lines of coordination between the two occurrences of Cicero in the uncoordinated proposition). In this way, we can distinguish between the semantic values of the two sentences. But in the underlying requirement-based semantics, there will only be appeal to the uncoordinated proposition and the difference between the two sentences will show up in how the proposition is specified. Thus whereas it will be a semantic requirement that 'Cicero = Tully' designate an identity proposition that relates Cicero to Cicero, it will be a semantic requirement that 'Cicero = Cicero' designate an identity proposition that relates Cicero to himself—where, in the second case, it is built into the semantics for the sentence that the individual in subject and object position should be the same.[6]

---

[5] We might see McDowell (1976), p. 42, for example, as proposing to derive sense from reference in some such way.

[6] As observed in Fine (2007a), p. 59, the semantics for predicates and plurals gives rise to some related issues, which are discussed in Fine (2007b), pp. 120–1.

Under each of these alternative views, the value-based semantics can be seen to arise from the attempt to reify certain semantic features of the expressions in question. The value-based semantics does not allow us to talk of the semantic features of an expression except in so far as these consist in the expression standing in a semantic relationship to an appropriate semantic value and so, when the features are not directly of this form, they must somehow be encoded as features that are. Thus instead of taking sentences to be true or false, we say that they designate the truth-values True and False; instead of taking 'Cicero' to refer to the most famous Roman orator (as opposed to the author of 'De Amicitia'), we say that it has a certain sense; and instead of taking 'Cicero = Cicero' to designate an identity proposition in which the individuals in subject- and object-position are the same, we say that it designates a coordinated identity proposition.

In each of these cases, the value-based model does not provide us with the most appropriate way to formulate the semantics. It looks as if the semantics is designative, but what we have are pseudo semantic values and a pseudo semantic relation; and it is only through applying some kind of translation-scheme to the requirements most directly delivered by the semantics itself that we can ascertain what the content of the semantics genuinely is.[7]

## 4. SEMANTICS AS A SET OF TRUTHS

Under the second of the two standard models, a semantics for a language is given by a theory, or set of theorems.[8] The intent is that these sentences should constitute the semantic truths for the language. Thus a semantics of this sort might contain the following sentences (either as axioms or theorems): ''Cicero' designates an individual just in case it is Cicero'; ''is an orator' is true of an individual just in case it is an orator'; and 'a sentence '$Pa$' is true just in case '$P$' is true of the individual designated by '$a$' '. From these sentences, the sentence ''Cicero is an orator' is true iff Cicero is an orator' will follow and will therefore also be a theorem of the theory.

---

[7] To some extent these difficulties may be alleviated by appropriately specifying the target function. In case sentences are taken to have the feature of being true, for example, designation may be taken to be the relation that holds between a sentence and a truth-value when the sentence is true and the truth-value is True or when the sentence is not true and the truth-value is False. But even when something like this can be done, it will not deliver exactly the right results, since the reference to pseudo values, such as True and False, will import extraneous material into the content of the semantic requirements.

[8] It is customary in logic to take a theory to be a set of sentences (or formulas) closed under logical consequence, whereas it has been common in discussions of theories of truth to take a theory to be an *axiomatized* theory, i.e. a theory that is equipped with a set of axioms from which the remaining sentences (or formulas) of the theory are logical consequences. Of course, 'theory' also has an informal use in which it is taken to be a set of propositions (not sentences); and it is perhaps some slippage between the informal and formal uses of the term that has made it more attractive to think of semantics as having the aim of providing us with a theory.

It is normally supposed that a semantic theory of this sort will be a theory of truth. Its vocabulary will include a truth-predicate and it will be a requirement on the theory (Convention T) that for each sentence *s* of the given language, there should be some sentence '*p*' of the theory which translates *s* and for which the biconditional '*s* is true iff *p*' is a theorem.[9] But there is, of course, no reason in principle why a semantic theory should take this particular form or be subject to this particular requirement. Any designative semantics of the sort previously considered, for example, might also be stated as a theory in which the sole semantic predicate was one of designation; and the requirement on the theory might be that for each meaningful expression *e* of the language, there should be an appropriate term *t* of the theory for which '*e* designates *t*' is a theorem.

I criticized the value-based account on the grounds that in specifying a function it was not clear what semantic information was being conveyed. A similar criticism can be leveled against the theory-based approach. For in specifying a theory, all we do is mention or characterize certain sentences; and, in so doing, we say nothing.

However, it might be thought to be relatively straightforward in this case to say what is being said. For what is being said is what we would be saying if we were to *use* the sentences of the theory (with their intended meaning) and not merely to mention them. Thus if ' 'snow is white' is true iff snow is white' is a theorem of the theory, then part of the semantic information implicitly conveyed in specifying the theory is that 'snow is white' is true iff snow is white.

But there is a peculiar difficulty in conceiving of the information in this way. For what information is conveyed by the sentences of the theory may be part of what was at issue in stating the theory in the first place. Consider the Fregean and referentialist positions on proper names. Each side can assent to the sentence ' 'Cicero' refers to Cicero' (or, more cautiously, to the sentence ' 'Cicero' refers to Cicero if it refers at all'); and they can therefore agree that it is a semantic fact that 'Cicero' refers to Cicero. The referential claim ' 'Cicero' refers to Cicero' will even serve to convey what each position is, given that the position is indeed correct. For the proposition expressed by the sentence ' 'Cicero' refers to Cicero', will be a 'singular' proposition, according to the referentialist, relating the name directly to the individual, whereas it will be a 'general' proposition according to the Fregean, relating the name to the individual via its sense.

It might be thought that this is a case in which the referentialist and Fregean are assenting to different, though homophonic, truths. But such a line is not at all plausible. Surely when each assents to the ordinary English sentence 'Cicero is an orator', they assent to the same sentence. And so why should it be any different for the meta-linguistic sentence ' 'Cicero' refers to Cicero'? In each of these cases, they assent to the same truth even though they adopt a different theoretical position as to what it conveys.

---

[9] For ease of reading, I have been sloppy over use-mention.

The situation is therefore one in which there is a difference in the semantic facts (with a singular referential fact in the one case and a general referential fact in the other) but no corresponding difference in the semantic truths; and a semantic theory, as it is usually conceived, will be powerless to state in what the difference consists.[10]

If we are to give adequate expression to the difference, then it is helpful—and perhaps essential—to import the notion of being a semantic fact or requirement into the very formulation of the semantics facts. For what the referentialist will want to say is that it is semantically required *of* Cicero that 'Cicero' refer to it or, to put it in quantificational terms, he will want to say that there is something which is Cicero and for which it is semantically required that 'Cicero' should refer to it ($\exists x(x = \text{Cicero} \,\&\, \text{s}\,(\text{'Cicero' refers to } x))$). In this way, we get at the singular semantic fact—but only, so to speak, from within the scope of a quantifier. The Fregean, by contrast, will wish to reject the quantificational claim (and might even find it meaningless). He may grant that it is semantically required that 'Cicero' refer to Cicero and even that it is semantically required that 'Cicero' refer to the most famous Roman orator, should 'Cicero' and 'the most famous Roman orator' have the same sense, but he will deny that it is semantically required that 'Cicero' refer to the very individual, Cicero, independently of how he is described.

In giving expression to the difference in this way, we must therefore make the transition from the first grade of semantic involvement, in which semantic necessity is treated as a predicate of sentences, to the third grade of semantic involvement, in which semantic necessity is treated as an operator on sentences into which we can quantify.[11] In requiring that a semantics be given by a theory we are in effect adhering to the first grade of semantic involvement and denying ourselves the expressive possibilities afforded by the third grade.

There is another shortcoming in the theory-based approach. For it only allows us to state semantic requirements simpliciter; it does not allow us to distinguish between the semantic requirements that arise from the meaning of certain expressions as opposed to others. Given that 'Charlie' refers to the name 'Cicero', for example, it does not allow us to distinguish the sensible view that it is a semantic requirement on 'Charlie' that it refer to 'Cicero' from the ridiculous view that it is a semantic requirement on 'Cicero' that 'Charlie' refer to it. If we wish to state localized requirements of this sort, then a semantic theory, as it is standardly conceived, will again be inadequate.

It is true that one might supplement the theory for the language as a whole with an indexed family of theories, one for each meaningful expression of the language. The sentence ''Charlie' refers to 'Cicero'' will then be a theorem of

---

[10] The case also shows that philosophers like McDowell (1977) must be mistaken in thinking that the meaning of a proper name might simply be given by means of a referential axiom. For such an axiom will remain neutral on the semantic facts that are in dispute between the Fregean and the referentialist.

[11] The analogy is, of course, with the three grades of modal involvement of Quine (1953).

the special theory for 'Charlie' though not of the special theory for 'Cicero'; and in this way, we might give expression to the difference in the relative requirements. But the expanded framework is barely workable. For we will need to navigate between different indexed theories, appealing to one in specifying another, and this will not be possible, at least with the desired degree of generality, unless we have a 'super-theory' in which the various relative requirements are explicitly made.

One might, of course, have an austere view in which it is no part of a theory of meaning to state such relative requirements. But the need to relativize such requirements can arise within a relatively austere program, such as Davidson's, in which they are not taken to be an immediate part of the task at hand. One familiar problem with Davidson's approach is to say when a T-theory (containing a correct T-theorem of the form '*s* is true iff *p*' for each sentence *s* of the object language) is interpretive, i.e. serves to interpret the language in question. To use an example of Davidson's,[12] we would not want an interpretive T-theory for English to contain the sentence:

'Snow is white' is true iff grass is green.

And so how are such sentences to be excluded?

The natural response to this problem, within our own framework, is to insist that the content of the T-theorems should be semantic requirements. Thus the only way for the above sentence to be part of an interpretive T-theory for English is for it to be a semantic requirement that 'snow is white' is true iff grass is green—which is not in fact the case.[13] Davidson would presumably be unhappy with using the notion of semantic requirement in this way and he appeals instead to general constraints on theory acceptance (Davidson 1984, pp. 26, 172–3). Any theory that we accept should be reasonably comprehensive, reasonably simple, etc.; and no T-theory for English could be expected to contain the offending biconditional without violating one or more of these constraints.

But there is another familiar problem that arises, once we have identified the interpretive T-theories.[14] For let us suppose that we have somehow identified a correct interpretive T-theory. Then not all of the resulting T-theorems will be interpretive, i.e. will serve to interpret the sentence in question. Indeed, given one such theorem in *p*:

*s* is true iff *p*,

---

[12] Davidson (1984), p. 25. Foster (1976), pp. 13–14 considers some related examples.

[13] Cf. Wallace (1978), who suggests that each axiom of the truth theory should be prefixed with the operator 'it is a matter of meaning alone that'. Foster's second problem for Davidson (Foster 1976, p. 19), that of making the knowledge of the truth theory appropriately reflective, is also solved if we bring the notion of a semantic requirement down into the object language.

[14] Lepore and Ludwig (2005, ch. 7) contains a general discussion and background to these two problems.

any $p'$ for which $p \equiv p'$ is a theorem of T will give another such theorem in $p'$:

   s is true iff $p'$.

In particular, let $Ax$ be the conjunction of a finite set of axioms for T (which Davidson assumes will exist). Then $p \equiv (p \,\&\, Ax)$ will be a theorem of T; and so in addition to the T-theorem above, we will also have:

   s is true iff $(p \,\&\, Ax)$.

Here we face not an ambiguity in the theory but an ambiguity in the T-theorems given the theory.

   No doubt, some ambiguities of this sort are relatively harmless. We should not be too concerned if the T-theorems for 'snow is white' also included:

   'Snow is white' is true iff snow is white & snow is white,

and we should perhaps not be too concerned if any logical equivalent of 'snow is white' were also allowed to occur on the right-hand side of the biconditional. But the case is quite different when the truth-conditions for a given sentence incorporate the whole theory of meaning of the language to which the sentence belongs. Surely the interpretive T-theory itself cannot properly be included in the truth-conditions of any given sentence?[15]

   A related problem arises in regard to the compositional determination of meaning. Davidson (1984, p. xiv) has claimed that 'the proof of such a theorem [the T-theorem for a given sentence] amounts to an analysis of how the truth or falsity of the sentence depends on how it is composed from elements drawn from the basic vocabulary'. But just as there is no such thing as *the* T-theorem for a given sentence, so there is no such thing as *the* proof of a given T-theorem. For any such theorem, there will be an infinitude of possible proofs, some involving unnecessary detours, some perhaps exploiting shortcuts that do not simply follow from what we take to be the compositionally determined meaning of the sentence, and some corresponding more or less exactly to what we take to be the compositionally determined meaning. Which, then, of the T-proofs of T-theorems are interpretive, i.e. properly determinative of the interpretation of the sentence in question?

   We may avoid the second of these problems—or, at least, largely mitigate it—by appealing to the notion of a relative semantic requirement. For we may insist that, in the case of any T-theorem, it should be a semantic requirement on the sentence $s$ that $s$ be true iff $p$. This will then exclude the monstrous biconditional above since, even if it is a semantic requirement on $s$ that $s$ be

---

[15] This is a striking form of an objection that has already been considered in the literature. I consider an analogous objection to the modal account of essence in Fine (1994), p. 6.

true iff $p$, it will not in general be a semantic requirement on $s$ that $s$ be true iff $(p \ \& \ Ax)$.

We are also able to avoid—or to mitigate—the third problem by appeal to the idea of a relative semantic requirement. For making the requirements relative imposes a natural discipline on how the requirements for a given expression are to be derived from the requirements on other expressions. If it is a requirement on 'not funny', for example, that it be true of exactly those things of which 'funny' is not true and if it is a requirement on 'funny' that it be true of exactly those things that are funny then, as we have seen, we may appeal to the Chaining Principle to show that it is a requirement on 'not funny' that it be true of exactly those things which are not funny. The relative requirements provide the organizational framework, so to speak, through which the compositional determination of meaning must flow.

However, it is not clear to me how either of the last two problems can be satisfactorily solved within Davidson's own framework. Lepore and Ludwig (2005, ch. 7) have suggested that they be solved by appealing to the notion of a 'canonical proof'. The hope is that, for any given semantic theory, we might provide a set of canonical proof procedures which are such that (i) for each sentence of the object language there will be a canonical proof of a corresponding T-theorem (constructed in accordance with the canonical proof procedures) and (ii) whenever there is a canonical proof of a T-theorem then both proof and theorem will be interpretive. I have my doubts as to whether this can always be done in a satisfactory or natural way. But even if it can, the proposal fails to provide any general explanation as to why particular proof procedures should be associated with particular theories. It would clearly be preferable if we could say what it was about a semantic theory that permitted certain proof procedures and not others; and the idea of 'chaining' provides at least one of the mechanisms by which this more general form of explanation might be achieved.

## 5. CONCLUSIONS

Two morals emerge from the previous discussion. The first is that semantics should be conceived as a body of semantic requirements or facts—and not as a body of semantic truths or as an assignment of semantic values. The second is that the notion of a semantic requirement should itself be imported into the content of those requirements. It is the key semantic meta-primitive and, although different approaches to semantics may differ on which other semantic primitives to adopt, they should all agree on using this higher level primitive as a basis for organizing the lower level semantic facts.

The problem with the alternatives is that they involve an element of indirection. If we are clearly to see what is said on the value-based designative approach, then we must propositionalize 'up' and attempt to ascertain which requirements are implicit in the assignment of semantic values; and if we are clearly to see what is said on the theory-based approach, then we must propositionalize 'down' and attempt to ascertain which propositions are expressed by the sentences of the theory. Although sometimes straightforward, there are cases in which there is serious ambiguity in what we should take the resulting propositions to be.

But why should the ambiguity matter? It should be conceded that, for certain purposes, it will not matter and, in this connection, we should distinguish between two broadly different aims that we might have in providing a semantics. According to the first, more linguistically oriented aim, the emphasis is on the compositional determination of meaning—we wish to ascertain how the meaning of a complex expression is to be determined on the basis of its simpler components. According to the second, more philosophically oriented aim, the emphasis is on giving fundamental expression to the semantic facts—to so express them that there is no more fundamental way (within the semantic realm) of conceiving what they are. Thus in regard to the first aim, it will be a matter of indifference whether we think of sentences as being true or false or as designating truth-values or whether we think of plural expressions as plurally designating various objects or as singularly designating a plurality, since the compositional import of these two ways of thinking will be the same. But in regard to the second aim, the differences will be momentous and our general stand on the semantic role of sentences or of plurals will be largely determined by the stand we take on these more particular questions.

The requirement-based approach allows us to avoid any indirection that might otherwise be involved in attempting to give fundamental expression to the semantic facts. Partly this is because it does not require us to package a semantic feature (such as truth or falsehood) as a semantic value (the True and the False); and partly it is because the focus is on the connection between the object language and the world, and not on how the semantic facts are themselves to be specified. But it is also because the notion of a semantic requirement may itself be of use in stating the semantic facts. Thus what most fundamentally distinguishes the referential position from Fregeanism is that it makes use of de re semantic facts, in which it is required of an object itself that it enter into certain semantic requirements. There is no appeal here to rigid designation or to some special relation of *direct* reference; and I suspect that this is not an isolated instance and that there are many other cases of interest in which the notion of a semantic requirement will be essentially involved in giving fundamental expression to the semantic facts.

# 4

# Modal Logic within Counterfactual Logic

*Timothy Williamson*

A fact of under-discussed significance is that metaphysical possibility and necessity can be defined in terms of counterfactual conditionals. Since such conditionals play a large role in our ordinary cognitive dealings with the world, whereas metaphysical possibility and necessity seem to be of interest mainly to philosophers, it is plausible that counterfactual conditionals provide a good starting-point for understanding metaphysical modality. Elsewhere, I have used the connection to derive the epistemology of metaphysical modality from the epistemology of counterfactual conditionals (Williamson 2005, 2007a). The concerns of the present paper are logical rather than epistemological. In particular, it derives the logic of metaphysical modality from the logic of counterfactual conditionals, and discusses some of the associated logical questions.

1

Our first task is to argue for equivalences between statements of metaphysical possibility and necessity on the one hand and statements involving counterfactual conditionals on the other. In order to do that, we formulate two plausible constraints on the relation between counterfactual conditionals and metaphysical modalities.

Henceforth, 'necessary' and 'possible' should always be understood as qualified by 'metaphysical'. As usual we symbolize them with $\Box$ and $\Diamond$ respectively. The counterfactual conditional and material conditionals are symbolized with $\Box\!\!\rightarrow$ and $\supset$.

The first constraint is that the strict conditional implies the counterfactual conditional:

NECESSITY      $\Box(A \supset B) \supset (A \Box\!\!\rightarrow B)$.

Thanks to participants in an Arché workshop on modality at St Andrews for stimulating discussion of an earlier version of this material. Some of the acknowledgements to Williamson (2005 and 2007a) are also relevant to the present paper.

Suppose that **A** could not have held without **B** holding too; then if **A** had held, **B** would also have held. In terms of possible worlds semantics for these operators along the lines of Lewis (1973a) or Stalnaker (1968): if all **A** worlds are **B** worlds, then any closest **A** worlds are **B** worlds. More precisely, if all **A** worlds are **B** worlds, then either there are no **A** worlds or there is an **A** world such that any **A** world at least as close as it is to the actual world is a **B** world.

The second constraint is that the counterfactual conditional transmits possibility:

POSSIBILITY     $(A \,\square\!\!\rightarrow B) \supset (\lozenge A \supset \lozenge B)$.

Suppose that if **A** had held, **B** would also have held; then if it is possible for **A** to hold, it is also possible for **B** to hold. In terms of worlds: if any closest **A** worlds are **B** worlds, and there are **A** worlds, then there are also **B** worlds. More precisely, if either there are no **A** worlds or there is an **A** world such that any **A** world at least as close as it is to the actual world is a **B** world, then if there is an **A** world there is also a **B** world.

Together, NECESSITY and POSSIBILITY sandwich the counterfactual conditional between two modal conditions. But they do not squeeze it very tight, for $\lozenge A \supset \lozenge B$ is much weaker than $\square(A \supset B)$: although the latter entails the former in any normal modal logic, the former is true and the latter false whenever **B** is possible without being a necessary consequence of **A**, for example when **A** and **B** are modally independent.

Although NECESSITY and POSSIBILITY determine no necessary and sufficient condition for the counterfactual conditional in terms of necessity and possibility, they yield necessary and sufficient conditions for necessity and possibility in terms of the counterfactual conditional. We argue thus. Let $\perp$ be a contradiction. As a special case of NECESSITY:

(1)  $\square(\neg A \supset \perp) \supset (\neg A \,\square\!\!\rightarrow \perp)$.

By elementary (normal) modal logic, since a truth-functional consequence of something necessary is itself necessary:

(2)  $\square A \supset \square(\neg A \supset \perp)$.

From (1) and (2) by transitivity of the material conditional:

(3)  $\square A \supset (\neg A \,\square\!\!\rightarrow \perp)$.

Similarly, as a special case of POSSIBILITY:

(4)  $(\neg A \,\square\!\!\rightarrow \perp) \supset (\lozenge \neg A \supset \lozenge \perp)$.

By elementary (normal) modal logic, since the possibility of a contradiction is itself inconsistent, and necessity is the dual of possibility (being necessary is equivalent to having an impossible negation):

(5)  $(\lozenge \neg A \supset \lozenge \perp) \supset \square A$.

From (4) and (5) by transitivity:

(6) $(\neg A \mathbin{\Box\!\!\rightarrow} \bot) \supset \Box A$.

Putting (3) and (6) together:

(7) $\Box A \equiv (\neg A \mathbin{\Box\!\!\rightarrow} \bot)$.

The necessary is that whose negation counterfactually implies a contradiction. Since possibility is the dual of necessity (being possible is equivalent to having an unnecessary negation), (7) yields a corresponding necessary and sufficient condition for possibility, once a double negation in the antecedent of the counterfactual has been eliminated.

(8) $\Diamond A \equiv \neg(A \mathbin{\Box\!\!\rightarrow} \bot)$.

The impossible is that which counterfactually implies a contradiction; the possible is that which does not. In (7) and (8), the difference between necessity and possibility lies simply in the scope of negation.

Without assuming a specific framework for the semantics of counterfactuals (in particular, that of possible worlds), we can give a simple semantic rationale for (7) and (8), based on the idea of vacuous truth. That some true counterfactuals have impossible antecedents is clear, for otherwise $A \mathbin{\Box\!\!\rightarrow} A$ would fail when $A$ was impossible. Make two generally accepted assumptions about the distinction between vacuous and non-vacuous truth: (a) $B \mathbin{\Box\!\!\rightarrow} C$ is vacuously true if and only if $B$ is impossible (this could be regarded as a definition of 'vacuously' for counterfactuals); (b) $B \mathbin{\Box\!\!\rightarrow} C$ is non-vacuously true only if $C$ is possible. The truth of (7) and (8) follows, given normal modal reasoning. If $\Box A$ is true, then $\neg A$ is impossible, so by (a) $\neg A \mathbin{\Box\!\!\rightarrow} \bot$ is vacuously true; conversely, if $\neg A \mathbin{\Box\!\!\rightarrow} \bot$ is true, then by (b) it is vacuously true, so by (a) $\neg A$ is impossible, so $\Box A$ is true. Similarly, if $\Diamond A$ is true, then $A$ is not impossible, so by (a) $A \mathbin{\Box\!\!\rightarrow} \bot$ is not vacuously true, and by (b) not non-vacuously true, so $\neg(A \mathbin{\Box\!\!\rightarrow} \bot)$ is true; if $\Diamond A$ is not true, then $A$ is impossible, so by (a) $A \mathbin{\Box\!\!\rightarrow} \bot$ is vacuously true, so $\neg(A \mathbin{\Box\!\!\rightarrow} \bot)$ is not true.

Given that the equivalences (7) and (8) are logically true, metaphysically modal thinking is logically equivalent to a special case of counterfactual thinking. Whoever has what it takes to understand the counterfactual conditional and the elementary logical auxiliaries $\neg$ and $\bot$ has what it takes to understand possibility and necessity operators.

As we shall check later, $A \mathbin{\Box\!\!\rightarrow} \bot$ is logically equivalent to $A \mathbin{\Box\!\!\rightarrow} \neg A$. Thus (7) and (8) generate two new equivalences:

(9) $\Box A \equiv (\neg A \mathbin{\Box\!\!\rightarrow} A)$

(10) $\Diamond A \equiv \neg(A \mathbin{\Box\!\!\rightarrow} \neg A)$.

The necessary is that which is counterfactually implied by its own negation; the possible is that which does not counterfactually imply its own negation.

Stalnaker (1968) used (9) and (10) to define necessity and possibility, although his reading of the conditional (with a different notation) was not exclusively counterfactual. Lewis (1973a, p. 25) used (7) and (8) themselves to define necessity and possibility in terms of the counterfactual conditional. However, such definitions seem to have been treated as convenient notational economies, their potential philosophical significance unnoticed (Hill 2006 is a recent exception).

If we permit ourselves to quantify into sentence position ('propositional quantification'), we can formulate another pair of variants on (7) and (8) which may improve our feel for what is going on. As we shall see below, on elementary assumptions about the logic of such quantifiers and of the counterfactual conditional, $\neg A \; \Box\!\!\rightarrow A$ is provably equivalent to $\forall p\,(p \; \Box\!\!\rightarrow A)$: something is counterfactually implied by its negation if and only if it is counterfactually implied by everything. Thus (9) and (10) generate these equivalences too:

(11) $\Box A \equiv \forall p\,(p \; \Box\!\!\rightarrow A)$

(12) $\Diamond A \equiv \exists p\, \neg(p \; \Box\!\!\rightarrow \neg A)$.

According to (11), something is necessary if and only if whatever were the case, it would still be the case (see also Lewis 1986a, p. 23). That is a natural way of explaining informally what metaphysically necessity is. According to (12), something is possible if and only if it is not such that it would fail in every eventuality.

Since the right-hand sides of (7), (9), and (11) are not strictly synonymous with each other, given the differences in their semantic structure, they are not all strictly synonymous with $\Box A$. Similarly, since the right-hand sides of (8), (10), and (12) are not strictly synonymous with each other, they are not all strictly synonymous with $\Diamond A$. Indeed, we have no sufficient reason to regard any of the equivalences as strict synonymies. That detracts little from their philosophical significance, for failure of strict synonymy does not imply failure of logical equivalence. The main philosophical concerns about possibility and necessity apply equally to anything logically equivalent to possibility or necessity. A non-modal analogy: $\neg A$ is logically equivalent to $A \supset \bot$, but presumably they are not strictly synonymous; nevertheless, once we have established that a creature can handle $\supset$ and $\bot$, we have established that it can handle something logically equivalent to negation, which answers the most interesting questions about its ability to handle negation. We should find the mutual equivalence of (7), (9), and (11), and of (8), (10), and (12) reassuring, for it shows the robustness of the modal notions definable from the counterfactual conditional, somewhat as the equivalence of the various proposed definitions of 'computable function' showed the robustness of that notion.

2

Let us now consider the issues more rigorously, within a formal language for counterfactual conditionals. No particular formal semantics will be assumed, although various sorts of model theory will occasionally be used in auxiliary roles. Rather, the emphasis will be on derivations within the object language using informally plausible principles.

For most purposes our object language will be L, which has countably many propositional variables **p**, **q**, **r**, . . ., the propositional constant ⊥ and two binary connectives, ⊃ and □→. Other truth-functional operators are introduced as metalinguistic abbreviations in the usual way; for example, ¬A is A ⊃ ⊥. 'A', 'B', 'C', . . . are metalinguistic variables ranging over all formulas.

Except when otherwise specified, we work in the following axiomatic system (where ⊢ means theoremhood):

| | |
|---|---|
| PC | If **A** is a truth-functional tautology then ⊢ **A** |
| REFLEXIVITY | ⊢ A □→ A |
| VACUITY | ⊢ (¬A □→ A) ⊃ (B □→ A). |
| MP | If ⊢ A ⊃ B and ⊢ A then ⊢ B. |
| CLOSURE | If ⊢ ($B_1$ & . . . & $B_n$) ⊃ C then |
| | ⊢ ((A □→ $B_1$) & . . . & (A □→ $B_n$)) ⊃ (A □→ C) |
| EQUIVALENCE | If ⊢ A ≡ A* then ⊢ (A □→ B) ≡ (A* □→ B). |

These axiom schemas and inference rules constitute a weak subsystem of David Lewis's 'official' logic of counterfactuals, VC (1986a, p. 132). PC, REFLEXIVITY, and VACUITY are his axiom schemas (1), (3), and (4) respectively, and MP is his rule of Modus Ponens (for ⊃). CLOSURE is his rule of Deduction within Conditionals (unlike Lewis, we allow $n = 0$, interpreting this case as the rule that if ⊢ C then ⊢ A □→ C; but that special case is anyway derivable from CLOSURE for $n = 1$ and REFLEXIVITY). EQUIVALENCE is a special case of Lewis's rule of Interchange of Logical Equivalents (incorrectly omitted from the original 1973a edition (1986a, p. ix)); Interchange of Logical Equivalents in its full generality is derivable from EQUIVALENCE, CLOSURE, PC, and MP (proof: by induction on the construction of formulas). One way in which this subsystem is weak is that it lacks Lewis's irredundant axiom schema (A & B) ⊃ (A □→ B), for, unlike the principles above, it is invalid when □→ is reinterpreted as strict implication in S5.

PC and MP simply encapsulate the background classical logic. REFLEXIVITY reflects the triviality that in developing a counterfactual supposition we can start with that supposition itself. The point of VACUITY is that ¬A is the 'worst' antecedent for A as consequent; if A is forthcoming even in that case, it is forthcoming in every case. To think of it another way, ¬A □→ A can be true only by being vacuously true, in which case A is true in every eventuality. CLOSURE means that in developing the consequences of a counterfactual supposition, we can include any logical consequence of the results obtained so far. EQUIVALENCE goes with the idea that differences between logically equivalent counterfactual suppositions are in effect differences only in the mode of presentation of the way that the world is being supposed to be.

CLOSURE and EQUIVALENCE are not quite as straightforward as they look. In a language with a rigidifying 'actually' operator @, p ≡ @p is arguably a logical truth. But if it is a theorem, each of CLOSURE and EQUIVA-LENCE separately (when combined with REFLEXIVITY) yields the theorem p □→ @p, which is false on many interpretations: 'If it had rained, it would have actually rained' is false if it did not rain. In the terminology of Davies and Humberstone (1980), CLOSURE and EQUIVALENCE preserve general validity (truth at every world of every model) but not real world validity (truth at the actual world of every model). Thus CLOSURE and EQUIV-ALENCE must be restricted to theorems derived solely by appeal to axioms and rules which preserve general validity. A similar restriction is needed on the standard rule of Necessitation (RN), that if A is a theorem so is □A, for even if p ⊃ @p is logically true, □(p ⊃ @p) may be false. For present purposes we can ignore this complication, since the languages under consid-eration lack operators such as 'actually' (see Williamson 2006a for further discussion).

For our immediate purposes, we must expand L to the language L+ by adding propositional quantifiers. That is, if p is a propositional variable and A is a formula of L+, ∀ p A is also a formula of L+. We extend the axiomatization by a corresponding axiom schema and rule (where A[B/p] is the result of substituting the formula B for all free occurrences of p in A, on the assumption that no variable free in B thereby becomes bound):

UINST  If p is any propositional variable then ⊢ ∀ p A ⊃ A[B/p].

UGEN  If p is any propositional variable not free in A, and ⊢ A ⊃ B then ⊢ A ⊃ ∀ p B.

This system, like that for L, satisfies the rule of substitution of proved material equivalents, in the sense that if ⊢ B ≡ B* then ⊢ A[B/p] ≡ A[B*/p] for any formula A and propositional variable p (proof: by induction on the complexity of A). Thus proved material equivalents are interchangeable in all relevant contexts. In the setting of possible worlds semantics, UINST and UGEN are sound when the propositional quantifiers are interpreted as ranging over all subsets of the set of possible worlds associated with the given model, but they will not yield a complete system, since they do not guarantee the existence of maximally specific possible propositions, true in exactly one world (for example, one cannot derive

∃ p (p & ∀ q (q ⊃ □(p ⊃ q)))). For present purposes, those stronger assumptions are unnecessary.[1]

Our first task is to show that three candidate definitions of □A in L+ are mutually equivalent: (i) ∀ p (p □→ A) (where p is not free in A); (ii) ¬A □→ A; (iii) ¬A □→ ⊥. First we establish the equivalence of (i) and (ii):

| | | |
|---|---|---|
| (1) | ∀ p (p □→ A) ⊃ (¬A □→ A) | UINST |
| (2) | (¬A □→ A) ⊃ (p □→ A) | VACUITY |
| (3) | (¬A □→ A) ⊃ ∀ p (p □→ A) | 2, UGEN |
| (4) | ∀ p (p □→ A) ≡ (¬A □→ A) | 1, 3, PC, MP. |

Now we establish the equivalence of (ii) and (iii):

| | | |
|---|---|---|
| (1) | (A & ¬A) ⊃ ⊥ | PC |
| (2) | ((¬A □→ A) & (¬A □→ ¬A)) ⊃ (¬A □→ ⊥) | 1, CLOSURE |
| (3) | ¬A □→ ¬A | REFLEXIVITY |
| (4) | (¬A □→ A) ⊃ (¬A □→ ⊥) | 2, 3, PC, MP |
| (5) | ⊥ ⊃ A | PC |
| (6) | (¬A □→ ⊥) ⊃ (¬A □→ A) | 5, CLOSURE |
| (7) | (¬A □→ A) ≡ (¬A □→ ⊥) | 4, 6, PC, MP. |

Thus (i), (ii), and (iii) are mutually interchangeable in all relevant contexts. It matters little which of them we use to define □A. However, the complexities of propositional quantification are best avoided when they are not needed, and (iii) is marginally simpler than (ii), so we shall treat □A as a metalinguistic abbreviation for ¬A □→ ⊥. We can therefore return to the propositional language L, and omit the quantifier rules. As usual in modal logic we treat ◊A as a metalinguistic abbreviation for ¬□¬A, which in our case is ¬(¬¬A □→ ⊥), which is equivalent by EQUIVALENCE to ¬(A □→ ⊥).

3

The next task is to check that once we define □ and ◊ as proposed, we can recover the constraints NECESSITY and POSSIBILITY within counterfactual logic. That is fortunate, for otherwise our position would be incoherent: those constraints would have been used to motivate interpretations of the modal operators which did not vindicate the constraints.

[1] See the pioneering works Fine (1970) and Kaplan (1970) for more technical detail on propositional quantification in modal logic. Williamson (1999) discusses its interpretation: interpreting it by means of quantification into name position in the metalanguage, over sets of possible worlds or anything else, is arguably only a rough approximation to its philosophically most significant interpretation, which involves ineliminable quantification into sentence position. Such subtleties are inessential for present purposes.

We prove them in our system as follows. First, NECESSITY:

| | | |
|---|---|---|
| (1) | $\Box(A \supset B) \supset (\neg(A \supset B) \Box\!\!\rightarrow \bot)$ | DEF$\Box$, PC |
| (2) | $(\neg(A \supset B) \Box\!\!\rightarrow \bot) \supset (\neg(A \supset B) \Box\!\!\rightarrow$ $(A \supset B))$ | PC, CLOSURE |
| (3) | $(\neg(A \supset B) \Box\!\!\rightarrow (A \supset B)) \supset (A \Box\!\!\rightarrow$ $(A \supset B))$ | VACUITY |
| (4) | $\Box(A \supset B) \supset (A \Box\!\!\rightarrow (A \supset B))$ | 1, 2, 3, PC, MP |
| (5) | $((A \Box\!\!\rightarrow (A \supset B)) \,\&\, (A \Box\!\!\rightarrow A)) \supset$ $(A \Box\!\!\rightarrow B)$ | PC, CLOSURE |
| (6) | $(A \Box\!\!\rightarrow (A \supset B)) \supset (A \Box\!\!\rightarrow B)$ | 5, REFLEXIVITY, PC, MP |
| (7) | $\Box(A \supset B) \supset (A \Box\!\!\rightarrow B)$ | 4, 6, PC, MP. |

Then, POSSIBILITY:

| | | |
|---|---|---|
| (1) | $\neg\Diamond B \supset (\neg\neg B \Box\!\!\rightarrow \bot)$ | DEF$\Diamond$, PC |
| (2) | $(\neg\neg B \Box\!\!\rightarrow \bot) \supset (\neg\neg B \Box\!\!\rightarrow \neg B)$ | PC, CLOSURE |
| (3) | $(\neg\neg B \Box\!\!\rightarrow \neg B) \supset (A \Box\!\!\rightarrow \neg B)$ | VACUITY |
| (4) | $\neg\Diamond B \supset (A \Box\!\!\rightarrow \neg B)$ | 1, 2, 3, PC, MP |
| (5) | $((A \Box\!\!\rightarrow B) \,\&\, (A \Box\!\!\rightarrow \neg B)) \supset$ $(A \Box\!\!\rightarrow \bot)$ | PC, CLOSURE |
| (6) | $((A \Box\!\!\rightarrow B) \,\&\, \neg\Diamond B) \supset (A \Box\!\!\rightarrow \bot)$ | 4, 5, PC, MP |
| (7) | $(\neg\neg A \Box\!\!\rightarrow \bot) \supset \neg\Diamond A$ | DEF$\Diamond$, PC |
| (8) | $(A \Box\!\!\rightarrow \bot) \supset (\neg\neg A \Box\!\!\rightarrow \bot)$ | PC, EQUIVALENCE |
| (9) | $((A \Box\!\!\rightarrow B) \,\&\, \neg\Diamond B) \supset \neg\Diamond A$ | 6, 7, 8, PC, MP |
| (10) | $(A \Box\!\!\rightarrow B) \supset (\Diamond A \supset \Diamond B)$ | 9, PC, MP. |

4

We now turn to deriving some basic principles of modal logic within counterfactual logic. The weakest normal modal logic is K, which is axiomatized by PC, MP, and the following axiom schema and rule:

K    $\vdash \Box(A \supset B) \supset (\Box A \supset \Box B)$

RN    If $\vdash A$ then $\vdash \Box A$.

We derive K in our system thus:

| | | |
|---|---|---|
| (1) | $\Box A \supset (\neg A \Box\!\!\rightarrow \bot)$ | PC, DEF$\Box$ |
| (2) | $\Box A \supset (\neg A \Box\!\!\rightarrow A)$ | 1, PC, CLOSURE, MP |
| (3) | $\Box A \supset (\neg B \Box\!\!\rightarrow A)$ | 2, VACUITY, PC, MP |
| (4) | $\Box(A \supset B) \supset (\neg B \Box\!\!\rightarrow (A \supset B))$ | Like 3 |
| (5) | $((\neg B \Box\!\!\rightarrow (A \supset B)) \,\&\, (\neg B \Box\!\!\rightarrow A)) \supset$ $(\neg B \Box\!\!\rightarrow B)$ | PC, CLOSURE |

| | | |
|---|---|---|
| (6) | $(\Box(A \supset B) \,\&\, \Box A) \supset (\neg B \,\Box\!\!\rightarrow B)$ | 3, 4, 5, PC, MP |
| (7) | $(\neg B \,\Box\!\!\rightarrow B) \supset (\neg B \,\Box\!\!\rightarrow \bot)$ | REFLEXIVITY, CLOSURE, PC, MP |
| (8) | $(\neg B \,\Box\!\!\rightarrow B) \supset \Box B$ | 7, DEF$\Box$ |
| (9) | $\Box(A \supset B) \supset (\Box A \supset \Box B)$ | 6, 8, PC, MP. |

Here is a derivation of RN:

| | | |
|---|---|---|
| (1) | A | Theorem by assumption |
| (2) | $\neg A \supset \bot$ | 1, PC, MP |
| (3) | $(\neg A \,\Box\!\!\rightarrow \neg A) \supset (\neg A \,\Box\!\!\rightarrow \bot)$ | 2, CLOSURE |
| (4) | $\neg A \,\Box\!\!\rightarrow \bot$ | 3, REFLEXIVITY, PC, MP |
| (5) | $\Box A$ | 4, DEF$\Box$. |

Thus all theorems of K are theorems of our system, under our definition of $\Box$.

We can prove something stronger: the modal principles derivable in our current system are *just* those derivable in K. More precisely, let $L_\Box$ be the language of propositional modal logic, built up from the propositional variables, $\bot$, $\supset$, and $\Box$ (treated as primitive). Let $^*$ be the mapping from $L_\Box$ to L that corresponds to our definition of $\Box$:

$^*p = p$ for each propositional variable $p$
$^*\bot = \bot$
$^*(A \supset B) = \,^*A \supset \,^*B$
$^*\Box A = \neg\,^*A \,\Box\!\!\rightarrow \bot$.

Then for any formula A of $L_\Box$, $^*A$ is a theorem of our system ($\vdash \,^*A$) if and only if A is a theorem of K ($\vdash_K A$). We have in effect already proved that if $\vdash_K A$ then $\vdash \,^*A$. The converse is trickier, because the proof of $^*A$ in our system may involve formulas such as $p \,\Box\!\!\rightarrow q$ that are not of the form $^*B$ for any formula B of $L_\Box$. We define an auxiliary 'unintended' mapping $^\wedge$ back from L to $L_\Box$:

$^\wedge p = p$ for each propositional variable $p$
$^\wedge\bot = \bot$
$^\wedge(A \supset B) = \,^\wedge A \supset \,^\wedge B$
$^\wedge(A \,\Box\!\!\rightarrow B) = \Box(^\wedge A \supset \,^\wedge B)$.

We note two easy lemmas. (I) For any formula A of L, if $\vdash A$ then $\vdash_K \,^\wedge A$. Proof: by induction on the length of proofs in our system. (II) For any formula A of $L_\Box$, $\vdash_K A \equiv \,^\wedge\!^*A$. Proof: by induction on the complexity of A. Now suppose that A is a formula of $L_\Box$ and $\vdash \,^*A$. By (I), $\vdash_K \,^\wedge\!^*A$. By (II), $\vdash_K A \equiv \,^\wedge\!^*A$. Therefore $\vdash_K A$, as required. Thus $\vdash \,^*A$ if and only if $\vdash_K A$.

The system K is far too weak to be an adequate logic of metaphysical possibility and necessity. The most saliently missing principle is that what is necessarily so is so:

T    $\vdash \Box A \supset A$.

We can derive T in our system by adding Lewis's 'weak centering' principle (schema (6) in his official logic of counterfactuals (1986a: 132); it is also axiom schema (a6) in Stalnaker 1968), which corresponds to modus ponens for the subjunctive conditional given the logic of the material conditional:

MPSUBJ      $\vdash (A \,\square\!\!\rightarrow B) \supset (A \supset B)$.

T is an immediate consequence of MPSUBJ:

| | | |
|---|---|---|
| (1) | $(\neg A \,\square\!\!\rightarrow \bot) \supset (\neg A \supset \bot)$ | MPSUBJ |
| (2) | $(\neg A \,\square\!\!\rightarrow \bot) \supset A$ | 1, PC, MP |
| (3) | $\square A \supset A$ | 2, DEF$\square$. |

By a proof along just the same lines as for K (with the same mappings), we can show that for any formula **A** of L$_\square$, *A is a theorem of our system extended by MPSUBJ if and only if **A** is a theorem of KT, the result of extending K (as axiomatized above) by T. Thus PC, REFLEXIVITY, VACUITY, MPSUBJ, MP, CLOSURE, and EQUIVALENCE induce the simple logic KT for metaphysical modality.

MPSUBJ is an immensely plausible principle. If we discover that *e* happened without *f*, doesn't that refute the claim that if *e* had happened, *f* would have happened?[2] Nevertheless, it is worth observing that the full strength of MPSUBJ is not needed to derive T. For if we merely add T itself to our original system (read by means of DEF$\square$), we cannot derive MPSUBJ. We can show this by giving an unintended model theory that validates PC, REFLEXIVITY, VACUITY, T, MP, CLOSURE, and EQUIVALENCE but not MPSUBJ. It is a 'possible worlds' semantics, but with the natural numbers playing the role of the worlds. The clause for $\square\!\!\rightarrow$ is this: **A** $\square\!\!\rightarrow$ **B** is true at all worlds iff either **A** is false at all worlds or **B** is true at the least world at which **A** is true ('least' in the sense of the usual ordering of the natural numbers; recall that every nonempty set of natural numbers has a least member); otherwise **A** $\square\!\!\rightarrow$ **B** is false at all worlds. Everything else is standard. It is routine to check (by induction on the length of proofs) that every formula of L derivable from PC, REFLEXIVITY, VACUITY, T, MP, CLOSURE, and EQUIVALENCE is true at all worlds in all such models. For example, in the case of T, suppose that $\square$A is true at a world, which is to say that $\neg$A $\square\!\!\rightarrow$ $\bot$ is true at that world; since $\neg$A $\square\!\!\rightarrow$ $\bot$ cannot be non-vacuously true, it must be vacuously true; thus **A** is true at every world. But not all instances of MPSUBJ are true at all worlds in all such models.

---

[2] One can accept a counterfactual when rationally unwilling to apply modus ponens to it, in the sense that on learning its antecedent one would reject the counterfactual rather than accept its consequent. For example, I accept 'If Oswald had not shot Kennedy, Kennedy would not have been shot', but if I come to accept 'Oswald did not shoot Kennedy', I will not conclude 'Kennedy was not shot'. But that is no threat to the validity of modus ponens. In circumstances in which both 'If Oswald had not shot Kennedy, Kennedy would not have been shot' and 'Oswald did not shoot Kennedy' are accepted, so is 'Kennedy was not shot'.

For example, let **p** be true at 0 but false at every other world. Then $\neg \perp \square \rightarrow$ **p** is true at every world, while $\neg \perp \supset$ **p** is false at 1.

A more controversial but still plausible principle about metaphysical modality is the characteristic axiom schema of the modal system S5, known as E:

E    $\vdash \Diamond A \supset \square \Diamond A.$

KTE is simply S5; in that system, matters of possibility and necessity are always non-contingent. We can also derive in it the characteristic principle of S4:

4    $\vdash \square A \supset \square \square A$

(Hughes and Cresswell 1996 provides appropriate background in modal logic.) If we read E directly in terms of our subjunctive definitions of the modal operators, $\square \Diamond A$ becomes a subjunctive conditional with a (negated) subjunctive conditional in its antecedent, which is quite hard to get a feel for. Here is a more natural equivalent of E in subjunctive conditional terms:

ES    $\vdash (A \square \rightarrow (B \square \rightarrow \perp)) \supset ((A \square \rightarrow \perp) \vee (B \square \rightarrow \perp)).$

The embedded subjunctive conditional has been moved into the consequent, where such embeddings occur somewhat more naturally. Informally, ES says that embedding one possible subjunctive hypothesis inside another cannot lead to an impossibility: even if **B** is incompatible with **A**, counterfactually supposing **B** within the counterfactual supposition of **A** takes one back out of the **A** worlds into the **B** worlds, not to an impossibility.

The generalization of ES to arbitrary sentences in place of the logical falsehood is much less plausible:

ES+    $\vdash (A \square \rightarrow (B \square \rightarrow C)) \supset ((A \square \rightarrow C) \vee (B \square \rightarrow C)).$

If I had been a French grocer then it would have held of me that if I had been a philosopher I would have been a French philosopher; but it is not the case that if I had been a French grocer I would have been a French philosopher, nor is it the case that if I had been a philosopher I would have been a French philosopher. In terms of Lewis's similarity semantics, suppose that **p** holds only at the counterfactual world $w$, **q** holds only at the actual world and at a third world $x$, closer to $w$ than the actual world is, and **r** holds only at $x$. Then $w$ is a **q** $\square \rightarrow$ **r** world, because the closest **q** world to $w$ is $x$, which is an **r** world; thus the actual world is a **p** $\square \rightarrow$ (**q** $\square \rightarrow$ **r**) world, since $w$ is the closest **p** world to the actual world; but the actual world is neither a **p** $\square \rightarrow$ **r** world (since the closest **p** world to the actual world, $w$, is not an **r** world) nor a **q** $\square \rightarrow$ **r** world (since the closest **q** world to the actual world is the actual world itself, which is not an **r** world). Thus ES+ is invalid in Lewis's semantics. By contrast, ES holds on Lewis's semantics provided that all worlds form a single similarity space (compare Lewis's uniformity condition (1986a, pp. 120–1)). For then **B** $\square \rightarrow \perp$ is false at every world if **B** is true at some world; thus if **B** $\square \rightarrow \perp$ is false at a world, so **B** is true at some world, then **B** $\square\!\rightarrow \perp$ is true at exactly the same worlds as $\perp$, so **A** $\square\!\rightarrow$ (**B** $\square\!\rightarrow \perp$) and **A** $\square\!\rightarrow \perp$ have the same truth-value at all worlds; thus ES holds (consequently, ES does not entail ES+). The plausibility of ES depends on the occurrence of a logical falsehood in the consequent.

Although we will not attempt to determine here whether ES should ultimately be accepted, it at least gives us a new perspective on the status of S5 (Salmon 1981, pp. 238–40; 1989; and 1993 argue that S4 and therefore S5 are invalid for metaphysical modality; Williamson 1990b, pp. 126–43 and 2000b, pp. 119–20 reply).

We still have to establish the equivalence of ES with E. First, we argue from ES to E in our original system:

(1)   $((\neg\neg\textbf{A} \square\!\rightarrow \perp) \square\!\rightarrow (\neg\neg\textbf{A} \square\!\rightarrow \perp)) \supset$
      $(((\neg\neg\textbf{A} \square\!\rightarrow \perp) \square\!\rightarrow \perp) \vee$
      $(\neg\neg\textbf{A} \square\!\rightarrow \perp))$                                    ES

(2)   $((\neg\neg\textbf{A} \square\!\rightarrow \perp) \square\!\rightarrow \perp) \vee (\neg\neg\textbf{A} \square\!\rightarrow \perp)$    1, REFLEXIVITY, MP

(3)   $\neg(\neg\neg\textbf{A} \square\!\rightarrow \perp) \supset (\neg\neg(\neg\neg\textbf{A} \square\!\rightarrow \perp)$
      $\square\!\rightarrow \perp)$                                          2, EQUIVALENCE, PC, MP

(4)   $\Diamond\textbf{A} \supset \square\Diamond\textbf{A}$                                    3, DEF$\Diamond$, DEF$\square$.

Now we establish the converse, again in our original system:

(1)   $\Diamond\textbf{B} \supset \square\Diamond\textbf{B}$                                    E

(2)   $\neg(\textbf{B} \square\!\rightarrow \perp) \supset (\neg\neg(\textbf{B} \square\!\rightarrow \perp)$
      $\square\!\rightarrow \perp)$                                          1, EQUIVALENCE, PC, MP, DEF$\Diamond$, DEF$\square$

(3)   $(\neg\neg(\textbf{B} \square\!\rightarrow \perp) \square\!\rightarrow \perp) \supset$
      $(\neg\neg(\textbf{B} \square\!\rightarrow \perp) \square\!\rightarrow \neg(\textbf{B} \square\!\rightarrow \perp))$    CLOSURE, MP, PC

(4)   $\neg(\textbf{B} \square\!\rightarrow \perp) \supset (\neg\neg(\textbf{B} \square\!\rightarrow \perp) \square\!\rightarrow$
      $\neg(\textbf{B} \square\!\rightarrow \perp))$                              2, 3, MP, PC

(5)   $\neg(\textbf{B} \square\!\rightarrow \perp) \supset (\textbf{A} \square\!\rightarrow \neg(\textbf{B} \square\!\rightarrow \perp))$    4, VACUITY, MP, PC

(6)   $((\textbf{A} \square\!\rightarrow (\textbf{B} \square\!\rightarrow \perp)) \,\&\, (\textbf{A} \square\!\rightarrow$
      $\neg(\textbf{B} \square\!\rightarrow \perp))) \supset (\textbf{A} \square\!\rightarrow \perp)$    CLOSURE, MP, PC

(7)   $(\textbf{A} \square\!\rightarrow (\textbf{B} \square\!\rightarrow \perp)) \supset ((\textbf{A} \square\!\rightarrow \perp) \vee$
      $(\textbf{B} \square\!\rightarrow \perp))$                                   5, 6, MP, PC.

Although PC, REFLEXIVITY, VACUITY, MPSUBJ, ES, MP, CLOSURE, and EQUIVALENCE together yield the full strength of S5, they still constitute a rather weak logic of counterfactuals. For example, they do not yield axiom schema (a7) from Stalnaker (1968), a strengthening of EQUIVALENCE:

(a7)   $\vdash ((\textbf{A} \square\!\rightarrow \textbf{B}) \,\&\, (\textbf{B} \square\!\rightarrow \textbf{A})) \supset ((\textbf{A} \square\!\rightarrow \textbf{C}) \supset (\textbf{B} \square\!\rightarrow \textbf{C}))$.

To check independence, consider another deviant semantics in which the possible worlds are the natural numbers. Let **A** $\square\!\rightarrow$ **B** be true at a world $w$ if and only if three conditions hold: (i) if **A** is true at $w$ then **B** is true at $w$; (ii) if

**A** is true at exactly one world then **B** is also true at that world; (iii) if **A** is true at a world $x$ and at some world $y$ such that $x > y$ then **B** is true at $x$. In particular, therefore, **A** $\Box\!\!\to \perp$ is true at all worlds if **A** is false at all worlds; otherwise **A** $\Box\!\!\to \perp$ is false at all worlds. Everything else is standard. It is routine to check that all theorems of our system are true in all such models. But (a7) fails: for if **p** is true at just 1 and 2, **q** at just 0, 1, and 2, and **r** just at 2, then **p** $\Box\!\!\to$ **q**, **q** $\Box\!\!\to$ **p**, and **p** $\Box\!\!\to$ **r** are true but **q** $\Box\!\!\to$ **r** false at 2 (since **q** is true and **r** false at 1, which is not the least world at which **q** is true). The same semantics shows that the complex axiom schema (5) of Lewis's official system VC (1986a, p. 132) is not derivable in our system (since (**q** & **p**) $\Box\!\!\to$ **r** is true but **q** $\Box\!\!\to$ (**p** $\supset$ **r**) false at 2). We might wish to add some of these further principles to our system.

Moderately natural counterfactual equivalents of other modal principles can also be provided. For example, the 4 schema $\vdash \Box$**A** $\supset \Box\Box$**A** is equivalent to this schema:

4S   $\vdash$ (**A** $\Box\!\!\to \perp$) $\supset$ (**B** $\Box\!\!\to$ (**A** $\Box\!\!\to \perp$)).

Similarly, the B schema $\vdash$ **A** $\supset \Box\Diamond$**A** is equivalent to this schema:

BS   $\vdash$ (**A** $\Box\!\!\to$ (**B** $\Box\!\!\to \perp$)) $\supset$ (**B** $\supset$ (**A** $\Box\!\!\to \perp$)).

The proofs are similar to those already given. The preceding observations merely begin the work of exploring the modal subsystems of logics of the subjunctive conditional. With luck, they will encourage others to explore the matter more thoroughly.

5

It may be objected to the preceding account that the assumption about vacuous truth on which it relies is wrong (Nolan 1997). According to the objector, some counterpossibles (counterfactuals with metaphysically impossible antecedents) are false, such as (a), uttered by someone who mistakenly believes that he answered '13' to 'What is $5 + 7$?'; in fact he answered '11':

(a) If $5 + 7$ were 13 I would have got that sum right.

Thus, contrary to the account, $\Box$**A** may be true while $\neg$**A** $\Box\!\!\to \perp$ is false. In the argument for their equivalence in section 1, the contentious premise is NECESSITY. If some worlds are metaphysically impossible, and **A** is true at some of them but false at all metaphysically possible worlds, while **B** is false at all worlds whatsoever, then every metaphysically possible **A** world is a **B** world, but the closest **A** worlds are not **B** worlds.[3] Similar objections apply to the other purported equivalences for the metaphysical modalities.

---

[3] Technically, NECESSITY fails on a semantics with similarity spheres for $\Box\!\!\to$ that include some impossible worlds (inaccessible with respect to $\Box$). Conversely, POSSIBILITY fails on a

If *all* counterpossibles were false, ◇**A** would be equivalent to **A** □→ **A**, for the latter would still be true whenever **A** was possible; correspondingly, □**A** would be equivalent to the dual ¬(¬**A** □→ ¬**A**) and one could carry out the programme of this paper using the new equivalences. But that is presumably not what the objector has in mind. Rather, the idea is that the truth-value of a counterpossible can depend on its consequent, so that (a) is false while (b) is true:

(b) If 5 + 7 were 13 I would have got that sum wrong.

However, such examples are quite unpersuasive.

First, they tend to fall apart when thought through. For example, if 5 + 7 were 13 then 5 + 6 would be 12, and so (by another eleven steps) 0 would be 1, so if the number of right answers I gave were 0, the number of right answers I gave would be 1.

Second, there are general reasons to doubt the supposed intuitions on which such examples rely. We are used to working with possible antecedents, and given the possibility of **A**, the incompatibility of **B** and **C** implies that **A** □→ **B** and **A** □→ **C** cannot both be true. Thus by over-projecting from familiar cases we may take the uncontentious (b) to be incompatible with (a). The logically unsophisticated make analogous errors in quantificational reasoning. Given the evident truth of 'Every golden mountain is a mountain', they think that 'Every golden mountain is a valley' is false, neglecting the case of vacuous truth. Since the logic and semantics of counterfactual conditionals is much less well understood, even the logically sophisticated may find similar errors tempting. Such errors may be compounded by a tendency to confuse negating a counterfactual conditional with negating its consequent, given the artificiality of the constructions needed to negate the whole conditional unambiguously ('it is not the case that if. . .'). Thus the truth of **A** □→ ¬**B** (with **A** impossible) may be mistaken for the truth of ¬(**A** □→ **B**) and therefore the falsity of **A** □→ **B**.

Some objectors try to bolster their case by giving examples of mathematicians reasoning from an impossible supposition **A** ('There are only finitely many prime numbers') in order to reduce it to absurdity. Such arguments can be formulated using a counterfactual conditional, although they need not be. Certainly there will be points in the argument at which it is legitimate to assert **A** □→ **C** (in particular, **A** □→ **A**) but illegitimate to assert **A** □→ ¬**C** (in particular, **A** □→ ¬**A**). But of course that does not show that **A** □→ ¬**A** is false. At any point in a mathematical argument there are infinitely many truths that it is not legitimate to assert, because they have not yet been proved (Lewis

semantics with some possible worlds excluded from all similarity spheres (see Lewis 1986a, p. 16 on universality). Inaccessible worlds seem not to threaten POSSIBILITY. For suppose that an **A** world *w* but no **B** world is accessible from a world *v*. Then if **A** □→ **B** holds at *v* on the usual semantics, there is an **A** world *x* such that every **A** world as close as *x* is to *v* is a **B** world. It follows that *w* is not as close as *x* is to *v* and that *x* is inaccessible from *v*, which contradicts the plausible assumption that any accessible world is at least as close as any inaccessible world.

1986a, pp. 24–6 pragmatically explains away some purported examples of false counterfactuals with impossible antecedents).

We may also wonder what logic of counterfactuals the objectors envisage. If they reject elementary principles of the pure logic of counterfactual conditionals, that is an unattractive feature of their position. If they accept all those principles, then they are committed to operators characterized as in section 1 that exhibit all the logical behaviour standardly expected of necessity and possibility. What is that modality, if not metaphysical modality?

A final problem for the objection is this. Here is a paradigm of the kind of counterpossible which the objector regards as false:

> (c) If Hesperus had not been Phosphorus, Phosphorus would not have been Phosphorus.

Since Hesperus is Phosphorus, it is metaphysically impossible that Hesperus is not Phosphorus, by the necessity of identity. Nevertheless, the objectors are likely to insist that in imaginatively developing the counterfactual supposition that Hesperus is not Phosphorus, we are committed to the explicit denial of no logical truth, as in the consequent of (c). According to them, if we do our best for the antecedent, we can develop it into a logically coherent though metaphysically impossible scenario: it will exclude 'Phosphorus is not Phosphorus'. But they will presumably accept this trivial instance of reflexivity:

> (d) If Hesperus had not been Phosphorus, Hesperus would not have been Phosphorus.

In general, however, coreferential proper names are intersubstitutable in counterfactual contexts. For example, the argument from (e) and (f) to (g) is unproblematically valid:

> (e) If the rocket had continued on that course, it would have hit Hesperus.
>
> (f) Hesperus = Phosphorus.
>
> (g) If the rocket had continued on that course, it would have hit Phosphorus.

Similarly, the argument from (d) and (f) to (c) should be valid. But (d) and (f) are uncontentiously true. If the objector concedes that (c) is true after all, then there should be an explanation of the felt resistance to it, compatible with its truth, and we may reasonably expect that explanation to generalize to other purported examples of false counterpossibles. On the other hand, if objectors reject (c), they must deny the validity of the argument from (d) and (f) to (c). Thus they are committed to the claim that counterfactual conditionals create opaque contexts for proper names (the same argument could be given for other singular terms, such as demonstratives). But that is highly implausible. (e) and (g) are materially equivalent because their antecedents and consequents concern the same objects, properties and relations: it matters not that different names are used, because the counterfactuals are not about such representational features. But then exactly the same applies to (c) and (d). Their antecedents and consequents too concern the same objects, properties and relations. That the antecedent of (c) and (d) is in fact metaphysically impossible does not radically alter their subject matter. The transparency of the counterfactual conditional construction concerns its general logical form, not the specific content of the antecedent.

Under scrutiny, the case for false counterpossibles looks feeble.[4]

6

The account of metaphysical modality in terms of counterfactual conditionals casts new light on a number of old issues. Consider the problem of quantifying into modal contexts. The present conception of modality makes quantification into the scope of modal operators tantamount to a special case of quantification into counterfactual contexts, as in (h) and (i):

(h) Everyone who would have benefited if the measure had passed voted for it.

(i) Where would the rock have landed if the bush had not been there?

Thus challenges to the intelligibility of claims of *de re* necessity are tantamount to challenges to the intelligibility of counterfactuals such as (h) and (i). But (h) and (i) are evidently intelligible.

To take another example, discussions of the epistemology of modality often focus on imaginability or conceivability as a test of possibility while ignoring the role of the imagination in the assessment of mundane counterfactuals. In doing so, they omit the appropriate context for understanding the relation between modality and the imagination. For instance, scorn is easily poured on imagination as a test of possibility: it is imaginable but not possible that water does not contain oxygen, except in artificial senses of 'imaginable' that come apart from possibility in other ways, and so on. Imagination can be made to look cognitively worthless. Once we recall its fallible but vital role in evaluating counterfactual conditionals, we should be more open to the idea that it plays such a role in evaluating claims of possibility and necessity. At the very least, we cannot expect an adequate account of the role of imagination in the epistemology of modality if we lack an adequate account of its role in the epistemology of counterfactuals.

---

[4] But see Kment (2006) for an interesting attempt to characterize the metaphysical modalities in terms of counterfactual conditionals within a framework which does allow for false counterpossibles.

# 5

# Is Timothy Williamson a Necessary Existent?

*David Efird*

Timothy Williamson (2002) has offered an argument for the claim that, necessarily, he exists, that is, that he is a necessary existent.[1] Though this argument has attracted a great deal of attention (e.g., Rumfitt 2003 and Wiggins 2003), I present a new argument for the same conclusion which reveals a new way of denying the soundness of Williamson's argument, one which denies not only that it is necessary that he exists but also that there are any true necessities about Williamson at all. In conclusion, given that it is contingent that Williamson exists, I nevertheless distinguish a sense in which he is, after all, a necessary existent: Williamson necessarily exists, though it is not necessary that he exists.

1

Williamson's (2002, pp. 233–4) argument is as follows.[2]

(1) Necessarily, if TW does not exist, then the proposition that TW does not exist is true.

(2) Necessarily, if the proposition that TW does not exist is true, then this proposition exists.

(3) Necessarily, if the proposition that TW does not exist exists, then TW exists.

I would like to thank Thomas Baldwin, William Crawley, Stephen Everson, Bob Hale, Barry Lee, Marie McGinn, Tom Stoneham, an anonymous referee, and especially Dorothy Edgington, Gonzalo Rodriguez-Pereyra, Ian Rumfitt, and David Wiggins for helpful comments and discussion. In addition, I would like to thank Aviv Hoffmann whose meticulous comments on what was to be the final draft of this paper led to substantial improvements. Most importantly, I would like to thank Timothy Williamson, whose most helpful guidance was in every sense necessary for whatever merit this paper has.

[1] To be fair, Williamson takes the argument to generalize, that is, to show that everything is such that, necessarily, it exists. However, in this paper, I am interested only in the argument for the claim that, necessarily, Williamson exists.

[2] As Williamson notes, his argument derives from Prior (1967, pp. 149–51); cf. Fine (1977, pp. 149–50; 1985, pp. 160–80) and Plantinga (1983, pp. 9–10; 1985, pp. 341–9).

From these premises, he concludes:

(4) Necessarily, TW exists.

Call this argument 'Argument A'.

As it stands, Argument A relies on the controversial assumption that propositions are individuals. But, as Ian Rumfitt (2003) has argued, this assumption is not essential to the argument if we employ Prior's (1957) concept of statability, where it is statable that *P* just in case there is a question whether *P*. Purged of this assumption, the argument then becomes:

(5) Necessarily, if TW does not exist, then it is true that TW does not exist.

(6) Necessarily, if it is true that TW does not exist, then it is statable that TW does not exist.

(7) Necessarily, if it is statable that TW does not exist, then TW exists.

From these premises, we can conclude:

(8) Necessarily, TW exists.

Call this argument 'Argument B'. Because Argument A does, but Argument B does not, rely on a controversial assumption for the same conclusion, Argument B seems to be stronger than Argument A in a dialectical sense.

We can further strengthen Williamson's argument by logically weakening the premises and showing that we can infer Williamson's necessary existence from any true necessity about him, such as a logical truth, or even one of the premises of Arguments A and B which are about Williamson, namely, (1), (3), (5), or (7). Consider any true necessity about Williamson, for example, that he is self-identical; from this assumption, we can conclude that, necessarily, Williamson exists. The argument proceeds as follows.

(9) Necessarily, TW is self-identical.

(10) If, necessarily, TW is self-identical, then, necessarily, it is true that TW is self-identical.

(11) If, necessarily, it is true that TW is self-identical, then, necessarily, it is statable that TW is self-identical.

(12) If, necessarily, it is statable that TW is self-identical, then, necessarily, TW exists.

From these premises, we can conclude:

(13) Necessarily, TW exists.

Call this argument 'Argument C'. Argument C is stronger than Argument B in a logical sense: Argument C is non-modally valid, while Argument B is only modally valid, and premises (10)–(12) of Argument C are entailed by premises

(5)–(7) of Argument B, given the K axiom, but not vice versa, and premise (9) of Argument C can be any true necessity about Williamson, including premises (5) and (8) of Argument B. However, Argument C is not stronger in a dialectical sense, since the reasons for accepting premises (10)–(12) of Argument C are simply those for accepting premises (5)–(7) of Argument B.[3]

What is important about Argument C is not that it is stronger, in a sense, than Argument B and so Argument A, but rather that it displays a new way of denying the soundness of Argument B, and also of Argument A. For the soundness of Argument C requires that there be some true necessity about Williamson, which could be that he is self-identical, or, more importantly, (1), (3), (5), or (7), with (10)–(12) modified appropriately. That there are no true necessities about Williamson, and so (1), (3), (5), and (7) are false, is the way of denying the soundness of Williamson's argument and its variations which I wish to defend in this paper. Before doing so, I will set it in the context of the best of the existing responses to his argument.

## 2

With any argument, there are three kinds of responses we can make to it: we can accept the conclusion, we can deny the conclusion by rejecting the reasoning, or we can deny the conclusion by denying at least one of the premises. Below, I outline what I take to be the best of the existing responses to Williamson's argument, concentrating on how they apply to Argument C. Each of the three responses requires a distinction to be made which is designed to render, respectively, (i) the conclusion less implausible (Williamson's), (ii) the argument invalid if the premises are true (Fine's), or (iii) one of the premises false (Rumfitt's).

Williamson, of course, accepts the conclusion, but as he himself notes, the conclusion seems pre-theoretically implausible:

It seems obvious that I could have failed to exist. My parents could easily never have met, in which case I should never have been conceived and born. The like applies to everyone. More generally, it seems plausible that whatever exists in space and time could have failed to exist. Events could have taken an utterly different course. Our existence, like most aspects of our lives appears frighteningly contingent. (2002, p. 233)

In order to deal with this implausibility, Williamson (2002; cf. Linsky and Zalta 1994, 1996, and Williamson 1990a, 1998, 2000a) distinguishes between logical and concrete existence: a logical existent is one which is in the range of the existential quantifier, a concrete existent is one which exists in space and time, and something could be a logical existent without being a concrete existent.

---

[3] Thanks to an anonymous referee for urging me to clarify the sense in which Argument C is stronger than Argument B and the sense in which it is not.

Making use of this distinction, Williamson explains that in the actual world, he is a concrete existent, but in worlds in which his parents do not meet and he is therefore never conceived and born, he is merely a logical and not a concrete existent; thus, Williamson is a contingent concrete existent but a necessary logical existent. The benefit of this response is that it allows for the simplest quantified modal logic, since such a logic requires the necessary existence of every object. The cost of the response is that in order to lessen the pre-theoretic implausibility of the conclusion, we must expand our ontology to include contingently non-concrete objects, thereby increasing qualitatively our ontological commitments. Though it is not obvious that this cost outweighs its benefits, it is not obvious that its benefits outweigh its costs. Consequently, it is worth exploring ways of denying Williamson's conclusion.

Of the responses which deny Williamson's conclusion, it seems to me that the strongest is Fine's (1985), which posits a distinction between inner and outer truth, a distinction which renders Williamson's argument valid just in case its premises are not true. He writes:

One should distinguish between two notions of truth for propositions, the inner and the outer. According to the outer notion, a proposition is true in a possible world regardless of whether it exists in that world; according to the inner notion, a proposition is true in a possible world only if it exists in that world. We may put the distinction in terms of perspective. According to the outer notion, we can stand outside a world and compare the proposition with what goes on in the world in order to ascertain whether it is true. But according to the inner notion, we must first enter with the proposition into the world before ascertaining its truth.   (Fine 1985, p. 163; cf. Adams 1981)

On this response, premises (10) and (11) are true only if the truth predicate has the following interpretations:

(10) If, necessarily, TW is self-identical, then, necessarily, it is true$_{\text{OUTER}}$ that TW is self-identical.

(11) If, necessarily, it is true$_{\text{INNER}}$ that TW is self-identical, then, necessarily, it is statable that TW is self-identical.

But the argument is then invalid on those interpretations. The benefit of the response is that it avoids the pre-theoretic implausibility of the conclusion and the ontological costs Williamson incurs by attempting to lessen this implausibility. The cost of the response, according to Williamson (2002), is that it requires possible worlds to be primitive, as opposed to the concepts of possibility and necessity themselves. Assuming Williamson is right, as it is not obvious that this is the appropriate order of analysis, it would be beneficial to explore an alternative way of denying Williamson's conclusion which allows for the concepts of possibility and necessity to be primitive.

Like Fine's response, this response to Williamson's argument and its variations requires making a distinction, but instead of a distinction in the truth predicate, the distinction is made in the modal operators, a distinction between the impossibly-not-the-case and the necessary. In order to motivate this distinction, I will consider Rumfitt's (2003) response to Williamson's argument which maintains that not all true necessities are necessarily true, which seems to be a special case of Fine's response, on which the truth predicate has a univocal truth$_{\text{INNER}}$ interpretation. Locating where I think Rumfitt's reply is unpersuasive will point the way to the response to Williamson's argument which I favour.

3

In response to Williamson (2002), Rumfitt (2003) argues that (5) is false if the necessity operator is taken to express metaphysical necessity and the truth operator is taken to be non-redundant. In order to explain Rumfitt's argument, I will reconstruct it in a way which makes it relevant to the argument from it being necessary that Williamson is self-identical to it being necessary that Williamson exists.

To begin, we note that from (10) and (11), we can conclude:

(14) If, necessarily, TW is self-identical, then, necessarily, it is statable that TW is self-identical.

On Rumfitt's view, (14) is false. A symbolized reconstruction of his argument is as follows, where 'T' stands for 'it is true that' and 'S' stands for 'it is statable that'. Assume:

(15) $\Box(TW = TW)$.

Rumfitt then assumes, with Prior, that statements about contingent existents are merely contingently statable. So, assuming Williamson is a contingent existent, it is contingently statable that Williamson is self-identical, which Rumfitt represents thus:

(16) $\Diamond \neg S(TW = TW)$.

From (15) and (16), it follows:

(17) $\neg[\Box(TW = TW) \supset \neg\Diamond\neg S(TW = TW)]$.

Given the duality of the modal operators:

(18) $\Box P \equiv \neg\Diamond\neg P$

we can conclude:

(19) $\neg[\Box(TW = TW) \supset \Box S(TW = TW)]$,

which says that though it is necessary that Williamson is self-identical, it is not necessarily statable that Williamson is self-identical.

Now because (14) follows from (10) and (11), if (14) is false, then either (10) or (11) is false. On Rumfitt's view, (10) is false. The argument is as follows. Rumfitt claims that the truth operator is non-redundant in modal contexts, and defines this non-redundant operator as follows:

(20)  $T(P) \equiv [P \, \& \, S(P)]$.

Assuming that the equivalence is necessary, we obtain:

(21)  $\Box(T(P) \equiv [P \, \& \, S(P)])$.

Applying the K axiom and *modus ponens* yields:

(22)  $\Box T(P) \equiv \Box [P \, \& \, S(P)]$.

Assuming that the necessity operator distributes over conjunction, we obtain:

(23)  $\Box T(P) \equiv [\Box P \, \& \, \Box S(P)]$.

From (23), we may conclude:

(24)  $\Box T(P) \supset \Box S(P)$.

A substitution instance of (24) is

(25)  $\Box T(TW = TW) \supset \Box S(TW = TW)$

which is (11). So given that (10) and (11) together entail (14), that (14) is false, and that (11) is true, (10) is false. Now if (10) is false, then so is (5), since (5) entails (10), together with the K axiom, which is not in question. This then in outline is Rumfitt's counter-argument to Arguments B and C.


4


Rumfitt's counter-argument comes in two phases: an argument for the falsity of (14) and an argument for the truth of (11). The crucial move in the first phase is the assumption that it is contingently stable that Williamson is self-identical and its formal representation as:

(16)  $\Diamond \neg S(TW = TW)$.

Given (16), the falsity of (14) follows simply and quickly from the assumptions that it is necessary that Williamson is self-identical and that the modal operators are duals.

The crucial move in the second phase is the assumption that the truth operator is non-redundant in modal contexts and its definition as:

(20)  $T(P) \equiv [P \, \& \, S(P)]$.

Given (20), the truth of (11) follows almost immediately. I wish to challenge both of these moves, taking the second one first.

Rumfitt's second move is motivated by his argument against the inference from '*P*' and 'O(*P*)'—where '*P*' is a sentence and 'O' is a sentential operator—agreeing in assertoric content to 'O' being redundant. This inference underlies Frege's (1915, pp. 322–3) argument for the redundancy of the truth predicate. Rumfitt's argument is as follows.

If 'O' is a redundant operator, then '*P*' and 'O*P*' are intersubstitutable *salva veritate* in every context. But consider the sentences:

> (i) It is metaphysically necessary that: if Blair is Prime Minister in 2002, then Blair is Prime Minister in 2002.
> (ii) It is metaphysically necessary that: if, actually, Blair is Prime Minister in 2002, then Blair is Prime Minister in 2002.

The former is true but the latter is false, since the latter, together with the (K) axiom, entails:

> (iii) If it is metaphysically necessary that, actually, Blair is Prime Minister in 2002, then it is metaphysically necessary that Blair is Prime Minister in 2002

which is false. So, '*P*' and 'Actually, *P*' are not intersubstitutable *salva veritate* in every context. So, the actuality operator is not redundant, particularly in modal contexts. There is then no reason to think that the truth operator is not like the actuality operator in being non-redundant in modal contexts.

The crucial move in Rumfitt's argument is his claim that while (i) is true, (ii) is false. (ii) is false, he thinks, because if the actuality operator is a rigidifying operator, then, given that Blair is Prime Minister in 2002, it is metaphysically necessary that, actually, Blair is Prime Minister in 2002, while it is not metaphysically necessary that Blair is Prime Minister in 2002.

Presumably, the argument supporting this inference is the following.

> (26) 'Blair is Prime Minister in 2002' is true with respect to the actual world, but not true with respect to every possible world.
> (27) 'Actually' is a rigidifying operator such that the truth-value of 'Actually, *P*' with respect to any possible world is the truth-value of '*P*' with respect to the actual world.
> (28) So, if '*P*' is true with respect to the actual world, 'Actually, *P*' is true with respect to every possible world.
> (29) So, 'Actually, Blair is Prime Minister in 2002' is true with respect to every possible world.
> (30) If '*P*' is true with respect to every possible world, it is necessary.
> (31) So, 'Actually, Blair is Prime Minister in 2002' is necessary.

But this sort of argument has not gone unchallenged. In particular, motivated by the thought that it is implausible that prefixing a contingently true sentence with the actuality operator renders the resulting sentence necessary, David Bostock (1988) denies that sentences which are true with respect to all possible worlds are necessary, presumably taking the argument from (26)–(31) to be a *reductio* of assumption (30).[4] But denying that sentences which are true with respect to all possible worlds are necessary is tantamount to surrendering theoretical control over the concept of necessity, since it is that assumption which underlies the semantics of modal logic, cf. Kripke (1963). Therefore, if we are faced with the choice of accepting (31) or denying (30), it seems we should accept (31) and learn to tolerate its implausibility.

But this is not the only option. In order to deny (31), we can deny (27). Now one way of denying (27) would be to deny that the actuality operator is a rigidifying operator, but this way of denying (27) has the same sort of cost as denying (30) because to do so would be to surrender the theoretical control we have achieved over the concept of actuality, cf. Kaplan (1989). Another way to deny (27) would be to grant that the actuality operator is a rigidifying operator, but, rather than being a strongly rigidifying operator, it is a weakly rigidifying operator.[5] That is, rather than taking the truth-value of 'Actually, *P*', for *any* sentence *P*, with respect to *any* possible world to be the truth-value of '*P*' with respect to the actual world, we take it that if a sentence, '*P*', is about an object *a*, which is true (false) with respect to the actual world, 'Actually, *P*' is true (false) with respect to every world in which *a* exists and neither true nor false in worlds in which *a* does not exist.

Now if the actuality operator is a weakly rigidifying sentential operator, then prefixing a contingently true sentence about a contingent existent with the actuality operator renders the resulting sentence both impossibly-not-the-case and not-necessary $[(\neg\Diamond\neg A(P(a))\ \&\ \neg\Box A(P(a)))]$. For example, 'Actually, Blair is Prime Minister in 2002' is both impossibly-not-the-case and not-necessary, because it is true with respect to all worlds in which Blair exists but neither true nor false with respect to the worlds in which Blair does not exist. With this semantics of sentences of the form 'Actually, *P*' we can block Rumfitt's second phase of his argument by allowing that 'actually' is a rigidifying operator, albeit weakly so, but denying that 'Actually, Blair is Prime Minister in 2002' is necessary.

We can then extend this semantics for the actuality operator to the statability operator in order to deal with the first phase of Rumfitt's argument. Now the

---

[4] He writes (1988, p. 357) that it seems to him "to be just obvious" that "the criterion of truth in all possible worlds is no longer an adequate criterion of necessity" since "[w]e cannot really turn a contingent proposition into a necessary one by adding such qualifications as 'actually' or 'in fact' or 'as things are'."

[5] For the distinction between strongly and weakly rigid designators, on which the present distinction is based, see Kripke (1980, pp. 48–9).

standard semantics for the stability operator is: for any sentence $P$ about an object $a$, $S(P(a))$ is true with respect to a world $w$ just in case $a$ exists in $w$ and false otherwise. This, presumably, is the semantics Rumfitt has in mind when he represents the contingent stability of 'Williamson is self-identical' as:

(16) $\Diamond\neg S(TW = TW)$.

However, following the above treatment of the actuality operator, we can give an alternative semantics of the stability operator on which (16) is false. On this semantics, for any sentence $P$ about an object $a$, $S(P(a))$ is true with respect to a world $w$ just in case $a$ exists in $w$ and neither true nor false otherwise; consequently, if $a$ is a contingent existent and $P$ is any sentence about $a$, then 'It is stable that $P$' is both impossibly-not-the-case and not-necessary $[(\neg\Diamond\neg S(P(a))\ \&\ \neg\Box S(P(a)))]$. On this semantics, then, (16) is false since there is no world with respect to which $\neg S(TW = TW)$ is true. The contingent stability of 'Williamson is self-identical' is rather represented formally as:

(32) $[S(TW = TW)\ \&\ \neg\Box S(TW = TW)]$

which is true. Given this semantics of the stability operator, we can then block the first phase of Rumfitt's argument, and we have, therefore, now blocked Rumfitt's argument in its entirety.

5

Having outlined an alternative semantics of the actuality and stability operators which blocks Rumfitt's argument, we can generalize this semantics which then yields a distinctive response to Williamson's argument and its variations. The generalized semantics is based on a Priorian (1957) semantics for quantified modal logic:

$\Box P(a)$    is true just in case: $P(a)$ is true with respect to every possible world and $a$ exists in every possible world.

$\Diamond P(a)$    is true just in case $P(a)$ is true with respect to some possible world in which $a$ exists.

Because the modal operators have asymmetrical strengths and weaknesses, and so are not duals, if $a$ is a contingent existent (E!$a$ & $\neg\Box$E!$a$), the conjunction $[\neg\Diamond\neg P(a)\ \&\ \neg\Box P(a)]$ can be consistent, as we found on the alternative semantics developed for the actuality and stability operators.

Furthermore, the clause for the necessity operator makes it clear that for a sentence $P$ about an object $a$ to be necessary, $a$ must be a necessary existent ($\Box$E!$a$); consequently, on this semantics, there are no true necessities about contingent existents, including logical truths, such as '$a$ is self-identical'. This then yields a distinctive response to Williamson's argument and its variations. Should we wish to take Williamson to be a contingent existent, the semantics tells us that we should deny premises (1) and (3) of Argument A, premises (5) and (7) of Argument B, and premise (9) of Argument C, since there are no true necessities about him on this semantics.

But, ironically, not only does this semantics yield a distinctive response to Williamson's argument and its variations, it also yields a sense in which, even if Williamson is a contingent existent (E!$a$ & ¬□E!$a$), there is also a sense in which he is a necessary existent (E!$a$ & ¬◇¬E!$a$) since there is no possible world with respect to which the statement 'Williamson exists' is false. But it is impossible for something to be both a necessary existent and a contingent existent. So then the question arises, how can we express in English the conjunction [E!$a$ & (¬◇¬E!$a$ & ¬□E!$a$)] which is consistent in the Priorian semantics?

My proposal is to connect this Priorian semantics with a certain way of drawing the *de re/de dicto* distinction in English. Typically, the distinction between the *de re* and the *de dicto* is drawn along the following lines. A sentence containing a single modal expression is a *de re* modal sentence just in case its logical form contains a name within the scope of the modal operator; a sentence containing a single modal expression is a *de dicto* modal sentence just in case its logical form does not contain a name within the scope of the modal operator. On this approach, no distinction is made between a sentence in which a modal expression figures as a sentential operator or as a predicate modifier, e.g. it classifies both 'Necessarily, Williamson exists' and 'Williamson necessarily exists' as *de re* modal sentences and gives them the same formal representation (□E!$a$). Seeing a distinction between these two sentences, Wiggins (1976, p. 294) draws the *de re/de dicto* distinction differently and gives the sentences different formal representations. On Wiggins's approach, a sentence containing a single modal expression is a *de re* modal sentence just in case the modal expression functions as a predicate modifier in its logical form; a sentence is a *de dicto* modal sentence just in case the modal expression functions as a sentential operator in its logical form. To represent formally *de re* modal sentences, Wiggins employs the 'nec' operator and the lambda calculus, so that the formal representation of a *de re* modal sentence $P$ about an object $a$ is [nec($\lambda x$)($P(x)$)], [$a$]; to represent formally *de dicto* modal sentences, Wiggins employs the '□' operator, so that the formal representation of a *de dicto* modal sentence $P$ about an object $a$ is □$P(a)$. So, on this approach, 'Williamson necessarily exists' is a *de re* modal sentence having the formal representation [nec($\lambda x$)(E!($x$))], [$a$], and 'Necessarily, Williamson exists' is a *de dicto* modal sentence having the formal representation □E!$a$.

The benefit of Wiggins's approach to the *de re/de dicto* distinction is that it preserves the grammatical structure of modal sentences in their formal representations; the cost of the approach is that it is unclear what logic we are to use to formalize arguments containing modal sentences since, at present, there is no developed modal logic making use of both the 'nec' operator and the '□' operator. We therefore need a materially adequate scheme for translating formulas containing the 'nec' operator to formulas containing the '□' operator. We could, of course, take [nec($\lambda x$)($P(x)$)], [$a$] to be materially equivalent to $\Box P(a)$, but this would be to render Wiggins's distinction between the *de re* and the *de dicto* a distinction without a difference. More promisingly, Wiggins suggests that if $a$ is a contingent existent and $a$ is essentially F, [nec($\lambda x$)(F($x$))] is true but $\Box$F$a$ is not, which seems to mirror the distinction previously drawn between the impossibly-not-the-case and the necessary.[6] Now if we accept the Priorian semantics, we can then define a scheme for translating formulas containing 'nec' to sentences containing '$\Diamond$' and '$\neg$': [nec($\lambda x$)($P(x)$)], [$a$] $=_{df.} \neg\Diamond\neg P(a)$. This then yields the following scheme for representing formally the four kinds of modal sentence:

'Necessarily, $a$ is F' is represented formally as: $\Box$F$a$.
'$a$ is necessarily F' is represented formally as: (F$a$ & $\neg\Diamond\neg$F$a$).
'Contingently, $a$ is F' is represented formally as: (F$a$ & $\neg\Box$F$a$).
'$a$ is contingently F' is represented formally as: (F$a$ & $\Diamond\neg$F$a$).

These formalizations give rise to the consistent conjunctive schema:

'$a$ is necessarily F and, contingently, $a$ is F' is represented formally as: [F$a$ & ($\neg\Diamond\neg$F$a$ & $\neg\Box$F$a$)].

As an instance of this conjunctive schema, we have: Williamson necessarily exists and, contingently, Williamson exists [E!$a$ & ($\neg\Diamond\neg$E!$a$ & $\neg\Box$E!$a$)]. So, to answer the title question, Williamson is, in a *de re* sense, a necessary existent, but he is not a necessary existent in the *de dicto* sense: Williamson necessarily exists, but it is not necessary that he exists.

---

[6] Wiggins seems to have this distinction in mind when discussing the necessity of identity:

> For the conclusion [the necessity of identity] is not put forward here as a necessarily true statement. (On this we remain mute.) It is put forward as a true statement of *de re* necessity. The thing that the proof comes down to is simply this: Hesperus is necessarily Hesperus, so, if Phosphorus is Hesperus, Phosphorus is necessarily Hesperus. (2001, p. 116)

I would, however, go further than Wiggins and not remain mute on whether the necessity of identity expresses a true statement of *de dicto* necessity: it does not. Employing the translation scheme developed below in the text, it is true that Hesperus is necessarily identical with Hesperus [($a = a$) & $\neg\Diamond\neg(a = a)$], so if Phosphorus is Hesperus ($b = a$), Phosphorus is necessarily Hesperus [($b = a$) & $\neg\Diamond\neg(b = a)$], but it is contingent that Phosphorus is Hesperus [$b = a$ & $\neg\Box(b = a)$]. So, true identities are *de re* necessary, but they are *de dicto* contingent.

# 6

# Metaphysical Dependence: Grounding and Reduction

*Gideon Rosen*

## 1. INTRODUCTION

This essay is a plea for ideological toleration. Philosophers are right to be fussy about the words they use, especially in metaphysics where bad vocabulary has been a source of grief down through the ages. But they can sometimes be too fussy, dismissing as 'unintelligible' or 'obscure' certain forms of language that are perfectly meaningful by ordinary standards and which may be of some real use.

So it is, I suggest, with certain idioms of metaphysical determination and dependence. We say that one class of facts *depends upon* or is *grounded in* another. We say that a thing possesses one property *in virtue of* possessing another, or that one proposition *makes* another true. These idioms are common, as we shall see, but they are not part of anyone's official vocabulary. The general tendency is to admit them for heuristic purposes, where the aim is to point the reader's nose in the direction of some philosophical thesis, but then to suppress them in favor of other, allegedly more hygienic formulations when the time comes to say *exactly* what we mean. The thought is apparently widespread that while these ubiquitous idioms are sometimes convenient, they are ultimately too unclear or too confused, or perhaps simply too exotic to figure in our first-class philosophical vocabulary.

Against this tendency, I suggest that with a minimum of regimentation these metaphysical notions can be rendered clear enough, and that much is to be

Earlier versions of this material were presented to audiences at the University of St Andrews, Stanford University, MIT, UCLA, and to the metaethics workshop at the Hebrew University's Institute for Advanced Study. I am grateful to everyone who participated in these discussions. Special thanks to Paul Audi and Steve Yablo for extensive conversation. Audi's views on these topics are developed in Audi (2007).

gained by incorporating them into our analytic tool kit. I make this proposal in an experimental spirit. Let us see how things look if we relax our antiseptic scruples for a moment and admit the idioms of metaphysical dependence into our official lexicon alongside the modal notions (metaphysical necessity and possibility, the various forms of supervenience) with which they are often said to contrast unfavorably. If this only muddies the waters, nothing is lost; we can always retrench. If something is gained, however, as I believe it is, we may find ourselves in a position to make some progress.

## 2. EXAMPLES

The first order of business is to identify our topic, so let's begin with some examples. The point here is not to defend the claims that follow, all of which are controversial. It is simply to insist that they are not gibberish, and hence that we must have some sort of grasp of the terms in which they are formulated. Thus a philosopher might say:

- The dispositions of a thing are always grounded in its categorical features (Prior, Pargetter, and Jackson 1982). A glass is fragile in virtue of the arrangement of the molecules that make it up, perhaps together with the laws of chemistry and physics. One of the aims of materials science is to identify the physical bases of such dispositions.

- If an act is wrong, there must be some feature of the act that *makes* it wrong. Any given act may be wrong for several reasons, and some of these reasons may be more fundamental than others. A breach of promise may be wrong because it is a breach of trust, and a breach of trust may be wrong because it is prohibited by principles for social cooperation that no one could reasonably reject. One central aim of moral theory is to identify the most fundamental right- and wrong-making features.[1]

- If it is against the law to keep a tiger as a pet in Princeton, there must be some constellation of non-legal facts in virtue of which this is so. One of the aims of jurisprudence is to identify in general terms the facts in virtue of which the legal facts are as they are. One distinctive claim of legal positivism is that the grounds of law are wholly social, consisting ultimately in the acts of officials and the social practices in which they are embedded (Hart 1961; Raz 1979). Antipositivists typically maintain that pre-institutional moral facts often play a role in making the law to be as it is.

- There are no brute semantic facts. If Jones means *addition* by '+', there must be some array of non-semantic facts in virtue of which this is what he means

---

[1] It has been clear at least since Sidgwick and Ross that this project is distinct from the analytic project of saying *what it is* for an act to be right or wrong (Sidgwick 1907; Ross 1930).

(Kripke 1982). These non-semantic grounds for the semantic facts may vary substantially from case to case. A name may mean what it does in virtue of some initial dubbing ceremony; a logical particle may mean what it does in virtue of its inferential role. The metaphysical part of semantics aims to catalog in general terms the various ways in which the semantics facts may be grounded in pre-semantic reality.

These are familiar-sounding claims, and they are all at least superficially intelligible. In each case some philosophically interesting class of facts is said to be grounded in, or to obtain in virtue of, some allegedly more fundamental class of facts, and some discipline is charged with identifying the detailed patterns of dependence. The surface intelligibility of these claims gives us some reason to believe that the idioms of dependence make good sense. This creates a defeasible presumption of intelligibility.

To this we may add: it would be very good if these notions were in fact intelligible, for we would then be in a position to frame a range of hypotheses and analyses that might otherwise be unavailable, and which may turn out to be worth discussing. Again, consider some provisional examples.

- It is sometimes said that meaning is a normative notion (Kripke 1982), and hence that any general case for antirealism about the normative implies antirealism about semantics. What could this mean? It might be the claim that every semantic fact ultimately obtains in virtue of some collection of normative facts, e.g., facts about the norms of 'correctness' for assertoric utterances.

- Some philosophers espouse a naturalistic metaphysics. What could this mean? The naturalist's basic thought is that certain peculiar aspects of *our* world—the human world—are not among the fundamental features of reality. Human beings think; most of nature doesn't. Human beings are governed by norms; most of nature isn't. These (more or less) distinctively human aspects of reality may be genuine; but according to the naturalist, they are not fundamental. As a first pass, then, we might identify metaphysical naturalism with the thesis that there are no brute normative or intentional facts, i.e., with the view that every such fact ultimately obtains in virtue of other facts. But of course this is compatible with each normative fact's obtaining in virtue of some other normative fact, and so on ad infinitum; and this is obviously incompatible with the naturalist's vision. Better to say that for the naturalist, every normative fact and every intentional fact is grounded in some constellation of non-normative, non-intentional facts, and if we take the 'in virtue of' idiom for granted, we can say this exactly. Every fact p, we may say, is associated with a *tree* that specifies the facts in virtue of which p obtains, the facts in virtue of which those facts obtain, and so on. A path in such a tree is *naturalistic* when there is a point beyond which every fact in the path is non-normative and non-intentional. A tree is naturalistic when every path in it is naturalistic. Metaphysical naturalism is then the thesis that every fact tops a naturalistic tree.

- Some properties are intrinsic, others extrinsic. How is this distinction to be drawn? There are numerous proposals, most of which seek to explain the notion in modal terms; but none is clearly adequate to the intuitive contrast. If we take the 'in virtue of' relation for granted, a straightforward proposal presents itself. Recall that one intuitive gloss on the contrast has it that a property F is intrinsic iff whether or not X is F depends entirely on how things stand with X and its parts, and not on X's relations to things distinct from X. If we read 'depends' in this formulation as a nod to the 'in virtue of' relation, we can make this idea explicit as follows:

    F is an intrinsic property iff, as a matter of necessity, for all x:

    If x is F in virtue of $\varphi(y)$—where $\varphi(y)$ is a fact containing y as a constituent—then y is part of x; and

    If x is not-F in virtue of $\varphi(y)$, then y is part of x.

    (The last clause ensures that *loneliness*—the property a thing has when there are no things distinct from it—is not deemed an intrinsic property.)

- Some philosophers believe that the aim of ontology is not simply to say what there is, but rather to say what *really* exists, or what exists in the most fundamental sense (Dorr 2005). Such philosophers may say: Of course the lectern exists; it's a thing; it's real. But it is not an *ultimate* constituent of reality; it is not *ontologically real*. What could this mean? Here is one possibility. Say that a fact is fundamental (or brute) if it does not obtain in virtue of other facts, and that a *thing* is fundamental if it is a constituent of a fundamental fact. Then we might say that fundamental ontology seeks a catalog of the fundamental things. When the fundamental ontologist says that the lectern is not 'ultimately real', all he means is that the various facts concerning the lectern—including the fact that it exists—ultimately obtain in virtue of facts about (say) the physical particles in its vicinity, facts that do not contain the lectern itself as a constituent.[2]

So far I have made two points, both preliminary: that we are often tempted to invoke the idioms of metaphysical dependence, which suggests that we often take ourselves to understand them; and that if we do understand them, we are in a position to frame a number of novel theses and analyses that appear to be worth discussing. Together these considerations supply us with some

---

[2] I discuss this conception of the project of fundamental ontology further in 'Numbers and Reality' (Rosen, MS). It is to be distinguished from another structurally similar approach, according to which the fundamental facts are the facts that do not admit of reduction or analysis, and the fundamental things are the constituents of facts that are fundamental in this sense. The two approaches will yield different verdicts if there are facts that are grounded in further facts, but which do not admit of analysis or reduction. This possibility is broached in Section 13 below.

reason to believe, and some reason to hope, that the idioms of metaphysical dependence—the grounding idiom, the 'in virtue of' idiom—are clear enough for serious philosophical purposes.

## 3. DOUBTS ABOUT THE IDIOMS OF DEPENDENCE

These considerations shift the burden: if the idioms of dependence are in fact unclear or otherwise unsuitable for demanding philosophical purposes, we need some account of what is wrong with them. We should grant immediately that there is no prospect of a reductive definition of the grounding idiom: We do not know how to say in more basic terms *what it is* for one fact to obtain in virtue of another. So if we take the notion on board, we will be accepting it as primitive, at least for now. But that is obviously no reason for regarding the idiom as unclear or unintelligible. Many of our best words—the words we deem fully acceptable for rigorous exposition—do not admit of definition, the notion of metaphysical necessity being one pertinent example. We should likewise concede that we have no explicit method for determining whether one fact is grounded in another, and that there are many hard questions about the extension of the grounding relation and the principles governing it that we cannot answer. But again, that is not decisive. We have no established routine for deciding whether some hypothesis represents a genuine metaphysical possibility, and the general principles of modality are matters of great controversy. But that does not mean that we do not understand the modal notions. It simply means that there is much about them that we do not know.

One slightly better reason for regarding the idioms of dependence with suspicion is the thought that while these idioms cannot be defined in modal terms, they are always dispensable in practice in favor of the idioms of modal metaphysics—entailment, supervenience, the apparatus of possible worlds, and so on—notions for which we have elaborate theories, and which are in any case more familiar. And yet it seems to me that this is not true at all. Consider again the debate over legal positivism. One side says that the legal facts are wholly grounded in the social facts; the other says that moral facts play a role in making the law to be as it is. Now try to frame this debate as a debate about a supervenience thesis. The antipositivist says that the legal facts supervene on the moral and the social facts taken together; but of course the positivist will agree. The positivist says that the legal facts supervene on the social facts alone—that possible words cannot differ in legal respects without differing in social respects. But the antipositivist need not deny this. For he may think that whenever two worlds are alike in social respects—whenever they involve the same actions, habits and responses of human beings—they must also agree in moral respects, *since the moral facts themselves supervene on the social facts broadly conceived.* But in that case the parties will accept the same supervenience claims. And yet they differ on an important issue, viz., whether the moral facts play a role in making the law to be as it is.

Perhaps the best reason for resisting the grounding idiom is the suspicion that despite its superficial intelligibility, the notion is ultimately confused or incoherent. To say that the notion is confused is to say that there are several distinct relations of grounding or dependence in the vicinity, and that uncritical invocation of 'the' grounding idiom conflates them. To say that the notion is incoherent is to say that every effort to set out the principles that govern it ultimately leads to absurdity or incoherence. This was the burden of Quine's critique of the modal idiom as he understood it, and we cannot rule out the possibility that something similar might happen here.

We should bear these possibilities in mind as we proceed, but it is impossible to say in advance whether the idioms we have been discussing really are problematic in these ways. I begin with the working hypothesis that there is a single salient form of metaphysical dependence to which the idioms we have been invoking all refer. The plan is to begin to lay out the principles that govern this relation and its interaction with other important philosophical notions. If the notion is confused or incoherent, we should get some inkling of this as we proceed. On the other hand, if all goes smoothly, we will have neutralized the main grounds for resistance, in which case there can be no principled objection to admitting the notion as intelligible, to be used in raising and answering philosophical questions insofar as this proves fruitful.


## 4. ONTOLOGICAL BACKGROUND AND NOTATION

The grounding relation is a relation among facts. We may say that A is F in virtue of B's being G, but this is shorthand for the claim that the fact that A is F obtains in virtue of (is grounded in) the fact that B is G.

I shall suppose that facts are structured entities built up from worldly items—objects, relations, connectives, quantifiers, etc.—in roughly the sense in which sentences are built up from words. For my purposes, facts might be identified with true Russellian propositions (cf. King 2007).[3] Facts are individuated

---

[3] Nothing in what follows depends on thinking of the fact that p as an item distinct from the proposition that p, which somehow makes that proposition true. My discussion is therefore silent on the question whether every true proposition has a truth-maker. I note, however, that the intuitive notion of a truth-maker presupposes the grounding idiom that is our focus. In this intuitive sense, x is a truth-maker for p iff p is true in virtue of x's existence, i.e., in virtue of the fact that x exists. Some writers replace this formulation with a modal surrogate, holding that the truth-maker for p is an item whose existence entails the truth of p. But this

by their constituents and the manner of their composition. This yields a very fine-grained notion. If p and q are distinct propositions, then the fact that p ∨ ~p is distinct from the fact that q ∨ ~q. And this is as it should be. The fact that p ∨ ~p might obtain in virtue of the fact that p. But p cannot possibly ground the fact that q ∨ ~q except in special cases.

I write [p] for *the fact that p*. When the enclosed sentence has internal syntactic structure, I shall assume that we are talking about a fact with constituents corresponding to the relevant symbols. Thus [Fa] will be a fact containing the property F and the object a as constituents.[4]

I shall write [p] ← [q] for: *the fact that p is grounded in the fact that q*. Since it will turn out that a given fact may be grounded in several facts taken collectively, the grounding relation is officially plural on the right. The general form of a grounding claim is thus

[p] ← Γ

where Γ is a non-empty, possibly infinite collection of facts. When [q] is one of several facts that together ground [p], we can say that [p] obtains *in part in virtue of* [q]. In general:

[p] $\mapsfrom$ Δ $=_{df}$ for some Γ, [p] ← Γ and Δ ⊆ Γ.


## 5. STRUCTURAL PRINCIPLES

It seems clear that the binary part of the grounding relation is asymmetric and hence irreflexive. Since the relation is plural on the right, we should accept general versions of these claims:

Strong asymmetry: If [p] ← [q], Γ then not: [q] ← [p], Δ

Strong irreflexivity: not: [p] ← [p], Γ.

The case for strong irreflexivity is clear enough. Just as no fact can make itself obtain, no fact can play a role along with other facts in making itself

---

threatens to collapse what appear to be real distinctions. If the truths of universal morality have truth-makers, they are distinct from the items that ground the truths of pure mathematics. But on the simple entailment account, everything is a truth-maker for every necessary truth. For a non-classical account of entailment and truth-making that avoids these difficulties, see Restall (1996).

[4] For expository purposes I shall assume that facts and propositions are structured like sentences in the language of the predicate calculus and its familiar extensions. This is entirely provisional. Nothing should be taken to hang on this assumption. I do not assume that every predicate corresponds to a property, or that every true sentence corresponds to a fact whose structure mirrors the syntactic structure of the sentence. The examples that follow must therefore be understood in a conditional spirit: *if there are facts of such and such a form, then* . . .

obtain. Strong asymmetry (which entails strong irreflexivity) is less evident. The thought is that when we cite grounds for [p], we cite facts that are strictly prior to [p] in a certain explanatory order. If [q] plays a role in making it the case that p, then [q] must be 'more fundamental' than [p], in which case [p] cannot play a role in making it the case that q. These principles are more perspicuous when formulated in terms of the notion of partial grounding:

Strong asymmetry: If [p] $\twoheadleftarrow$ [q] then not: [q] $\twoheadleftarrow$ [p]

Strong irreflexivity: Not: [p] $\twoheadleftarrow$ [p].

If [q] is part of what makes it the case that p, then [p] contributes nothing to making it the case that [q]; and [p] plays no role whatsoever in making it the case that p.

The grounding relation is not obviously transitive, but I shall assume transitivity in a strong form.

Strong transitivity: if [p] $\leftarrow$ [q], $\Gamma$ and [q] $\leftarrow$ $\Delta$ then [p] $\leftarrow$ $\Gamma$, $\Delta$.

If the most fundamental relation in the vicinity is not transitive, then $\leftarrow$ picks out its transitive closure.

The relation is presumably not connected. Barring some enormous surprise in metaphysics, it seems clear that the fact that 5 is prime neither grounds nor is grounded by the fact that wolverines are fierce. So partial grounding is at best a partial order on the domain of facts.

We should not assume that the relation is well founded. That is a substantive question. It may be natural to suppose that every fact ultimately depends on an array of basic facts, which in turn depend on nothing. But it might turn out, for all we know, that the facts about atoms are grounded in facts about quarks and electrons, which are in turn grounded in facts about 'hyperquarks' and 'hyperelectrons', and so on ad infinitum. So we should leave it open that there might be an infinite chain of facts [p] $\leftarrow$ [q] $\leftarrow$ [r] $\leftarrow$ . . .

We must emphatically reject a principle that is plausible in other formally analogous contexts. The grounding relation resembles a relation of consequence or entailment. And in most contexts we suppose that if $\Gamma$ entails p, then so does $\Gamma$ together with q—where q can be any sentence or proposition. The analogous principle of *monotonicity* does not hold in the present context. Intuitively, if [p] is grounded in $\Gamma$, then *every fact in* $\Gamma$ plays some role in making it the case that p. Holding this fixed, monotonicity would entail that each fact plays a role in grounding every fact. And that is just not so.

The failure of monotonicity is a general feature of explanatory relations. Suppose that C caused E, and hence that E occurred in part because C occurred. It does not follow that E occurred in part because C and X occurred, where

X is an arbitrary event. This would entail that X played some role in bringing E about, which need not be the case. Since the grounding relation is an explanatory relation—to specify the grounds for [p] is to say why [p] obtains, on one version of this question—we should expect monotonicity to fail in the present context.

## 6. INTERACTIONS WITH LOGIC: EASY CASES

Some of the clearest examples of grounding involve facts that stand in simple logical relations. Thus it seems quite clear that if there are disjunctive facts, then a disjunctive fact is grounded in its true disjuncts. If Fred is in New York, then Fred is either in New York or Rome. Moreover, the fact that Fred is in New York or Rome obtains *in virtue of the fact that Fred is in New York*. In general:

($\vee$): If p is true, then $[p \vee q] \leftarrow [p]$.[5]

If Feldman is both a doctor and a lawyer, then the fact that he is either a doctor or a lawyer obtains in virtue of each of its disjuncts. This is a harmless form of metaphysical overdetermination.

For similar reasons, it seems clear that existential facts are grounded in their instances. If Jones voted for the anarchists, then someone voted for the anarchists. And if we ask *in virtue of what is it the case that someone voted for the anarchists?*, one good answer will be: *someone voted for them in virtue of the fact that Jones voted for them*. In general:

($\exists$): If $\varphi(a)$ is true, then $[\exists x \, \varphi x] \leftarrow [\varphi a]$.[6]

If an existential fact has several instances, it is fully grounded in each. This is another form of harmless overdetermination.

Conjunctive truths are made true by their conjuncts, not individually, but collectively. In general, neither [p] nor [q] has what it takes to make it the case that $p \wedge q$. But just as several knights together can surround the castle, several facts together can ground a single fact:

($\wedge$): If $p \wedge q$ is true, then $[p \wedge q] \leftarrow [p], [q]$.

---

[5] This is compatible with there being cases in which a disjunctive fact obtains even though neither disjunct is true. To exclude this, we could accept a stronger principle:

($\vee+$) If $p \vee q$ is true, then either $[p \vee q] \leftarrow [p]$ or $[p \vee q] \leftarrow [q]$.

[6] Again, we could accept a stronger principle:

($\exists+$) If $\exists x \, \varphi x$ is true, then for some y, $[\exists x \, \varphi x] \leftarrow [\varphi(y)]$.

## 7. THE ENTAILMENT PRINCIPLE

These examples illustrate a principle that has been implicit in our discussion all along. If [p] is grounded in [q], then q entails p. Stated more generally:

Entailment:  If [p] ← Γ then □(∧Γ ⊃ p).[7]

The facts that ground [p] together ensure as a matter of metaphysical necessity that [p] obtains. This is one respect in which the grounding relation differs from causal and other merely nomic forms of determination. On the present view, there is a difference between the materialist who holds that the facts about phenomenal consciousness are grounded in, and hence necessitated by, the neurophysiological facts that underlie them, and the dualist for whom the neural facts merely cause or generate conscious states according to contingent causal laws.[8]

## 8. THE GROUNDING OF UNIVERSAL FACTS

As Russell noted, universal truths are not entailed by the conjunction of their instances (Russell 1918). Even when a, b, . . . amounts to a complete inventory of the universe, the premises Fa, Fb, . . . do not entail ∀xFx, since the premises taken together are consistent with their being some item distinct from a, b, . . . that is not F. Given the Entailment Principle, we cannot say that a universal truth is grounded in its instances taken together.[9]

---

[7] Γ is a list of facts and is therefore unsuitable to serve as the antecedent of a conditional. ∧Γ is the conjunction of the propositions that correspond to the facts in Γ.

[8] Should we distinguish the materialist for whom the phenomenal facts are *grounded* in the neural facts together with contingent psychophysical laws from the dualist for whom the phenomenal facts are merely *caused* by the neural facts according to psychophysical laws? We should. The difference will be clearest if the dualist allows that the relevant causal laws may be indeterministic, for in that case the underlying facts will not necessitate the phenomenal facts. But even if the laws are deterministic there is room for a distinction. In a deterministic physical universe, the initial state of the universe and the laws together necessitate every subsequent state. But we would not say that the current state of the universe obtains *in virtue of* the initial state together with the laws, at least not in the sense of that notion that I wish to isolate. In that sense, the grounding relation is a *synchronic* relation. When [p] is a fact wholly about how things are at any given time, then any fact that grounds [p] must also concern that time. Now this observation by itself does not preclude assimilating *simultaneous deterministic causation* (of the sort that might exist in the mind–body case) to grounding. But it strikes me as much more natural to keep causal relations on one side — as external relations among wholly distinct states of affairs — and grounding relations on the other. If that is right, then it is one thing to say that physical states synchronically *cause* phenomenal states according to deterministic laws, and another to say that the physical states and the laws together suffice to *ground* the phenomenal facts.

[9] We could evade this argument if we could assume that the inventory of objects is fixed as a matter of metaphysical necessity, for then the premises Fa, Fb, . . . would entail ∀xFx. On this gambit, see Williamson (1998) and Linsky and Zalta (1994).

Must we then say that every universal fact is a brute fact? Not at all. In special cases it will often be clear that a given universal fact is grounded in more basic universal facts. Thus if all Fs are G, it follows that all Fs are G or H. And in such cases we should say: All Fs are G or H in virtue of the fact that all Fs are G. The interesting question is whether universal facts might be grounded in facts that are not themselves universal. Let me mention some possibilities.

## (a) Universal facts grounded in essences

Every triangle has three angles. Why? Because it lies in the *nature* of a triangle to have three angles. *Part of what it is* to be a triangle is to have three angles. That is why, as a matter of fact, every triangle has three angles. Indeed, that is why as a matter of *necessity* every triangle has three angles.

Let us follow Kit Fine in writing $\Box_x p$ for: *it lies in x's nature that p*, or (as Fine sometimes puts it) *p obtains in virtue of what it is to be x*, or *in virtue of x's identity* (Fine 1994, 1995).[10] In the example we might have:

$\Box_{\text{triangularity}} \forall x(x \text{ is a triangle} \supset x \text{ has three angles})$.

The proposal is that this claim about the nature of a property might ground a simple universal generalization according to the following principle:

Essential grounding: If $\Box_x p$ then $[p] \leftarrow [\Box_x p]$.

When p is a universal generalization, this gives us one way in which a universal generalization can be grounded in a truth that is not itself a universal generalization.[11]

## (b) Universal facts grounded in strong laws

Now consider a rather different case. Why is it that, as a matter of fact, any two bodies attract one another with a force inversely proportional to their square distance and proportional to their masses? It is natural to say that this mere

---

[10] The 'in virtue of' in these informal glosses of Fine's key notion is not exactly the relation we have been discussing under that rubric. Our relation is a relation among facts or truths, whereas Fine's relation, if it is a relation at all, is a relation between a given truth and the *items* whose natures ground that truth. It is an open question whether Fine's primitive $\Box_x p$ might be defined in terms of our grounding relation together with other materials. The most straightforward approach would be to identify some class of propositions involving x—x's essence—and then to define $\Box_x p$ as follows:

For some subset $\Gamma$ of x's essence, $[p] \leftarrow \Gamma$.

But this is problematic for a number of reasons. In particular, it entails that no basic proposition can be an element of x's essence. And it is unclear whether that is a welcome consequence. I hope to expand on these issues elsewhere.

[11] We should presumably also accept a stronger principle:

Strong essential grounding: If $\Box_x p$ then $\Box p \leftarrow \Box_x p$.

regularity corresponding to Newton's law of gravitation holds *because it is a law of nature that bodies attract one another in this way*. This is controversial as a matter of philosophy, of course. The so-called Humean view would reverse the explanatory order, insisting that the nomic fact obtains in part because every body happens to attract every other body in a certain way (Lewis 1973b). But proponents of the anti-Humean view will say that the nomic facts (the laws of nature) explain the mere regularities that correspond to them (Armstrong 1983). Moreover, as the anti-Humean understands these matters, this is not mere causal explanation or anything of the sort. P's lawhood *ensures* p's truth as a matter of metaphysical necessity. In our idiom, we might understand the anti-Humean's fundamental claim as a claim about that in virtue of which certain universal truths obtain:

> Natural Necessity: If it is a strong law of nature that p, then [p] ← [It is a strong law that p].

Where p is a universal generalization, this gives another way in which a universal fact may be grounded in a fact that is not itself universal.[12]

## (c) Accidental regularity

In the cases we have discussed so far, a universal fact is grounded in a broadly modal fact—a fact about laws or essences. In these cases, the generalization holds *because it must*. A generalization that is not so grounded is (in one good sense) an accidental regularity. We have seen that some accidental regularities are grounded in others. Can we say anything general about how such generalizations might be grounded?

As noted above, a complete inventory of instances Fa, Fb, . . . fails to entail, and so fails to ground the corresponding generalization. But even when [∀xFx] is a thoroughly accidental regularity, it is entailed by its instances together with what D. M. Armstrong calls a *totality* fact: the fact that a, b, c, etc. are all the things there are (Armstrong 1997). The totality fact is itself a universal fact:

> [∀x(x = a ∨ x = b ∨ . . .)].

But it is a universal fact of a special kind. And so we might say that when [∀xFx] is an ordinary accidental regularity, it always grounded at least in the following way:

> [∀xFx] ← [Fa], [Fb], . . . [∀x(x = a ∨ x = b ∨ . . .)].

---

[12] This pattern of explanation may be extended to regularities that are not themselves laws, but which are the consequences of laws. For example, it might be a law that all Fs are G, and a law that all As are B; and yet it might not be a law that everything that is either F or A is G or B. Nonetheless, the universal regularity—∀x((Fx ∨ Ax) ⊃ (Gx ∨ Bx))—might be grounded in the two laws taken together.

On this approach, there will be at most one ungrounded universal generalization, namely, the totality fact itself.[13]


## 9. THE GROUNDING OF MODAL TRUTHS

The truths concerning metaphysical possibility and necessity are either analyzable or they are not. If they are—that is, if there is a way of saying in more basic terms *what it is* for a truth to be necessary—then the account will entail an account of the grounds of necessity. Thus, if Lewis is right about the nature of modality, then any fact of the form $[\Box p]$ reduces to a fact of the form [For all worlds w, p/w], where p/w is the result of restricting the quantifiers in p to parts of w (Lewis 1986b). On such a view it will follow, given a principle to be annunciated shortly, that $[\Box p]$ obtains in virtue of the fact that every world is a p-world. Alternatively, if a conjecture of Kit Fine's is correct, the modal facts may be analyzed as follows:

$[\Box p]$ reduces to $[\exists X \ \Box_X p]$.

In words: For it to be necessary that p just is for there to be some things, X, such that p holds in virtue of the natures of the Xs. On such a view it will follow that the facts about metaphysical necessity obtain in virtue of certain existentially general facts about the natures of things, which in turn hold, given our principle governing existential generalizations, in virtue of their instances.

Now many writers are skeptical about the prospects for a reductive analysis of modality. Fine himself worries that his essentialist account will omit what metaphysical necessity has in common with other forms of necessity—specifically normative necessity and nomic necessity—which cannot be analyzed in this way (Fine 2002). He thus entertains the possibility that metaphysical necessity might be analytically basic. We may note, however, that even if Fine is right about this, the facts of metaphysical modality might nonetheless be *grounded* in existentially general facts about essences according to the following principle:

If $\Box p$ is true, then $[\Box p] \leftarrow [\exists X \ \Box_X p]$.

Just as a Moorean may regard the moral facts as unanalyzable while insisting that each moral fact is grounded in facts about (say) the distribution of happiness, so Fine might regard the irreducible facts of metaphysical modality as systematically grounded in the essences of things.

---

[13] If the existence of one thing can be grounded in the existence of others, then the totality fact need not be basic. The basic fact in the vicinity might simply itemize the *ontologically fundamental* items and assert the completeness of the inventory.

## 10. THE GROUNDING–REDUCTION LINK

The discussion in the previous section assumes a principle that we must now make explicit. The principle connects what I have called 'reduction' or 'analysis' with the grounding idiom. We may put it roughly as follows.

If p reduces to q and p is true, then [p] ← [q].

But now we must say something more about reduction.

As I understand the notion, reduction is a metaphysical matter. To say that p reduces to q is not to say that p and q are synonymous, or that q gives the meaning of p. It is give an account of what it is for p to obtain. When we ask what it is for a substance to be a metal or for a curve to be continuous or for a person to be responsible for an action, we are not asking questions about what ordinary speakers or even experts have in mind. We are asking questions about the natures of the properties and relations in question.

These examples suggest a tight connection between reduction and what is sometimes called *real definition*. The objects of real definition are *items*—typically properties and relations, but possibly also items in other categories. When a philosopher asks the old Socratic questions—What is knowledge? What is justice?—she is asking for definitions, not of words, but of things. This suggests that the canonical form of a real definition should be this:

X =<sub>df</sub> . . .

But without significant distortion we may think of reduction and real definition as a relation among *propositions* that contain the target items as constituents. Instead of asking, 'What is knowledge?', we can ask: 'What is it for a person to know that p?' And the answer, if there is one, will take the following form: For all x, p, for x to know that p just is for it to be the case that $\varphi(x,p)$. In general, real definitions of properties and relations, which are normally expressed by verbal formulae of the following sort:

To be F just is to be $\varphi$.

might just as well be expressed as follows:

For all x, for it to be the case that Fx just is for it to be the case that $\varphi x$.

On this approach, reduction or analysis is a relation among propositions, and real definitions of items are given by general schemata for such reductions.

Some notation may help. Let us write ⟨p⟩ as a name for the structured Russellian proposition that p. As above, where *p* has internal structure—where *p* is *Rab*, for example—we suppose that the name, ⟨Rab⟩, picks out the proposition with the corresponding structure (if there is one). Let us write

⟨p⟩ ⟸ ⟨q⟩

for *p reduces to q*, or more long-windedly: *for it to be the case that p just is for it to be the case that q*, or *p's being the case consists in q's being the case*. The real definition of a relation R then takes the following canonical form:

For all x, y, . . . ⟨Rxy . . .⟩ ⟸ ⟨$\varphi$xy . . .⟩

where $\varphi$ is a complex that does not contain R as a constituent. Items in other categories admit of analogous definitions. To define a unary function f is to assert a claim of the form:

For all x, y ⟨f(x) = y⟩ ⟸ ⟨$\varphi$(x,y)⟩.

And one way to define an object a is to assert a claim of the form:

For all x, ⟨x = a⟩ ⟸ ⟨x = g(b)⟩.

For example, someone might propose that to be the number 2 just is to be the successor of 1. In our notation:

For all x, ⟨x = 2⟩ ⟸ ⟨x = s(1)⟩.

In some special cases we may want to say that one state of affairs reduces to another even though no constituent of the reduced state of affairs admits of this sort of explicit definition. Thus a neo-Fregean philosopher of mathematics who accepts this notion of reduction may wish to claim that propositions of the form

⟨the number of Fs = the number of Gs⟩

reduce to corresponding propositions of the form

⟨there is a one-one function *f* from F to G⟩.

Moreover, they may wish to claim this without insisting that there exists an explicit definition of 'number of' that would permit the reduction of arbitrary propositions in which this function figures (Wright 1983; Hale and Wright 2003; Rosen and Yablo, MS). One virtue of the general policy of conceiving of reduction as a relation among propositions is that it leaves room for semireductionist proposals of this kind.

The principle connecting grounding and reduction may now be formulated as follows:

Grounding–Reduction Link: If ⟨p⟩ is true and ⟨p⟩ ⟸ ⟨q⟩, then [p] ← [q].

In words: If p's being the case consists in q's being the case, then p is true in virtue of the fact that q. The prima facie case for the Link comes from examples.

To be a square just is to be an equilateral rectangle, let us suppose. This means that if ABCD is a square, then it is a square in virtue of being an equilateral rectangle. To be an acid just is to be a proton donor. So HCl is an acid in virtue of the fact that HCl is a proton donor. Suppose Lewis is right; suppose that for a proposition to be necessary just is for it to hold in all possible worlds. Then it is a necessary truth that whatever is green is green, and if we ask what *makes* this proposition necessary, the answer will be: It is necessary in virtue of the fact that it is true in every world.

These instances of the Grounding–Reduction Link have a certain ring of plausibility. We do think that correct analyses support explanatory claims, and it is natural to suppose (having come this far) that these explanations point to metaphysical grounds of the sort we have been discussing. But the Link presents us with a real puzzle. After all, if our definition of square is correct, then surely the fact that *ABCD* is a square and the fact that *ABCD* is an equilateral rectangle are not different facts: they are one and the same. But then the Grounding–Reduction Link must be mistaken, since every instance of it will amount to a violation of irreflexivity.

If we wish to retain the Link, we must insist that reduction is a relation between distinct propositions. There is some evidence that this is in fact how we conceive the matter. Thus it sounds right to say that Fred's being a bachelor consists in (reduces to) his being an unmarried male, but slightly off to say that Fred's being an unmarried male consists in (or reduces to) his being a bachelor. This asymmetry corresponds to an explanatory asymmetry. Fred is a bachelor because (or in virtue of the fact that) he is an unmarried man, but not vice versa. On the assumption that the explanatory relation in question is a relation between facts or true propositions, this asymmetry entails that the reduced proposition and the proposition to which it reduces must be distinct.

The trouble comes from our commitment to the thesis that facts and propositions are individuated by their worldly constituents and the manner of their combination. For surely the *property* of being a bachelor just is the *property* of being an unmarried male (if the analysis is correct). And this means that any proposition or fact in which the former figures just is the corresponding proposition or fact in which the latter figures. But if the operation of replacing an item in a fact with its real definition yields the same fact again, this operation cannot possibly yield a fact in virtue of which the original fact obtains. And this means that the Grounding–Reduction Link must be mistaken.

We can resist this line of thought by insisting that the operation of replacing a worldly item in a fact with its real definition never yields the same fact again. It yields a new fact that 'unpacks' or 'analyzes' the original. To see that this is plausible, consider an example involving the real definition of an individual.

Suppose for the sake of argument that to be the number two just is to be the successor of 1. In our notation,

For all x, $\langle x = 2 \rangle \Leftarrow \langle x = s(1) \rangle$.

One might accept this while rejecting the exotic view that the number 2 somehow contains the number 1 as a part or constituent. Simply from the fact that 1 figures in the *definition* of 2, it does not follow that 1 is a part of 2. But now propositions (and facts) are individuated by their constituents. So we can readily accept the definition while insisting that in general $\langle \ldots 2 \ldots \rangle$ and $\langle \ldots s(1) \ldots \rangle$ are distinct propositions. The former contains 2 as a constituent, but need not contain the successor function or the number 1; the latter contains *successor* and the number 1, but need not contain the number 2.

Now turn to an example involving properties. We have supposed that to be a square just is to be an equilateral rectangle, i.e.,

For all x, $(\langle \text{Square } x \rangle \Leftarrow \langle \text{Equilateral } x \wedge \text{Rectangle } x \rangle)$.

But it does not follow from this that the property of being square contains the properties that figure in its definition as constituents. To be sure, it is somewhat natural to think of a conjunctive property as some sort of construction from its conjuncts, for in these cases we may think: Whenever the conjunctive property is present, each of its conjuncts is also present, and this would be explicable if the conjunctive property were some sort of aggregate of its conjuncts. But in general, the thesis that a property is composed of the items that figure in its definition is not so plausible. Suppose that for a thing to be grue just is for it to be green or blue. Should we suppose that wherever grue is present, green and blue are also present? Obviously not, since this would entail that each is present whenever the other is. Instead we should say that while green and blue may both figure in the definition of grue, the property of being grue does not contain either of these properties as a constituent. Rather grue stands to green and blue as the value of a function stands to its arguments. And as Frege stressed, this relation is not one of part to whole (Frege 1904). We are therefore led to say that while the proposition that a is grue reduces to the proposition that a is green or blue, these propositions are nonetheless distinct. The former contains *grue* but not *green* as a bona fide constituent, whereas the latter contains *green* but not *grue*.[14]

---

[14] Note that we do not reject the straightforward identities:

The property of being grue = the property of being green or blue

The property of being square = the property of being an equilateral rectangle.

And this means that there is a sense in which we must accept the following identity

$\langle \ldots$ the property of being grue $\ldots \rangle = \langle \ldots$ the property of being green or blue $\ldots \rangle$.

But the sense in which this identity holds is one in which the proposition designated on the right does not contain green or blue as constituents. Language may mislead us here. Consider the noun phrase:

If we go this route, we can retain the Grounding–Reduction Link. When we reduce ⟨p⟩ to ⟨q⟩, we reduce a relatively simple proposition to a distinct, relatively complex proposition. There is then no bar to supposing that the truth of the complex proposition *grounds* or *explains* the truth of the relatively simple proposition of which it is the reduction.

## 11. DETERMINABLES AND DETERMINATES, GENERA AND SPECIES

It may be useful to bring this apparatus to bear on another topic. Consider a bright blue ball. The fact that the ball is blue is presumably not a brute fact. It might be grounded in microphysical facts about the ball's surface, or in facts about its dispositions to reflect light. But let us suppress the scientific subtleties and pretend that the colors are simple properties with no deep nature. Still, the fact that the ball is *blue* is not a brute fact. Suppose that our ball is a uniform shade of blue—let it be cerulean. Then it seems quite natural to say that the ball is blue *in virtue of being cerulean*. Another ball might be blue *for a different reason:* it might be blue in virtue of being cobalt blue. If we ask, What is it about these balls that makes them blue?, we get different answers in the two cases. And this suggests a general principle.

> Determinable–Determinate Link:  If G is a determinate of the determinable
> F and a is G, then [Fa] ← [Ga].[15]

Now contrast this case with a superficially similar case. Every square is a rectangle but not vice versa. Square is thus a more *specific* property than

*the proposition that 2 is prime.* Since 2 is the successor of 1, we could pick out the same proposition by means of the noun phrase: *the proposition that the successor of 1 is prime.* But this would be misleading in many contexts, since the same noun phrase would more naturally be used to pick out a different proposition, viz., ⟨prime s(1)⟩. The same thing can happen with predicative expressions and with noun phrases of the form *the property of being φ.* Since grue is the property of being either green or blue, the proposition ⟨grue a⟩ might be picked out by the noun phrase: *the proposition that a has the property of being either green or blue.* But this would be misleading, since the same phrase might also pick out the proposition ⟨blue a ∨ green a⟩, which contains green and blue as constituents.

In general, when a functional term *f(a)* occurs in the name of a proposition, ⟨. . . *f (a)* . . .⟩ the expression as a whole will naturally be taken to pick out a complex that contains f and a as constituents. That is the convention with which he has been operating in this paper. But it may also denote a complex that contains only the *value* of f on a in the relevant position. English expressions like *the property of being green or blue* are functional expressions in this sense, and this means that whenever such a term occurs in the name of a proposition, the expression as a whole may designate a proposition containing the relevant *arguments* for the function in question (green and blue) or a proposition containing only the *value* of that function for these arguments (grue). The use of a simple name for the property in question—*grue*, for example—tends to block the former reading and is therefore useful.

[15] We might prefer a stronger claim: If F is a determinable and a is F, then there is some determinate G of F such that [Fa] ← [Ga]. For speculative doubts about this, see Rosen and Smith (2004).

rectangle, just as cerulean is more specific than blue. Indeed, there is a sense in which square, like cerulean, is a maximally specific property in its family: Just as any two things that are cerulean must be *exactly* the same color, so any two things that are square must be exactly the same shape. The relations between the more determinate property and the less determinate one are thus rather similar in the two cases.

And yet there is a difference. Square is not a determinate of rectangle. It is rather a species of the genus, in one traditional sense of these terms. In this traditional sense, a species is defined as the conjunction of genus and differentia. In our notation:

For all x, ⟨Species x⟩ ⇐ ⟨Genus x ∧ Differentia x⟩.

To be a square (species) just is to be an equilateral (differentia) rectangle (genus). The determinate–determinable relation is rather different, as is well known. Cerulean cannot plausibly be defined as a conjunction of blue and some other property $\varphi x$.

For all x, ⟨Cerulean x⟩ ⇐ ⟨Blue x ∧ $\varphi x$⟩.

What could possibly complete the formula?

Does this difference make a difference? Perhaps. As noted, a ball may be blue in virtue of being cerulean. By contrast, it seems quite wrong to say that *ABCD* is a rectangle in virtue of being a square. If we ask what it is about the figure *ABCD* that makes it a rectangle, the answer must be something like this: the thing is a rectangle because it is a right quadrilateral. The fact that its sides are equal—the fact responsible for its being a square—simply *plays no role* making the figure rectangular. The striking fact, then, is that despite the similarities between the determinable–determinate relation on the one hand and the genus–species relation on the other, there is this difference: the determinate grounds the determinable, but the species does not ground the genus.

Our principles yield a straightforward explanation of the latter fact. Suppose that S is a species of the genus G, and that a is S (and therefore G). Now suppose for reductio that a is G in virtue of being S.

(1) [Ga] ← [Sa].

Since S is a species of G, we know that for some differentia D,

(2) ⟨Sa⟩ ⇐ ⟨Ga ∧ Da⟩.

Given the Grounding–Reduction Link, this entails:

(3) [Sa] ← [Ga ∧ Da].

Our principle governing conjunctions, (∧), then assures us that

(4) [Ga ∧ Da] ← [Ga], [Da].

And so by two applications of transitivity, it follows that

(5)  [Ga] ← [Ga], [Da].

But this is a violation of strong irreflexivity.

The intuitive point is straightforward. Since a species in the old-fashioned sense is defined by genus and differentia, a thing must belong to the species in part because it belongs to the genus. But then it cannot also belong to the genus in virtue of belonging to the species. The explanatory arrows in this area all point in the same direction. By contrast, nothing prevents a thing from possessing a determinable property in virtue of possessing some determinate thereof.

## 12. EXPLAINING THE DETERMINABLE–DETERMINATE LINK

Our framework thus provides an easy account of why an object belongs to a given species in virtue of belonging to the corresponding genus, and not vice versa. Can we also explain why it is that when a thing possesses a determinate property like cerulean, it possess the corresponding determinable (blue, colored) in virtue of possessing that determinate?

The most straightforward approach would begin by reducing determinable properties like blue to disjunctions of their determinates. In general, we might say:

Where F is a determinable property with determinates $G_1, G_2, \ldots,$
for all x, $(\langle Fx \rangle \Leftarrow \langle G_1x \vee G_2x \vee \ldots \rangle)$.

We could then derive the Determinate–Determinable Link via the Grounding–Reduction Link and the principle governing disjunctions, $(\vee)$.[16]

I can think of no decisive reason to reject this 'disjunctivist' approach, but a suggestive line of thought weighs against it. Suppose that Smith is familiar with many shades of blue but has never seen cerulean and has no conception of it. At this point Smith has no way of thinking about cerulean. We can even imagine that he is constitutionally incapable of thinking of it, perhaps because he lacks the neurons that would have to fire in order for him to perceive or imagine this particular shade. Would this deficit prevent him from knowing *what it is* for a thing to be blue? Needless to say, it would not prevent him from being competent with the word 'blue', or from knowing a great deal about the color blue. But would it prevent him from knowing everything there is to know about the *essence* of the color? Recall that we are operating under the pretense that

---

[16] The claim is not that any old disjunction of properties suffices to define a determinable with the disjuncts as determinates. It is simply that when F is a determinable, whatever that comes to, it reduces ipso facto to the disjunction of its determinates.

colors are sui generis properties, and hence that one might know their natures without knowing anything about the physics of light or surfaces. Relative to this pretense, it is natural to suppose that you and I know everything there is to know about the nature of blue, or that we could know this simply on the basis of reflection and simple experiments.[17] But if we know this, so does Smith, who does not and perhaps cannot think of cerulean. And if he knows the nature of the color blue, the exhaustive disjunction that we have been discussing cannot be a correct account of that nature.[18]

This argument exploits uncertain intuitions about what it takes to *know* the nature of a thing in order to rule out a proposed account of the nature of that thing. This strategy is obviously somewhat perilous, and so we should not place to much weight on these considerations. It is worth noting, however, that these worries do not undermine the most salient alternative proposal.

This salient alternative appeals to higher-order properties. The various determinate shades of blue all have something in common. They are all *blues*—as in, 'Some blues are more saturated than others'—or *shades-of-blue*. Similarly, the determinate masses, shapes, positions, pitches and so on are all unified collections of properties. Each mass property, e.g., the property of weighing exactly 2kg, is a *mass*. In light of this we may conjecture that each determinable property F of ordinary individuals is associated with a second-order property of properties: the property of *being an F-determinate*. On the alternative account, the determinable F is then defined as follows:

For all x, ($\langle Fx \rangle \Leftarrow \langle \exists G$ G is an F-determinate $\wedge$ Gx$\rangle$).[19]

To be blue is to instantiate some *shade-of-blue*. To have mass is to have *a* mass, i.e., *some* mass or other, e.g. 2kg. We may then derive instances of the Determinable–Determinate Link by means of the Grounding–Reduction Link and the principle governing the grounding of existential truths, ($\exists$).

This 'existentialist' approach is not vulnerable to the epistemic objection we raised against the previous disjunctivist proposal. Anyone who is in a position to know what it is for a thing to be blue should be in a position to think of a given property as a shade-of-blue. So perhaps this account is to be preferred.

However we proceed, we will have a straightforward account of why a thing possesses a determinable property in virtue of possessing some determinate

---

[17] Cf. Johnston (1992, p. 138): 'The *intrinsic nature* of canary yellow is *fully revealed* by a standard visual experience as of a canary yellow thing (and the same goes, *mutatis mutandis*, for the other colors).'

[18] A less fanciful example: If someone proposes that *to have mass* is to have either $m_1$ or $m_2$ or . . . where the $m_i$s are all of the determinate masses, we may object that our incapacity to think about the vast majority of these masses (thanks to our finitude) does not prevent us from knowing what there is to know about the nature of mass.

[19] This is not objectionably circular. The second-order property of being an F-determinate is supposed to be definitionally prior to the first-order property F, and neither it nor its definition involves F as a constituent, orthography notwithstanding.

thereof, and the account will not generalize to the case of genus and species. A genus may be equivalent to the disjunction of its possible species. But it will not be correctly defined by this disjunction. That would invert the definitional order, in which the species is defined by reference to the genus and not vice versa. Likewise, each genus G may be associated with a second-order property, *being a species-of-G*. But it would be a mistake to define the genus by reference to this property, saying that for a thing to be rectangle (say) just is for it to instantiate some property that is a *species-of-rectangularity*. That would be to miss the much better definition in terms of genus and differentia.

## 13. MOOREAN CONNECTIONS

The discussion in the previous section illustrates an important phenomenon. In many cases, when one fact obtains in virtue of another we can begin to explain why this grounding fact obtains by pointing to one or more constituents of those facts whose natures 'mediate' the connection. This ball is blue in virtue of being cerulean. Why does the latter fact ground the former? Because (a) the ball is cerulean, and (b) as a matter of necessity, whenever a thing is cerulean, it is blue in virtue of being cerulean. And why does (b) hold? Because (c) cerulean is a shade-of-blue and (d) it lies in the nature of the color blue that whenever a thing instantiates a shade-of-blue, it is blue in virtue of instantiating that shade.[20] Anyone who knows these facts should find it totally unsurprising that our ball is blue in virtue of being cerulean.

In this sort of explanation, particular grounding facts are explained by appeal to ordinary facts (e.g., [the ball is cerulean]) together with general, broadly formal principles of grounding—e.g., for all x, if x is cerulean then [x is blue] ← [x is cerulean]. These formal principles are then explained by appeal to further facts—e.g., [cerulean is a shade-of-blue]—together with essential truths about the natures of at least one of the items in question.

We seem to see a similar pattern in other cases. The disjunctive fact [p ∨ q] is grounded in [p]. Why? Let's make the explanation as explicit as possible. [p ∨ q] is grounded in [p] because

    (a)  p is true

    (b)  [p ∨ q] is a disjunctive fact with p as one of its disjuncts

    (c)  In general, if p is true, then [p ∨ q] ← [p].

And why is (c) true? Because:

    (d)  $\Box_\lor$ For all p, q: (if p is true, then [p ∨ q] ← [p]).

----

[20] This assumes the second account of the nature of blue given above. The 'disjunctivist' would give a different answer at this point.

The last claim is a claim about the nature of disjunction. The general law identified in (c)—that a disjunction is grounded in its true disjuncts—is not a mere regularity or a law of nature. It is an essential truth. Disjunction may be indefinable, in the sense that there may be no account in more basic terms of what it is for p ∨ q to be the case. Nonetheless it seems quite plausible that it lies in the nature of disjunction that disjunctive truths should be so grounded. On this view, to know the nature of disjunction is not simply to know the conditions under which a disjunctive proposition is true. It is to know something about what *makes* such propositions true. Anyone who knows the nature of disjunction in this sense should find it totally unmysterious that our original disjunctive fact [p ∨ q] is grounded in the truth of its true disjunct, in this case p.

We see a similar pattern when we attempt to explain why some particular conjunctive fact is grounded in its conjuncts, or why some regularity is grounded in a law, or why some claim of metaphysical necessity is grounded in a general claim about essences. This law grounds that regularity because (a) the law holds, and (b) it lies in the nature of (strong) lawhood that when a law holds, the corresponding regularity holds in virtue of that law. The fact that triangles *must* have three angles is grounded in the fact that it lies in the nature of triangles to have three angles. Why? Because (a) triangles are essentially three-angled, and (b) it lies in the nature of *necessity* that if p is an essential truth, then p is a necessary truth in virtue of being an essential truth.

The examples suggest the following two-part conjecture.

> Formality: Whenever [A] ← [B], there exist propositional *forms*[21] $\varphi$ and $\psi$ such that
>
> (i) A is of the form $\varphi$; B is of the form $\psi$; and
> (ii) For all propositions p, q: if p is of the form $\varphi$ and q is of the form $\psi$ and q is true, then [p] ← [q].

> Mediation: Every general grounding principle of the form (ii) is itself grounded in, and hence explained by, an essential fact of the form (iii):
>
> (iii) $\Box_X$ (For all propositions p, q: if p is of the form $\varphi$ and q is of the form $\psi$ and q is true, then [p] ← [q])

> where the X's are constituents of the propositional forms in question.[22]

---

[21] Propositional forms are properties of propositions, like the property of being a conjunctive proposition. It is convenient to think of them as the result of replacing one or more constituents in a proposition with schematic items of some sort. Thus if we start with a determinate proposition, say ⟨A ∨ B⟩, we can generate various propositional forms: ⟨α ∨ β⟩, ⟨A ∨ β⟩, and even ⟨α * β⟩, where * is a schematic connective. If we think in these terms, then we may speak of the constituents of a propositional form as the real, non-schematic items that figure in it. Thus the propositional form ⟨α ∧ β⟩ would have conjunction as a constituent.

[22] Note that the connection between (ii) and (iii) is an instance of the principle we earlier called *Essential Grounding*: For all p: If $\Box_X p$, then [p] ← [$\Box_X p$]. In the spirit of the present section, we

Note that this proposal is a proposal about how the facts about grounding are themselves grounded. Every true instance of this sort of pattern will yield a claim involving multiple occurrences of ←, e.g.,

$([A \vee B] \leftarrow [B]) \leftarrow$

[B], [⟨A ∨ B⟩ is of the form ⟨φ ∨ ψ⟩], [□$_\vee$ (if p is of the form ⟨φ ∨ ψ⟩ and ψ is true, then [p] ← [ψ])].

We have not explored principles involving multiple occurrences of ←, but this example suggests that such principles sometimes make good sense.

Are these conjectures plausible? I can think of no likely counterexample to Formality. If Fred is handsome in virtue of his symmetrical features and deep green eyes, then anyone with a similar face would have to be handsome for the same reason. Particular grounding facts must always be subsumable under general laws, or so it seems. It would be interesting to know why this is so.

Mediation is much less obvious. It is closely analogous to Kit Fine's thesis that the modal facts are grounded in facts about the essences of things, and counterexamples to Fine's thesis would yield counterexamples to mediation. Consider a version of non-reductive materialism in the philosophy of mind according to which every fact about phenomenal consciousness is grounded in facts about the material organ of consciousness (in our case, the brain) even though no phenomenal property is reducible to any neurophysiological property or to any functional property that might be realized by a brain state. On this sort of view, I might be in pain in virtue of the fact that my c-fibers are firing, even though my being in pain would not *consist in* the firing or my c-fibers, nor in any disjunctive state of which c-fiber firing was a disjunct, nor in some existentially general state of which c-fiber firing was an instance. According to this non-reductive materialist, the *nature* of pain is exhausted by its phenomenal character; and yet, when my c-fibers are firing, I am always in pain in virtue of this fact *in the same sense in which a thing is square in virtue of being an equilateral rectangle.*

As another example, consider a Moorean position in metaethics according to which moral properties like *right* and *good* are indefinable, and yet every right act is right in virtue of possessing some right-making feature. To be more concrete, suppose that there is only one such feature, and that it is a natural feature: suppose that every right act is right in virtue of the fact that it would produce more happiness than any other option open to the agent. This view entails and to some extent explains the supervenience of the moral on the non-moral while

---

may ask: what grounds *this* general principle. And here a relatively natural answer suggests itself. It lies in the nature of *essence* that essentialist truths of the form □$_X$p should ground the corresponding fact that p. Part of what it is for it to be the case that □$_X$p is for this fact to ground the fact that p. *Essential Grounding* is thus a law of grounding that is mediated by the nature of one of its constituents in the sense that we are presently trying to capture. Thanks to David Enoch on this point.

insisting that morality concerns a sui generis domain that in no way reduced to, or consists in, facts that might be formulated in other terms.

These views endorse general grounding principles of the sort required by Formality:

> For all x, if x's c-fibers are firing then [x is in pain] ← [x's c-fibers are firing].
>
> For all agents x and actions A, if x's doing A would maximize happiness then [A is right] ← [X's doing A would maximize happiness].

But when we cast about for some item whose nature might explain these general laws, we find no likely suspects. By hypothesis, the 'higher-level' properties (*pain*, *rightness*) do not have natures that make contact with the lower level properties invoked in the law. To put the point in epistemic terms, we are imagining views on which one might know everything there is to know about the nature of pain or rightness without knowing the first thing about c-fibers or happiness. The only alternative is that these grounding principles might be explained by reference to the natures of the relevant lower-level properties. Someone might suggest, for example, that while it does not lie in the nature of *pain* to be grounded in c-fiber firing, it lies in the nature of c-fiber firing that facts about it always ground states of pain. On this sort of view, the analgesic neuroscientist who knew everything about the detailed physiology of c-fibers and their role in the functional economy of the organism but who knew nothing about pain would have an incomplete understanding of *what it is* for a c-fiber to fire. But this is implausible. Of course he would obviously fail to know something important about c-fibers. But it is hard to see why his understanding of the *essence* or *definition* of this particular neurological kind should be defective.

Can we rule these positions out on principled grounds? The most promising strategy is to lean heavily on Fine's account of necessity—to insist that whenever p is a necessary truth, p must be grounded in the nature of some thing or things. The views in question are incompatible with this principle, since they posit general grounding principles which are presumably necessary if true at all, but which do not derive their truth from the natures of any of their constituents.

This poses a challenge for these views, but the case is not conclusive. Fine's position locates the ground of metaphysical necessity in a special stratum of fact—the facts about the essences of things. An alternative position would identify the basic grounding principles as a further source of absolute necessity. On Fine's account, a truth is necessary (roughly speaking) when it is a logical consequence of the essential truths. On the alternative account, the necessary truths would be the consequences of the essential truths together with the basic grounding laws. This may seem untidy, but it is not clearly objectionable. I thus conclude, rather tentatively, that we cannot rule out the possibility of Moorean connections—general principles affirming that facts of one sort are grounded in facts of another sort, but which cannot be explained in terms of the essences of any of the items in question.

## 14. CONCLUSION

Philosophers often speak as if they believed that some facts obtain in virtue of others. We have indulged freely—some might say extravagantly—in this way of speaking, and having done so we may ask: Is there any reason not to take this idiom seriously? To do so would be to give oneself license to ask philosophical questions and to frame philosophical theses in terms of it, while conceding that one cannot define the grounding idiom in more basic terms. My strategy for approaching this question was simply to *use* the idiom for the purpose of framing general principles, and then to show how those principles might interact with other principles that we accept. My thought was simple: if the grounding idiom is seriously problematic, this project should eventually break down. We should find ourselves landed in confusion or incoherence, accepting contradictory principles or not knowing what to say or how to proceed. My preliminary conclusion is that we do not find ourselves in this predicament. I have not tried to produce a complete theory of the 'in virtue of' relation. I have simply attempted to state some principles that might ultimately figure in such a theory. My claim is simply that at this stage we have no reason to doubt that an adequate theory of this sort might be attainable.

The project of rehabilitating the grounding idiom is analogous, as I see it, to the project begun in the 1960s for the rehabilitation of traditional notions of necessity and possibility—a project that is now more or less complete, and whose value is beyond dispute. The rehabilitation of the modal idiom did not proceed by definition or reduction. Definitions were sometimes proposed, but they were never widely accepted. Nor did it depend for its success on systematic axiomatization, as is shown by the fact that questions of *de re* modality—Could this lectern have been made of ice?—are widely regarded as intelligible despite the absence of a single generally accepted system of quantified modal logic. Rather it proceeded by pointing out that once the relevant notions have been distinguished from others with which they are frequently confused (analyticity, apriority) we understand them well enough: we simply find ourselves with tolerably clear intuitions—i.e., beliefs—about necessity and possibility and moderately effective strategies for extending our knowledge by means of argument and analogy (Soames 2003). Systematic theory-building is obviously desirable; but it is not a prerequisite for regarding the modal notions as legitimate resources for philosophy.

The same goes, I believe, for the idioms of grounding, and also for the idioms of reduction and essential truth that I have invoked in this discussion. Needless to say, ye shall know them by their fruits. The strategy of acquiescing in these ways of speaking will be vindicated when they are put to use in making sense of some independently puzzling domain. I hope that I have provided grounds for optimism about this project; but I do not pretend to have done more. My argument is principally addressed to those who resist these notions on the ground that they simply *do not understand them*. We have seen that it is possible to lay down a battery of plausible principles involving the disputed idiom and to develop arguments involving those principles. We have seen that it is possible to frame questions in this idiom that seem to be discussable. Given all of this, I ask: What would it take, beyond this, to establish the grounding idiom as a legitimate resource for metaphysics?

# 7

# On the Source of Necessity

*Ross P. Cameron*

## 1. BLACKBURN'S DILEMMA

Simon Blackburn raises a dilemma for anyone who attempts to identify the source of necessity. He says,[1]

Suppose an eventual answer [to the question 'What is the source of necessity?'] cites some truth F, and so takes the form: '□A because F'. . . Now, either F will claim that something *is* so, or it will claim that something *must* be so. If the latter, there is no problem about the *form* of the explanation, for one necessity can well explain another. But . . . there will be the same bad residual 'must' . . . And there is no escape from the overall problem that way. Suppose instead that F just cites that something *is* so. If whatever it is does not *have to be* so, then there is strong pressure to feel that the original necessity has not been explained or identified, so much as undermined.

Before we proceed we should note two curious things in Blackburn's presentation of the dilemma. First, Blackburn is assuming that what we will appeal to as the source of necessity is the *truth* of some proposition (F). But this is certainly not forced on us, and it would be thought by many, I think, to be undesirable. What accounts for the source of necessity, one might think, is some *thing*. This would be the truthmaker theorist's thought: there is some thing, or things, in virtue of which there are necessary truths. If this is one's preferred account, Blackburn's dilemma doesn't get off the ground: it doesn't make sense to ask whether this thing, or these things, are necessary, for they are the wrong type of thing to be classified as necessary or contingent.

Suppose, for example, one believed in a thing N, the necessity maker, such that for every necessary truth p, p is necessary in virtue of the existence of N (so the truthmaker for [Necessarily, p][2] is N). N accounts for the source of necessity, if

Thanks to Bob Hale, and the other members of the Arché modality project at the University of St Andrews, for many helpful discussions.

[1] Blackburn (1999, p. 635).
[2] I use '[p]' to refer to the proposition that p.

there is such a thing. And if Blackburn asks whether N is necessary or contingent one should reply that it is neither, because it is not a true proposition, and it is only true propositions that are necessary or contingent. One can legitimately ask, of course, whether N is a necessary or contingent *existent*:[3] that is, whether the proposition [N exists] is necessary or contingent. But the legitimacy of this question is of no help to Blackburn, for there is no regress looming if we answer that N exists necessarily. For what makes it true that N exists necessarily? N, of course!—N is the necessity maker, all the necessary truths are necessary in virtue of it. There is no sense of a "bad residual 'must'". We know the answer to all questions of the form 'Why is p necessary?'—the answer is: in virtue of the existence of N. Blackburn's regress only starts if we are forced whenever we wish to account for why there are necessary truths to appeal to some necessary truth; but if we believe in the necessity maker we need make no such appeal, we only appeal to the existence of a certain thing. Nor is the original necessity in any sense undermined if N is a contingent being. For it certainly does not follow from the contingent existence of the necessity maker that the necessary truths could have failed to be necessary. It may be necessary that had N not existed there would be something else to fulfil the necessity maker role: that is, even if the thing which is actually the necessity maker only exists contingently, it may be necessary that there be *some thing or other* in virtue of which all the actual necessary truths are necessary. And what would make that necessary? N, of course, for it is the necessity maker.

Nevertheless, it would be interesting if Blackburn's dilemma established that we had to believe in truthmakers to account for the source of necessity. So let us grant for the sake of argument that we wish to account for the source of necessity by appealing not to the existence of some thing but to the truth of some proposition, and ask whether Blackburn's dilemma is troubling on this assumption.

The second curiosity is that Blackburn says that the form of the explanation we are considering is □A because F. But that is the explanation of the necessity of a *particular* proposition, A, whereas one might only be concerned with the explanation for why there are necessities *in general*. To be sure, one way of explaining why there are necessities in general is to explain why there is a particular necessity; since obviously if there is a necessary proposition then there are necessary propositions. But there's no reason to suppose that an answer to the question 'why are there any necessary truths?' *must* be of the form 'because A is necessary, and A is necessary because of F'. So if Blackburn's dilemma requires that the explanation be of such a form then there is perhaps a point of resistance there.

---

[3] And one may, of course, use the words 'Is N necessary?' to ask this; but that is not what Blackburn would be asking were he to ask the question that sets up his supposed dilemma.

Some might think that Blackburn's question is the right one; that the demand for an explanation of the source of necessity should be understood as a demand for an explanation for why the particular necessary truths are necessary, as opposed to explanation for why there are necessities in general. After all, sometimes a demand for explanation is only taken to be appropriate if the facts in question could have been otherwise. And it is open to think that the fact that there are necessary truths could *not* have been otherwise even if the facts that particular truths are necessary could have been: accepting that necessarily some propositions are necessary does not commit one to accepting that some propositions are necessarily necessary. But this can't have been Blackburn's reason for focusing on the explanation for the necessity of some particular proposition rather than for there being necessities in general because, as we will see below, the contingency horn of his dilemma makes use of the characteristic axiom of S4 and assumes that the necessary truths are necessarily necessary.

Nonetheless, let us examine Blackburn's dilemma as regards attempts to identify the source of the necessity; I will flag when I think it is relevant that he is not considering the view which attempts only to explain why there are necessities as opposed to why there are some *particular* necessities.

## 2. THE CONTINGENCY HORN

First let us concentrate on the contingency horn of Blackburn's dilemma. Why is there "strong pressure" to think that if the fact we cite to explain why there are necessary truths could itself have been false then we are undermining the necessity of the proposition(s) in question? I presume Blackburn's thought is along the following lines. If F, which is to explain why there are necessities, is contingent then it might have been false. (So far so good!) So consider the world in which it is false; in that case the source of necessity is lacking. But how can the source of necessity be lacking? Necessity is necessity; truth in *all* worlds.

As Bob Hale has pointed out,[4] this reasoning seems to presuppose one of two principles: either that if the source of necessity were lacking then the necessities would no longer be necessary, or that they might not be necessary.[5] If that is right then the contingency of the source of necessity leads to the possibility that the necessary truths are not necessary. That is, the argument has one of either the following two forms.

---

[4] Hale (2002, pp. 302–3).
[5] It is obviously false that if the source of necessity were lacking, the necessary truths would not be *true*, since there are no circumstances under which the necessary truths would not be true.

| | | | |
|---|---|---|---|
| 1 | (1) | $\Box$p because q | Assumption |
| 2 | (2) | (A because B) $\to$ ($\neg$B$\Box$$\to$ $\neg$A) | Assumption |
| 1,2 | (3) | $\neg$q $\Box$$\to$ $\neg$$\Box$p | From 1,2 $\to$E |
| 4 | (4) | $\Diamond\neg$q | Assumption |
| 1,2,4 | (5) | $\Diamond\neg\Box$p | From 3,4. |

Or

| | | | |
|---|---|---|---|
| 1 | (1) | $\Box$p because q | Assumption |
| 2* | (2*) | (A because B) $\to$ ($\neg$B$\Diamond$$\to$$\to$$\neg$A) | Assumption |
| 1,2* | (3*) | $\neg$q $\Diamond$$\to$$\neg$$\Box$p | From 1,2* $\to$E |
| 4 | (4) | $\Diamond\neg$q | Assumption |
| 1,2*,4 | (5) | $\Diamond\neg\Box$p | From 3*,4. |

5 follows from 3 and 4 or 3* and 4 according to the Lewisian semantics for counterfactuals. $\neg$q $\Box$$\to$ $\neg$$\Box$p is true at a world $i$ (according to a system of spheres \$) if and only if either (1) no $\neg$q-world belongs to any sphere S in \$$_i$, or (2) some sphere S in \$$_i$ does contain at least one $\neg$q-world, and the material conditional $\neg$q $\to$ $\neg$$\Box$p holds at every world in S. 4 tells us that there is a sphere $S_1$ in \$$_i$ to which there belongs a $\neg$q-world, call it W. The material conditional $\neg$q $\to$ $\neg$$\Box$p must be true at every world in $S_1$, a fortiori it must be true at W. So $\neg$$\Box$p is true at W, which means that $\neg$$\Box$p is possible.

    p $\Diamond$$\to$ q =$_{df}$ $\neg$(p $\Box$$\to$ $\neg$q), so $\neg$q $\Diamond$$\to$ $\neg$$\Box$p =$_{df}$ $\neg$($\neg$q $\Box$$\to$ $\neg$$\neg$$\Box$p) =$_{df}$ $\neg$ ($\neg$q $\Box$$\to$ $\Box$p). So from 3* we can infer that both the sufficient conditions for the counterfactual $\neg$q $\Box$$\to$ $\Box$p must be false. In particular then we can infer that there is no sphere S in \$$_i$ such that there is at least one $\neg$q-world and that the material conditional $\neg$q $\to$ $\Box$p is true at every world in S. But again, from 4 we can infer that there is a sphere S* in \$$_i$ such that there is a $\neg$q-world. In that case it must be that the material conditional $\neg$q $\to$ $\Box$p is not true at every world in S*; so the consequent must be false at some world in S*. i.e. there is a world in S* at which $\neg$$\Box$p is true; so $\Diamond\neg$$\Box$p.

    As I said above, there seems then to be a tacit reliance on the characteristic principle of S4, $\Box$p $\to$ $\Box$$\Box$p, to get trouble from the conclusion at 5. For there is no problem with it being possible that p is not necessary unless we think it follows that p is not necessary, and that is just the contraposition of the S4 axiom.

    Incidentally, I don't think it matters here that Blackburn's argument concerns the explanation for the necessity of a particular proposition as opposed to an explanation for there being necessities in general. For if either 2 or 2* is correct then if that which explains why there are necessities in general is lacking then there might not have been any necessary truths. Given S4 that cannot be true; S4 says there must be some necessary truths because, in particular, the actual necessary truths must be necessary. (Actually we should be more careful: it follows from S4 that *if* there are some actual necessary truths then there are necessarily some necessary truths. But the antecedent is easily discharged, since the S4 axiom itself is an actual necessary truth if it is true.)

The commitment to the S4 axiom in generating a problem means that Blackburn is forced into accepting the principle at 2 rather than the principle at 2*, because use of the principle at 2* is incompatible with the S4 axiom. 2* says that if A is true because of B then had B not been the case A might not have been the case. Now if A is itself a necessary truth then that principle cannot be true. Might counterfactuals are existentially committing in a way that would counterfactuals are not; to assert the might counterfactual 'p $\Diamond\rightarrow$ q' is to commit oneself to the existence of a world at which p is true and q is true. In that case any might counterfactual with a necessary falsehood as its consequent is false, since there is no world at which necessary falsehoods are true. As Hale puts it[6]

> Suppose $\Box$B. Then $\Box\neg\neg$B, whence it is (vacuously) true that A $\Box\rightarrow$ $\neg\neg$B, and *hence* [given that p $\Diamond\rightarrow$ $\neg$q $=_{df}$ $\neg$(p $\Box\rightarrow$ $\neg\neg$q)] *false that . . .* A $\Diamond\rightarrow$ $\neg$B, whatever proposition A is taken to be.

Hale concludes that the might counterfactual is no good when we are concerned with explaining necessities, it is only (if at all) good when we are concerned with explaining contingencies. What this shows is that acceptance of the might counterfactual is incompatible with the S4 axiom. We're concerned with explaining necessities: but there is an ambiguity in the phrase 'explaining necessities', it may mean that the A in 'A because B' is necessary, or it may mean that it is of the form $\Box$p. In our case we can presume only that A is of the form $\Box$p, because the dilemma concerns an explanation of the form '$\Box$p because q'. Hale's trouble with the might counterfactual arises if A itself is necessary, in this case if it is necessary that $\Box$p, and that only follows if the S4 axiom is true. It is perfectly okay for one who embraces the contingency horn to accept the might counterfactual, but then she will have to deny S4 and, hence, have no problem with Blackburn's conclusion, which was that the necessities are undermined because they might not have been necessary; the denier of S4 does not take this to undermine the original necessity.

In summary: the principle at 2*, if true at all, is only true when A is a contingent truth. In the case we are concerned with, A is a truth of the form $\Box$p, so Blackburn can only make appeal to 2* if he thinks that truths of the form $\Box$p are contingent, i.e. if he thinks $\Diamond\neg\Box$p. But that is, of course, to deny the S4 axiom, which says that no truth of the form $\Box$p is contingent. So Blackburn can have 2* *or* the S4 axiom, but he can't have both; so the second version of the argument is unconvincing.

Blackburn needs to rely on 2 then, which says that if A is true because of B then had B not been the case A *would* not have been the case. This counterfactual does not commit us to the existence of a world at which A is true, so assertion of 2 is compatible with the S4 principle. But, of course, to assert that counterfactual *and* the claim that there is a world at which B is false commits us to the existence

---

6 Hale (2002), p. 303.

of a world at which A is not true. Since one who embraces the contingency horn, by definition, is one who asserts that there is a world at which the relevant B is false, that means that one who embraces the contingency horn, if they accept the principle at 2, is also committed to thinking that there is a world at which the relevant A is false. Since the relevant A is a truth of the form $\Box p$ then, as above, the theorist who embraces the contingency horn is committed to the contingency of some necessary truth, and therefore to the denial of the S4 principle. And I suppose that must be Blackburn's problem: that one cannot hold all of the S4 axiom, principle 2, and the claim that the source of necessity may have been lacking; but if the first two of these are plausible then it must be the last that goes.

How to respond? Well, it's always an option to deny S4; although we would want to be given a reason for *why* it fails (a reason that doesn't amount simply to wanting to avoid this horn of the dilemma). But really what should be first to go out of the three incompatible principles is principle 2. It is not in general true that if that which explains some true proposition p were lacking then p would be false, because in general it is the case that p *might* have been true for some other reason. Hale gives the following example:[7] suppose I shoot at a balloon, and you shoot at it in-between the time that I shoot and the time the balloon bursts. The balloon burst because I shot it. But it is not true that had I not shot the balloon would not have burst; it might still have been burst by your shot.

Are we entitled to assert the stronger claim: that the balloon *would* still have burst because it *would* have been burst by your shot? If so then principle 2* is false, even in the case of contingencies, because the previous would counterfactual is incompatible with the might counterfactual 'If I hadn't shot the balloon might not have burst'. But I don't think we can make that stronger claim; it's not true that had I not shot the balloon *would* still have burst; for in those circumstances you *might* have chosen not to shoot as well, or your gun *might* have misfired, or the bullet from your gun *might* have been displaced as a result of quantum indeterminacy, or etc. Such possibilities suggest the truth of principle 2* as it concerns contingencies; if (some contingent) p is true because of q, then had q been false, p might have been false; but it might also have been true. So there is nothing we can say about what the truth of contingent propositions *would* have been had the source of their truth been lacking. I conclude that Blackburn has not shown that any grounding of the necessary in the contingent is doomed to failure: principle 2 is not in general true, and acceptance of principle 2* goes hand in hand with rejection of the S4 axiom, which makes Blackburn's conclusion unproblematic.

Of course, this doesn't show that no problem faces the contingency theorist. For all that's been said, it may turn out that any plausible grounding of the necessary in the contingent is such that the S4 axiom plausibly holds as a result, and is such that were the contingent facts doing the grounding false, the actual

---

7 Hale (2002), p. 302.

necessary truths wouldn't be necessary. Any attempt to sit on the contingency horn has to show that these conditions don't hold.

## 3. THE NECESSITY HORN

The problem on the necessity horn is that if that which explains why there are necessities is necessarily true then we have a "bad residual 'must'". Now here I think it is crucial to distinguish the question 'why are there any necessities?' from the question 'why are the necessary propositions necessary?' because Blackburn's worry, and any response to it, will look quite different in either case. (The questions are obviously different. The legitimacy of the questions presupposes that an informative answer can be given. But it is a perfectly coherent possibility that an informative answer can be given as to why there are any necessary propositions at all but no informative answer given as to why some particular proposition is necessary, and vice-versa.)

Consider first the attempt to explain, for every necessary truth, why it is necessary. The problem seems to be that we land either in circularity or an infinite regress: we can explain the necessity of $p_1$ by appeal to a necessary truth $p_2$, but now we must explain the necessity of $p_2$; if we make appeal to the necessity of $p_1$ in explaining the necessity of $p_2$ then our explanation is circular, so we must explain the necessity of $p_2$ by an appeal to the necessity of some new proposition $p_3$. But now, of course, we must explain the necessity of $p_3$. We can never make appeal to the necessity of a proposition previously mentioned on pain of circularity, so we must always make appeal to the necessity of some new proposition, which leads to regress.

Now consider the attempt to explain why there are any necessary truths. If I do this by appealing to some necessary truth, p, then the worry here seems not to be that I have invited the same question again—for a demand for an explanation as to why p is necessary is not the same as the demand for an explanation for why there are any necessary truths—but rather that I have presupposed the truth of what I was intending to explain. I have relied on the fact that there are necessary truths to explain why there are necessary truths; it is as if I have attempted to explain why there is something rather than nothing by saying 'well my parents gave birth to me, which is why I exist; hence I exist, hence there is something rather than nothing'. That is true; but obviously it is not a good explanation, for it presupposes the truth of what is to be explained when it makes appeal to the existence of my parents. So the worry here does not so much seem to be a threat of regress or circularity, but rather that a good explanation can never get off the ground. Let me deal with this latter worry first. Bob Hale has argued that it can be dispelled because we can give explanations for why there are necessary truths which do *not* presuppose the existence of necessary truths in the way that appeal to my parents presupposes that there is something rather than nothing.

Hale[8] makes a distinction between *transmissive* and *non-transmissive* models of the explanation of the necessity of some particular proposition p by appeal to some other necessary proposition. A transmissive explanation of the necessity of p is one in which the necessity of the explanans plays an explanatory role. A non-transmissive explanation of the necessity of p, by contrast, is when it is merely the *truth* of the explanans that explains the necessity of the explanandum, *even if the explanans is indeed necessary*; i.e. that while q might indeed be necessary, it is not the *necessity* of q that explains the necessity of p but merely the *truth* of q. In that case, if I give a non-transmissive explanation of why there are any necessities I do not presuppose what is to be explained: even though I have made use of a necessary truth q in the explanation, I have not presupposed that there are any necessary truths in the explanation, because the fact that q is necessary played no role in the explanation.

An example of a transmissive explanation of the necessity of a proposition p would be a proof[9] of p from premises that are themselves necessary.[10] A proof of p from true premises explains why p is true; but coupled with the information that the premises of the proof are not merely true but necessary, we have an explanation of the necessity of p. The necessity of p is explained by the premises, but not merely by their truth: the necessity of the premises plays a crucial role in the explanation, for their necessity *transfers* to the conclusion. An example Hale takes to be a non-transmissive explanation of the necessity of a proposition is as follows: the explanandum is the proposition that necessarily the conjunction of two propositions A and B is true only if A is true and B is true, the explanans the proposition that conjunction just *is* that binary function of propositions which is true iff both its arguments are true.[11] The explanans is necessary, to be sure; but, Hale thinks, the necessity of the explanans is not doing any explanatory work in explaining the necessity of the explanandum. What explains the necessity of the fact that a conjunction is true only if both conjuncts are is merely the *truth* of the fact that conjunction is the function which is true iff both its arguments are true; no appeal to the necessity of the latter fact is necessary to explain the necessity of the former fact, even though the latter fact is indeed necessary.

I think Hale is right to claim that there can be explanations of the necessity of a proposition that do not rely on the necessity of the explanans even if the explanans is in fact necessary; but I am doubtful about the particular example he gives. It does not seem to me that the claim that conjunction just *is* that binary function of propositions which is true iff both its arguments are true explains the necessity of the proposition that the conjunction of two propositions A and B

---

[8]  Hale (2002), p. 202.
[9]  I am using the term 'proof' somewhat loosely, so that if there are undischarged assumptions at the final line it can still count as a proof.
[10]  Hale (2002), pp. 308–9.      [11]  Hale (2002), p. 312.

is true only if A is true and B is true. Consider the impossible world, w, where one of A and B are false but in which the conjunction A&B is true. Does the fact that conjunction just *is* that binary function of propositions which is true iff both its arguments are true explain why w is impossible? I can't see why it would. Sure, conjunction is that binary function of propositions which is true iff both its arguments are true; but in w such a function can have a false argument but yield a true value. That is impossible, of course; a function which is true iff both its arguments are true cannot possibly have a false argument but yield a true value. But is this impossibility explained by conjunction being the function it is? I think not; for it is that function in w as much as it is in the actual world. It is simply that in w it is behaving in an impossible manner. But the source of this impossibility (and therefore the corresponding necessity of the negation) is so far left unexplained.

To put what I think is the same point slightly differently: isn't the reason w is impossible not to do with how conjunction in fact behaves, but rather with the fact that conjunction behaves the way it does *necessarily*: that as a matter of necessity a conjunction yields truth only when both its arguments are true? But that is not to explain, or to give grounding to, the necessity in question: it is merely to restate it.

But while I deny that Hale's proposed explanation here is a non-transmissive explanation, that is because I do not think it is an explanation, not because I think explanations need be transmissive. I think there *can* be non-transmissive explanations of necessity. Consider, for example, the Lewisian answer to the source of necessity. Lewis says that □p is true because p is true at every world.[12] Now that latter fact is, according to the Lewisian, necessary;[13] but the necessity of the proposition is playing no role in the explanation of the necessity of p, merely the truth of the proposition—'Necessarily, p' is *analysed* as 'at every world, p', and so it is the latter fact alone, as opposed to the necessity of the latter fact, that explains the necessity of p—and so we have a non-transmissive explanation of the necessity of p, and hence of the claim that there are some necessary truths.

If non-transmissive explanations are possible it follows that we can have an explanation for why there are some necessities that does not presuppose that there are necessary truths. Why are there some necessities? Because of some *truth* q. And even if q is in fact necessary, my explanation for why there are any necessary truths can stop here; no further demand for explanation is invited for

---

[12] Lewis (1986b).

[13] See Divers (1999a) for a Lewisian treatment of the modal status of claims concerning the plurality of worlds.

I have appealed only to the truth of some proposition, not the necessity of any proposition. As Hale puts it[14]

[E]ven if . . . an explanation '□p because q' of the kind suggested cannot be correct unless (one thinks that) q is itself necessary—so that the necessity of the explanans is in a sense presupposed—it does not follow that it is presupposed in a relevant way, i.e. in a way that compromises the explanation. It would do so if the explanation worked by transmitting the necessity of the explanans to the explanandum, but that it does not do.

In short, then, we start from the *truth* of the proposition that q, something which does not call out for explanation,[15] and use this to explain the necessity of some other proposition p, which in turn explains the truth of ∃p□p—the claim that there are necessary truths.

   Hale's non-transmission model aims to show us how we can explain why there are necessary truths without leaving a "bad residual 'must' ", but has it anything to say about the demand to explain the necessity of the *particular* necessary truths? It seems not (nor does Hale claim otherwise). If my goal is to give an explanation for the necessity of each necessary truth, and I begin by explaining the necessity of some necessary proposition p by an appeal to the necessary truth q, then the demand for an explanation for the necessity of q arises *whether or not the necessity of q was relevant to the explanation of the necessity of p*. When our goal is to give an explanation of the necessity of p, for all necessary propositions p, it seems we have *no choice* but to make appeal to some contingent proposition at some stage as the explanation for the necessity of some proposition if we want to avoid circularity or regress. But how bad a conclusion is this? Suppose one wants to avoid appeal to a contingency, how worried should we be about the looming circularity or regress that Blackburn threatens us with? I think at least in some cases the answer is 'not very'. Consider again the Lewisian answer to the source of necessity: p is necessary because p is true at every world. I argued that even though it is necessary that p is true at every world, the necessity of this proposition is not involved in the explanation of the necessity of p, merely its truth. But of course while we might at this point be able to claim that we have explained why there are necessary truths we cannot claim that we have explained the necessity of every necessary truth. In particular there is a necessary truth—at every world it is true that p—whose necessity has not been explained. What explains the necessity of this proposition? The fact that at every world it is true that at every world it is true that p. This too is necessary. Why? Because at every world it is true that at every world it is true that at every world it is true that p. We are clearly heading down a road with no end, but should we be worried about this regress? Is it vicious? I think not. There is no mystery about why any necessary truth is necessary. We are told the general reason why necessary truths

---

[14] Hale (2002), p. 314.
[15] At least it does not call out for explanation in *this* context: a context in which we are aiming to explain *necessity* as opposed to mere *truth*.

are necessary: because they are true at every world. If modal realism is correct then no necessary truth is left mysteriously unexplained, even if we face regress when we try to explain the necessity of every necessary truth (what else would we expect given that there are infinitely many necessary truths?). I conclude then that there is not in general a problem with the kind of regress Blackburn threatens when we attempt to explain the necessity of every necessary truth.

## 4. NEO-CONVENTIONALISM

I have argued, following Hale, that Blackburn's dilemma does not show us that any realist account of the source of necessity will be flawed: both horns of Blackburn's dilemma can in principle be resisted. But it's one thing to show that there are moves available to block the dilemma and another thing entirely to give a plausible account of the source of necessity where such moves look attractive. I showed how the Lewisian realist can sit happily on the necessity horn; but I, like most of us, am unwilling to embrace Lewis's vast ontology of concrete possibilia in order to provide an ontological grounding for the modal. In this section, then, I want to show how my preferred answer to the source of necessity doesn't fall victim to Blackburn's dilemma.

In previous work[16] I have defended a kind of conventionalism about modality. You might expect me, then, to sit on the contingency horn. Traditional conventionalism says that [p is necessary] is true in virtue of the obtaining of some linguistic convention; since it's not necessary that this convention was in place, or indeed that any conventions are in place, the source of necessity is grounded in contingent facts about the world. There is no problem from Blackburn's dilemma, however, because the traditional conventionalist will deny the S4 axiom: p is necessary in virtue of certain conventions being in place; but p isn't *necessarily* necessary, it could have been false that p is necessary; p would have been contingent had certain other conventions been in place.

But while traditional conventionalism isn't defeated by Blackburn's dilemma, it is nevertheless implausible.[17] It's just not true that the necessary truths are true in virtue of certain linguistic conventions obtaining. Every true sentence is true in virtue of the world being the way the sentence says it is. Now sure, in the case of a sentence, S, which expresses a necessary truth, there is a sense in which all that has to happen for S to express a truth is for S to mean what it does. But we shouldn't conclude from that that S is true solely in virtue of meaning. It is sufficient to fix the truth-value of S that we fix the meaning of S *because* the world is necessarily the way S says it is; it's not that the world is necessarily the

---

[16] Cameron (forthcoming). Cf. Sider (2003).
[17] Hale (2002) discusses traditional conventionalism in some detail.

way S says it is because it is sufficient to fix the truth-value of S that we fix the meaning of S.

The only sentences that can properly be said to be true in virtue of the obtaining of certain linguistic conventions are the subset of the contingent truths that are *about* linguistic conventions: such as [There are conventions] or [such and such a convention is in place]. These are 'true in virtue of convention' in the same sense as [There are humans] is true in virtue of the existence of humans. So traditional conventionalism is hopeless.

I hold a different kind of conventionalism, and I sit on the necessity horn of Blackburn's dilemma rather than the contingency horn. I believe that there are both possible and impossible worlds: abstract entities that represent ways things could have been and abstract entities that represent ways that things couldn't have been. The problem of the source of modal truth is the problem of explaining what it is about the possible worlds that makes them possible: what it is that all the possible worlds have that all the impossible worlds lack that accounts for the former but not the latter representing ways things could have been.

But when viewed that way it seems that the problem presupposes that there is some natural distinction between the possible worlds and the impossible worlds: that the world carves a joint between the possible and the impossible, and that we latch onto this natural distinction with our modal vocabulary. If that were so, then we would indeed face the challenge of saying what it is about the possible worlds that makes them fall on one side of the joint rather than the other. But maybe it's not so: maybe our modal vocabulary isn't latching on to some natural distinction between the possible and the impossible; maybe we are latching on to some highly unnatural distinction, and there is nothing more to a world's being a possible world than that it falls on one side of this unnatural distinction and not the other. This is what the neo-conventionalist[18] thinks.

There are many cases in which we can learn from the analogies between time and modality, and I think this is one of those cases. Consider the question as to the source of presentness: what makes the present time present, and other times past or future? What is it that the present has that other times lack that explains the *presentness* of the present? Is this a serious problem? It depends, seemingly, on whether we are A-theorists or B-theorists. The A-theorist and the B-theorist differ on whether or not there is a natural distinction between the present and the non-present. The A-theorist thinks that the world carves a natural joint between the privileged present time on the one hand and the non-present times on the other; the B-theorist, on the other hand, thinks that in singling out the present time from the non-present times we are not latching on to some natural

---

[18] The terminology is from Sider (2003). In Cameron (forthcoming) I called the view 'deflationism'.

distinction in the world but that we are merely carving up the world unnaturally on the basis of our perspective on it.

The neo-conventionalist treats the distinction between the possible and the impossible much like the B-theorist treats the distinction between the present and the non-present. And just as there is only a puzzling metaphysical question as to the source of the distinction between the present and the non-present for the A-theorist, so there is only a puzzling metaphysical question as to the source of the distinction between the possible and the impossible for the theorist who thinks that there is a natural distinction here.

It is incumbent upon the A-theorist to say *what it is* that makes the present time privileged. We want to be pointed to some metaphysical difference between that time and the other times that explains why it gets special treatment. That's what seems so wrong about the moving spotlight theory: here one time is privileged, but all the times are on a par ontologically. Contrast this with presentism, where the difference in treatment has a clear ontological explanation: the present time is privileged because it is the only time that *exists*. The B-theorist, on the other hand, does not face the same challenge. There's nothing special about the present time—we just single one out as present based on our perspective on the world: 'the present' doesn't pick out some special, ontologically privileged, time, it simply picks out the time that contains your reading of *this* sentence. So why are the non-present times not present? Just because they fall on that side of the unnatural distinction we decided to use to carve up the times.

Similarly, if there is some natural distinction between the possible worlds and the impossible worlds then it is incumbent on the modal metaphysician to say *what it is* that makes the possible worlds possible. That's a very hard question to answer if there is such a natural distinction. (At least, it's a hard question to answer unless you are Lewis. For Lewis, the metaphysical difference between the possible and the impossible is that the possible *exists*. But for the majority, who take possible worlds and impossible worlds to be on a par, this will not do.) But if the distinction between the possible and the impossible is not a natural one—if it does not reflect a joint in reality—then the question is easy to answer. What makes the possible worlds *possible*? Just that they fall on that side of the unnatural distinction that we decided to use to carve up the worlds.

Suppose I am presented with a group of people and I point to an arbitrary sub-group of them and call them the Fs, with the remaining members of the group being the non-Fs. If you ask me in virtue of what a non-F is a non-F the answer is obviously just that they weren't in the group I singled out as the Fs; there is nothing more to be said. Likewise, if I single out a sub-group of all the worlds, not by pointing to them explicitly but by mentioning certain features of them—such as representing the mathematical truths as true, not making false actually true kind identities, etc.—and I call the worlds in this sub-group the possible worlds, there is nothing more to be said about why they are the possible worlds than that they are in the group I singled out to be called that. Explanation stops there. We would only owe a further explanation if we thought that the distinction we were drawing was latching on to some natural joint between the worlds; then we would need to account for why some worlds had this natural property and others didn't. This is exactly what the neo-conventionalist rejects.

It's tempting to think that the neo-conventionalist should sit on the contingency horn. After all, isn't [There are some necessary truths] true in virtue of the fact that we draw this unnatural distinction between the worlds? Isn't [p is necessary] true because we drew the distinction where we did? And isn't it contingent that we drew the distinction where we did, or even that we drew a distinction at all?

I think that reasoning's mistaken. [There are some necessary truths] is *not* true in virtue of the fact that we draw this unnatural distinction between the worlds; it's true in virtue of the fact that some propositions are true at each of the possible worlds. [p is necessary] is *not* true because we drew the distinction where we did; it's true because p is true at each of the possible worlds. The whole point of *neo*-conventionalism was to abandon the hopeless idea of a proposition being true in virtue of the obtaining of some convention.[19] The neo-conventionalist doesn't think that [Necessarily, p] is true because of our convention to call some but not all of the worlds possible; [Necessarily, p] is true simply because p is true at every possible world. The point of neo-conventionalism is to allow this answer to be an *informative* answer, by removing the mystery over the distinction between the possible worlds and the impossible worlds.

So the explanation for the source of necessity is just that there are some propositions that are true at every possible world. The work neo-conventionalism is doing is allowing this to be a good explanation. For the theorist who thinks that there is a natural distinction between the necessary and the impossible it is *not* a good explanation, because the phenomenon that we are trying to explain—why there is a distinction between the necessary and the contingent—is presupposed in the appeal to the distinction between the possible worlds and the impossible worlds. This is not presupposed by the neo-conventionalist because the distinction between the worlds is not carved by tracking some prior modal truths: it is carved according to our perspective—we simply call certain worlds 'impossible' because they deviate from the actual world in matters we consider important.

Necessity has its source in necessary truths, then. For even though it is a contingent matter that we divided the worlds up as we did, or even that any division was made, this does not make it contingent that p is true at every possible world. That's because whether or not p is necessary at some world w depends on whether or not, at w, p is true at every possible world according to the way we *actually* carve up the worlds into the possible and the impossible. It doesn't matter how the modal vocabulary is used *at w*; what matters is how the modal vocabulary is actually used.

---

[19] Unless it is a proposition whose subject matter is the obtaining of some convention.

But while the necessary has its source in truths which are themselves necessary, it should be clear that the necessity of the explanans is playing no role in the explanation. What explains the truth of [There are necessary truths] is just that there are some propositions which are true at every possible world; that the explanans is itself necessary plays no role in the explanation. Likewise, what explains why p is necessary is simply that p is true at each of the worlds we call the 'possible worlds'. That it's necessary that p is true at each of those worlds plays no part in the explanation, even though it is true. And these necessary truths are themselves explained by the fact that they are true at every possible world; and *that* necessary truth is explained by the fact that *it* is true at every possible world; and so on. The necessity of every necessary truth, p, is explained simply by the truth that p is true at every possible world, never by the necessity of that fact. So we have a non-transmissive explanation of the necessity of every necessary truth, and a non-transmissive explanation of why there are any necessary truths. And so we have a complete account of the source of necessity that avoids Blackburn's dilemma.

# 8

# The Reality of Modality

*Anna Sherratt*

## 1. BACKGROUND

It is true that there might have been a blue swan, that triangles must have three sides, and that twice two is necessarily four. But what makes these propositions true? What is the source of modal truth? One approach to this question explains modality by appeal to possible worlds, either concrete or abstract. Another grounds modal truth in facts about essence; it is possible for there to be a blue swan because swans are not essentially white. An alternative, however, is to reject the presupposition that there is anything in the mind-independent, objective world capable of explaining necessity and possibility. According to this view, modality is something internal that we project onto the external; modal truth is mind-dependent. Adopting an inevitably controversial label, I will call this position *modal anti-realism.*

Modal anti-realism is not the most popular approach to the philosophy of modality. Nonetheless, it has enjoyed a fair share of attention, with no shortage of candidate anti-realist theories. Here are some examples. Hume's explanation of causal necessity has clear anti-realist inclinations. If one billiard ball hits another then, other things being equal, the second billiard ball *must* move. Why? In part because, when we see the impact, we form the expectation that the second billiard ball will roll away from the first. More recently, Simon Blackburn has proposed a 'quasi-realist' account of necessity.[1] According to Blackburn, when we say that the proposition $2 + 2 = 4$ is necessarily true, the function of our utterance is to express our failure to make sense of the idea that the proposition should ever turn out false. Meanwhile, Gideon Rosen mentions (but does not endorse) a

Versions of this paper were presented at the Arché Fourth Modality Workshop, University of St Andrews and at the Institute of Philosophical Research, National Autonomous University of Mexico. Thanks to audiences for their many helpful suggestions. Thanks are also due to Bob Hale and to an anonymous referee from Oxford University Press, both of whom provided extensive and challenging comments on earlier drafts.

[1] Blackburn (1987).

'conceptualist' version of his modal fictionalism.[2] The fictionalist maintains that a proposition of the form *possibly p* is true if and only if according to the fiction of the plurality of worlds, there exists a world at which *p*. The conceptualist fictionalist adds that this fiction gains its authority through being 'an explicit formulation of our imaginative habits'. Finally, Crispin Wright suggests that we should explore the feasibility of judgment-dependent accounts of modal truth.[3] According to the simplest such account, a proposition *p* is possible if and only if a suitable subject in suitable conditions judges that *p* is possible.

Modal anti-realism can claim two *prima facie* advantages over its rivals. Realist accounts of modality are often charged with cluttering up our ontology with cumbersome objects. In contrast, anti-realism attempts to explain modality by appeal to certain features of the human mind — features, we might hope, whose existence we are already committed to. The idea, then, is that anti-realism offers us modality at no extra ontological cost. The second sort of advantage is epistemological. Realist accounts of modality are often supposed to have difficulty explaining the possibility of modal knowledge. If, for instance, modal truth depends upon facts about causally-isolated concrete worlds, it is unclear how we could achieve justified beliefs about what is necessary and what is possible. In contrast, modal anti-realism suggests a simple and promising epistemology. If modal truth depends upon facts about the human mind, we can hope to find out about modality by investigating these facts: modal knowledge becomes a sort of self-knowledge.[4]

These advantages, together with the success of anti-realist strategies in other areas of philosophy, certainly make modal anti-realism worth investigating. My aim in this paper, however, is to argue that almost all such theories face a serious difficulty. This problem should lead us to be wary of anti-realist accounts of modal truth. We should incline, that is, towards accepting the reality of modality. In arguing my point, I take as a sample anti-realist theory Peter Menzies's account of modality.[5] In Sections 3, 4, and 5 below, I argue that Menzies's theory faces a grave and insurmountable difficulty. In the last sections of the paper, I work at showing that this objection will generalize to apply to any genuinely anti-realist approach.


## 2. MENZIES AND THE IDEAL CONCEIVER

Menzies's theory begins from the observation that there is a connection between what we can conceive, and what might be the case. If I can conceive of a flying

---

[2] Rosen (1990), p. 353.      [3] See e.g. Wright (1992), p. 111.

[4] Or so, at least, in the simplest cases. Some versions of modal anti-realism will require a more complicated account of modal knowledge. For instance, in the Wright-inspired version of modal anti-realism, we achieve knowledge of what is possible by finding out what a suitable observer in suitable conditions would judge to be possible. It probably requires more than introspection to work out which observers and conditions are suitable.

[5] Menzies (1998). I focus on Menzies's account because he offers an unusually explicit and detailed version of modal anti-realism.

hamster, this gives me reason to believe that such a creature is possible. But the connection is not infallible: sometimes we suffer from modal illusions. I may, for instance, be unable to conceive of a regular polygon with exactly 735 sides; I may be able to conceive of a barber who shaves everyone who does not shave himself. This happens, says Menzies, when we suffer from *cognitive limitations*, such as lack of concentration and inadequate reasoning. These limitations sever the connection between conceivability and possibility. The appropriate analogy, then, is with the case of colour. In most circumstances, if a pillar-box seems red to me, then it is red. But inadequate lighting, hallucinatory drugs, and colour blindness all can produce colour illusions. Likewise, if I can conceive of the truth of a proposition, then that proposition is possible—unless, of course, some cognitive limitation has led to a modal illusion.

From these observations, Menzies produces his *ideal conceiver theory*. Call a subject who suffers from none of the cognitive limitations which we regard as discounting acts of conceiving, an *ideal conceiver*. Then Menzies's idea is that what is necessary or possible depends upon the conceivings of an ideal conceiver. More precisely, Menzies endorses the following biconditional: $p$ is possible if and only if an ideal conceiver could conceive that $p$. Or, as I shall sometimes write it:

IC   $\Diamond p \leftrightarrow ICp$.

(Assuming that necessity and possibility are standardly interdefinable, this entails a corresponding account of necessity: $p$ is necessary if and only if an ideal conceiver could not conceive the negation of $p$. My focus, however, will be mainly on IC.) Menzies's ideal conceiver theory raises pressing questions. We may worry, for instance, that since IC employs the modal concept *could* on its right-hand side, Menzies's theory is viciously circular. We may also wish to know more about the nature of conceiving. Menzies has interesting things to say in response to these questions, but the details need not concern us here. They are peculiar to Menzies's account and therefore orthogonal to my overall purpose. Two issues, however, do deserve closer attention since they will be crucial to the discussion that follows.

The first involves the nature of the ideal conceiver. If Menzies's account is to serve as a substantive account of modality, the ideal conceiver must not be specified simply as a being that can conceive of all and only the possible. Such a specification would render IC trivially true. Menzies's idea, of course, is that he can avoid such triviality by appeal to the notion of a cognitive limitation. His claim is that if a proposition is possible, then someone who is not affected by limitations of reasoning, memory, attention, or what-have-you will be able to conceive of its truth. This claim is not trivial, but substantive and controversial. Relatedly, an ideal conceiver should not be regarded as some sort of conceiving machine, with infinite cognitive resources. Such an approach would lead to epistemological disaster: we would have few means of finding out what such an alien creature could conceive of, and thus little hope of acquiring modal knowledge. Instead, Menzies's idea is that an ideal conceiver should be somebody like you and me, but who is operating in optimum conditions. Indeed, Menzies claims, in many circumstances we *are* ideal conceivers.[6] Suppose that I conceive that there is a black dog outside my window. This act of conceiving is so simple that it is unlikely that any cognitive limitation will threaten the connection between conceivability and possibility. So in this case, at least, I have good grounds for thinking that the situation that I have conceived of is, in fact, possible.

The second point involves aprioricity, a theme that will be important throughout this paper. Menzies maintains that IC should be *a priori* knowable. Why? While Menzies does not spell out his reasoning, the usual line of thought in this context is as follows.[7] Suppose that a biconditional such as IC is true. Then there seem to be two possible explanations for this. The first is that our idealized conceivings are very accurate reflectors of what is necessary and what is possible. That is, they have what Crispin Wright would call an *extension-tracking role*. The second explanation is that what is necessary or possible depends upon, or is constituted by, what is ideally conceivable. That is, our idealized conceivings have an *extension-determining role*. Menzies, of course, favours the second explanation. How, though, is he to ensure that IC is read in this fashion? The answer is to insist upon its aprioricity. The thought is that if our abilities to conceive really do determine the truth or falsity of modal propositions, this fact should be accessible merely by reflection upon the concepts involved. In contrast, if our idealized conceivings merely track possibility, in the same way as our senses track the presence of medium-sized physical objects, we would need empirical investigation to find out that this is the case. By insisting that IC is a priori, Menzies ensures that it is understood in the fashion that he intends.

## 3. THE TRANSPARENCY OBJECTION

The ideal conceiver theory is an account of modality. But it also tells us something rather surprising about what the actual world is like. The ideal conceiver theory commits us to the view that every true proposition is ideally conceivable. We arrive at this conclusion as follows. Menzies endorses the following claim:

IC: $\Diamond p \leftrightarrow ICp$.

It is uncontroversial that a proposition is true only if it is possible:

T: $p \rightarrow \Diamond p$.

IC and T jointly entail a claim that I will call the *transparency thesis*:

TT: $p \rightarrow ICp$.

---

[6] Menzies (1998), p. 372.       [7] See e.g. Wright (1992), pp. 114–17.

According to the transparency thesis, if $p$ is true, then $p$ can be conceived by an ideal conceiver. To put it rather metaphorically, the ideal conceiver theory, together with the uncontroversial T, entails that the actual world is transparent to our idealized abilities to conceive.

Can we accept that the transparency thesis is true? This seems an optimistic conclusion. It seems an epistemic possibility that there are truths about the actual world so strange that even an ideal conceiver could make no sense of them. Colin McGinn has speculated that the truth about the mind–body problem is like this.[8] The human mind, he suggests, is 'cognitively closed' with respect to the property of the brain responsible for consciousness. We simply do not have, and could never attain, the conceptual resources to grasp this property—any more than a monkey could grasp, say, the property of being an electron.[9] Locke thought something similar about matter: since our ideas of the world are constrained by our limited perceptions, humans can no more understand the true nature of matter than a blind man can truly understand colour.[10] Other examples of this phenomenon might be provided by some of the wilder interpretations of quantum theory. Suppose that it turned out that certain particles are literally located in two different places at the same time. Then this, arguably, would be a truth about the world that is inconceivable, even to someone operating in ideal conditions. Of course, I do not claim that any of these speculations are correct. But while we remain open to their truth, we should feel uneasy about accepting the claim that every proposition is ideally conceivable.

I want to sharpen this initial unease into a more focused objection to the ideal conceiver theory. To do so, I will remain neutral about the truth of the transparency thesis. The important point concerns its epistemic status. Even if the transparency thesis is true, this cannot be known a priori. Why not? Because in order to know that every true proposition is ideally conceivable, we need to know which propositions are true. In order to know, for instance, that the truth about matter is ideally conceivable, I need to know what the truth about matter *is*. Most truths about the world can only be discovered through empirical investigation. So the transparency thesis, even if true, can only be known a posteriori. The argument here is not intended to depend upon the more general claim that in order to know that every true proposition has property P, we need to know which propositions are true. Clearly, this would not be plausible: I can know, for instance, that all true propositions are true without knowing which the true propositions are. Rather, the point is that there appears to be no conceptual link between the conceivability of $p$ and the fact that $p$ is true. Therefore, we could only find out that the transparency thesis is true by noting, on a case-by-case

---

[8] McGinn (1989).     [9] McGinn's example (1989, p. 351).
[10] Locke (1690), bk II, ch. iv.

basis, that each true proposition is ideally conceivable.[11] However, we can only do this once we know what the true propositions are—and this is something that cannot be known a priori.

Unfortunately, the ideal conceiver theory entails that transparency is knowable a priori. To see this, recall that IC, together with the uncontroversial T, entails that transparency is true. Menzies claims that IC is a priori knowable. T is surely a priori too: merely by reflecting on the relevant concepts, I can find out that every true proposition is possible. So transparency is entailed by two a priori propositions. Since this entailment is itself knowable a priori, the transparency thesis should also be a priori. The thrust of the paragraph above, however, is that transparency, even if true, can only be known through empirical investigation. So clearly something has gone wrong. The obvious culprit is the aprioricity of IC. In order to maintain the a posteriori status of transparency, we should deny that IC is knowable a priori. To do so, however, is to reject the notion that idealized conceivability plays a role in determining modal truth. And to reject this is to dismiss Menzies's ideal conceiver theory.

Since the objection to Menzies trades on the transparency thesis, I will call it the *transparency objection.* The next section sets out this argument in more formal terms and offers some elaboration and defence.

## 4. ELABORATION

We can present the transparency objection more formally by using the notation 'AP$p$' to express the claim that $p$ is knowable a priori.

| | | |
|---|---|---|
| 1. | AP ($\Diamond$p $\leftrightarrow$ ICp) | Assumed for *RAA* |
| 2. | AP (p $\rightarrow$ $\Diamond$p) | premiss |
| 3. | AP (p $\rightarrow$ ICp) | 1, 2 |
| 4. | $\neg$AP (p $\rightarrow$ ICp) | premiss |
| 5. | $\neg$AP ($\Diamond$p $\leftrightarrow$ICp) | 1, 3, 4, by *RAA.* |

Premiss 2 is the claim that T is knowable a priori. In this context, I take this to be beyond reproach. Premiss 4 denies that transparency can be known a priori. In defence of this claim, I note again that in order to know a priori that every true proposition is ideally conceivable, we would need to know something about which propositions are true—and this can only be discovered through a posteriori investigation. The move from premisses 1 and 2 to premiss 3 depends upon the assumption that a priori knowledge is closed under a priori knowable

---

[11] Or perhaps we would not need to do this for every true proposition. Perhaps we could instead note that the transparency thesis holds true of a suitable sample of true propositions and then conclude, through induction, that all true propositions are ideally conceivable. But this would not help: we would not be able to decide which propositions should be included in the sample without some empirical investigation of which propositions are true.

entailment. That is, if A entails B, A is a priori, and the relation between A and B can be known a priori, then B is a priori knowable too. Perhaps there are contexts in which this assumption is disputable—but it is unproblematic here.

Here are some comments about this argument. First, note that the nature of the ideal conceiver is doing a lot of work in motivating the thought that we cannot know a priori that the transparency thesis is true. If the ideal conceiver were specified as a being that could conceive of all and only the possible, then it would be easy to know a priori that every true proposition is ideally conceivable. And if we were to permit our ideal conceivers to have infinite cognitive resources, perhaps the apriority of transparency would be rather more plausible. As we saw earlier, however, Menzies cannot take either of these routes. The first leads to triviality; the second to epistemic disaster.

Second, it might be argued that someone who harbours anti-realist inclinations about the actual world might be more sympathetic towards the apriority of transparency. Suppose that we adopt a pseudo-Kantian view of truth: we maintain that the contents of the actual world are somehow constrained by the limits of human understanding. Then we might have grounds to know a priori that every true proposition is ideally conceivable. Perhaps, then, Menzies could reconcile himself to the apriority of the transparency thesis by embracing a more global form of anti-realism. An initial reaction is to dismiss this stance as heroic but misguided. It is one thing to hold that the metaphysical possibility that there is a black dog outside my window depends upon some aspect of the human mind. It is another thing altogether, and a much less plausible one, to maintain that the presence of an *actual* black dog is partly constituted by something mental. To put the point another way: if anti-realism about modality turns out to be unsustainable unless combined with some form of anti-realism about truth, the former will become a much less appealing position.

There may, however, be more to be said about the relation between these two anti-realisms. The claim that the truth about medium-sized physical objects depends upon what we can conceive is unpalatable. But perhaps a weaker version of anti-realism about truth will be enough to defend the apriority of transparency. Consider, for instance, the Dummettian claim that there are no evidence-transcendent truths.[12] That is, if $p$ is true, then $p$ is, in principle, knowable. This claim is, arguably, more plausible than the pseudo-Kantian position sketched in the previous section. But it may still be strong enough to explain the apriority of transparency. The reasoning here would be as follows. If $p$ is true, then, according to the Dummetian view, $p$ is knowable. But if $p$ is knowable, then $p$ is ideally conceivable. So every true proposition is ideally conceivable. The suggestion, then, is that the transparency thesis is entailed by the Dummettian position. Provided that it is knowable a priori that there are

---

[12] Proposed e.g. in Dummett (1976).

no evident transcendent truths, the transparency thesis will also be knowable a priori.

It is doubtful, though, whether this line of argument will prove helpful. First, even if Dummettian realism is more plausible than the pseudo-Kantian position, it would still be disappointing to find that it is an essential component of modal anti-realism. We might hope to endorse the view that modality is mind-dependent without being committed to any sort of stance about the nature of non-modal truth. More importantly, the reasoning that took us from Dummettian realism to the transparency thesis is highly dubious. The crucial step involves the claim that if $p$ is knowable then $p$ is ideally conceivable—but how is this to be defended? Perhaps the idea is that in order to know that $p$, an individual must believe, or at least understand, the proposition that $p$. Inconceivable propositions, however, can be neither believed nor understood. In the context of the ideal conceiver theory, however, this strategy would be mistaken. It is clearly possible to understand, and even believe, necessary falsehoods. I understand the proposition that the square root of two is rational—and might even, in a misguided moment, believe it to be true.[13] Somebody who adopts the ideal conceiver theory, however, must reject the claim that necessary falsehoods are ideally conceivable. So she must deny that believability or understandability entails ideal conceivability. Without this connection, however, we are left with no obvious way of defending the inference from in principle knowability to ideal conceivability. And without this inference, Dummettian realism cannot save Menzies's theory.

The transparency objection presents a real problem for Menzies's ideal conceiver theory. If there is an a priori connection between possibility and conceivability, there will be an a priori connection between actual truth and conceivability, too. Unless we endorse a strong form of anti-realism about the actual, we are unable to accept this conclusion. Shortly, we will see that this problem is not at all peculiar to Menzies's position; similar difficulties will be faced by almost any form of modal anti-realism. First, though, we will consider how a rather radical modification of Menzies's theory will allow him to escape the actuality objection. The resulting position, although flawed, is of some independent interest.

## 5. MODAL DISJUNCTIVISM

Suppose that, like Menzies, we want to maintain that there is an a priori connection between what is possible and what is ideally conceivable. We also want to deny that there is an a priori connection between what is actual and what

---

[13] Further examples of this phenomenon are provided by necessary a posteriori truths. It certainly seems that someone can believe that water is not $H_2O$, or that tigers are not animals. Since the propositions believed in these cases are impossible, Menzies must deny that believability entails ideal conceivability.

is ideally conceivable. Given the connection between the actual and the possible, how are we to do this? Perhaps by adopting a disjunctive theory of possibility. The idea would be that there are two ways that a proposition $p$ can be possible. $p$ can be possible because an ideal conceiver could conceive that $p$. Or $p$ can be possible simply because $p$ is true. That is:

D   $\Diamond p$ iff $ICp \lor p$.

I'll call someone who offers D as their theory of possibility, a *modal disjunctivist*.[14] Modal disjunctivism can sidestep the transparency objection. D and T do not entail the problematic transparency thesis. Instead, they jointly entail the following claim: $p \to ICp \lor p$. Since this claim is trivially true, its aprioricity should not worry us.

Modal disjunctivism is an independently interesting position. A couple of remarks about it are in order. First, disjunctivism should count as a form of anti-realism about modality, since it maintains that modal truth depends upon facts about the mind. But the dependence is only partial: some propositions are possible because they are ideally conceivable, while some propositions are possible because they are true. Despite its hybrid nature, disjunctivism retains the epistemological and ontological advantages that we associate with modal anti-realism. Indeed, it may even be able to claim some epistemological advantage over Menzies's view. Sometimes we find out that a proposition is possible by discovering that it is true. I may, for instance, discover that it is possible for space to be unbounded but finite only when some physicist tells me that this is in fact the case. Unlike the original version of the ideal conceiver, modal disjunctivism respects, and explains, this phenomenon. Second, there may be precedents for the disjunctive account found elsewhere in the philosophy of modality. Some ersatzers about possible worlds offer theories which are, at least implicitly, disjunctive. According to one variety of ersatzism, $p$ is possible if $p$ is a member of a maximal set of consistent sentences. But the actual world is not a maximal set of consistent sentences. So the ersatzer needs to recognize a second sufficient condition in order to make her account of possibility complete: $p$ is possible if and only if $p$ is a member of a maximal set of consistent sentences, or $p$ is actually true.[15]

The disjunctive position avoids the actuality objection. Nonetheless, it fails as an account of possibility.[16] To see this, first assume that the transparency thesis

---

[14] If the modal operators are standardly inter-defined, D implies a conjunctive account of necessity: p is necessary if and only if an ideal conceiver could not conceive that ¬p, *and* p is true.

[15] Note, though, that there are many forms of ersatzism which do not need to adopt a disjunctive strategy. Consider, for instance, the ersatzer who maintains that a proposition $p$ is possible if and only if $s$ expresses the proposition $p$ and there is a maximal set of consistent sentences that has $s$ as a member. This position ensures that all true propositions are possible without yielding the result that the actual world is a set of sentences.

[16] In the following, I am indebted to John Divers.

is false (we will relax this assumption shortly). This entitles us to suppose that there is a proposition $p$ which is true, but not ideally conceivable. Now make two further, plausible assumptions. The first is that there exists a further proposition $q$ which is false, but ideally conceivable. The second assumption is that $p$ and $q$ are compossible. If we want to fill in the example, we could suppose $p$ to be some strange quantum truth, and $q$ to be the false claim that there is a black dog outside my window. Since $p$ is true and $q$ is ideally conceivable, D ensures that $p$ is possible, and that $q$ is possible. But now consider the further claim:

$r$    $p \wedge q$.

It seems uncontroversial that a conjunction is ideally conceivable only if its conjuncts are ideally conceivable. So since $p$ is not ideally conceivable, neither is $r$. Moreover, it is certainly uncontroversial in any normal logic that a conjunction is true if and only if its conjuncts are true. So since $q$ is false, $r$ is false too. $r$, then, is neither true nor ideally conceivable. So D tells us that $r$ is impossible. But this contradicts our original assumption that $p$ and $q$ were compossible. So D must be rejected.

Now to relax the assumption that transparency is false. I argued in Section 3 that the transparency thesis is not a priori knowable. That is, we cannot know a priori that every true proposition is conceivable by an ideal conceiver. I now claim that since transparency is not knowable a priori, neither can we know a priori that there do not exist two propositions, $p$ and $q$, specified as above. We arrive at this conclusion through a process of elimination. What grounds could someone have for rejecting the problematic scenario? Well, suppose that we believe that there are no unrealized possibilities: every possible proposition is actually true. Then this thesis, together with an endorsement of disjunctivism, will lead us to reject the claim that $q$ is false but ideally conceivable. Or suppose that we hold that all truths are interdependent: an actually false proposition could not be true without all actually true propositions being false. Then this thesis will lead us to reject the claim that $p$ and $q$ are compossible. But both of these suppositions are absurd: there are unrealized possibilities and it is not the case that all truths are interdependent. What other reason could we have for rejecting the problematic scenario? Surely, only a belief in transparency; a belief that all true propositions are ideally conceivable. This would enable us to deny that there exists a proposition $p$ which is true but which cannot be conceived by an ideal conceiver. The transparency thesis, however, can only be known a posteriori. So we have no a priori grounds for rejecting the problematic scenario.[17]

---

[17] Some care is needed about the reasoning here. I do not wish to claim that appeal to the transparency thesis is, strictly speaking, the *only* remaining way to rule out the problematic scenario. It is logically possible to reject the thesis of no unrealized possibilities, reject the thesis of interdependence, and yet still deny that there exists two propositions $p$ and $q$ such that $(p \wedge \neg ICp) \wedge ((\neg q \wedge ICq) \wedge \Diamond (p \wedge q))$. We could do this, for instance, by adopting the following restricted version of the interdependence thesis: for any two propositions $p$ and $q$, if

From this point, we can quickly argue to the a posteriori status of D. As we have already seen, if D is true, there cannot exist two propositions $p$ and $q$ which are specified in the problematic fashion. This entailment is a priori knowable. So if D itself were knowable a priori, we would have a priori knowledge that the problematic scenario is not realized. But we do not have such knowledge. So D is not knowable a priori. The final stage of the argument against disjunctivism runs as follows. If D is to offer us a genuine theory of possibility, it should be a priori knowable. This echoes the reasoning of Section 2: if there really is a constitutive connection between the right-hand side of D and the left, we should be able to discover this merely by reflecting upon the concepts involved. Since D is not knowable a priori, disjunctivism fails as a serious theory of possibility. Or more precisely: disjunctivism is incompatible with the claim that the transparency thesis is not knowable a priori. Like Menzies's original position, it should therefore only be attractive to someone who holds a strongly anti-realist view of truth about the actual.

## 6. GENERALIZING

In this section, my more ambitious aim is to show that the transparency objection is not a problem uniquely faced by Menzies. Almost anybody who contends that modal truth is mind-dependent will face a similar difficulty. In a nutshell, the problem is as follows. The modal anti-realist thinks that modal truth is mind-dependent. She will therefore maintain that there is an a priori biconditional connection between the possible and the mental. Yet this, together with the uncontroversial T, commits her to the existence of an a priori connection between the actual and the mental. Since we are unwilling to accept this connection, we should reject modal anti-realism.

An example illustrates the problem. Suppose that we adopt a simple form of linguistic conventionalism. We maintain that $p$ is possible if and only if $p$ can be expressed by a sentence that is permitted by our linguistic conventions:

LC   $\Diamond p \leftrightarrow Cp$.

LC together with T entails a new form of transparency thesis. It entails that every true proposition can be expressed by a sentence that is permitted by our linguistic conventions:

TT*   $p \rightarrow Cp$.

---

$p$ is not ideally conceivable and $q$ is false, then $p$ and $q$ are not compossible. But I can see no non *ad hoc* reason for endorsing such a claim. The argument of this paragraph, then, is supposed to be an abductive one. The best reason (and, indeed the only plausible reason) for thinking that the problematic scenario does not obtain is a belief that transparency is true. We do not know a priori that transparency is true. So we do not know a priori that the scenario does not obtain.

Since transparency* is entailed by two a priori propositions, it should be knowable a priori too. But it is not. In order to know that every true proposition can be expressed in our language, we need to know which propositions are true. For instance, we cannot be confident that our linguistic rules allow us to express the truth about matter until we know what the truth about matter *is*—and this can only be discovered through empirical investigation. In order to secure the a posteriori status of transparency*, we must deny that LC is a priori. But to do so is to reject the claim that modal truth depends upon our linguistic conventions.

I have chosen an easy target to make my point. But the problem is a general one. If there is an a priori biconditional connection between the modal and the mental, there will be an a priori connection between the actual and the mental, too. And this is something that we are unwilling to accept. To offer one more example, suppose that the modal anti-realist endorses a response-dependence theory of modality. She maintains that *p* is possible if and only if *p* is judged to be possible by a suitable subject in suitable conditions. Since this biconditional is intended to have an extension-determining role, it should be a priori knowable. So the anti-realist will be committed to the existence of an a priori truth of the following claim: *p* is true only if *p* is judged to be possible by a suitable subject in suitable conditions. But the only person who should be willing to accept such a claim is someone who is an anti-realist about the actual world—someone, that is, who maintains that our modal judgements play a role in determining which propositions are true. We are reluctant to accept such a position. So we should reject the proposed account of modality.

The transparency objection, then, does not just pose a problem for Menzies. It presents a difficulty for almost all versions of modal anti-realism. But not quite all: there are two forms of anti-realism that will escape; I conclude with a discussion of these positions.

*One-way modal anti-realism.* Throughout, I have presented the anti-realist as accepting the existence of a biconditional connection between the modal and the mental. Suppose, however, that she chooses to reject this assumption. Suppose, for instance, that Menzies merely claimed that:

> IC*: ICp → ◊p.

It might be argued that if this one-way claim is true and a priori, modal truth is mind-dependent. If the ideal conceivability of *p* offers an a priori guarantee that *p* is possible, then there is a constitutive link between conceivability and possibility. Yet this form of anti-realism escapes the transparency objection. IC* and T fail to yield the problematic transparency thesis.

I accept that the modal realist who rejects the existence of a biconditional connection between the modal and the actual will be immune from the transparency objection. The transparency objection, then, does not show that all versions of modal anti-realism fail. But I doubt if many anti-realists will be tempted by this strategy. There are a couple of reasons for this. The first problem is a technical one. A common view is that at least some modal truths are knowable a priori. It is knowable a priori, for instance, that there might have been a flying hamster. If $\Diamond p$ is knowable a priori, however, IC* will be both trivially true and trivially a priori. And a trivial claim cannot serve as a substantive theory of modality.[18] The second problem with IC* is that it leaves us rather dissatisfied. All truths which are ideally conceivable are possible. But some possible truths are not ideally conceivable. We are left wondering what the one-way anti-realist can say about these truths: when $\Diamond p$ and $\neg ICp$, what makes $p$ possible? It is hard to see how she can provide a satisfactory answer to this question which neither compromises her anti-realist inclinations, nor invites a version of the transparency objection. Of course, neither of these two worries are by any means conclusive against the one-way anti-realist. But they do go some way to explaining why most anti-realists prefer to postulate a biconditional connection between the mental and the modal.

*A posteriori anti-realism.* The transparency objection also depends heavily upon the assumption that this biconditional is supposed to be a priori. Suppose, however, that the anti-realist rejects this assumption. She accepts that there is a biconditional connection between the mental and the modal, but she denies that this connection is knowable a priori. Then, again, she can avoid the transparency objection. Suppose, for instance, that the linguistic conventionalist maintains that LC is true, but not a priori. Then she will avoid the problematic conclusion that transparency* is a priori true. And perhaps the mere a posteriori truth of transparency* is something that we can live with. The anti-realist who pursues this strategy, however, faces a challenge that has already been mentioned. There are two possible explanations for the truth of a biconditional such as LC. It could be the case that our linguistic conventions determine modal truth. Or it could be the case that our conventions have evolved in a way that mirrors modal reality. Without appeal to apriority, how is the modal anti-realist to ensure that her biconditional claim is understood in the former fashion?

There may be a number of ways to answer this question. Here I will briefly discuss, and dismiss, the most obvious. The modal anti-realist might claim that the biconditional linking the modal and the mental is a necessary a posteriori truth.[19] Its necessity, she might maintain, is enough to grant the biconditional

---

[18] Note that this objection cannot be easily dismissed by noting that some modal truths (those about natural kinds, for instance) are only knowable a posteriori. In order to avoid the objection, the one-way anti-realist would need to maintain that *all* modal truths are only knowable a posteriori—otherwise, there will be at least one modal truth of which her theory cannot give a non-trivial account. Admittedly, this view is not without its advocates. Bob Hale, for instance, argues that all truths about possibility are only a posteriori knowable (see Hale 2003).

[19] Caution is needed here. If the anti-realist's biconditional contains certain rigidifying operators, their necessity is likely to become trivial. If the proposition $p$ is true, then the proposition *actually* $p$ is necessarily true. For instance, the claim LC*: $\Diamond p \leftrightarrow p$ can be expressed by a sentence

an extension-determining role. The trouble with this strategy, however, is that it invites a new, and equally worrying, version of the transparency objection. Suppose that the linguistic conventionalist maintains that the biconditional LC is necessarily true. LC together with T entails transparency*. T, surely, is necessarily true. Since transparency* is jointly entailed by two necessary propositions, it should be necessary too. But this claim is unattractive: there are no non-trivial necessary connections between the truth and our linguistic conventions. If we are lucky, every truth about the world can be expressed in our language. But there are plenty of possible worlds where this is not the case; worlds, for instance, where we have not developed the linguistic apparatus to express irrational numbers. Since we do not believe that generalized transparency is necessarily true, we should reject the claim that LC is necessary. Left with neither necessity nor apriority, there is no obvious way to express the thought that modality constitutively depends on our conventions.

It would be interesting to take this thought further. As we have seen, the claim that $p$ is possible if and only if Mp, where M is some suitable predicate, is not sufficient to express the thought that modality is mind-dependent. We further need to grant this biconditional some special property, such as necessity or apricity—a property, that is, that ensures that the biconditional is understood as stating that the extension of the predicate 'is possible' constitutively depends upon the extension of the predicate M. The trouble is that whatever this property is, it is likely to be inherited by the claim 'p → Mp'. And this conclusion is likely to be distasteful—at least to those who are realists about the actual world. If this line of reasoning could be defended, it would provide a conclusive demonstration that all forms of biconditional modal anti-realism are unacceptable. But I leave this more ambitious thought for future exploration.


## 7. CONCLUSION

Not all versions of modal anti-realism face the transparency objection. The anti-realist who denies that there is a biconditional connection between the mental and the modal will escape. So will the anti-realist who accepts the existence of a biconditional connection, but who denies that this connection is a priori knowable. The thrust of the paragraphs above, however, is that neither of these strategies is attractive. My final conclusion, then, is as follows. All published versions of modal anti-realism face a serious, and apparently insurmountable, objection. There exists room in logical space for anti-realist theories that escape

---

that is permitted by our actual linguistic conventions. If LC* is true, then it will also be necessarily true—yet this does not establish that our conventions play an extension-determining role. (It is for this sort of reason that Wright prefers to use the notion of apricity in this context. See Wright 1992, pp. 114–17.)

this objection. But much more work needs to be done if such theories are to be viable—and it is unclear what form these developments could take. The prospects, then, do not look good for the modal anti-realist. We do, of course, want a theory of the nature of modality that offers us a parsimonious ontology and an unproblematic epistemology. But we should concentrate on developing such a theory within the context of a broadly realist approach to modal truth.

# 9

# IBE, GMR, and Metaphysical Projects*

*Scott A. Shalkowski*

## 1. INTRODUCTION

Philosophical theories abound. We have theories of justice, the nature of the mental, accounts of the semantics for natural language, the aesthetic value of abstract art, and many more. Beyond the value of satisfying the curiosity of the idle and keeping mental hands busy and free from mischief, why should we value philosophical theories? Of course, not all philosophical theories are themselves idle. It matters greatly to how one can live one's life well whether one's rulers are Marxist, Rawlsian, or Nozickian. Many theories, particularly some metaphysical theories, do seem to be idle, however. Those who believe in immanent universals carry on in their non-philosophical lives indistinguishably from trope theorists. Nothing in their disagreement has anything to do with the price of eggs.

John Stuart Mill, however, might ask us not to be hasty in our denigration of high-level metaphysical theories. Better a dissatisfied Socrates than a satisfied pig, and all that. Socrates himself exhorted us to recognize that our character can be harmed even when that harm involves no suffering on our part; lying diminishes the liar, even if there were no experiential hell to pay. So, a modern Socrates might encourage us to see that more things are to be valued than those that affect the price of eggs. The quality of our character matters and the quality of our intellectual lives matters as well.

Philosophers, save committed empiricists, think that theories are to be valued not only because they have empirical consequences and that one theory is to be preferred to another on the basis of conditions other than their relative merits for predicting and controlling nature. Good theories systematize our beliefs, they point to explanatory facts which enhance our understanding of why things are

* Thanks go to Chris Daly for commenting on an early draft and to Leeds colleagues for offering helpful suggestions on early, half-formed ideas in an informal presentation, and to participants in the Modality Project sponsored by the Arché Research Centre for the Philosophy of Logic, Language, Mathematics and Mind at the University of St Andrews.

the way they are. Metaphysicians, understandably, are attracted to what enhances our understanding precisely because the price of eggs is so distant from the metaphysician's concerns. Naturally, then, if metaphysical theories are valued because they enhance our understanding because they, in turn, speak of deep explanatory phenomena, then one theory is to be preferred over another when (at least when other relevant factors are equal) one provides a better explanation than its competitors.

Once upon a time in Analytic Philosophy, philosophical explanation was taken to be of a quite specific kind. It was conceptual analysis. Explanation was quite directly connected to understanding because an explanation was nothing more than explaining something to someone in order for that someone to understand relations between concepts, to enhance their linguistic capabilities.

Once upon a somewhat later time, David Lewis at least appeared to flirt with conceptual analysis. In chapter 4 of *Counterfactuals* (Lewis 1973b), he gives what came to be known as the paraphrastic argument for his thesis that there are many concrete possible worlds. Though he continued to endorse the argument, it confers no serious epistemic warrant on his key ontological thesis and, so, plays no role in the mature development of his metaphysical programme in *On the Plurality of Worlds*.[1] There the main general strategy was to use something like an inference to the best explanation (IBE). What provides good reason to believe that there is a plurality of concrete worlds is that the plurality, were it to exist, would provide a good explanation of the truth conditions for modal discourses including counterfactual conditionals, of causal relations, of the nature of properties, of the nature of propositions, and more. Lewis did not think that he was the only one with explanations of these things. He did, however, think that he was the only one who had a single metaphysical system according to which all of these things were explained on the very same metaphysical basis. The strategy provided a two-fold advantage to Lewis. First, only one general ontological revision was necessary in order to realize great philosophical gains; admit a plurality of worlds and all these things will be added unto you: modality, causation, properties, propositions, etc. Second, the strategy promises to provide a general legitimization of metaphysics and in the current intellectual and cultural environments in the West, the strongest available. Inference to the best explanation is thought to be a commonly-used mode of inference in science. If metaphysicians, and philosophers more generally, really do use this form of inference, then at least part of the Quinean hope of casting philosophy as continuous with science is realized, even if for a most unQuinean thesis. There is no small irony in one who is regarded by many as the most speculative of contemporary metaphysicians claiming argumentative kinship with our scientific colleagues.

---

[1] Lewis (1986b). He continued to endorse the argument, though not that it was sufficient to establish genuine modal realism rather than ersatzism about worlds, cf. Chihara (1998), p. 86 n. 22.

In what follows I will explore the prospects of treating metaphysical justifications as, ultimately, of a piece with those used in science. Though it is not uncontroversial that such inferences are properly used in science, some of the key features that count toward their legitimacy in science are distinctly lacking in their metaphysical counterparts. Legitimizing metaphysics still demands some fresh thinking.

## 2. THE STRUCTURE OF THE CASE FOR IBE

Instances of IBE take a theory's being the best explanation to count for something. To count for what, exactly? It is to count for adopting that theory. But theories, like children, can be adopted for a variety of reasons. There is a very long history of theories being adopted for reasons of truth and a reasonably long history of theories being adopted for reasons of use. Reasons are sometimes epistemic, sometimes pragmatic. IBE is proposed as a general kind of inference involving epistemic reasons; it is to provide us with reasons to adopt a theory as more likely to be true than its competitors and not merely as a tool useful for accomplishing some non-alethic goal.

Now, what constitutes being the best theory? If we are in search of the truth, then clearly the theory that is the best culmination of that search is a true theory. To be satisfied with a false theory is to stop too soon and to fail to reach the goal. If, however, IBE is to be a respectable form of inference *to* the truth of a theory, then it would be foolhardy for an advocate of IBE to make truth a condition *on* the best theory to which one infers by its use. To do so consigns all instances of IBE to begging the relevant question. Adopting a theory as true on the basis of IBE would, thus, depend on the prior acceptance of a premise stating that the theory is the best, which itself involves the theory being true.

This, of course, is not news to advocates of IBE. Conditions on the best theory must involve only conditions other than truth, but which are markers of truth. Markers of truth are supposed to be conditions like simplicity, coherence, informational content, and explanatory power. The latter two conditions must not be back doors by which a truth condition re-enters as a constitutive condition on the best theory, but advocates finesse this point with aplomb.[2] The danger, by no means trivial, is that the more secure the gate against truth entering as constitutive of the best theory, the more tenuous the link between reasons for thinking that by virtue of being the best explanation it is most likely to be true. Simplicity is a theoretical virtue, let us grant, but it is an instrumental virtue. Simple theories are easier to work with, so recognizing that a theory is simple

---

[2] See Lipton (2004).

provides one with a reason to work with the theory, but this is a conclusion of a piece of practical reasoning. Wondering why reality should be simple, is the familiar response at just this point. The closer we get to a Grand Unified Theory, the greater the practical virtues of our theory, but its greater probability over competitor theories requires argument.

Peter Lipton makes the case for linking the various conditions on what constitutes the best theory with likely truth on the basis of past instances of judging theories that meet those conditions to be the best and inferring them to be true. Theories so judged have with sufficient consistency turned out to be true theories, or at least theories that we now deem to be further along to the road to the truth than their relevant competitors that possessed less optimal balances of the theoretical virtues.[3] IBE is reliable on the basis of past instances of reliability from a theory's being best to its being true. Such an argument is an inductive justification of abductive arguments. Humean worries about induction aside, so long as the meta-argument is not, ultimately, an IBE, there is no systematic trouble regarding the style of argument. The problem is at the level of the premises of the meta-argument. If we do not keep firmly in mind the difference between epistemic and pragmatic grounds for adopting a theory, it is easy to miss the substantial question of whether we do and should take conditions on a best theory to be conditions the recognition of which should be taken to warrant adopting the theory as true.

The meta-argument, nevertheless, remains in danger of begging the question. If one thinks that the conditions on best theories are themselves instrumental virtues only and warrant only the instrumental adoption of the best theory, then the premises are either false—because our forebears did not themselves infer truth from virtue—or else they tell us of repeated mistakes by both us and our forebears whenever we did infer truth from virtue. In either case, the historical premises of the meta-argument do no useful work to bolster the case for IBE as a form of argument conferring epistemic warrant.

All is not lost for inferrers from best explanations, even if the case is the worst for such reasoners, i.e., if the historical data are insufficient to decide whether past uses of IBE have been inferences to the truth of the best theories or whether they were merely inferences to the practicality of using the best tool to hand at the time. We can now decide to rectify this indeterminacy for ourselves and our successors. We can engage in slightly more self-conscious analysis of current and future scientific reasoning and make explicit inquiries of those who engage in it. We can be sure that they are apprised of the distinction between adopting a theory for epistemic reasons and adopting it on pragmatic grounds. That will help us to settle what our attitudes are regarding theories that we now take to be the best. The sociological point, however, is the easy component. The harder component is the truth of the best theories which are the concern of the premises

---

[3] Lipton (2004), ch. 11.

of a new and improved meta-argument that will be useful in the future. If our overall, final, conclusion is to be that IBE is a reliable form of inference and the basis for that conclusion is to be that in a sufficiently great proportion of cases, constrained as necessary to yield reliability, when we recognize that a theory was best and we infer that it is true it turns out to be true, then we must have some means of determining that the theory inferred on the basis of IBE really is true. Furthermore, we must be able to package that basis in some argument form other than IBE.

It is at exactly this point that empiricist critics of IBE play their best card. Empiricists are not, generally, unhappy about inferring the truth of conclusions. There's more to intellectual life than getting experience to turn out the way one wants. There is no problem, for instance, in inferring that there is a mouse living with us even when we have not yet seen it. There is, further, no problem with inferring that there is a mouse living with us because the hypothesis that we have a resident rodent is the best explanation of the scratching we hear at night and of the remnants of food being dragged from their improper resting places the night before, etc. An empiricist can rest reasonably happily with this inference because we have a very well-developed theory of rodents and their behaviour and much of that is confirmed by a wealth of observation of both rodent anatomy and rodent behaviour. The range of cases for which IBE is deemed acceptable is precisely the range of those for which it is, ultimately and perhaps ideally, dispensable. It is acceptable to use IBE to conclude, perhaps tentatively, that we have a mouse and that we should probably do something about it. This is acceptable especially when, for reasons of inconvenience or even sheer laziness, it is not worth taking the extra effort to conduct a direct inspection of the premises, given the potentially great nuisance of ensuring, as we must, that were there any mice around we would inspect the premises when the mice were not away on holiday and that they could not escape when we began our inspection. Availing ourselves of IBE allows us to reach a reasonable conclusion that warrants further action. Those wishing to cause no direct harm to rodents can then resolve to clean the kitchen more thoroughly prior to retiring for the night; those with less concern for the mice and perhaps more concern for those on whom the now-hungry mice would be thrust might invest in mouse traps to eliminate the unwanted residents. When trappers end up catching a mouse, the theory deemed to be the best and inferred to be true because it was best is now confirmed by observation. We now have a rescue of the meta-argument used in support of IBE that is acceptable to the empiricist. IBE is perfectly acceptable, at least as a stop-gap measure, when the conclusion of an IBE concerns observable objects. IBE can be shown to be reliable, at least in principle, on an inductive basis but only when we have sufficiently many historical cases concerning the use of IBE to empirically-testable conclusions. Precisely because we do not need to use IBE to gain sufficient epistemic warrant for those conclusions can we take our independent access to those conclusions as confirming that IBE is, indeed, reliable. Were there no such independent access to the relevant sub-conclusions, then there could be no inductive justification for IBE.[4]

The advocacy of IBE is supposed to separate scientific realists and anti-realists. Realists maintain that when we use IBE to infer that the atom has a structure somewhat like our solar system, as did Bohr, the form of inference is no different from what all parties agree is acceptable in the case of the mouse. Reasoning now by analogy, the realist urges us to find IBE perfectly acceptable when we use it to draw conclusions about objects not amenable to observation.

Anti-realists, however, should urge caution, and they do. To recommend any form of inference on good grounds we need to have *some* grounds for recommending it. With deductive arguments, we appeal to *a priori* considerations. All the cajoling one might do to help a hapless undergraduate understand the rules of natural deduction aside, all such efforts end in the *a priori* insight that the rules guarantee the preservation of truth when moving from premise(s) to conclusion. The justification of inductive inferences, however, is not *a priori* in this way. It is only the testing of hypotheses arrived at on the basis of inductive inferences that exposes the limits of those argument forms. Concluding that a population contains n% Fs is warranted on the basis of the sample from that population containing n% Fs is not justified *a priori*. We have arrived at a complex body of conditions about the size, randomness, stratification, etc., of the sample that must be satisfied before the evidence of the sample is thought by trained experts to warrant the conclusion. Even this, of course, is overly simplified. Sophisticated statistical inferences recommend that we accept the conclusion as having a given probability and the conclusion itself should, ideally, be expressed in terms of a range of likely percentages. So, that a suitable sample of a population contains n% Fs warrants the conclusion that with probably $P_1$ the population has $n \pm m$% Fs. We have acquired this body of sophisticated inductive principles on the basis of testing inductive inferences; such testing demands that we have some manner of determining the truth or falsity of the conclusions of those simpler arguments other than through those very same inferences. Similar form aside, the empiricist is justified in complaining that when it comes to IBEs that involve conclusions about unobservable entities, we are no better off than we were prior to our inductive testing of simple statistical

---

[4] Thus the inductive defence of IBE shares a common structure with the Indirect Realist's defence of ordinary perceptual claims. In our case, the defence of IBE has this structure: T is deemed to be best amongst its competitors; at least most of the time when a theory has been deemed to be best amongst its competitors it is true; therefore, T is likely to be true. The paradigmatic Indirect Realist inference is: I seem to see external object, O, in front of me. Most of the time when I seem to see external objects, there are the relevant external objects; therefore, probably O is in front of me. In each case, the problem is this: by their own lights, how is the inferrer from best explanation and the indirect realist entitled to their second premise? The case is fatal to the indirect realist. It is not fatal to the inferrer from best explanations, so long as the domain over which IBE is applied is the domain of the observable.

arguments. On philosophical grounds alone the empiricist maintains that we have yet produced no non-question-begging reasons for thinking that IBE is reliable concerning unobservables. Nor, by the very nature of the case, could we have anything similar; the conclusions concern unobservables, thus prohibiting any parallel independent access.[5]

The philosophical case is bolstered by the work of cognitive scientists. There is a wealth of information about how inferential heuristics that seem natural to many are really quite unreliable. Simple statistical fallacies, anecdotal evidence taken to trump sophisticated scientific studies, contrary evidence discounted when it conflicts with cherished beliefs, and the like, show that quite often we engage in poor inductive inferences. There could be no proper role for the cognitive scientist when it comes to the evaluation of inference were there no way to break out of inferential circles and land ourselves into observational circumstances. To maintain that all cognitive activity is caught within inferential circles is to leave no room at all for the cognitive scientific enterprise; the cognitive scientist could never observe the (in)correctness of belief formed using the heuristics in a meaningful way were there no access to the facts of the case independent of those inferences. If other inferences are relied upon, then there would be no means of adjudicating between the deliverances of distinct inference rules without observation. Here I offer no argument against this very anti-scientific position. I do, however, note that the advocates of IBE are very poorly placed to advance their cause by denying the prospects of being in situations that should be characterized as observational rather than inferential.

There are other complaints registered against the use of IBE. 'Best' here is not intended to denote the ideal final theory at the end of some ideal process

---

[5] The appeal to other *a posteriori* justifications will be of no use here. The very same argument ushered for thinking that no sufficient case for the quite general reliability of IBE has been made will simply reappear concerning these argument forms that are to be brought in to the rescue. For the case to be warrant inducing, there must be a history of testing that the inferences have, in fact, taken us to the truth. If naïve and sophisticated forms of these new arguments must be distinguished and if their domains of application must be carefully circumscribed, so be it. The empiricist should still maintain that not only has there been no good case made for the general reliability of these argument forms, there could be no such case. The situation is not very unlike the meta-argument that had been popular among anti-theistic philosophers of religion: a series of weak theistic arguments cannot be cobbled together to constitute a strong theistic argument. This quick dismissal of cumulative case arguments was so facile as to gain currency beyond its merit, ignoring scientific arguments as it did. When a philosopher bothered to say more about the kinds of theistic arguments that were said to be defective and why the cobbling together of weak/invalid arguments of those sorts could not yield a strong/valid theistic argument, the case at least became respectable to merit serious scrutiny, as it has received lately. In the case before us, however, the parallel complaint is not of the simple, unpersuasive sort. Rather, the complaint is that there is no way of showing that the inferences are reliable when concerned with unobservables. The case given regarding IBE just replays itself about any other form used to reach a conclusion that one might have reached via IBE. If we have no reason to think that any of the mutually-supporting family of arguments is at all reliable in a given domain, then using several of them provides no warrant for the others.

of empirical investigation. If it were, there *could* be no inductive case for thinking that IBE is reliable, because at no time in the past have we possessed the best theory or, only marginally better, if we did we never knew that it was the ideal final theory. So, only by accident have we ever inferred the truth of the best theory. All the other times have been, at best, cases when we were deceived into thinking that we possessed the best theory. For this reason, 'best' is to denote merely the best, if such there be, of our current crop of theories that purport to explain some phenomena. We can grant that if the lot is very poor indeed, then being the best of that lot is insufficient to warrant adopting the best theory as true. None of the prospects is even remotely up to the job in that case. Here, again, is the problem. If we are ever to hold with good reason that our best explanation is not merely the best of a very bad lot, then there must be some basis for linking the satisfaction of the theoretical virtues with a sufficient probability of being true. The empiricist's case is strong once again. In the absence of *a priori* justifications, we are left with inductive justifications which will demand that we can recognize that the conclusions of at least some inferences are true to enable us to determine when and where these forms of inference are reliable. Absent any such basis, there is literally no warrant for concluding that our best explanations are anything but the best of a bad lot. Even if the best explanation counts as excellent on the front of satisfying the relevant theoretical virtues, without independent access to the facts of the case on individual applications of IBE, we have no warrant for thinking that excellent explanations thereby have their likelihood raised at all.

## 3. THE CASE FOR GMR

Our interest in IBE is not because of its apparent centrality in the case for realist commitments to unobservables. Our interest is in the relevance to the prospects of engaging in metaphysics. The form of modal inference is unexceptional, but it has no significance for those who worry that metaphysics is an ill-conceived enterprise. Their worry is that there is something defective in the enterprise we call 'metaphysics'. According to the logical positivists and the Wittgenstein of the *Tractatus*, that defect was that we mistake nonsense for sense. Each proposed a general theory of meaning according to which statements that could not be verified, or those that did not vary truth value over some range of possibilities, failed to express genuine propositions.

The positivist and the Tractarian case against metaphysics is quite sweeping and threatens to undermine much of the philosophical enterprise as many of us know it, since metaphysicians are not the only philosophers who concern themselves with what cannot be observed. Would that ethical, meta-ethical, epistemological, aesthetic, and religious claims could be sorted out as easily as scientific claims can be, even though the latter are often not so easily sorted. The case just put forth for doubting that IBE has a warrant-inducing character when concerning unobservables has a somewhat more limited application than the positivists' and Tractarian cases. The limit arises because the allegation does not attach itself to the propositions to which one infers via IBE. So far as I have presented the case, the empiricist may have no qualms about unverifiable or unfalsifiable propositions just because they are unverifiable or unfalsifiable. Humean empiricists wished to distinguish propositions concerning relations of ideas from those concerning matters of fact precisely so that they could find space for genuine propositions that are not verifiable in any ordinary sense. The empiricist case against the use of IBE when unobservables are concerned applies only to the use of the inference when concerned with that domain of objects. It is a complaint that such an argument form cannot be shown to be reliable over that domain combined with the thesis that argument forms that are not *a priori* justified demand empirically-based warrant.

The empiricist's concerns, then, do not apply even to metaphysicians generally, much less to the entire philosophical enterprise. The concerns mooted are much more limited and they apply only to philosophers who wish to justify their philosophical claims with IBE-style arguments. They are, then, prey to the empiricist considerations against the scientific realists' use of IBE, for their conclusions are no more amenable to observation than are the contentious claims made by the realist about neutrinos.

It is a sign of professional weakness that in most areas of philosophy, at least among those who claim the label 'analytic', little meta-philosophical work has been done to make quite explicit the nature of our enterprise and what conditions need to be satisfied for us to have successfully made the case for a philosophical conclusion.[6] Most of us know that the heady days of conceptual analysis have passed, but there is not much said regarding what else we might be up to when philosophers do what philosophers do.[7] Surely many have had the discomfort of answering an honest inquirer who asks what it is we philosophers do. It's not conceptual analysis; it's not the recollection of our clear sight of the Forms prior to our fall to Earth; it's not the end result of using our highly trained rational intuitions of *a priori* truth, it's not empirical psychology. Mostly we have quite good ideas about what it is we don't do, but not many ideas about what it is we do. We have mostly fallen into the chicken sexing approach to philosophy. "I can't really explain what it is that I do, nor how I manage to do it, nor how we

---

[6] For a more detailed discussion of related issues, see Williamson (2006b).
[7] The most notable exception is Frank Jackson; see Jackson (1998).

manage to recognize those who are better and those who are worse at doing it. If, however, you watch us do it enough, you will learn what it is that we do, you will learn how to do it, and you will better discern the experts." That we have somewhat more than this to say to people in the context of discussions about the nature of reasoning goes some way to explain why we are less troubled than perhaps we should be by the difficulty many have in saying what it is we do.

As in many ways, David Lewis was a notable exception on this count. He was quite explicit that his metaphysical claims were to be justified in a way not unlike scientific claims. Lewis was a Quinean in his preference for things extensional as well as in his preference to see philosophy as continuous with science. His flirtations with mathematical platonism arose both out of his reluctance to tell mathematicians that, really, they do not know what they are talking about, and out of his attraction to the Quine–Putnam Indispensability Argument. According to this argument ontological commitments to mathematical objects such as numbers and sets are warranted because reference to such entities is indispensable to our best scientific theories. Lewis saw continuity with science not merely there, but also in the kind of argument that can be used to warrant metaphysical theories. In particular, IBE can be used to warrant metaphysical theories. It is precisely in finding Genuine Modal Realism (GMR) to be a simple, coherent, systematic, and extremely powerful metaphysics that leads Lewis to conclude that it has a greater claim on our assent than any competitors. Most of the competitors are one-trick ponies anyway while Lewis's is a robust jack-of-all-trades. There are non-reductive accounts of modal discourse, actualist theories of causation, theories of properties, and theories of propositions. Only those who propose alternatives to GMR that are somewhat parasitic upon its structure, as are fictionalist accounts of possible worlds, promise as much integration and explanatory power. Those who utilize possible worlds but who reverse the order of explanation as in ersatzist accounts of worlds, lose some elegance and comprehension in the process.[8]

---

[8] Even though Lewis presents his case for GMR as an instance of IBE, one might strengthen this a bit and make the case for GMR to be an indispensability argument. Certainly, with respect to the semantics of modal discourse, Lewis thinks that one important feature possessed by his account of the semantics for modal discourse is that a possible worlds-based meta-language has greater expressive power than those meta-languages that involve primitive modality. He can say things that the modalist cannot say and these things left unsayable by the modalist are things we can, indeed, say or at least understand. This looks like the beginnings of an indispensability argument. GMR is warranted because the quantification over Lewis-style possible worlds is indispensable to an adequate semantics for modal discourse. Of course, it is open to someone to show that such quantification is not indispensable because the things that Lewis thinks are sayable really are not; they are mere nonsense. Alternatively, the modalist might produce a more satisfactory account of the propositions that seemed to give quantification over worlds its foothold. Lewis's winning this particular dispute would be sufficient to cast the case for GMR as an indispensability argument. When we consider a sufficiently big philosophical picture, we would see that we cannot do without possible worlds. If the case for the semantics of modal discourse

The clear and devastating implication for Lewis's use of some version of IBE is that the empiricist's complaint against the scientific realist resurfaces with a vengeance. We know that non-deductive arguments have limited ranges of reliability. Furthermore, we determine the ranges of reliability and the conditions of their reliability only by way of empirical means, requiring as it does an independent access to the facts of the supporting cases. This prevents IBE and other inductive forms having any grounds within the desired domain of application: the unobservable. This is exactly the situation with any use of IBE to provide support for GMR. This verdict is not merely the result of those with empiricist leanings screwing up their faces and complaining that the modal realist offends empiricist scruples. That offence does occur, but the case to be answered is stronger and more motivated than that. The charge is that arguments, to be taken as reliable, must receive justification on either *a priori* or *a posteriori* grounds. No *a priori* justification looks to be forthcoming for IBE and the only *a posteriori* justification depends on IBE being applied to domains concerning observables. That there is an analogy between uses concerning observables and uses concerning unobservables is an inadequate answer to the empiricist's complaint. There is an analogy between any proper use of a non-deductive argument form and a demonstrably improper use of that form. Given that we know that many non-deductive argument forms are not universally reliable, the burden really is on one who maintains that the method used in a given context is reliable in that context and under those conditions of application. This is precisely what the Lewis-style modal realist cannot provide for any use of IBE to support GMR. And, of course, the case is more general, applying as it does to any use of IBE to support philosophical claims not restricted to the observable. It is not only the metaphysician who is discomfited by this result. The metaphysical project demands that we provide some other way of understanding the justifications we produce for the characteristic claims made by those who engage in that project.

## 4. PIECEMEAL ENGAGEMENT

While the previous sections provide significant difficulties for the use of IBE as the chief form of defence for metaphysical theories, it is worth pursuing the case at the level of the details, since the grand-scale inductive case for using IBE depends on small-scale details about the truth of theories inferred on the basis of IBE. The first detail in favour of Lewis's defence of GMR is that it does not depend on GMR being the best theory in every domain over which it is to

---

can be repeated for causation, or properties, or propositions, etc., so much the better. I put this construal of the argument to one side since it receives fuller treatment in Bueno and Shalkowski (2004).

be genuinely explanatory. Indeed, a theory might be best overall, even though it loses to some competitor or other each individual case. The same applies to the possession of the individual theoretical virtues. So, GMR might be bested by another theory when it comes to the semantics for modal discourse and it might be bested by a second regarding causation, by a third when it comes to properties, and by a fourth on propositions. Nevertheless, GMR might be judged Best in the Show because of its account of all of these domains taken as a package, while other theories have no obvious ability to carry their respective metaphysical explanation in one domain into others. Likewise, other theories might be simpler, or more coherent with prior judgements, but GMR might score sufficiently well on the range of virtues to, once again, come out Best in the Show.

In order for the details of the case to be made, it must be that GMR produces a sufficiently plausible account of the things metaphysicians find in need of explanation. It must be that for each proposed explanation in a given domain there is sufficient discipline on what counts as a good explanation of the data for us to call the winners in each case. The grand IBE that a supporter of GMR wants to use depends on some shared standards regarding the data and the form of proper explanations, otherwise the resulting IBE could be no more than preaching to the modal realist choir. That there are obstacles is brought out by considering a particular case.

One of the virtues that is alleged to accrue to Lewis's GMR is that it provides us with an account of propositions. On his view, propositions are properties. Properties, according to Lewis, are sets of individuals, normally construed as entities like Socrates and Man O' War as well as substances like snow and kinds like donkeys. Properties are sets of individuals, many of which we care not one whit about, but others we do. One set of individuals contains exactly the right individuals to be the set of snub-nosed philosophers and contains our very own Socrates. Another set contains all and only the Triple Crown Winners and includes our very own Man O' War. Propositions turn out to be properties that are instantiated only by entire worlds.[9] Intuitively, and to state the idea exactly backwards, the relevant set is the set of all worlds in which the relevant proposition is true. So, the proposition expressed by normal speakers of English via the sentence 'Snow is white' is the set of all white snow worlds. The propositions expressed by 'Donkeys talk' is the set of all talking donkey worlds.

So, GMR provides us with a story to tell about propositions. There are some obvious conveniences. First, once we have the story about properties in place and we have the brainwave that there could be properties that are possessed only by entire worlds, and we link this brainwave with one way of thinking about truth, i.e., that it is the world that makes a truth bearer true or false, then we can see the nature of the truth bearer as a special kind of property: a property of worlds.

---

[9] Lewis (1986b), p. 53.

It is tempting to say that once the ontology of GMR has been granted and the virtues of the GMR story in the domain of properties are acknowledged, then it is no great ask to adopt this account of propositions. Tempting though this is, it is against the spirit of the IBE case for GMR. That case requires that we appreciate the adequacy of the totality of explanations offered by GMR over some appropriate range of data and, furthermore, appreciate that this adequacy surpasses that of all competitors. Only then do we make the inference to GMR and take on the attending ontological commitments. This subtle, but important, point must be kept in mind when looking at the individual piecemeal issues. For unless we have some handle on how to judge these issues in the small, we have no basis for making assessment in the large.

As is typical with theories, while there are conveniences, there are also inconveniences in this theory. Unqualifiedly necessary propositions get the same set of worlds—the entire domain of the GMR theory. Unqualifiedly impossible propositions get the same set of worlds—the null set of that same domain. These, as should be expected, are simply special instances of the general case. Universally-instantiated properties are the universal GMR set of individuals; necessarily co-extensive properties collapse into one, since each is the same set of individuals; impossibly-instantiated properties are the null set of GMR individuals. Here is the first cost to be reckoned for the GMR account of propositions: it surely looks like we are not merely speaking redundancies when we maintain that there are multiple necessarily true propositions and multiple necessarily false propositions. This should not be surprising, since we think that we are not proving redundancies when we prove that the sum of the internal angles in Euclidean triangles is $180°$ and then go on to prove that when two line segments intersect on a Euclidean plane opposite angles are equal. One concerns the sum of three angles, the other the comparison of two. No amount of conceptual unpacking promises to bring the enlightenment that these propositions are not two but one. The GMR account of the nature of propositions shows its first infelicity.

There are others. When we are doing the piecemeal work, we assume that we have some handle on the topic under discussion. We assume that when philosophers talk about propositions we know that they are not talking about the kinds of things that when loaded into a box change the reading on the scale on which the box rests. We assume that we speak an analogy when we speak of constructing a new compound proposition out of two simpler propositions. We know it is an analogy because construction is normally a physical activity, but even if we were reluctant to give the grubby priority over the Platonic, we know that this is at best analogical language or, worse, just misleading. Those who believe in things like proposition believe them to be entities of a certain sort. They are often said to be abstract entities, perhaps because they stand in no causal relations. This abstractness proscribes us from taking seriously any talk of construction, even by way of mental activities. Propositions are also said to be eternal and immutable things. If eternal, then we poor temporal beings cannot manage to bring them into existence with our feeble attempts at creation and if immutable, they cannot be brought into any new relations with each other. That much of what we know about propositions does not look troublesome for GMR.

What does generate some difficulty, however, is that propositions are the contents of our beliefs and the bearers of truth. The GMR story looks like it just simply says the wrong kind of thing in this connection. Regardless of how the complications go to finesse the apparent structure of propositions in terms of things comprising (perhaps among other things) sets of worlds, propositions are still fundamentally just sets of worlds, even if sets with bells on. Sets, like Socrates and Man O' War, can be the objects of our beliefs but they cannot be the content of our beliefs. Sets themselves possess no truth values, while the entire raison d'être of propositions is to be the kind of thing that bears truth value, sometimes available for discovery.[10]

Here we would be well served were we possessed of a useful prolegomenon for our metaphysical research. Such a prolegomenon would impose some disciple on the structure of a solution to the problem of the nature of propositions. The worry here is not an unfamiliar one. Theory proposals are the proverbial dime a dozen. Proposing a theory of propositions is dead easy. Go ahead. Try it. All could easily outdo the White Queen and propose a few dozen prior to breakfast. It is not worth your bleary-eyed bother, though, because there is so little point unless the proposals brought with them some decent chance of surviving scrutiny. The odds are very great that what we propose will not survive that scrutiny, which explains why even philosophers obsessed with metaphysical concerns busy themselves with other things prior to breakfast.

It is not uncommon for those discussing GMR to observe that one philosopher's modus ponens is another's modus tollens. In other contexts, this is perfectly fair. When different people confront an argument some will find the premises overwhelmingly warranted and others will not. Some will find the conclusion beyond the pale of any rational belief; others not. The specifics of one's epistemic situation guide the proper reaction. If the truth of the premises is far more plausible than the falsehood of the conclusion, use modus ponens and adopt the conclusion. If the falsehood of the conclusion seems far more likely than the truth of all the premises, use modus tollens and reject a premise.

Here, however, the observation is distracting. True, were one already in a position to find the ontology of GMR congenial and also to find that it really does provide sufficiently good explanations of a range of other objects or phenomena, then the modus ponens move would be warranted. If you have already paid the ontological cost—whether willing or not, whether the cost was high or

---

[10] The point about bearing truth was first made by Alvin Plantinga in Plantinga (1987), p. 207.

not—then there is little if any additional cost to taking this GMR story to be the story about propositions. You have already paid for the meal; you might as well now eat it.

The IBE strategy for GMR, though, prevents us from being in this situation. I do not pay the price for the ontology until I am already convinced that the piecemeal stories it provides are individually sufficiently good to constitute GMR being the best explanation. Then I adopt the entire ball of wax, not just the ontology, but the attending stories about modal discourse, causation, properties, and propositions. If the implausibilities are sufficiently great for the piecemeal stories, we never arrive at a state where the modus ponens option is the right one. If at each stage we find the GMR story implausible, either because the ontology itself seems to be made out of whole cloth or because the piecemeal stories simply offend against what we know about the piecemeal data, then we are forever in the position of finding each piecemeal story implausible and using modus tollens to reject GMR.

The modus ponens/modus tollens issue does arise for the verdicts we render in each of the piecemeal cases as well, though. For which should we opt: given that propositions are sets, it turns out that some sets bear truth values or given that sets do not bear truth value, propositions are not sets? Of which are we entitled to be more sure? The issue must be one of epistemic entitlement since if we are always in good intellectual conscience permitted to use the modus ponens route and infer from theory to previously implausible consequence, then we are left with no ability to assess theories; our constraints have left us. Even if we grant that there is more in heaven and earth than dreamt by philosophers or physicists, intellectual enterprises are not "no holds barred" affairs.

The problem is how to proceed without begging questions against one another. The GMR-ist can certainly hold ground and insist that even at the level of specific cases the story is right and that we have yet another example of how reality is more surprising than we thought; it does turn out that some sets are true and some are false. More than two can play this game and we can propose theories that someone like Lewis would find implausible because of their fantastic consequences, for a kind of role reversal. If there is no more to be said in the specific cases, we just cannot proceed. The more often and the more significantly we must say that prior to the development of the theory in question we really did not understand the thing or phenomena investigated, the more we must face scepticism. We were pretty sure that propositions bore truth values and that sets did not. If these are things we do not know about these objects, should we not be even less sure of the theory itself? If we knew so little about sets, propositions, and truth bearing that we were wrong about sets not bearing truth, is there really anything we know about these objects and that relation?

The moral derived about IBE and non-deductive arguments generally applies here as well. So long as we are trapped in the domain of inference alone, we have no way whatsoever of determining when the arguments we use are reliable.

We have no idea whether we have exceeded their domains of applicability. If we do not know this, then not only do we know that there is the prospect of error forced upon us by the abductive argument form, but there is the added prospect that we are simply barking up the wrong tree, building castles in the air, or in the case of metaphysics, spinning theories that have no bearing at all on reality. We have no reason to think that we have not simply re-defined the problem at hand in a way that fits the theory, rather than adopting a theory that solves a problem by illuminating the facts of the case. The six blind men and the elephant, each arriving at conclusions about their subject quite different from the others, at least had some useful data that could act as a check upon theory development. This is just what we do not have regarding GMR supported by IBE.

## 5. METAPHYSICAL PROJECTS

The first moral to be drawn is that there is little hope to be found in the use of IBE to settle metaphysical questions. There is no reason to think that it is reliable in the cases for which metaphysicians might wish to use it. There is no *a priori* ground for thinking IBE is reliable in any case; truth is not among the criteria of best theories so that we can discern the markers of truth from truth; we are trying to infer the truth of the theory, not infer from it. We are, then, left with pragmatic standards and there is no *a priori* connection between ease of use and truth. *A posteriori* justifications demand that we have some access to the facts of the case in the relevant domain so that we have some good reason to think that our inferences are reliable over the domain. So, the metaphysician must face some cold, hard realities. Continuity with the sciences is not the path to legitimacy nor the means by which we can resolve our disagreements. That was a procedural blind alley down which Lewis led us. If not some variation on IBE, what then?

There is always the Jacksonian route. Those of us that engage Lewis can return to our analytic heritage and construe philosophical questions as, ultimately, about conceptual analysis. The difficulty, well known in the era after *Naming and Necessity*, is that our questions and our answers seem to be an admixture of *a priori* and *a posteriori* issues. We are, again, in a state where less discipline is imposed on our philosophical work than would be useful. If the conceptual is limited to the content of our understanding of concepts prior to the activity of philosophical analysis, then there is always the risk of indeterminacy. Our questions are just not the questions of our non-philosophical brethren, so it is no surprise if their handling of concepts prior to confronting explicit philosophical issues is insufficient to settle our questions. The same is true for most philosophers.

There are other options. We can loosen the constraint that the content of concepts of which we are masters is transparent to us. Externalist accounts of meaning do this to some extent. There may be well-disciplined ways of arriving at the conclusion that not all meaning is in the head and that in some cases of linguistic knowledge—knowledge of what we ourselves mean—we must respect our elders/superiors/etc. It had better be, though, that the analysis by which we come to this conclusion does not depend on external content at every stage. It can't be experts all the way down. At some point we must stop at what's in the head or at innocent enough refinements thereof. On this count, semantics and epistemology merge. Externalist theories of warrant may have a role to play in our accounts of knowledge, but they cannot be the whole story. At least when we engage in philosophy, we need some internally-accessible insight into warrant. Theorizing depends on it.

Conceptual analysis, however it is construed, has the advantage over IBE arguments because it relies upon the *a priori*. Wholly internalist accounts of meaning and analysis will rely on the *a priori* alone with the rejection of substantive metaphysics. Externalist account of meaning and analysis permit substantive metaphysics. The arguments of previous sections do not touch inferences from conceptual content. Perhaps Lewis should have stuck with his paraphrastic argument. This advantage accrues to any sufficiently rich knowledge that is *a priori*, whether packed into conceptual content or not, so the rationalists can take heart. We are back to the classic divide regarding philosophy: empiricism vs. rationalism, conceptual analysis vs. substantial metaphysics.

Three matters demand the attention of serious metaphysicians. The first is the proper space to be given to explanation in metaphysics. Disputes over the Principle of Sufficient Reason and whether the contingent physical universe are acceptable stopping places for explanation are disputes over the proper stopping place for explanation. Another that bears on the acceptability of GMR is whether modal metaphysics is acceptable or does all modality require a categorical basis? An answer here spills over to whether there are irreducible counterfactuals of freedom, whether phenomenalism is an acceptable account of material being, and whether modalism is preferable to any reductive theory. In all cases, answers depend on the requirements of a proper explanation and whether metaphysics is about giving explanations.

Another matter that requires attention is the matter of resolving differences. Many who reject Lewis's GMR ontology express their rejection in terms of the bloatedness of the ontology, as though its sheer size were the problem. Many of them, though, are mathematical platonists happy with the Cantorian hierarchy of sets; many are realists about universals and are content with as many of these as may be necessary, sometimes leaving it up to the state of future inquiry to determine the nature and number of the genuine universals. It is not, then, the size of the ontology that troubled Lewis's critics; it was that there was, by the lights of the advocate of GMR, no good epistemic access to the existence and the content of the postulated worlds. The concerns seem not to have been articulated well or often but the underlying worry should have been that there was too much theory upon which our access depends. One need not be an empiricist to be worried that the problem with IBE in metaphysics is that the access to any special objects is just through the theory that postulates the objects. This is closely related to the concern sometimes expressed about our access to the sub-atomic: our access to the objects is so dependent on the theory that says that there are such objects with various characteristics, that the observations hardly count as non-question-begging data points in favour of the theory. Structural realists are realists about structure precisely because they think this theory-dependence of access prohibits warranted realism about the objects.

In the case of modal metaphysics, even in the absence of a grand account of the constraints on well-behaved metaphysical inquiry, some progress could be made were there some suitable observability. Once some *a priori* principles are in hand, we can determine that water is $H_2O$ because we have ways of determining that we have water without doing electrolysis and we can know that we have containers of oxygen and hydrogen without combining them to obtain water. Likewise with lightning and discharges of static electricity. So, were there some access to Lewis's worlds, the modalist might well admit that modality is reducible upon having reasonable beliefs about the number and nature of worlds independently of GMR. That our only access to the number and nature of the worlds is through the modal judgements we make is reason for the modalist to think that reification is done for no good reason. The nominalist might find the realist about universals reifying unnecessarily for the same reason. The chair is red. On that we all agree. That it is red because it instantiates the universal of Redness looks fishy. Access to the facts spoken about on one side of the account is gained only *via* what is unexceptional. An attribute is turned into an object, which would be fine were we able to sometimes peek at the objects without recourse to the attributes. Those without a reifying disposition cannot see the point of the reification. Those with the disposition insist that something is missing without the reification—a demanded explanation.

All of this assumes that the data to be explained are the facts about modality, the grounding of the modal truths. A third subject that requires attention, though, regards the scope of the data to be explained. If the primary data are the ways in which we modalize, then no theory that aspires to provide the truth conditions for modal claims thereby has any advantage over a theory that yields no such truth conditions. Error theories accompanied by the right kind of psychological explanation may explain modalizing at least as well as modalist or possible worlds theories. If the data are the modal truths, then error theories are at a distinct disadvantage, immediately disqualified as eligible theories from the outset.

Metaphysics need not be Kantian, but perhaps it needs to be kantian. A bifur-cation between the phenomenal and noumenal realms may not be necessary; fixed categories of thought and perception may not be necessary. The meta-physician needs an account of when something like transcendental arguments are appropriate, though. With a good theory of what demands explanation, the proper form of explanation, as well as the data to be explained, we would be in a position to discern when we should pursue the necessary preconditions of some observables or some intellectual activity like modalizing and when we should not. Without this kantian basis, metaphysics looks like a project in need of some discipline. Such a kantian framework would not rehabilitate IBE for metaphysics. It would render it unnecessary, returning to metaphysics a basis for theory construction without the need for observational access.

# 10

# Modal Commitments

## *John Divers*

In this paper, my aim is to promote interest in an issue which I take to be both badly neglected and crucial to the proper configuration of our modal philosophy: the issue is that of the function of modal judgment. In §1, I expand upon what it is that we lack in lacking a serious account of the function of modal judgment. In §2, I consider, and reject, various attempts to resist the demand for an account of the function of modal judgment. In §3, I propose a functional constraint which allocates to one's conception of the function of modal judgment a crucial role in constraining the accumulation of philosophically substantial commitments in theorizing about modality. In §4, I attempt to pinpoint precisely the different sources of the different kinds of commitment that are accumulated in modal theorizing. In §5, I attempt to illustrate, in the case of de dicto necessity, the potentially radical impact of implementing the functional constraint in light of this awareness of the precise sources of the modal theorist's commitments.

## 1. THE LACUNA

The major theme of this paper is that our philosophical understanding of modality is disastrously inhibited by our lack of any remotely developed account of the function of modal judgment. Indeed, I take it that we are doubly inhibited in lacking an account of the function of modal judgment. First, because the question of function is an intrinsically important question that any comprehensive theory of modality must answer satisfactorily. Secondly, because an account of the function of modal judgment ought to serve as a major constraint, if not the primary constraint, on the accumulation of substantial commitments—metaphysical (ontological), epistemological, semantic (conceptual), etc.—in modal philosophy. In unqualified form, the functional constraint to be proposed is as follows: that a theory of modality ought to be no more substantial than is required in order to account for the body of modal assertions that we have to make in order to achieve whatever it is that our modalizing achieves for us.

In this section, I try to indicate what I take the lacuna in the modal case to consist in. To that end, I begin by presenting some formative questions about our modalizing. I will then indicate the kinds of answer that are available to the question of function in the cases of various other discourses that attract philosophical interest.

## 1.1  Some Formative Questions

It is a matter of fact that our philosophical and non-philosophical talk is saturated with modalizing: talk of necessity, contingency, possibility, and impossibility in all its guises (can, cannot, must, must not, might, might not, could, could not); talk of the essential and the accidental; talk of potential and ability; talk of what counterfactually would or might have been the case; even talk of what is necessary but might not have been; and talk of what might have been possible but isn't. If this modalizing is worth doing then—no doubt—it's worth doing well, and—no doubt—it is a practice of which we (non-quietist) philosophers should strive to produce an ontological, epistemological, conceptual, inferential, and semantic account. But the antecedent claim is not trivial. In what sense, exactly, is modalizing worth doing? And the consequent also merits scrutiny. What is it to modalize well rather than badly? Hereby we fall upon a cluster of formative questions that circumscribe the issue of the function, purpose, or role of modal judgment.[1]

Which aspects of our practical or intellectual conduct are facilitated by our modalizing, and how so? Does our modalizing facilitate by allowing us to do more efficiently what we could do otherwise (but less efficiently) or by being indispensable in some stronger sense? If a creature knew all those facts about the actual world which could be stated in non-modal terms, would she have any use for modal judgment?[2] Could we contrive a *schmodalizer*—a creature that we train to join in our community and its modal language-games undetected, despite its being equipped initially with only non-modal concepts and non-modal beliefs? If I have the faculty that allows me to detect the facts about (say) unactualized possibility and you lack that faculty, how, if at all, will your commerce with the actual world go better than mine? Or how would things go for you if you were cautious in that you systematically abstained from making judgments of necessity and impossibility?[3] Does *all* of our modalizing have an identifiable purpose, or is the work done only by a special part of the discourse with the remainder—even if perfectly meaningful—functionally epiphenomenal or redundant? When we

---

[1] That many of these questions will be posed in modal terms is a potential distraction, but one which (I hope) can be put aside on the promise that this point will be addressed in §2.1.

[2] This question is derived from Spinoza's discussion in and around Proposition XXXIII of Book I of his *The Ethics*. See Spinoza (1677), pp. 106–7.

[3] This question is derived from Wright (1980), ch. 23.

do give an account of why we go in for certain kinds of modal judgment, which other kinds of modal judgment are encompassed in that account and which stand in need of an independent account?

## 1.2 Comparitors

At least some of these formative questions are answerable for other discourses and practices that capture philosophical attention. For in many, if not all, such cases we do have a decent account of function and answers to the (analogous) formative questions proceed from that account. Here are some examples.

We have all sorts of interests in being able to infer conclusions about the concrete world from premises about the concrete world. Many such inferences are facilitated by the introduction and application of the special discourse of *mathematics*—both in everyday dealings with common objects and in the realm of the sciences. It is, of course, a moot point whether mathematics is, in some sense, absolutely indispensable in this respect. But what no one doubts is that the practice of applied mathematics *at the very least* makes more economical, convenient, and practically manageable our inferential practices. Exactly how and why mathematics improves our lot in this respect is, of course, philosophically controversial.[4] But that mathematics has (at least) this function is not controversial.

We have a special sort of interest in being able to infer conclusions about the observable part of the concrete world from premises about the observable part of the concrete world. An important sub-class of these inferences, those that fall within the realm of certain sciences, are facilitated by the introduction of discourse about unobservable, *microphysical* things. In this case, the idea that the special discourse is dispensable, even "in principle", has gone out of fashion. But, in any event, the conviction is universally shared that our inferences about the observable part of the world are facilitated when supported by talk of underlying, unobservable, microphysical parts of the world. Exactly how and why microphysical theorizing improves our inferential lot is, of course, philosophically controversial.[5] But that microphysical theorizing has (at least) this function is not controversial.

We have a special sort of interest in being able to infer conclusions about the behaviour of agents in the world from premises about their behaviour. An important sub-class of those inferences, those that fall within the realm of folk psychology, are facilitated by the ascription of *propositional-attitudes*. In this case, the idea that the discourse is ultimately dispensable does have its advocates. But again there is a thesis of purpose or utility that no one disputes, and that is that our present and actual practices of behaviour prediction—in our present and actual state of knowledge—would deteriorate significantly, if

---

[4] For one detailed account, see Field (1980, 1989).
[5] For one detailed account of this function, see van Fraassen (1980).

not fall apart altogether, were they to proceed without talk of belief, desire, and intention. That point stands even though it may be philosophically controversial exactly how, and why, propositional-attitude ascription improves our predictive lot.[6]

We have a special sort of interest in being able to influence the attitudes and practical conduct of others. One important way in which we seek to do so, and succeed in doing so, is by using moral discourse—slightly more controversially, by adducing what are, prima facie, moral reasons. Again, it may be moot whether our moralizing provides a unique or indispensable means of influencing the conduct of others. But that (at least some) moral talk actually plays this role, and could not easily be supplanted in that role by clearly non-moral talk, is not in serious doubt. Exactly how and why moral talk is especially efficacious in the influence of conduct is, of course, philosophically controversial: but that it has some such role is far less controversial.[7]

Thus, in the cases presented as examples—mathematics, the microphysical, propositional attitudes, and the moral—we have a conception of some important function that the discourse and practice serves in our practical and intellectual lives. Of course, one could say more in many of these cases. Perhaps in the moral case, for example, only a much richer and heterogeneous account of function will do—one that incorporates separate accounts of the functions of each of the following: the ascription of thin evaluative concepts; the ascription of thick evaluative concepts; the ascription of obligations and permissions (responsibilities and rights); the ascriptions of moral character traits; the moral evaluation of actions, etc. Perhaps in the mathematical case, for another example, we have one story to tell about the function of arithmetical discourse (talk of natural numbers) but must tell another story about the function of analysis (talk of real numbers)—and perhaps we may have to appeal to deep but contingent facts of the world in doing so. But these observations help rather than hinder the present point. For if there is much more to say, and more to understand, about function in the cases that we have considered, all the better then for the contrast between this embarrassment of riches and the (presently alleged) poverty of our account of function for the modal case.

I do not doubt that we could also make similar points about the function of many other philosophically interesting discourses.[8] So what is there to say, and what do we understand, about the matter of the function of modal judgment?

---

[6] For more detailed accounts of this function see e.g. Fodor (1987) and Dennett (1981).

[7] For accounts of this function see e.g. Mackie (1977) and Blackburn (1998).

[8] It would be easy to identify comparable and important functions that are served by various other discourses and (or) to point towards specific philosophical accounts of how the functions in question are discharged—talk of the spatial, of the temporal, of colour, of sensations, of truth, and of meaning, etc.

## 1.3 Some Proto-Thoughts about the Modal Case

It is a striking fact that the question of the function of modal judgment has been marginalized in contemporary modal philosophy. Going back some decades now, the most widely influential, and widely cited, works of modal philosophy have almost nothing explicitly, and barely more implicitly, to say about the question of function.[9] In fact, the philosophers who have attempted to engage with the question of function tend to be those who have engaged—either as champions or critics—directly with Quine on the point or (otherwise) with non-cognitivism about the modal.[10] But we can collect from that source, and from some other thoughts that are or have been in the air, various proto-suggestions about the function of various kinds of modal judgment.

The function of modal judgment may be thought to "have something to do with": the need to take, and subsequently express, a certain kind of epistemic attitude (usually some kind of super-confidence) to the truth of certain propositions or to the reliability of certain inferences (necessity); the need to recognize, and subsequently to mark, a special kind of limit to our thinking—especially, our conceivings or imaginings (impossibility); the need to limit the range of relevant options in planning or evaluating courses of practical conduct, or the need to distinguish behaviour that is blameworthy or praiseworthy (possibility); the need to distinguish cases in which certain moral-psychological states, such as guilt and regret, are merited, or the need to distinguish those true generalizations about the past which are projectable into the future (counterfactuals). There are also further, non-instrumental, and quasi-transcendental thoughts about the function, or rather the role or status, of modal judgment. Among such thoughts are that modal judgments (facts,

---

[9] Thus consider, for example, Kripke (1972), Plantinga (1974), Stalnaker (1976), Lewis (1973b, 1986b), Armstrong (1989), and Rosen (1990). It is difficult to resist speculating that the lack of concern with the function of modal judgment is not unconnected to the desire, common to these philosophers, to do their modalizing as though—but maybe not just as though—it were a matter of reporting facts about a realm of special modal objects (viz. possible worlds). When this picture is construed realistically, it naturally inspires various sorts of worry about how modal judgment, so understood, should have any bearing on our attitudes to, or engagement with, the actual world. See e.g. Blackburn (1984, pp. 213–17; 1986; 1993, pp. 73–4).

[10] In Quine, scepticism about the function of modal judgment is intertwined with a more general scepticism about the modal and with other more general themes. For salient primary sources see e.g. the revised versions of 'Reference of Modality' (Quine 1961, pp. 139–59) and of 'Three Grades of Modal Involvement' (Quine 1976, pp. 158–76): for further guidance through the Quine corpus on function-directed and other scepticism about modality, see Hookway (1988, ch. 7) and Føllesdal (2004). For concern with the function of modal judgment that pertains to Quinean scepticism or to non-cognitivism about the modal see e.g. Wittgenstein (1964), Craig (1975, 1985), Wright (1980, pt IV; 1986, 1989, 1992), Blackburn (1984, 1986, 1993), Forbes (1985, ch. 9), Hale (1989, 1999), Hart (1989), and McFetridge (1990c).

truths) are "presupposed by" certain of our practices—for example, reference, individuation, or explanation.[11]

In face of the suggestions, and their state of development, I think it is fair to say that our understanding of any specific kind of modal judgment is in a relatively poor state when compared with the other cases that have been cited. I also think it is fair to say that the range of proto-answers to the question of function in the modal case is so strikingly heterogeneous as to undermine thoroughly the notion that we have even a proto-story to tell about function which speaks to the *entire range* of modal assertion that we, in fact, go in for. But I will go no further in seeking to convince that our understanding of the function of modal judgment is in a relatively poor state. Moreover, I will not attempt to provide here a direct answer to the question of what the function of modal judgment is. For to develop, and to examine seriously and comprehensively, the proto-suggestions about the function of modal judgment, and to attempt to provide, in each case, direct answers to our formative questions, is an enormous task which lies far beyond the scope of this paper. So, while I will allude to some specific and direct answers to the various questions of the function of modal judgment, my hope is to illustrate the consequences and qualities of function-driven theories of modality at a level of some generality. My main concern is to chart the consequences of adopting a policy which allocates a crucial role to *some such* conception of the function of modal judgments via a functional constraint that I will discuss in some detail (in §3). Before turning to the functional constraint, however, I consider (in §2) various suggestions to the effect that the demand for an account of function, comparable to those indicated in the other cases, is misplaced, or at least may be avoided, in the case of modal judgment.

## 2. AVOIDING THE QUESTION

When posed a difficult question, it is a philosophical reflex to consider whether it might be dismissed, avoided, or dealt with indirectly. In this section, I consider various such responses to the question of the function of modal judgment.

### 2.1 Circularity

We will consider various versions of the suspicion that our modalizing is—somehow—too deep a feature of our intellectual practices to be susceptible to the kind of account of function that is available in other cases. In its first version, this suspicion is articulated along the lines that the project of

---

[11] Here I take the liberty of not attributing directly or specifically any of the suggestions, since some are not obviously attributable to any specific source, and others could be attributed only with extensive qualification.

enquiring into the function of modal judgment—that is, modal judgment *in particular*—is vitiated by a special, and vicious, explanatory circularity.

Certainly, reflection on the formative questions that were listed would suggest that we naturally form, and cannot easily avoid forming, the function-relevant questions in modal terms—for example, counterfactual questions (how would things be were we to abstain from modalizing?) and questions of possibility (could we otherwise achieve at all, or achieve as efficiently, what we actually achieve by our modalizing?). Equally, the various suggestions about the function of modal judgment are of the form that the making of such judgments is hypothetically necessary—necessary in order to X. Now, one response to this observation would be to dispel the appearance of vicious circularity by attempting to reformulate the questions in non-modal terms. But I see no reason why we should do so since, I will argue, the suspicion of vicious circularity is ill-founded.[12]

What may be a legitimate constraint of non-circularity on an account of the function of modal judgment—and mutatis mutandis for the other cases—is the following: that the relevant explanation of modal judgments *in general* should apply (or may be extended to apply) in those special, reflexive, cases where the subject of our modalizing is our own modalizing. In light of that constraint, vicious circularity is constituted by the occurrence of brute or inexplicable occurrences of modal locutions in the *explanans* when those modal locutions also occur in the *explanandum*. But the present constraint does not require, nor would it be legitimate to require, that an account of the function of modal judgment must take place in a modal vacuum—that we must not modalize in giving an account of the function of modal judgment. That the requirement to abstain from modalizing is too strong is made more plausible by the consideration of a different project in modal philosophy—that of giving a thoroughly non-modal analysis of the modal concepts.[13] Comparison with the project of analysing the modal concepts offers both an illuminating analogy and an illuminating disanalogy. The analogy is that it is mistaken to require that we abstain from modalizing altogether in providing an explanation of modality—whether it is an explanation of function or of conceptual content. When the kind of explanation in the offing is that of aiming to provide a thoroughly reductive analysis of the modal concepts, then (perhaps) we are bound to assert that our favoured analyses of the modal concepts, as with any analyses, are necessary. And if the aim is to have a non-modal analysis of the modal concepts, then we cannot help ourselves to *irreducible* modal concepts. The appropriate requirement, then, is that our talk of the necessity of our analyses

---

[12] To poison the well at the outset, I think that there is no more to the present allegation of vicious circularity of explanation than there is in the superficial allegations that an account of the function of propositional attitude ascription is stymied by our commitment to *believe* (ah-ha!) what we ascribe; or that an account of the function of truth-predications is stymied by our commitment to hold that our favoured explanation is (ah-ha!) *true*.

[13] See Lewis (1986b).

should itself, ultimately, fall to (broadly) the same analysis of modality that such talk of necessity is supposed to facilitate. The appropriate circularity constraint, which applies to *both* conceptual explanation and functional explanation, is a higher-order constraint which generalizes, uniformly, over different kinds of explanation. This constraint rules out modalities figuring in the *explanans* if they themselves are inexplicable *in the contextually relevant sense*: the contextually relevant kind of explanation of the modal (whether functional or conceptual) should be applicable to whatever modalizing figures in the *explanans*. However, this second-order constraint emphatically does *not* forbid the occurrence of unanalysable modal concepts in the explanans when it is the function of modal judgment that is up for explanation. When the relevant kind of explanation is of function, the kind of explicability that is required in the name of non-circularity is explicability of function. When the relevant explanation is the reductive analysis of concepts, the kind of explicability that is required in the name of non-circularity is analysability (in non-modal terms) of concepts. It would be to confuse two distinct applications of the second-order constraint to read it as requiring that the kind of explicability required of modal elements of the *explanans* is analysability (in non-modal terms) of concepts when the relevant kind of explanation is one of function.[14] In any event, no clearly plausible constraint against vicious circularity rules out the ineliminable appearance of modal terms in the explanation of modal function.

## 2.2  The instrumental models

We should beware of illicitly presupposing that an appropriate or adequate account of the function of every discourse, or of modal discourse in particular, must be, in some sense, an *instrumental* account. The worry may be inspired by the (correct) observation that the examples that have been presented of accounts of function for the various non-modal discourses are uniformly instrumental. Indeed, in all of our non-modal examples we advert to one of two instrumental models of function which it is useful to distinguish: on one model, the sentences of the discourse are *inferential* instruments and on the other model, they are *conduct-guiding* instruments.[15]

---

[14] Brief reflection on the non-modal cases considered earlier should clearly establish the general principle that reductive analysability of the relevant concepts is not required for an adequate (non-circular) answer to the question of the function of the relevant judgments. Consider the cases of spatial and of temporal judgment, where the concepts in question are very strong candidates for being resistant to reductive analysis, but where we have a very clear and simple story to tell about (basic) function. Consider also the various admonitions against the analysability of the concept of truth (Frege and others) and their apparent consistency with the popular view that the truth predicate has some special prosentential or compendious expressive function (as in, "Everything that the Pope says is true").

[15] I do not intend the terms "inferential instrument" or "conduct-guiding instrument" to carry the traditional instrumentalist or non-cognitivist connotation on which such a sentence would not

The notion of inferential instrument is elaborated as follows. We are (sometimes) interested in drawing conclusions from premises when all are stated in terms entirely free of X-vocabulary (mathematical, microphysical, psychological). But we find that our inferences are, in one way or another, facilitated when we introduce X-vocabulary in the form of further bridging premises that mix X-vocabulary with other vocabulary. The notion of conduct-guiding instrument is elaborated thus. We are sometimes interested in guiding or influencing the practical (or intellectual) conduct of ourselves and others, and we find that we are (somehow) better able to do so when we adduce reasons or considerations in the form of sentences couched in a special X-vocabulary (moral—or perhaps more generally normative).[16]

Perhaps an adequate account of the function of (certain) modal judgments is available which conforms to one of these two instrumental models. It is a prominent theme among the earlier collected suggestions about the function of modal judgment, and reflecting their antecedence in the literature on modal non-cognitivism, that (certain) modal judgments have a conduct-guiding role.[17]

---

be truth-evaluable. On one hand, many philosophers hold that it is perfectly consistent to associate the sentences of a given discourse (microphysical, moral, etc.) with one or both of these sorts of function while also assigning them fully cognitive semantic status (see e.g. van Fraassen 1980 and Mackie 1977). On the other hand, even those who wish to hold that there is a connection between having either kind of instrumental function and "non-cognitive status" need not hold that recognition of this special status requires us to deny that the sentences in question are properly called "true" or "false" (see e.g. Blackburn 1984, 1993 and Wright 1992). Indeed, throughout the paper, I assume that the most competitive and interesting expressions of non-cognitivist thought are quasi-realistic, in that they do not take the traditional form of denying truth-aptitude, truth-value, etc. to the declarative sentences of modal sentences (or whichever other sentences are relevant).

[16] The pre-eminent example of discourse as conduct-guiding instrument is that of moral discourse. There is a sense in which it is uncontroversial that at least some moral talk has this function. Those who reject moral non-cognitivism typically do so *not* because they deny that moral talk has (at least sometimes) a conduct-guiding role, but rather on the grounds that moral discourse *need not have non-cognitive status* in order to function in that way. Those who reject internalism in moral psychology typically do so *not* because they deny that moral commitments stand in some special relation to action, but rather on the grounds that the connection in question is not the internal, absolutely necessary, connection that the internalist takes it to be. But wherever we have a live non-cognitivist or internalist position, whether in the moral case or not, we may find examples of discourses that are cast in the role of conduct-guiding instrument.

[17] There is, of course, a substantial tradition of modal non-cognitivism, and so the idea that modal talk has a conduct-guiding role is already familiar. Sometimes the non-cognitivist thought is that the role in question is that of guiding practical conduct or action—thus talk of broadly causal necessity has been cast as expressive of confidence in a method A for making it the case that B. But more usually the role allotted to modal discourse is that of guiding our *intellectual* conduct. Modal talk is cast as expressive of our own policy in certain matters of intellectual conduct—policy that we adopt in the regulation of our own intellectual conduct and which we commend to others. For example, judgments of impossibility have been taken to be expressive of resolution to count nothing as legitimate evidence against, or as expressive of resolution to immunize from revision come what may (or at least on empirical grounds): thus, certain strands in the thought of Quine and of the later Wittgenstein. So if we seek to cast modal judgment in the role of conduct-guiding instrument, we have some positive proposals to consider.

And although it is not as prominent, or explicit, a theme that the function of modal judgment is to play a distinctive inferential role, we can certainly cast various pieces of (historical) modal philosophy in that light.[18] However, it would be a rather quick move to insist that the instrumental models exhaust the range of adequate responses to the question of function. And perhaps we ought to consider the prospect that the modal case is, in this respect, exceptional, or at least different from the others that we have considered, in that it admits or merits a response to the question of function that proceeds other than by the identification of an instrumental role—either of one of the two kinds identified or, indeed, at all. There are, then, various such suggestions to consider. But I note in advance of considering these suggestions that we would learn something important about our modalizing should it turn out that it was exceptional in meriting an entirely non-instrumental account of function.

## 2.3  The bluntly cognitive response

A bluntly cognitive response to the question of the function of modal judgment has it that the function of modal judgment is to tell it how it modally is—to get the modal facts right, to state the modal truths. The response is as compelling as it is unhelpful. We should put aside the worry that the bluntly cognitive response says something wrong about modal discourse in order to emphasize how it misses the point.[19] For one might say of any of the discourses (mathematical, moral, etc.) for which we have already offered an account of function *qua instrument*, that *a* function qua *illocutionary role* of its declarative sentences is to describe the X-facts, to state the X-truths, etc. So, perhaps in succumbing to an ambiguity of the term "function" which has now been exposed, the bluntly cognitive response seems to leave untouched the question of which instrumental function, if any, is discharged by the discourse in question. It may be, of course, that the bluntly cognitive response is expressive of a stronger conviction—viz. that *no more* than the illocutionary response is available by way of an adequate answer to the question of function in the modal case. But if so, let the stronger thesis be made

[18] Here are two examples. We can recover or reconstruct from Kant the suggestion that the role of necessitated universal generalizations is to furnish warrant for non-necessitated but genuinely universal generalizations: we are warranted in asserting a spatiotemporally unrestricted universal generalization only when we can "descend" deductively to it from its, a priori established, necessitation (Kant 1781, Divers 1999b, §3). We can recover more straightforwardly from the Sixth Meditation of Descartes (1641) the idea that two kinds of modal judgments function pairwise as inferential instruments that allow us to establish the negation of a non-modal hypothesis via modus tollens—thus: if $p$ then necessarily $p$; possibly not-$p$; so not-$p$. In a special, and familiar, application of the latter, the aim is to establish the actual distinctness (non-identity) of certain things (objects, properties) when the hypothesis, $p$, takes the form of a (certain kind of) identity statement.

[19] What I advise that we put aside here is the traditional non-cognitivist option of finding that it is wrong to allow modal sentences the semantic and illocutionary appearances that are associated with the cognitive—telling it like it is, stating truths, describing the facts, etc.

explicit and let us hear the explanation of why the modal is supposed to have this special status.

## 2.4 The essentiality of modal thought

One reason for thinking that no instrumental account is available of the function of modal judgment is that we can "make nothing of" the kinds of counterfactuals that we would have to be able to formulate and evaluate in order to arrive at such an account. How would things be if we were to lose the capacity to make modal judgment? How would a creature think, and at what disadvantage would it be, if it were capable of thinking, but not of thinking modally? Perhaps we simply cannot make anything of the non-modal ways of thought hypothesized. And perhaps there is an adequate basis in that consideration for the metaphysical thesis that thought is essentially modal: that there could not be a non-modal way of thought, in that any creature capable of thought at all has to be capable of modal thought. Clearly, these claims—the impossibility of our making anything of a non-modal way of thought and the impossibility (tout court) of such a way of thought—are large and complex. But perhaps we need not explore these theses in too much detail in order to undermine the idea that there is a sound argument from them to the conclusion that it is (somehow) a mistake to seek an instrumental account of the function of modal judgment. Here are three kinds of problems that threaten any such argument.

First, it is implausible that we can make nothing of a non-modal way of thought. One source of prima facie evidence for the counter-claim is located with considerations about the syntactic and semantic status of modal vocabulary. We can give a completely non-modal syntactic and semantic account of fairly rich languages (theories, logics) in the following sense: we can construct syntactically rich languages and give non-trivial (even intended) interpretations of them in which no object-language expression is assigned any modal content and, indeed, wherein no terms of the meta-language are explicitly modal. We might reach higher, but take as a relatively safe example the standard languages of first-order predicate logic with non-modal predicates. In that way, and to that extent, we can make perfectly good sense of a non-modal language. But a related point, which is perhaps of even greater significance, is that we cannot contrive, or make sense of, a *purely modal* language. Modal discourse shares with logical discourse (and perhaps others) the feature that it does not come in a "pure" version. There are no proper atomic modal predications of individual subjects. We might say that it is possible that *a* is *F*, or *a is possibly F*, but not simply that *a is possible* (other than degenerately or elliptically, when we mean that it is possible that *a* exists). To introduce modalizing to a system of representation, we have to introduce it *on top of* something else. And this essentially dependent status of modal elements of vocabulary *requires* that such a non-modal basis be in place before those modal elements can be introduced. So, these reflections suggest, not only is the idea of an intelligible and semantically coherent non-modal language perfectly in order, but it is *required* that there be such languages in order that there are intelligible and semantically coherent modal languages.[20]

In response to these observations based on syntactic and semantic status, perhaps we should consider whether there is a richer and more exacting sense of "making something of" a non-modal way of thought than that which is captured in the rather narrow linguistic criteria that were implicit in the recent argument. After all, one could, it may seem, rehearse all of the foregoing considerations, concerning syntactic and semantic compositionality, and thereby "establish" that non-spatial, non-temporal, or non-causal ways of thought are (respectively) possible or intelligible to us. But even if so, that would not rid many of the conviction that there is a deeper sense in which we can make nothing of a non-spatial (non-temporal, non-causal) way of thought. If creatures lacked all spatial and temporal and causal concepts, with grasp of which concepts could we credit them even if we could assign various extensions to their putative predicates? These are good and interesting questions. But for immediate purposes we need note only that the intended analogy with these other, putatively essential, categories of thought is counter-productive, and this is the second point.

Secondly, then, even if we accept that certain categories are essential to thought, there is no clear connection between that status and instrumental function for related judgments. Aside from the modal case, which is presently moot, the categories of judgment that are best candidates (spatial, temporal, causal) for being essential to (all) thought are all instrumentally intelligible *as well*. Despite the depth of such categories of judgment, it seems that there are counterfactuals that we may perfectly reasonably assert and which (partially) constrain an instrumental (conduct-guiding) function in each case. If we didn't make spatial judgments, then we would fall down and bump into things. If we didn't make temporal judgments, then we wouldn't be able to coordinate various kinds of cooperative action, etc. So even among the candidates for the essential categories of thinking, modal judgment still stands out as exceptional in lacking, thus far, a compelling instrumental account of its function.

Thirdly, allow that there are certain broad and deep features of our thinking that do have some claim to lying so deep as to make unintelligible a (putative) way of thought that lacks them. But even if we can pin down such cases, what has to be negotiated very carefully is any contentious transition from a claim

---

[20] One might think that the considerations aired here would support just as well, or as badly, the view that a way of thought which lacks various specific and clearly logical elements—negation, conditionalization, disjunction—is possible or intelligible. Note, though, that it would be one thing to establish the inessential status of any one element and another to establish that a purely atomic way of thought—one with no compositional elements—is possible. Fine, if so. It strikes me as perfectly reasonable that we may make something of a way of thought that lacked an element of negation or disjunction. As in the modal case, we might explore the deep question of the function of negative judgment, or of disjunctive judgment, precisely by considering the ways in which such an impoverished thinker would, subsequently, be disadvantaged.

about the "essentiality" of these deep features of our thinking to any claim about the level of modal commitment that is needed to sustain them. In face of a hypothesis that a certain kind of modal judgment is necessary for the (efficient) discharge of the function in question, we are at liberty to test the hypothesis by asking, first, whether a less substantially committing modal attitude will do the job and, secondly, whether a non-modal attitude will do.[21]

## 2.5 Modalizing by implication

One might seek to build a fast track to the inevitability of our modalizing along the observation that all of our thoughts—even our non-modal thoughts—have modal implications or entailments.[22] Thus, the observation may unfold: every proposition that we think is either necessary or contingent; there are necessary truths that limn the boundaries of every concept that features in our thoughts; whenever we assert that $p$ we are thereby committed to asserting that it is possible that $p$. The observation is correct in that *once we go in for modalizing* we seem bound to accept some, if not all, of these suggested modal implications of our thinking. But the proviso is crucial. For nothing in these observations amounts to an argument as to why we are bound to go in for modalizing in the first place. Perhaps *if* we are forced to judge whether it is necessary or contingent that—say—everything is what it is and not another thing—we have no serious option but to judge it necessary. But—with Quine to Kripke—whence this force to add any modal ingredient to the judgment at all?[23]

## 2.6 Free modalizing

The last two of the indirect responses that I will consider to the question of the function of modal judgment are made in rather a different spirit. The theme common to these responses is that the commitments entailed by the accommodation of our actual modalizing may be justified by means of *some* kind of appeal to function even if we cannot identify a (specific) function for modal judgments.

The first response is based on the idea that acceptance of the commitments required to accommodate our modal judgments may be forced upon us independently of the consideration that these commitments stand in that relation to the modal case. In particular, might it not arise that we have an account of the function in the case of some non-modal discourse, the accommodation of which requires us to take on commitments which—it turns out—suffice to

---

[21] On the sources of different kinds of commitment in modal theorizing see further §4.

[22] The thought in question will have to be formulated in a way that immunizes it from trivialization via the classical entailment of all necessary propositions by any proposition whatsoever.

[23] Quine (1981), pp. 173–4.

accommodate our actual modalizing? Perhaps the two sorts of discourses that look best suited to fund indirectly the commitments of our modalizing are those of the intensional and the intentional—perhaps individually or, more plausibly, conjointly. Imagine that we have a good account of the function of talk of various kinds of intensions (properties, propositions, etc.) and intentionality (thinking about, talking about, etc.). Imagine further that we have a story to tell about the ontology, epistemology, logic, and semantics of our functionally efficacious talk of intensions and the intentional. Perhaps this is a rather minimal or insubstantial story, or perhaps it is—as is more familiar—a very substantial story. Thus, for example, one might begin with the following sort of thought. Once we have postulated sufficiently many and various entities to be the objects of thought, and sufficiently many and various entities to be collected into sets to give us all of the properties and propositions, thereby we have postulated sufficiently many and various objects to be the possibilia (and perhaps the impossibilia).[24] In any event, it is then worth considering whether we can identify within the resources required by the story, sufficient resources to fund a story about the ontology, epistemology, logic, and semantics of our modalizing. In the best-case scenario, the independently gathered resources would be sufficient to vindicate all of our de facto modalizing—the entire body of kinds of modal assertion that we in fact go in for. For then, no matter what account is offered of the function of modal judgment, and so long as the function is discharged by *some* part of the body of de facto modal assertion, we know that we have a theory that is substantial enough to account for that function. We cannot rule out that these resources are excessive in that they may be funding *more* modalizing than is functionally driven. But we are also committed to these "excessive" resources anyway (at least pro tem) since (we take it) commitment to them is required in the name of providing adequate functionally driven accounts of our talk of the intensions and of the intentional.[25]

There is a point to this response that is well taken. We can indeed see how we *could*, thus, come by a comprehensive theory of modality without confronting directly the question of the function of modal judgment and yet remain confident in some measure that the resources invoked were—in an appropriate sense—no more substantial than they had to be. But, three comments occur.

First, it hardly need be added that substantial work would have to be done to show that a theory of modality does so emerge from a theory of intensionality, intentionality, or of anything else. Secondly, were it to be shown that an adequate theory of modality did so emerge from the theories of certain other discourses, that in itself would be a significant, and perhaps surprising result.

---

[24] I take it that this is the methodological order of play which marks the Meinongian tradition. See e.g. Priest (2005), ch. 1.

[25] We should also take note, for future reference, of the prospect of intra-modal funding: the case where some kinds of modalizing, for which we have no functional account, are funded, in the fashion described, by other kinds of modalizing, for which we do have a functional account.

Thirdly, while such a story of emergence would speak to the worry that a comprehensive theory of modality was excessively substantial, the intrinsically interesting question of whether modal judgment has an identifiable function would remain outstanding.

## 2.7 Entrenchment as evidence of function

A final attempt at avoidance has it that we may be warranted—indeed, that we are warranted—in claiming that modal judgment has (de facto) some characteristic function even though we have no account of that function to offer. The warranting considerations are the longevity, width, and the depth of entrenchment of modal talk both within and across natural languages. The subsequent thoughts are: (a) that it is radically implausible that so robust and pervasive a way of talking (and thinking) should survive were it an idle, non-functional, wheel in our conceptual scheme and (b) we are in a position to make that claim even in the absence of an account of what the function is.[26] Moreover, this claim about function lends a kind of support to the kind of modal theorizing that sets out to preserve, or vindicate, all of the kinds of modal assertions in which we actually indulge.[27] For, in the absence of an account of the precise nature and precise locus of our functioning modal judgment, to risk giving up on any kind of modal judgment that we actually go in for, would be to risk giving up on a kind of modal judgment which is in fact functionally efficacious.

An adequate response to this line of thought must make at least the following points.

First, we can take the point that the survival and entrenchment of modal talk is, indeed, evidence of some functional utility. And, indeed, we may think it correspondingly unlikely that thorough reflection and a full state of information would lead us to conclude that *no* modal talk serves *any* distinctive and indispensable function.[28] But this gives us no clue as to which elements of our modalizing are crucial—no clue as to which elements are doing work and which are merely epiphenomenal.

Secondly, and reflecting an attractive supervenience principle, we can take the point that whatever function or functions are served by our body of de facto modal assertion will be preserved should we resolve to sustain—to eschew revision of—that body of assertion. But this, of course, gives us no clue as to whether the function of our modal discourse—whatever it is—might be sustained, more economically, on the basis of a subset of the modal assertions that we actually go in for.

---

[26] I take it to be no part of this story that the function of modal discourse is undetectable or ineffable: it may be just that as things stand we don't have an account.

[27] That is to say, the orthodox kind of modal theorizing. See §3.1 below.

[28] Although a genuinely open enquiry must be prepared for such a discovery. See §3.2 below.

Thirdly, we may even take the point that the present response provides a justification—if any is needed—for proceeding in modal philosophy in the absence of a substantive account of the function of modal discourse. But, obviously enough, it still leaves us wanting an answer to the legitimate and fundamental question of what the function of modal judgment is.

Fourthly, while de facto considerations of longevity, ubiquity, and entrenchment of a vocabulary can count as evidence of a characteristic associated utility, these considerations should not be taken as *constitutive* of functional utility in any interesting sense. Certainly, and obviously, the more ubiquitous and more entrenched a way of speaking is, the greater the cost associated with abandoning it, and the greater the utility, *qua convenience*, associated with persevering with, rather than abstaining from, that way of talking. But there comes a point at which such centrality, and the corresponding inconvenience of revision, is *merely* de facto, or merely psychological, and of no philosophical significance. Thus consider the 'entrenchment' of personal pronouns, the definite article, etc.

In sum, the ubiquity and entrenchment of modal talk is indeed strong prima facie, but defeasible, evidence that modal talk has some function. But these evidential facts, in themselves, do not close, or significantly channel, any philosophically interesting question about the existence or identity of that function.

## 3. THE FUNCTIONAL CONSTRAINT

In this section, I outline and seek to explore and promote a methodological stance which allocates to one's conception of the function of modal judgment a crucial role in constraining the accumulation of philosophically substantial commitments in theorizing about modality. Exploration of this function-driven approach is of interest at the very least in that it stands in marked contrast to the prevailing approach.

### 3.1 The function-driven approach versus the orthodoxy

On the prevailing approach we buy completely into the body of de facto modal assertion. This comprises all the kinds of assertion that the folk and the philosophers are inclined to make: assertions of unactualized possibility, necessity, impossibility, counterfactual dependence—restricted and unrestricted, de re and de dicto, simple and iterated, etc. The regulating principle is that, by and large, we are to accommodate the truth of assertions of *all* such kinds. Thus, we begin by aiming to construct a comprehensive metaphysical and semantic theory to accommodate all such kinds of de facto modalizing as truth. We may subsequently consider such questions as how we know these (putative) modal truths and, if time permits, why we are concerned with them at all.

On the alternative approach that is presently commended, we begin by asking which aspects of our modalizing serve identifiable purposes and then constrain our accumulation of substantial philosophical commitments—ontological, semantic, conceptual, epistemological, etc. to these. More specifically, the *functional constraint*, baldly stated, is as follows: one ought to accept no more substantial a theory than is required in order to account for the body of (functionally) de jure modal assertion. The body of de jure modal assertion comprises the kinds of modal assertion that we (in some sense) *need* to make in order to serve whatever are the legitimate and identifiable purposes of our modalizing.[29]

When the two approaches are so contrasted, the following dual prospect opens up: (a) that the body of de facto modal assertion exceeds *to some extent* the body of de jure modal assertion and (b) that the excess is crucial and marginal—i.e., by attempting to accommodate precisely these excessive, functionally unvindicated, assertions one acquires theoretical commitments (ontological, epistemological, etc.) beyond those that suffice to deal with the de jure assertions. The advocate of the functional constraint, whose part I now take, finds this prospect intellectually unacceptable and takes the view that commitments so acquired are unjustified. As she views matters, the orthodox approach demonstrates an easily anticipated connection between failure to pay due attention to the question of the function of modal judgment and risking the accumulation of gratuitously substantial commitments in modal theorizing. On the orthodox approach, the question of the function or purpose of modal judgment is ignored, downplayed, or marginalized. Consequently, the distinction between the bodies of de jure modal assertion and de facto modal assertion is equally neglected. And so, in turn, is the prospect of developing theories of modality that are far less substantive than those orthodox theories that—more or less reflectively—gear themselves to the accommodation of the body of de facto modal assertion.[30]

---

[29] From the standpoint of the present distinction between assertion de jure and de facto, we are better placed to note a further and radical non-direct response to the question of the function of modal judgment. The response in question consists in applying to the modal case in particular a generalized quietism. This generalized quietism finds that it is a mistake to set out on a line of enquiry that may, even in principle, find a serious discrepancy between the body of de jure assertion and that of de facto assertion with respect to any given discourse that is entrenched in a network of linguistic and associated practices. For along with the prospect of such a serious discrepancy goes a cluster of unacceptable ideas: that such a discourse is fundamentally not in order; that we could somehow discover that practices which are so entrenched are, nonetheless, ill-motivated, unnecessary, unjustified, and (in principle) apt for significant revision. I note this quietist move. If this quietism is genuinely generalized, I have nothing to say to impede it. But if our modalizing in particular is supposed to merit this quietist attitude, then we should seek out the specific reasons why this is so.

[30] I take as typical of the commitments of orthodox contemporary theories of modality, some subset of the following: ontological commitment to an infinity of concrete non-actual objects or to an infinity of abstract, actual (and perhaps sui generis and simple) objects or to primitive relations of necessitation; commitment to the primitive status of modal concepts or concepts expressed by "according to" or "true at" or "accessible from", etc. The epistemological commitments of various modal theories are frequently less clear since the question is more frequently avoided.

By way of elaboration, and defence, of the functional constraint, I will comment on its relationship to antirealism and to revisionism about modality. To anticipate, my claim will be that the functional constraint facilitates, but by no means demands, acceptance of theories of modality that are relatively insubstantial or revisionary.

## 3.2 The functional constraint and revision

The functional constraint is not essentially revisionary, but it opens the door to the prospect of revision. The immediate prospect is that philosophical enquiry will fail to find that all of our de facto modalizing is justified by serving an identifiable and valuable purpose. The effect of the functional constraint is that at those points where extensive enquiry discloses no purpose in making certain kinds of modal assertion, the modal theorist is released from the obligation to provide a philosophical package which underwrites the truth of, and our knowledge of, those modal propositions which are the contents of our (merely) de facto assertions. There is then a question of how this theoretical position relates to the practice of modalizing. The natural answer to that question is that where we, as theorists, find no point in making certain kinds of modal assertion, but risk the accumulation of extra commitments by accommodating them as de jure modal assertions, we ourselves should (at the very least) abstain from making those assertions and recommend abstention (at the very least) to others. So the functional constraint naturally issues revisionary recommendations concerning whatever emerges as the body of *merely* de facto modal assertions. However, while the functional constraint builds on a distinction in sense—as it were—between "de jure modal assertion" and "de facto modal assertion", it does not presuppose any particular distinction in extension, nor any distinction in extension at all. Nor, therefore, does the functional constraint presuppose anything about the extension of the body of merely de facto—dispensable—modal assertion. At the outset of an enquiry into function, the extent of de jure modal assertion, and so that of its complement—the body of merely de facto modal assertion—is simply moot. At one end of the spectrum of outcomes lies the prospect that the body of de jure modal assertion coincides with that of de facto modal assertion.[31] At the opposite end of the spectrum lies the (ultra-Quinean) prospect that the extent of the body of de jure modal assertion is zero. To the extent that any specific outcome of the application of the functional constraint is prima facie unlikely, it is unlikely that we will find conclusive reason to endorse as de jure the entire

---

[31] At least this is the most extreme prospect at the optimistic end of the spectrum which I will actively consider. I suppose that investigation may, in principle, disclose that the body of de jure modal assertion goes beyond that of de facto modal assertion—that once we are clear about the function of modal judgment we will realize that we ought to indulge in kinds of modal assertion in which we do not presently indulge. I acknowledge this prospect, but will not pursue it here.

body of de facto modal assertion. But the built-in predisposition towards revision is no stronger than that.

### 3.3 The functional constraint and antirealism

The functional constraint is not essentially antirealistic. Theories that are regulated by a conception of function are often antirealistic theories in the broad sense that they are intended to avoid the ontological commitments that realists associate with the standard pattern of assertion of the declarative sentences of the discourse. In this category of functionally regulated antirealistic theories we find various versions of non-factualism, error-theory, and agnosticism.

In the case of non-factualist (non-cognitivist, quasi-realist) versions of anti-realism, the question of function, and often something very like our functional constraint, is the primary regulator of theory construction.[32] In a second kind of case, an error-theoretic or agnostic interpreter seeks broadly to preserve or vindicate actual patterns of assent and dissent over theories or the sentences of a discourse by explicating these in terms of certain norms that are weaker than those of knowledge, belief, and truth. Thus, for example, Mackie (1977) on that which promotes human welfare impartially considered as the criterion of assent in the moral; Field (1980, 1989) on conservativeness as the criterion of assent in mathematics; van Fraassen (1980) on empirical adequacy as the criterion of assent in microphysical theorizing. The primary constraint under which such subsidiary norms are introduced is precisely the following: that it should be *sufficient* for the discourse to discharge its characteristic function that those theories, or sentences, that merit our assent should satisfy the subsidiary norm, but not *necessary* to discharge that function that they should be (held) true. A third kind of case in which considerations of function take a central role is when agnosticism or error-theory makes no play with any subsidiary norm but prescribes a revision of actual patterns of assent and dissent with belief, knowledge, and truth in view. In these cases, the agnostic or error-theorist admits and prescribes an assertion deficit: she cannot admit as assertable—nor, therefore, can she assert—many claims that the realist and the folk are prepared to assert, and she advises the folk to align their practices with her own. The burden of explanation taken on by such a revisionary interpreter is precisely that of explaining why this assertion deficit does not matter. And what *not mattering* amounts to in such cases is just making no *functional* difference—there is nothing that we do with the concepts in question that we prevent ourselves from doing by abstaining from assertion of the controversial sentences.[33]

---

[32] See Blackburn (1984, 1986, 1993). One might say that the spirit in which the functional constraint is presently promoted is that of endorsing this element of non-cognitivist methodology, but without buying into so much as the intelligibility of the traditional non-cognitivist conclusions that our ascriptions of truth-values and other cognitive predications are erroneous.

[33] See Divers (2004).

The question then naturally arises whether acceptance of a regulative role for an account of function, and acceptance—in particular—of the functional constraint under consideration, amounts to loading the dice against ontologically realistic, or otherwise substantive, theories. The question is delicate. On one hand, it is eminently possible for the functional constraint to generate, as the minimal functionally adequate theory, a theory whose commitments are very substantial. Perhaps, for example, a full-blooded ontological Platonism, paired with a non-natural epistemology, *is the least substantial* philosophical package that will properly account for the function of mathematical discourse. On the other hand, there is a sense in which the functional constraint clearly does impose considerations of economy on our acceptance of theories: where two competing theories are functionally adequate, the functional theory commends to us the less substantially committed. So the functional constraint involves a bias against relatively substantial theories just in the sense that any preference for relatively economical theories starts any relatively substantial theory at relatively unfavourable odds. This feature of the methodology is made explicit, but will not be defended here.

## 3.4 Non-functional constraints on theory construction

The functional constraint has it that one ought to accept no more substantial a theory than is required in order to account for the body of (functionally) de jure modal assertion. One way in which the functional constraint may prove controversial is in its implication that considerations of function have a unique or decisive role in constraining the accumulation of commitments in our modal theorizing. For one might think that there are other considerations that ought to count as data which are weighty enough to require theoretical accommodation—and, moreover, accommodation which may entail substantial commitments beyond those entailed by accommodation of the data on function. In that regard, and given the over-arching claim that considerations of function have not been given their due, we ought to weigh the kinds of consideration that have loomed large, and which have been taken to justify the accumulation of substantial commitments, in modal theorizing. There are, at least, three such kinds of consideration that ought to be distinguished but which stand in complex inter-relations to one another: (1) the phenomenology of modal judgment; (2) modal intuitions; and (3) communally sanctioned judgments of truth-value. A decent account of these categories and their inter-relations would involve us in a lengthy detour which I cannot afford to take here. But without taking such a detour, some points are available in response to the suggestion that the functional constraint does not do justice to these further considerations.

First, there is nothing in the functional constraint that rules against the idea that there are legitimate non-functional data. But what the functional constraint does require is that either: (a) the commitments generated by the accommodation of non-functional data should already—as it were—be justified by the accommodation of functional data or (b) that the "accommodation" of the further data should take some form other than accepting as true any propositions that are not de jure, functionally assertible, but which are presented as true by phenomenology, by intuition, or by communal assent. Clearly, (a) is the more irenic prospect. But (b) is perhaps the more important in underlining the point that *accommodation* of the data need not take the form of placing maximal cognitive trust in assent as the hallmark of truth and knowledge.

Secondly, the real challenge to the legitimacy of the functional constraint is that non-functional considerations might merit the acceptance as true of propositions that we have no functional reason to accept as true. But in that regard, we should note that the further non-functional considerations do not always agree on which modal propositions they present as true. Indeed, there are both intra-categorical and inter-categorical tensions. As an example of intra-categorical tension, consider the intuitions which present as true certain claims of (a posteriori) necessity of identity—it is necessary that Hesperus = Phosphorus, it is necessary that Water = $H_2O$, etc. While these intuitions are philosophically widespread, they are not ubiquitous, and the contrary intuitions of contingency are taken seriously enough to require extensive, often subtle, and error-imputing explanation.[34] As an example of inter-categorical tension, consider the incontestable fact that there simply is no communally sanctioned view of the truth-value of any such modal proposition, even if (reflective!) intuition or phenomenology delivers an internally unanimous verdict one way or the other. The main point is two-fold: (i) the primary role accorded to functional considerations would be threatened most seriously in cases where the further considerations co-operate to elect unanimously certain modal propositions as truths but (ii) it is not obvious how many propositions will be presented as such.

Thirdly, perhaps the correct, and certainly the irenic, thing to say is that all of the considerations that have been adduced are legitimate sources of data for modal theorizing—that the conflicting claims of the various sources have to be balanced against one another and against considerations of theoretical cost, etc. In that case, one approach which is methodologically legitimate is to treat the functional constraint as a constraint on the accumulation of commitments which is defeasible in light of claims from other sources. Another reason for prosecuting the functional approach to the hilt is that this will compensate for the lack of consideration recently accorded to it in modal theory construction. Yet another reason is that it will be illuminating to discover exactly which kinds of consideration (functional, intuitive, phenomenological, etc.) are responsible for promoting the costly modal propositions—those whose acceptance as true

---

[34] Most notably in Kripke (1972, lecture III) and then in the literature on the relationship between conceivability and possibility, e.g., Gendler and Hawthorne (2002).

(and known) is driving our accumulation of ontological and other substantial commitments in the theory of modality. So there are plenty of reasons for prosecuting the functional constraint even if one is not convinced of the primary and decisive role that it allocates to considerations of function.

## 3.5 The theory of modal concepts

There is one region of our modal theorizing in which it may seem (especially) wrong to allow that theory construction should be dictated by anything other than communally sanctioned judgments of truth-value (patterns of assertion). The broad, and perhaps rather vaguely bounded, region in question is that of the theory of our modal concepts, or the theory of meaning of our modal language.[35] The nub of an objection to the functional constraint then has is that the truth-conditions of the folk's modal utterances are fixed by what they hold true (what they believe, etc.) and not by any considerations about which purposes they recognize, or which purposes their assertions serve. However, the objection incorporates several presumptions and confusions that have to be unpicked.

First, there are two kinds of theories of concepts that ought to be distinguished.[36] The first kind of theory is conservative, descriptive, or hermeneutic: its aim is to say what the folk actually mean, and meant all along, by the uses they make of the words in question. It hardly needs emphasis that it is a controversial and difficult matter what form such a theory should take and what constraints should shape it. But no matter. The second kind of theory is potentially revisionary, prescriptive, and reconstructive. In this second case, the theorist postulates some role or function for the discourse in question and then essays what is—by default—a stipulative definition of the terms in question which she takes to best serve, or makes the best of, the subjects' practice in relation to that function. The motivating thought here is counterfactual: if the subjects were to use their words with this new, improved, hygienic meaning, then there would be an overall improvement in their X-ing. Perhaps the improvements would be, as it were, first-order, in that they would—by the theorist's lights—speak more truly, or attain more frequently whatever other norm is relevant to the success of their talk, or would emerge as better or more reliable inferers. Perhaps the improvements would be second-order or theoretical. Their X-ing would become, conceptually, metaphysically, epistemologically, or semantically more perspicuous. Perhaps, the best reconstruction of meaning would be one that optimized some balance of first-order and second-order improvements. But the upshot of the reconstructive project would be a reason to recommend to the

---

[35] I do not take the theory of modal concepts and the theory of modal language to be interchangeable: thus see Divers and Melia (2002, 2006). But I trust that the fiction of interchangeability does no harm in the present context.

[36] Here I follow, at least in spirit, the distinction influentially drawn by Burgess and Rosen (1997). But some such distinction goes back at least to Carnap (1950b, ch. 1) on explication, etc.

subjects that they resolve to use the relevant discourse with the new and improved senses attached to their expressions. This theorist engaged in the reconstructive project has, as such, no interest in the question of whether the concepts so introduced are the same concepts that are identified by the hermeneutic project as those that the folk expressed all along, or whether the functionally driven meanings now assigned to the sentences are the same meanings as those identified by the hermeneutic project as having attached to the sentences as always used by the folk. Perhaps the reconstructive project is more deserving of the name "conceptual synthesis" and the hermeneutic project more deserving of the name "conceptual analysis". But in any event there is a kind of theory of concepts that is legitimately constrained primarily by a conception of function rather than by the facts about the subject's judgments about the truth-values of their sentences.

Secondly, let us confine our attention exclusively to a theory of meaning of the hermeneutic kind just described. We might expect such a theory of meaning to issue, in part, biconditionals that assign truth-conditions to sentences of the object-language—biconditionals of such forms as:

It is possible that $p$ iff. . .
It is necessary that $p$ iff. . .

Now even if these biconditionals are filled out in such a way that existential or otherwise substantial truth-conditions are assigned to the modal sentences, assertion of the biconditionals (qua meaning hypotheses or whatever) does not commit the theorist to assertion of their right-sides. The theorist (here, qua interpreter) does not, by assigning truth-conditions to sentences, accrue the commitments that are incumbent on those who hold that the sentences in question are true. The theorist qua interpreter is at liberty, within some margins, to find that the folk imbue their sentences with meanings which leave them in various sorts of error if they proceed to assert those sentences. And to refuse to join them in doing so.

Hence there is no obvious or immediate consideration emerging from the need to provide, as part of a comprehensive theory of modality, a theory of modal concepts that undermines the legitimacy of the functional constraint.

## 4. ON THE PRECISE SOURCE OF VARIOUS COMMITMENTS

Putting aside, for the present, the functional constraint, there are some very general but crucial points to be registered in response to the following questions. How do we as theorists of modality acquire substantive commitments in constructing our theories of modality? Which, precisely, are the sources of the various kinds of commitment that ensue from modal theorizing?

First, I propose, a comprehensive philosophical theory of modality will have at least three distinguishable kinds of sub-theory as parts: a semantic or conceptual theory, an epistemological theory, and a metaphysical (ontological) theory. At the interface of these interrelated sub-theories is a conception of the truth-conditions of modal sentences which the theorist endorses and which she commends to others. A conception of truth-conditions is, thus, a very important part of our modal theorizing: but it requires us to assert only conditional claims—more specifically, biconditional claims. Typically, our assertions are of this form not only when we offer a statement of truth-conditions, but also when we offer an explicit definition of any term, or an explicit analysis of any concept—thus, for example:

(a) "It is necessary that $Fa$" is true iff $A$

(b) "If it had been the case that $P$ then it would have been the case that $Q$" is true iff $B$

(c) It is necessary that $P$ iff $C$

(d) $P$ is S4-valid iff $D$

(e) $L$ is S5-complete iff $E$.

It does not matter whether these biconditionals are part of a notional metalanguage, nor whether they are elements of a systematic semantic or metalogical theory (a "possible-worlds semantics"), nor whether the theoretical context is hermeneutic or reconstructive. The point is that they are *biconditionals* and, as such, one is committed to very little in asserting them. That is not to say that one is committed to nothing. And that point is underscored when the business at hand is (something like) that of providing an analysis of a concept. For in that case, especially, one might think that the theorist who gives a certain account of the content, or identity, of a concept is (thus) committing herself to the intelligibility of such a concept, and is (thus) committing herself in principle to providing an account of how the concept is acquired and its possession manifested. So one way in which a theory of modality can be substantially committed is by being committed to endorsing, and vindicating, the good standing of certain kinds of concept. And, from Hume through Quine, one important historical source of empiricist scepticism about modality has been, precisely, scepticism about the good standing of modal concepts. The story about how a modal theorist acquires conceptual commitments is, no doubt, sketchy. But I hope that it is enough to support a crucial, contrastive, thesis. The thesis is that no substantial, and distinctive, *ontological* or *epistemological* commitments are accumulated by endorsing (asserting) those theories of modality, and those parts of theories, that consist in truth-condition-stating (and other) biconditionals.[37] Yet, a significant part

---

[37] Obviously enough, the assertion of the semantic-cum-conceptual claims raises a question about the ontological and epistemological commitments of the semantic-cum-conceptual theory. But that is a more general question and a question that doesn't only arise when the explananda are modal (versus mathematical, moral, etc.)

of what falls under the headings of "the analysis of modal concepts", and even of "possible-worlds semantics", involves the assertion of no more than relevant biconditionals: statements of truth-conditions, validity-conditions, completeness conditions, etc. Thus, I claim, no substantial ontological and epistemological commitments flow from those parts of those projects that do not go beyond commitment to such biconditionals.[38]

Secondly, then, we should consider as a potential source of substantial ontological and epistemological commitments, those parts of those modal theories that involve assertion of non-conditional claims. Imagine, then, that our theorist is committed, by his analysis-cum-semantics of modal sentences, to a biconditional such as:

(f) It is possible that $P$ iff there is a possible world at which $P$.

The idea, recently anticipated, is that our theorist is still at least one serious step away from being committed to whatever she would be committed to (ontologically or epistemologically) by asserting the right-side of (f). The further step that is required is that of asserting (in some instance) the left-side of (f), but then, commitment does follow to the assertion of the right-side of (f). And given that—as presently intended—the content of what is asserted is taken as transparent, the commitments in question are (at least) ontological commitment to the existence of a possible world at which $P$ and epistemological commitment to a vindicatory account of the implied claim to know the existence of such things.[39] So the proper source of substantial ontological and epistemological commitments in our modal theorizing is commitment to assert *some* (non-conditional) modal claims.

Thirdly, then, we must consider exactly which range of modal assertion involves ontological and epistemological commitments: and thereby we uncover an important distinction between the ontological and epistemological cases. Imagine, to continue the recent case, that one is committed to the standard possible-worlds analysis of possibility claims, as in (f) above, and—indeed—to the local network of analyses that reflect the classical inter-definitions of the sentential modal operators:

(g) It is necessary that $P$ iff at every possible world, $P$

(h) It is impossible that $P$ iff there is no possible world at which $P$.

---

[38] It is important here to distinguish two elements of standard semantic or metalogical theories of modal logics. One element of these theories is the definitional, biconditional element: A is X-valid iff . . ., etc. The other element is that which consists in claims about the extensions of various concepts (predicates): that these formulas are X-valid (or valid simpliciter), these systems are X-complete, etc. But even within the class of theses about extensions, only some entail existential claims. Classically, theses about INvalidity, UNsoundness, and INcompleteness are claims about the existence of countermodels and counterexamples of various kinds: theses about validity, soundness, and completeness are universal generalizations and, as such, entail no existential consequences. See Divers (2006).

[39] So right-sides are taken in the present context at face-value and not apt to reinterpretation.

The crucial point is that within any such network of analyses, only some modal claims are treated as (implicitly) existential: others are non-existential.[40] So in the present case, even those who accept the possible-worlds analyses, and are prepared to accept various claims of necessity and impossibility, would not be committed to asserting anything that involved a commitment—or, at least, any immediately demonstrable ontological commitment—to the existence of possible worlds. And since such assertion brings no commitment to the existence of possible worlds, it brings no commitment to provide a theory about how we know of the existence of possible worlds. So we find that even *assertion of many modal claims*—those claims that are not treated as implicitly existential claims—is not an immediate source of ontological commitment.

The situation with epistemological commitments, however, is different. For, I take it, the theorist who takes herself to be in a position to assert those claims that turn out to be negative existentials (presently, necessities and impossibilities) thereby brings upon herself a commitment to tell an epistemological story—a story about how one is justified in asserting those claims despite their existential innocence.

Fourthly, the story that has emerged so far is a story that has focused on contents. But a further, and essential, part of the account of the precise sources of various commitments requires us to consider, and to be very careful about, the nature of *attitudes* towards those contents. It has been claimed that a theorist of modality acquires substantial, and non-conceptual, commitments by (both) asserting a certain view about the truth-conditions of modal sentences, and by asserting *certain* sentences so interpreted. Here I take it that one is prepared to assert a sentence with a given truth-conditional content just in case one has a belief with that truth-conditional content. And while that formulation harbours various subtleties and difficulties, I appeal to it here by way of negotiating the formulation of subsequent points in terms of belief rather than assertion. The upshot is that the source of both epistemological and of ontological commitment is *belief*. If the question then is how one might avoid such commitments, the answer, obviously enough, is by not having the relevant beliefs. But then the most elementary distinction of scope becomes absolutely crucial to circumscribing precisely the source of the modal theorist's commitments. Letting *P* stand for an arbitrary modal sentence, and adopting the psychological vernacular, the (ontologically and epistemologically) committing attitude (type) is, then:

(B)  X believes that *P*.

---

[40] This really is just one example of such a network of analyses, and it is by no means inevitable that it is possibility claims that should be the primary source of ontological commitment. An alternative semantics that sought to reflect in detail, and comprehensively, the conviction that the truth of (certain) necessity claims requires the existence of necessary connections among (conceptual or non-conceptual) things would make assertions of necessity, and not possibility, the primary source of ontological commitment.

The stronger sufficient condition for not believing that $P$—the falsehood of (B)—is (B+):

(B+) X believes that not-$P$.

The weaker, more inclusive, sufficient condition for the falsehood of (B) is (B*):

(B*) It is not the case that X believes that $P$.

The obvious psychological difference is that the attitude of agnosticism about $P$ fulfils condition (B*) but does not fulfil condition (B+). And the difference between the two cases in terms of the commitments they impose is also enormous.

In the first place, consider the case in which $P$ stands for the kind of sentence which is interpreted as existential in content. Then, if the theorist is in the stronger position (B+) she will be committed, via her network of analyses, to further modal beliefs. For example, if $P$ stands for an arbitrary possibility sentence, then the attitude captured by (B+) is that of the theorist believing, and being committed to assert, that it is not possible that $P$ and, consequently—via her analytic commitments—that it is impossible that $P$, and that it is necessary that not-$P$. By the reasoning of the earlier section, that is enough to commit our theorist to the provision of an epistemology for the impossibility and necessity—more generally, for the negated contents. In the second place, consider the case in which $P$ stands for the kind of sentence which is interpreted as negatively existential in content. Then, if the theorist is in the stronger position (B+) she will be committed, via her network of analyses, to further modal beliefs. So, as in the preceding case, she will be committed to an epistemology for the negated contents (in the case envisaged, claims of possibility). But she will also be committed ontologically since she will, in this case, be committed—through denying negative existentials—to a positive existential (in the case envisaged, the existence of some possible world). But in neither of these cases—where $P$ is taken as an existentially committing modal claim or otherwise—is one who adopts the weaker stance of (B*) committed thereby to believing anything. So, it emerges, adopting the stronger attitude (B+) entails a range of epistemological and ontological commitments that are not entailed by adopting the weaker attitude—the agnostic attitude of not-believing or declining to assert versus the harder attitude of believing the negation or asserting the contrary (denying).

The picture that unfolds, then, has as an interesting aspect a certain hierarchy of sources of philosophical commitment in modal theorizing. One contracts *conceptual* commitments from the body of modal claims that one finds intelligible. One contracts *epistemological* commitments from the body of modal claims that one believes. One contracts *ontological* commitments from the body of modal claims that one believes *and* which one interprets as having existential content. Consequently, one may avoid both epistemological and ontological commitments by not-believing in the agnostic way rather than by believing-not.

## 5. AN ILLUSTRATION: THE CASE OF DE DICTO NECESSITY

According to the functional constraint, one ought to accept no more substantial a theory than is required in order to account for the body of (functionally) de jure modal assertion, where the body of de jure modal assertion comprises the kinds of modal assertion that we (in some sense) *need* to make in order to serve whatever are the legitimate and identifiable purposes of our modalizing. In combination with the claims that have recently been made about the precise sources of various commitments, the prospect raised by the functional constraint is that we ought not to accept a theory of modality whose ontological commitments are very substantial at all. This prospect is promoted by two observations. The first observation is that when function demands the assertion of, or belief in, modal claims, it may not thereby demand assertion of modal claims that involve the theorist in substantial ontological commitments. The second observation is that function may demand only that we do not assert (believe) a certain modal claim rather than that we assert (believe) its negation. By way of an illustration of this point, I conclude by sketching the form of a theory of de dicto necessity.[41]

Imagine that we are in possession of a very good story about how we benefit—either practically or intellectually, but distinctively—from treating certain non-modal propositions as necessary. Thus we have an account of the function of (some) judgments of de dicto necessity, where the intended conception of "de dicto" is syntactic: an occurrence of a modal operator is de dicto just in case the expression that lies immediately within its syntactic scope—the thing it operates on—is a closed sentence.[42] Moreover, I will take it that it is a non-negotiable part of what it is to treat a proposition as necessary that we should believe its necessitation.[43] The two related questions I want to raise are these: (i) how far would such a story (dealing with belief in the necessity of propositions) reach and (ii) how extensive, in principle, are the commitments that might flow from such a story?

In the first place, it seems that one might have a perfectly good story about the function of de dicto necessity judgments that simply did not speak to the question of whether judgments with various other kinds of modal content even

---

[41] Here I generalize on points made earlier in Divers (2004, §6).

[42] So this conception of the de dicto is very inclusive, admitting, for example, necessity (and possibility) claims that are "about" particular things: the closed sentence may contain proper names, demonstratives, kind terms, etc.

[43] I should emphasize that I will not be appealing here to any attenuated notion of assertion or belief: I will not be contrasting assertion with quasi-assertion nor contrasting belief with quasi-belief or acceptance. The only distinction I ask for here is that between full-blooded, out-and-out, ontologically committing assertion and belief—on one hand—and simply not so believing or so asserting on the other.

have a function. In fact there are two sub-cases of judgment contents that are, prima facie, functionally independent.

The first sub-case is that of semantically cognate but functionally independent contents. The notion of semantically cognate judgments is explicated (roughly) as follows. It may be that the best semantic theory that we have for assigning truth-conditions to de dicto necessity claims thereby also provides, ad hockery aside, truth-conditions for certain other kinds of sentence—sentences involving de dicto occurrences of other modal operators, sentences involving de re occurrences of various modal operators, and sentences involving the occurrence of one modal operator inside the scope of another. If so, then these other judgments are semantically cognate with judgments of de dicto necessity. And if one takes as a model any standard semantic theory of quantified modal logic, that is how it turns out. Now there are two points about these semantically cognate judgments. The first point is that one might have a story—even a good story—about why we treat certain propositions as necessary without having a story about the function of the semantically cognate judgments. And according to the functional constraint, then, we would lack any direct justification for asserting any such claim.[44] The second point is that it is quite consistent with that outcome—and indeed built into the notion of semantically cognate judgment—that we should regard the other judgments as perfectly meaningful, and of having an account of their truth-conditions to offer. The gap we may find is between taking ourselves to be in a position to say that much and taking ourselves to be either entitled or compelled to claim that the truth-conditions are fulfilled. In sum, certain modal judgments—semantically cognate modal judgments—may be no more than a semantic epiphenomenon of the functionally efficacious modal judgments.

The second, and easier, sub-case is where a certain type of modal judgment is not even semantically cognate with the judgments of the given kind. That is to say, roughly, that one might have an optimal semantic theory of the given judgments that did not encompass judgments of the further kind by assigning truth-conditions to them (or even recognizing them as part of the object-language). Thus for example, it might be that counterfactual conditionals are semantically independent of judgments of de dicto modal judgments. And in such cases it seems, if anything, even more obvious that one could have a story—even a good story—about the function of the given judgments that was simply silent on the function of counterfactual conditional judgments.

So, a good story about the function of judgments of de dicto necessity might, in principle, stand quite independently of the availability of a story about—for example—any judgments of de re modality, judgments involving

---

[44] I say "direct" justification in seeking to make room for the following indirect case. We may "need" to assert a modal proposition because we are committed to regarding it as a consequence of another modal proposition that we have a direct, functionally righteous, warrant to assert.

iterated modality, or counterfactually conditional judgments. And in light of the functional constraint, the prospect then opens up that one might have a theory of de dicto necessity that did not entail any of the further commitments that would be entailed by the need to assert any of these other kinds of judgment.

In the second case, we should consider what the commitments of a theory of de dicto necessity are, and particularly so in relation to immediately related semantically cognate judgments of de dicto possibility and de dicto impossibility.

I have already accepted as part of the profile that our theorist would be committed to being a self-ascriber of various beliefs—beliefs such as:

(a)  X believes that (It is necessary that $P$ iff $Q$)

(b)  X believes that (It is necessary that $P$).

Now imagine that we are working within the confines of a standard possible-worlds semantic account so that the content clause of (a) has a non-existential expansion—thus:

(a\*)  X believes that (It is necessary that $P$ iff at every possible world, $P$).

The need to deploy judgments of de dicto necessity in their correct functional role will, I have supposed, call for belief in some such necessities. And the functional constraint enjoins us to accept such ontological commitments as are functionally compelled. But no ontological commitments in the form of commitment to possible worlds flow from the (hypothesized) need to assert any de dicto necessity claim (so interpreted). Nor will any such commitments be entailed by the need (if any) to assert judgments in the semantically cognate cases of de dicto impossibility or de dicto strict conditionals. So whatever function is served by the making of these de dicto modal assertions we can have at no ontological cost. Furthermore, we can also have for nothing whatever function requires us to distinguish operationally—as it were—between judgments we treat as necessary and judgments that we don't. For the cognitive reflection of that operational distinction is that we believe that some propositions are necessary and we lack the belief(s) that others are necessary. But neither ontological commitment nor epistemological commitment flows from the constraint that one should *lack* the belief that a proposition is necessary (by contrast, of course, with the constraint that one should believe that a proposition is *not* necessary). So the position, as it stands, is this. One could have a good theory of the function of judgments of de dicto necessity, a theory that required belief in (and assertion of) all sorts of de dicto necessities, strict conditionals, and impossibilities—and one could *even* harness that theory to a standard possible-worlds semantic theory (quite literally and seriously construed) while bringing upon oneself no commitment to the existence of possible worlds. To that extent, I claim, the liberating and exciting effect of the functional constraint is to allow us to entertain seriously the prospect of a functionally vindicated and ontologically minimal theory of modality until, and unless, the functional case for extending the body of modal belief is made.[45]

## 6. A BRIEF SUMMARY

We don't have a very good answer to the question of what the functions of the various kinds of modal judgment are. But it is a good question, intrinsically, and one that cannot easily be dismissed. Moreover, want of an account of function disposes us to construct theories of modality that respond too readily to data about actual usage, intuition, and phenomenology and not readily enough to considerations about the point of making modal judgments. The upshot is that theories of modality are apt to be excessively substantial. In conjunction with some answer to the question of the function of modal judgment, the functional constraint on the construction of modal theories promises less substantial theories than those to which we have become accustomed. Even in the absence of the functional constraint, there is much to be learned about how substantial a theory of modality need be: for much can be learned simply by being careful about what the precise sources of our conceptual, epistemological, and ontological commitments are. But when we ally the results of those reflections to the functional constraint, I believe that a weighty burden of proof lies on those who would sustain their preference for ontologically (and otherwise) substantial theories of modality. For there is no story at all about why functionally effective modalizing requires the assertion of those modal judgments that are specifically responsible for the generation of the ontological commitments in question.

---

[45] The crucial case to be considered is that of belief in (non-actualized, de dicto) possibility claims (so long as it is these that are treated as the implicitly existential contents). I cannot attempt here to anticipate and meet the various ways in which a case might be made for the functional indispensability of beliefs about possibility. But a natural development of the dialectic is reflected in the following two points. First, it is surely the case that planning or decision-making requires us to have some conception of a relevant range of alternatives. But how are we disadvantaged if we take the relevant range as that which we do not believe to be impossible? Secondly, it is surely the case that we have an interest in distinguishing those inferences that are necessarily truth-preserving from those that are not. But why, exactly, should it ever matter that I am in a position to assert that a form of inference lacks this feature (assert that it is invalid) rather than simply decline to assert that it has this feature (refuse to assert that is valid)? How will taking the stronger line put a different range of inferences at my disposal? Won't I simply deploy and eschew the very same forms of inference depending exactly on which cases I believe to be valid (and independently of whether I distinguish the invalid among the complement)? See Divers (2006, §7).

# Response to John Divers

## Daniel Nolan

The question of the function of modal judgement is an interesting philosophical issue, and John Divers's paper (Chapter 10, above) has persuaded me that it has not received the attention it deserves. I think it is an important and interesting question even apart from any more ambitious claims that are made about its role in settling other issues about modality. Even if we became convinced that the story about function put no constraints whatsoever, epistemologically or metaphysically, on a theory of modality, it would still remain an interesting question about one of the pervasive and perhaps fundamental things we do in our cognitive lives.

Divers's paper is primarily concerned with establishing the legitimacy and importance of the question of the function of modal judgement, and disposing of some "quick answers" that might incline you to think there was not much of importance to be found here. There is too much that is thought-provoking to try to cover everything, so in these comments I want to talk about three things. The first two are challenges to Divers's project. Should sorting out the function of modal judgement be a job for philosophers in the first place? When we think about the question of function in other areas of theory, don't we realize that it should not play a very central role in modal theorizing? Then I'll end with something perhaps more constructive: a quite general kind of answer we should consider to Divers's central question.

## 1. SHOULD PHILOSOPHERS BE DOING THIS?

On the face of it, why people do certain particular things, and why certain social institutions exist, sound like questions for the social sciences. In particular, questions about why we make certain sorts of judgements look like psychological ones, or perhaps sociolinguistic ones if we focus on the practice of making public utterances expressing and evaluating these judgements. We need not assume that there is just one function, or a unified story about function for the whole, so the question "what are the functions of modal judgement?" is likely to be controversial, thorny, and might well repay some observation of people actually

Thanks to anonymous referees and to Carrie Jenkins for discussion.

modalizing. It's a lesson we learned slowly in the modern and contemporary period, but often if you want to find out how these conventional activities work and what they are aimed at, getting out of the armchair and having a look is usually important. Indeed, some empirical work has been done on modal judgement: a landmark is Jean Piaget's two pioneering volumes in developmental psychology *Possibility and Necessity* (1981, 1983), and if I were a psychologist or sociolinguist, I hope I would know of more.

Something like that would be the challenge, I take it. In fact, even though the function of modal judgement is an eminently a posteriori issue, I think philosophers do potentially have a useful role to play in answering it. There are a variety of things that can be usefully done from the armchair, even on empirical questions. There is useful ground clearing to be done in distinguishing different questions, suggesting initially plausible hypotheses for further scrutiny, assembling reminders about some of the kinds of phenomena to take into account, and so on. That does not sound like much in the abstract, but I think it can sometimes take us quite some way in a field that is in its infancy, and the investigation of the functions of modal judgement seems to me to be such a field.

One might object that discovering the function of modal judgement is a philosophical issue, because it is a normative one: we are not being asked just to work out when, in fact, people make modal judgements, or what in fact the effect of modalizing is, but rather what we *should* be modalizing for (if anything), what *good* it does us (if any). I agree that part of the question of the function of modal judgement is normative, but I would disagree with the view that this moved it out of the reach of the social sciences. Perhaps the natural sciences can avoid studying the normative, but most social sciences cannot: they are up to their neck in theories about function. It is an interesting question in the philosophy of social sciences *how* empirical investigation can shed light on normative questions, but that is what it seems to be doing.

So we should keep in mind that decent answers to questions about the function of modal judgement may have to await input from psychologists, sociologists, and others. Nevertheless, I think we (and particularly Divers) can probably get on and do some useful work before we call in the non-philosophers.

## 2. IS THE FUNCTIONAL CONSTRAINT TOO STRONG?

The second challenge is to the central role that Divers wants to suggest for considerations of function when we are formulating the rest of our theory of modality. Divers suggests a "functional constraint":

[O]ne ought to accept no more substantial a theory than is required in order to account for the body of (functionally) de jure modal assertion. The body of de jure modal assertion comprises the kinds of modal assertion that we (in some sense) *need* to make in order to serve whatever are the legitimate and identifiable purposes of our modalizing.

222          *Daniel Nolan*

First a comment about this as a piece of advice about how to proceed: it might be counterproductive to insist on a story about what a set of judgements are good for before we have a good story about what they amount to. If you don't understand a topic, you are unlikely to be able to perfectly understand what the information is good for, as anyone who has filled out a grant application aimed at non-specialists can probably tell you. Of course we do not need to treat this constraint as a starting point, and I'm not sure Divers wants us to: perhaps it is best seen as standing in a dialectical relationship to our theorizing—we have a stab at what is going on, and from that vantage point we work out if some of our commitments are unneeded for what seems to be the relevant purposes, and back again, simultaneously improving our understanding of modality and the role of modal judgement.

Even so, I think it is implausibly strong. When trying to work out how to constrain theories, I often think it's better to start with examples where we seem to have been doing pretty well—maybe the analogies won't transfer across, but if not it would be interesting to hear what the dissimilarities might be. So let's consider astronomy, and let's go back to its infancy. In ancient times, what was the function of astronomical judgement? Well, there were a few star-gazers, theologians, and other theorist types who really cared about the stars and planets themselves, but a lot of people wanted to know about two things: astrological stuff, about how the stars and planets were going to affect them, and "applied astronomy" such as treating the heavens as a navigation aid, as a calendar, etc. Suppose our proto-astronomer Diveros told us that astronomy should be subjected to a functional constraint: that we should not endorse any astronomical judgements that did not serve the "legitimate and identifiable purposes" of our astronomical judgements. Let's finally suppose we, anachronistically, manage to work out that we should reject astrology, or at least be agnostic about it.

Here are two ways of doing astronomy: coming up with tables of where the lights are in the sky when, on the one hand, and speculating about what the lights are and what relationships they stand in to each other, on the other. The latter involves a lot of theorizing that seems to go beyond the function of astronomical judgement, at least insofar as that is given by navigation and time-keeping purposes. But of course trying to work out what the planets are doing up there is by far the better way of coming up with a good astronomical theory: even if people like Ptolemy added instrumental glosses to their theory, it was the glory of Greek astronomy that it speculated about the nature of the planets, and came up with orbits and all the rest.

Okay, so maybe some planetary speculation was called for because we had a hunch we could improve the tables that way. (I doubt that hunch was particularly justified until planetary theorizing was fairly advanced, but no matter.) Should we, on grounds of function, stick to coming up with an instrumentally understood planetary theory that saves the phenomena? In the early modern period, instrumentalism and realism clashed again. Perhaps Divers, with Osiander, would urge us to treat the Copernican shift as a mere instrument. An attempt by Galileo or Newton to go beyond function and try to work out a plausible physics of the celestial bodies seems rather uncalled for, at least by the best accounts of the functions of astronomical judgement at the time of Osiander. (Unless just getting it right about the heavenly body is an important function of theoretical astronomy—but this sounds rather like the "bluntly cognitive" response Divers finds unsatisfactory.)

But let's face it, if your account of astronomical method condemns Newton's *Principia* as poor astronomical theory construction—in this case, because it took on too many commitments that took us beyond the pre-established "function" of astronomical judgement—then that is a *reductio* of the functional constraint, not a problem for Newton's astronomical theory. The fact that Newton's theory went well beyond what we need to tell the time or find out which way is north does not tempt anyone I've ever met, at least, to think we should be instrumentalist about it.[1] Perhaps we could try to say that while it fails to be good astronomy, it is good physics because of some function of physics it serves well—but frankly, sugaring a cyanide pill doesn't make it more appealing.

Consider another example (at less length). Suppose I worry that geology has lost its way—too much contemporary geology does not directly serve the "functions of geological judgement". Let us just suspend judgement about a lot of geology, and just keep the stuff that will find us oil or uranium or tell us when volcanoes are likely to erupt, and that sort of thing. Who's with me? Why not? You might think one of the main functions of geology is to get it right about how the Earth's crust, and perhaps below, is arranged. This "bluntly cognitive" function would serve to rule out most functionalist clamour to suspend judgement, of course, but if Divers is right, citing this sort of function "misses the point" and should be set aside.

Another reason we might be suspicious of imposing functional constraints on either astronomy historically or geology today is the somewhat holistic nature of the enterprise. To have the best geological theory about the location of oil deposits, we need to bring in all sorts of information about tectonic shifts, past land levels rising and falling, geological movements in different sorts of rock, and so on, and a lot of that information may have been first discovered and tested in areas that appeared to be only of "academic interest". And we should not burn, or cease believing, the unnecessary knowledge today, either, since progress on topics that may eventually serve an instrumental purpose may come from study of rocks or formations or movements that are far from mainstream interest today. The path that led us to our current understanding of the solar system and beyond, and abilities to predict astronomical phenomena beyond the dreams of the ancients, depended on a diverse range of enquiries interacting in ways that could not have been predicted in advance, including

---

[1] Perhaps Bas van Fraassen is an exception.

investigation into many phenomena, terrestrial and celestial, that seemed to be of no practical interest. Likewise with our understanding of our planet and its geology.

If this sort of epistemic holism is right in astronomy and geology, might it be right in the theory of modality? If it is, and I'm inclined to think that it is, we should try to work out what's right, and then work out what can be useful to us. Of course we do not need to wait until theoretical inquiry is finished before beginning the practical inquiry, and we don't, but even those uninterested in the theory of modality for its own sake should be cautious about dispensing with sections of modal theorizing as not currently useful for today's practical purposes. To get it right about the things that practically matter, I'm afraid we have to investigate matters that are not otherwise of practical interest—as test cases, as sources of insight, as reminders. At least that's true in astronomy and geology, and if it's not in the theory of modality, I would like to hear the reasons why.

What does this say about the functional constraint? It could be read as consistent with it—lots of modal judgements do serve a function, it's just that they serve those functions indirectly as being part of our overall project of inquiry. They help get the practical bits right (whatever they are). Of course, if we want to count any modal investigation as "functional" in this sense, fine, but then we've saved the functional criterion at the cost of eviscerating it, since the most academic mucking around with Kripkean essentialism of origin for tables or the modal profiles of tropes might get a free pass quickly once some modalizing, somewhere, is legitimated by reference to some instrumental purpose, and it is established that it matters that we get things right.


## 3. MODAL DESIRES

The third thing I want to cover in my comments is a suggestion for a kind of function that we might propose for modal judgements, and one that might make for a quick answer to the question of the function of a lot of modal judgements.

Often when we want to know what a piece of theorizing is for, or why we should do it, we are told about how it serves some desires of ours. Why do we collect information about water use, or theorize about water use in Britain? Well, for a variety of reasons, but one of the important ones is because we want supplies of clean water for drinking, bathing, industrial purposes, etc., and we want water for irrigation, feeding stock, and so on. The purpose of tracking water use in Britain is, in part, to enable us to get what we want, water-wise. We have many desires about water, and we seek to satisfy them. Analogously, we have a lot of modal desires. We desire to keep some possibilities open and close others off. We desire that some things have to happen, and other things do not have to happen. Since Divers brought up subjunctive conditionals, the field of desires with conditional content is very wide: I want it to be the case that if you steal from me, you go to prison, for example.[2] (Incidentally, there's a big problem for expressivism about conditionals waiting here: how could they express the contents of desires?)

Now, to satisfy these desires with modal content, it's very likely that we would need to make modal judgements. Finding out how the world is, modally speaking, is one of the first steps to changing it to suit us. There are more indirect connections too: sometimes when I care about something, I want to know how it stands, even if I cannot do much about it. (I want to know how tsunami reconstruction is going in Indonesia, even though there's not a lot I plan to do about it either way.) Even for modal matters that we cannot easily affect, if we want them to be some way rather than another, modal judgement seems called for to find out how they are.

So here is one story about the function of modal judgement: it is to tell us how things stand with respect to matters that we have desires with modal content about. Of course, this invites some further questions: What modal matters do we care about? Do we need all of our modalizing to answer to this need? The answer is pretty clearly *yes* if the desires include those of modal theorists: I want to know how things stand modally, de re as well as de dicto, alethically as well as epistemically and deontically, even if nobody else does. But maybe a lot of it is dispensable to answer to the desires of the people on the street. (There is presumably a controversy to be had whether the people on the street care about what is metaphysically necessary or not, for example.)

There is another set of further questions Divers may want to ask us. What is the function of modal desires? Should we have them? Should they obey a functional constraint: that we should only have, or attempt to satisfy, those modal desires that we *need* to have "in order to serve whatever are the legitimate and identifiable purposes of our modalizing"?

But here the ground might shift a bit, especially for a Humean. I'm inclined to think that sometimes, indeed, often, having a desire for something gives one an identifiable purpose for getting it. The question about purpose makes sense for those modal desires that are instrumental for a non-modal goal—then it seems perfectly appropriate to ask whether they are suited for their purpose, and whether there might be a better thing to want in order to serve that goal. But we have been given no reason to think all our modal desires are instrumental, and I think it is very plausible that some of them are not. My desire to be free, for example, seems to me a modal one—it is a desire, at least in part, for a cluster of abilities, and absence of necessities constraining me—but I'm not sure I want

---

[2] Okay, maybe I'm more of a softy than that. But steal too much, and I want you to go to prison.

that purely instrumentally.[3] Being free rather than a slave or a prisoner or a serf helps me get other things I want, but it's a good state to be in as well. Likewise my desire to have various cognitive abilities—it's not just instrumentally valuable for me that I'm not a vegetable.

There are further interesting lines of inquiry open here as well: What modal desires of ours are non-instrumental? What are the ways modal desires could be instrumental for non-modal ends? Thinking about the function of modal desires opens up interesting questions. But I do think we should be very careful imposing a functional constraint on our modal desires. If I want something, I don't want to have to wait until the philosophers have finished analysing its status, whether it is instrumental, whether my wanting it serves some purpose we would endorse: I want it now. So *pro tem* at least, we have one available story about the function of a lot of modal judgement: we make judgements about those topics because we have practical concerns about some modal matters. And while further investigation is fascinating, I don't want to stop caring until the philosophers tell me it's okay to be interested.

---

[3] A referee pointed out that in some of the classic Frankfurt cases—where I do what I want when I $\varphi$ but evil scientists stand ready to take over to ensure I $\varphi$ whether I want to or not, for example—what is undesirable is not anything about what I in fact do, but only about what *would* happen were things otherwise.

# PART II
# EPISTEMOLOGY

# 11

# Permission and (So-Called Epistemic) Possibility

*Stephen Yablo*

It is just possible that I can explain the structure of this paper by comparing it to a Soviet-era joke, based apparently on a remark of John Kenneth Galbraith's.

> Worker to party official: Tell me, what is the difference between Capitalism and Communism?
>
> Party official: Good question, comrade. It's this. Under Capitalism, you see, man exploits man. Under Communism, it's the other way around.

The joke operates on several levels. "The other way around" presumably means that under communism, *man* exploits *man*; and that sounds exactly the same as what was said about capitalism. Second, though, it's not as though we can't hear a difference between the first "man exploits man" and the second; one has the sense it's different men in the two cases. Third, though, that difference overlays a deeper similarity; one group exploiting another makes for a lot of the same unpleasantness as the other group exploiting the first.

Now consider the sentence, or sentence-fragment, *that may be*. It too can be read in two ways. On the one reading, it indicates that a certain state of affairs, $\varphi$ let's call it, is not ruled out. On the other reading, it *also* indicates that $\varphi$ is not ruled out.

*This* is a *distinction*? Just as in the exploitation joke, it's hard to see what difference there could be between $\varphi$'s not being ruled out and, well, $\varphi$'s not being ruled out. But, and this is the second point of analogy, it's not as though we can't hear a difference between different utterances of "Such and such is not ruled out". Compare "Sabotage is not ruled out," said by an FAA investigator after

I am grateful to Seth Yalcin, Eric Swanson, Bob Stalnaker, Thony Gillies, Kai von Fintel, Caspar Hare, Carrie Jenkins, Kit Fine, George Bealer, Andy Egan, Tim Williamson, Josh Dever, Nicholas Asher, David Beaver, Cleo Condoravdi, Alejandro Peréz Carballo, Paolo Santorio, and participants (beyond those already mentioned) in the Arché Conference on Modality (St Andrews, 2006), especially my excellent commentator David Efird, and the Austin Workshop on Epistemic Modals (University of Texas at Austin, 2006).

the plane crashes, and "Sabotage is not ruled out" said by a rebel leader six months before the crash. The investigator is saying that sabotage is not ruled out *descriptively*, as it would be if she'd asserted, "There was no sabotage". The rebel leader is saying that it is not ruled out *prescriptively*, as it would be if she'd commanded her underlings not to engage in sabotage. Yet, and this is the third point of analogy, just as the two things it can mean for man to dominate man have at a deeper level a lot in common, the two things "That may be" can mean have at a deeper level a lot in common. The descriptive reading, "That may be *so*," has a lot in common with the deontic reading, "That may be *done*." That anyway is what I'll be arguing in this paper.

What does it matter, though, if the one "may" has properties in common with the other? It matters because descriptive (often called *epistemic*) "may" is *extremely confusing*; and the questions we are driven to as we attempt to understand it are questions that, as it happens, have been much discussed in connection with deontic "may".

The standard semantics for "it may be (or might be, or it is possible) that $\varphi$"[1] has it expressing something in the vicinity of the speaker's failing to know that $\sim\varphi$. Thus Moore:

> It's possible that I'm not sitting down now . . . means 'It is not certain that I am' or 'I don't know that I am'[2]

More sophisticated versions allow the knower(s) and/or the information against which $\varphi$ is tested to vary:[3]

> It is possible$_A$ that $p$ is true if and only if what $A$ knows does not, in a manner that is obvious to $A$, entail not-$p$.[4]

> "It is possible that $p$" is true if and only if (1) no member of the relevant community knows that $p$ is false, and (2) there is no relevant way by which members of the relevant community can come to know that $p$ is false.[5]

There is undoubtedly something right about the standard semantics. But there are things wrong with it too.

One problem is that it gets the subject matter wrong. When I say, "Bob might be in his office," I am talking about Bob and his office, not myself or the extent of my information.[6] Suppose the building is on fire and everyone has been told

---

[1] I will generally use "might" rather than "may" for so-called epistemic possibility.
[2] Moore (1962), p. 184.
[3] DeRose (1991); Hacking (1967); Teller (1972); von Fintel and Gillies (2008).
[4] Stanley (2005), p. 128.    [5] DeRose (1991), pp. 593–4.
[6] It might seem this worry could be sidestepped by putting speaker's knowledge into the mechanism by which the content is generated, rather than the content itself (as in Kratzer 1981). Speaker's knowledge would play the same sort of role in the evaluation of "might"-claims as speaker's attention plays in the evaluation of "you"-claims. Andy Egan has convinced me that

to leave. I am afraid that Bob might still be in his office. I am not afraid that I don't know he's elsewhere.

Two, the proposed truth-conditions, at least in their naïve Moorean form, are too weak. The mere fact that I don't myself know that $\sim\varphi$ doesn't make it true in my mouth that $\varphi$ might be so. Suppose you question my claim on the basis that Bob was just seen stepping onto a plane. It would be no reply at all to say that my information really was as limited as I suggested; I really and truly didn't know that Bob was not in his office. Evidently the information that needs to comport with $\varphi$ for a might-claim to be correct can extend beyond what the speaker personally knows at the time of utterance. The proposal should really be that "it might be that $\varphi$" is true iff $\varphi$ is not ruled out by any *pertinent* facts—where the test of pertinence is presumably that the speaker is prepared to acknowledge that she was mistaken if these facts really do/did obtain.[7]

But, and this is the third problem, the truth-conditions are now so strong that speakers generally have no idea whether they are satisfied—so strong that speakers should refrain from asserting that $\varphi$ might be so. The principle here is that I should not assert that $\chi$, if (a) I am aware of a $\psi$ such that $\chi$ is false if $\psi$ is true, and (b) I consider $\psi$ entirely likely to be true. When $\chi$ is "it might be that $\varphi$", I am virtually always aware of a $\psi$ like that, viz. "somewhere out there, there is evidence that rules $\varphi$ out". $\psi$ meets condition (a) because I freely accept that my might-claim is mistaken if $\varphi$ is ruled out by the evidence, including evidence I don't myself possess. I freely accept, for instance, that if Bob was seen getting on a plane at 11:55, then it is not true that Bob might now (at noon) be in his office. $\psi$ satisfies condition (b) because I do not, when I say that it might be that $\varphi$, take myself to know that my evidence is relevantly complete; *obviously* I might be missing something which makes $\varphi$ highly unlikely.[8] It is clear to me, when I say that Bob might be in his office, that evidence not in my possession might well show he is somewhere else. But now, if I think it entirely possible that there is evidence that exposes my statement as false, how in good conscience can I make the statement? Who would dare make a might-claim, if the claim was entirely likely to be wrong?

The fourth problem with the standard semantics is that it is too *epistemic*. I have a thing about the sanctity of the ballot box, imagine, so when you ask me whether I am going to vote for Kucinich, I say, "I might or I might not," despite knowing perfectly well what I've decided, and not trying to hide the fact that I

---

there is still a prima facie problem, since the Kratzer-proposition is at root a consistency claim, and consistency-claims have the wrong evidential and modal properties.

[7] For more on these issues, see Egan (2007); Egan, Hawthorne, and Weatherson (2005); MacFarlane (2003, forthcoming); von Fintel and Gillies (2008).

[8] If that kind of knowledge were required, I would not say "it might be that $\varphi$ and it might be that $\sim\varphi$" unless I thought that $\varphi$ was *objectively undecidable*, in the sense that all the evidence in the world left it an open question whether $\varphi$.

know. (I am lying if I say I don't know whether I'll vote for Kucinich, but it is not a lie to say I might vote for him or I might not.) Or suppose that I run into a creditor who demands that I give him a check by the end of the day. I know perfectly well that I am going to do what he asks—I have the check in my pocket—but still I say, "I might or I might not; it might have to wait until tomorrow," for the loan is not strictly due until Friday. I say it not because I don't know I'll give him the check today, but because I reserve the right not to; it's not a limit in my information I'm indicating, but rather a limit in what I'm prepared to commit to. One final example. Imagine I am pitching a story line to a Hollywood mogul. "Now comes the good part," I tell him. "The Raskolnikov character brutally murders the pawnbroker." "Not a chance, not if we want PG-13," comes the reply. "OK," I say in a concessive spirit, "so he might just rough her up a bit." The "might" here is not to indicate the limits of my knowledge; there is nothing to know in this case, since the movie almost certainly won't get made. It's to indicate the limits of my proposal.

A fifth problem is more logical in nature. Suppose $\varphi$ is consistent with all pertinent information. Then so is everything $\varphi$ entails. One would expect, then, that if $\varphi$ entailed $\psi$, "it might be that $\varphi$" would entail "it might be that $\psi$". One would expect, for instance, that "Bob might be in his office" would entail "Bob might be in his office or in an opium den". And yet "Bob might be in his office or in an opium den" makes a stronger claim, to the effect that Bob might be in the one place *and* in addition he might be in the other. There is of course a similar puzzle about permission: how is it that "you can go or stay" entails (or seems to) that you can do whichever you want, that is, it is open to you to go *and* it is open to you to stay?[9]

The sixth problem I learned from Seth Yalcin. An advantage sometimes claimed for the standard semantics is that it explains the paradoxicality of "$\varphi$ and it might be that $\sim\varphi$". To say that is to say in effect, "$\varphi$ but I don't know that $\varphi$". And that's just Moore's paradox. The usual line on Moore's paradox is that the Moore-sentence is *unassertable* even though there's no reason it can't be true. The proof it's a problem of assertability rather than truth is that there's nothing to stop me from *supposing*, say in the antecedent of a conditional, that $\varphi$ and I don't know it; "if a piano is unbeknownst to me falling on my head, I am in for a big shock." One would expect, then, that "$\varphi$ & it might be that $\sim\varphi$" would be supposable too. And it isn't. "If a piano is falling on my head but it might not be falling on my head, . . ." makes no sense. The sixth problem is that "$\varphi$ & it might be that $\sim\varphi$" is not coherently supposable, and the standard semantics offers no explanation of this.

So the traditional "static" semantics for epistemic modals has its problems. This has led some to propose a *dynamic* semantics; the meaning of "might $\varphi$" is given

---

[9] Kamp (1973); Zimmermann (2000).

not by its truth-conditions but its effect on context or shared information. The most popular version of this is Frank Veltman's *default semantics*.[10] Veltman says that "might $\varphi$" uttered in information state S returns that same information state S if S is consistent with $\varphi$, and returns the null information state if S is not consistent with $\varphi$. Both parts of this seem prima facie at odds with the way "might" is used.

Consider first the idea that "might $\varphi$" returns the null state when S is inconsistent with $\varphi$. Suppose it is understood all around that John, Paul, George, and Ringo will be at the party. Then Yoko runs in with the news that Ringo might not be able to make it. Ringo's not making it is inconsistent with John, Paul, George, and Ringo being there. All our information is demolished, then. Intuitively, though, the information that John, Paul, and George will be at the party remains when we learn that Ringo might not attend.[11]

The idea that "might $\varphi$" returns S if $\varphi$ is consistent with S seems questionable, too. It's consistent with John, Paul, George, and Ringo being at the party that Ringo or Elton John stays away; for it might be Elton John that stays away. Nevertheless, if Yoko runs in with the news that Ringo or Elton John might not be attending, we will hardly keep on assuming that all four Beatles will be there. Rather our shared information is weakened to: John, Paul, and George will be at the party.

It seems from these examples that "might $\varphi$", uttered in information state S, has or can have the effect of cutting S down to a weaker information state S′; and it can have this effect both when $\varphi$ is consistent with S and when $\varphi$ is inconsistent with S. If we model information states with sets of worlds, then the effect of "might $\varphi$" is to add on additional worlds. The question, of course, is *which* additional worlds. The reason for looking at *deontic* modals is that the analogous question about them was raised years ago by David Lewis, in a paper called "A Problem about Permission".

Lewis starts by describing a simple language game. The players are Master, Slave, and Kibitzer, though we'll be ignoring Kibitzer (he's used to it). Master issues commands and permissions to Slave, thereby shrinking and expanding what Lewis calls the *sphere of permissibility*, the set of worlds where Slave behaves as he's supposed to. Behaving as he's supposed to is Slave's only purpose in this game, and given how we defined the sphere of permissibility, that comes to behaving so that the actual world lies within that sphere. Slave can't stay within the sphere, though, unless he knows where the sphere is. Let's try to help him with this: how does the sphere evolve?

---

[10] Gillies (2004); Veltman (1996).

[11] The counter-response is that we would take steps to avoid this disaster by scaling back to an information state consistent with Ringo's non-attendance. I agree that this is what we would do; the question is whether scaling back should be understood as a repair strategy used when disaster threatens, or as part of "might"'s basic semantic functioning. See Fuhrmann (1999). Thanks here to Thony Gillies.

When the game begins, all worlds are permissible. Now Master begins issuing commands and permissions. Our job is to figure out the function that takes a given sequence of commands (written !$\varphi$) and permissions (written i$\varphi$) to the set of worlds permissible after all those commands and permissions have been given. That fortunately boils down to two simpler-seeming sub-tasks: first, figure out the effect of a *command* on the sphere of permissibility, second, figure out the effect of a *permission* on the sphere of permissibility.

You might think the second sub-task would be the easier one: a sphere of *permissibility* would seem to be more directly responsive to *permissions* than commands. But it's actually the first sub-task that's easier. Suppose the going sphere of permissibility is S and Master says "Mop that floor!" Then the new sphere S′ is the old one S, restricted to worlds where the floor gets mopped. The rule stated generally is

$$!\varphi: S \rightarrow S \cap |\varphi|,$$

or to formulate it as an identity:

(C) $!\varphi(S) = S \cap |\varphi|$.

The left-to-right inclusion here ($!\varphi(S) \subseteq S \cap |\varphi|$) follows from two extremely plausible assumptions:

(c1) commands shrink (i.e. don't expand) the sphere,

and

(c2) commands to $\varphi$ make *all* $\sim\varphi$-worlds impermissible

The right-to-left inclusion ($!\varphi(S) \supseteq S \cap |\varphi|$) follows from (c1) and a third plausible assumption

(c3) commands to $\varphi$ make *only* $\sim\varphi$-worlds impermissible.

All this is treated by Lewis as relatively undebatable, and nothing will be said against it here; it serves as the background to the problem to come.

That problem concerns permission. If commands go with intersection, the obvious first thought about permissions is that they would go with unions:

$$i\varphi: S \rightarrow S \cup |\varphi|,$$

or, the corresponding identity

(P) $i\varphi(S) = S \cup |\varphi|$.

The left to right inclusion ($i\varphi(S) \subseteq S \cup |\varphi|$) is hard to argue with; it follows from

(p1) permissions expand (i.e., do not shrink) the sphere,

and

(p2) permission to $\varphi$ renders only $\varphi$-worlds permissible.

But the right to left direction requires along with (p1) the principle

(??) permission to $\varphi$ renders *all* $\varphi$-worlds permissible.

And while it is hard to argue with

(p3) permission to $\varphi$ renders *some* $\varphi$-worlds permissible,

(??) seems clearly wrong. Lewis explains why:

Suppose the Slave had been commanded to carry rocks every day of the week, but on Thursday the Master relents and says to the Slave, 'iThe Slave does no work tomorrow'. . . . He has thereby permitted a holiday, but not just any possible sort of holiday . . . [not] a holiday that starts on Friday and goes on through Saturday, or a holiday spent guzzling in his wine cellar . . .    (2000, p. 27)

So (??) allows in too much. (p3) on the other hand, although correct, can't be the whole story. Not any old expanded sphere which contains $\varphi$-worlds will do, for the one whose sole $\varphi$-world has Slave staying on holiday through Saturday won't do. So the situation is this:

Some worlds where the Slave does not work on Friday have been brought into permissibility, but not all of them. The Master has not said which ones. He did not need to; somehow, that is understood.    (2000, p. 27)

If it's understood, there must be a way we understand it: there must be a rule or principle of sphere-evolution that captures our shared implicit understanding of how permissions work.

Now we reach the problem of Lewis's paper. What is that rule? Or to put it negatively, what exactly is wrong with a rule R that tells us that having been permitted to take Friday off, Slave can take that and other days off? Lewis looks at five answers.

## (1) R lets in more worlds than necessary

Putting in a Saturday-off world enlarges the sphere more than necessary to allow Friday-off worlds. It's a "gratuitous enlargement" in the sense of adding more worlds than necessary.

Lewis replies that any reasonable enlargement will be gratuitous in that sense, since the only non-gratuitous enlargements add in just a single world. This is fair enough, but it is not, I think, the "real" problem. If it were, then limiting ourselves to non-gratuitous (single-world) enlargements would address it. And it doesn't; for we could pick as our single world a world where Slave takes Saturday off too.

### (2)  R lets in worlds more remote than necessary

Including Saturday-off worlds is a gratuitous enlargement in a *qualitative* sense. We should allow in only the *closest* worlds where the permitted action is done.

This, Lewis says, is too restrictive. Suppose Slave had previously been ordered to carry rocks around. Then he is forced to spend his vacation lifting weights! For weight-lifting worlds are closer to rock-carrying worlds than lying-around-at-the-beach worlds are to rock-carrying worlds.

One can put the problem like this. A permission should cleanly cancel relevant earlier commands; but on the present approach supposedly cancelled commands continue, from beyond the grave as it were, to exert an effect. The *clean cancellation requirement*, as I will call it, will come up again.

### (3)  R lets in worlds more impermissible than necessary

Allowing in Saturday-off worlds is a gratuitous enlargement, not in a qualitative but a prescriptive sense. We should put in the *least impermissible* worlds where the permitted action is done. Taking Friday and Saturday off was more impermissible than taking Friday off, so two-day-off worlds remain outside the sphere.

The objection Lewis offers is that this "solution" just restates, indeed aggravates, the problem: figuring out how comparative impermissibility evolves under the impact of commands and permissions is if anything harder than figuring out how straight permissibility does.

But there's again a prior worry, I think—a version of the clean cancellation problem. Suppose Master first says not to eat any animals, then relents and permits Slave to eat lobster. Before lobster-eating was permitted, it was less impermissible to nibble on lobster than to eat a whole one. So afterward is it only permissible to nibble on lobster?

### (4)  R lets in worlds more disagreeable to Master than necessary

Allowing in Saturday-off worlds frustrates Master's known or guessable purposes.

Lewis objects that either Slave knows Master's purposes or he doesn't. If he does, there's no need for commands; he can work unsupervised. If he doesn't, then the principle cannot be what's guiding him.

Once again, there's a prior worry. Let's say Master has frequently ordered Slave to carry rocks up the hill. Presumably she did this because she wants the rocks up the hill. But the Friday-off worlds that best serve the purpose of getting them up the hill are ones where Slave invites his friends to a game of "let's see who can carry more rocks up the hill". This is again a version of the clean cancellation problem.

## (5) R lets in worlds violating more commands than necessary

This takes a bit more explanation. It's a given that Master doesn't issue commands and permissions unless she needs to. She doesn't issue the command to $\varphi$ if it is already impermissible for Slave not to $\varphi$; and she doesn't issue permission to $\varphi$ if it is already permissible for Slave to $\varphi$. In particular, then, Master would not have permitted Slave to take Friday off unless taking Friday off would otherwise have been an act of disobedience, an act in violation of some explicit or understood command. So, proposal: the effect of permitting $\varphi$ should be to invalidate any commands that forbid $\varphi$-ing—that are inconsistent with $\varphi$—while leaving other commands in place. The problem with an update rule that lets Saturday-off worlds into the sphere is that it invalidates more commands than necessary. To make Slave's taking Friday off permissible, it's enough to invalidate the work-*Friday* command; the work-Saturday command doesn't care if Slave takes Friday off, so it should be left in place.

Call this update rule the *remainder* rule because it defines $S^+$ as the set of worlds satisfying the commands that remain when the $\varphi$-inconsistent commands are knocked out. Lewis doesn't like this rule either; here is why. Clearly, to apply the rule, we need there to be a list of commands $\psi_1, \ldots, \psi_k$ such that a world is permissible iff it complies with all of them, that is,

$$S = |\psi_1| \cap |\psi_2| \cap \ldots \cap |\psi_k|.$$

For the way the rule works is we delete from this list all the $\psi_i$s inconsistent with $\varphi$, and let the commands that remain define $S^+$. If the $\varphi$-incompatible commands are $\psi_{j+1}, \psi_{j+2}, \ldots \psi_k$, the new sphere is

$$S^+ = |\psi_1| \cap |\psi_2| \cap \ldots \cap |\psi_j|.$$

Where is the initial set of commands supposed to come from, though, the one we thin out to arrive at the reduced command-set that defines the $S^+$-worlds? It would be one thing if "$i\varphi$" were the first permission uttered; for then Master's earlier utterances were all commands and we can let the $\psi_i$s be those commands. Ordinarily, though, "$i\varphi$" is preceded by commands *and other permissions*. One could try considering just the commands that have already been given, ignoring the permissions, but these will not define the current sphere of permissibility, because the update effects of the permissions will have been ignored.

It seems, then, that we are driven to *contriving*, reverse-engineering if you like, a package of commands that define the current sphere. Unfortunately the relation between S and commands defining S is one–many; lots of packages will issue in the same sphere of permissibility. How does Slave know which package to use? It makes a difference, because the effect on S of permitting $\varphi$ varies enormously with our choice of implicit commands $\psi_i$.

Suppose that the current sphere S = the worlds where Slave works all day, every day from Monday to Sunday; and that we arrived at that sphere by a series of enlargements and contractions that offer no clues to what the right $\psi_i$s, the right implicit commands, are. Slave *might* think that initially, before he is given Friday off, the commands in effect are

$\psi_1$: Slave carries rocks on Monday.

$\psi_2$: Slave carries rocks on Tuesday.

$\psi_3$: Slave carries rocks on Wednesday.

$\psi_4$: Slave carries rocks on Thursday.

$\psi_5$: Slave carries rocks on Friday.

$\psi_6$: Slave carries rocks on Saturday.

$\psi_7$: Slave carries rocks on Sunday.

The one command here inconsistent with "Slave takes Friday off" is "Slave carries rocks on Friday". Suspending that one command leaves the commands to work other days still in place. Clearly on this way of doing it, Slave has *not* been permitted to take other days off, which was the desired result. But Slave might also think that the implicit commands are

$\chi_1$: Slave carries rocks on weekdays.

$\chi_2$: Slave carries rocks on the weekend.

Now the $\varphi$-inconsistent rule, the one to be cancelled on the present hypothesis, is "Slave carries rocks weekdays". But then the sphere of permissibility expands to include all worlds where Slave works on the weekend. And that seems crazy. Master meant to give Slave Friday off, but not Monday–Thursday as well.

Lewis's objection in a nutshell is that the implicit commands are too unconstrained for the remainder rule to be of any use. He may be right in the end. I wonder, though, whether there are constraints he is missing—constraints that don't come into view until you raise his sort of problem in the starkest possible terms. Let's look then at the most extreme cases of badly chosen implicit commands. At the one extreme we have commands *each* of which is inconsistent with $\varphi$; at the other we have ones *none* of which is inconsistent with $\varphi$. An example of each-inconsistent is

$\theta_1$: Slave carries rocks every morning of the week.

$\theta_2$: Slave carries rocks every afternoon of the week.

Neither of these is compatible with Slave taking Friday off. Cancelling the $\varphi$-inconsistent commands, then, is cancelling all commands whatsoever. If all commands are canceled, then everything is permitted. Master wanted to let Slave take Friday off, but winds up giving Slave his freedom.

Now consider commands none of which individually requires Slave to work Friday, but whose *joint* effect is to require Slave to work every day of the week. For instance,

$\sigma_1$: Slave carries rocks every morning if any afternoon.

$\sigma_2$: Slave carries rocks every afternoon if every morning.

$\sigma_3$: Slave carries rocks some afternoon.

$\sigma_1$ allows Slave to take Friday off, provided he never carries rocks in the afternoon. $\sigma_2$ allows him to take Friday off, provided he omits to carry rocks some morning. $\sigma_3$ allows him to take Friday off, provided he carries rocks some afternoon. Each of the $\sigma_i$s is consistent with $\varphi$, so none of them is canceled on the present rule. But then the sphere of impermissibility never changes. Master tried to give Slave permission to take Friday off, but it turns out he still has to work on Friday.

What can we conclude from this? The remainder rule—the one that says to cancel all and only pre-existing commands that forbid $\varphi$—can give *very silly results*. But we can make that work in our favor, by using the silliness of these results as a way of tightening up the rule. Call a command-list *reasonable* if running it through the remainder rule yields an expansion satisfying (p1)–(p3) above.

(p1) permissions expand (do not shrink) the sphere, and
(p2) permission to $\varphi$ renders *only* $\varphi$-worlds permissible.
(p3) permission to $\varphi$ renders *some* $\varphi$-worlds permissible.

It is not hard to establish the following (proof in Appendix to the chapter):

FACT: If S is defined by a reasonable list of commands, then $S = |{\sim}\varphi| \cap |\psi|$ for some $\psi$. Equivalently, any reasonable command list is of the form (up to equivalence) "You must not $\varphi$," "You must $\psi$".

This transforms the problem in a helpful way. Before we had one equation in several unknowns (corresponding to the several choices of implicit commands $\psi_i$). Now we have something very like one equation in one unknown. For we know what S is; that's just the present, pre-permission-to-$\varphi$, sphere of permissibility. And we know what $|{\sim}\varphi|$ is; that's just the worlds where the permitted behavior does not occur. The one unknown here is $|\psi|$, that is, the new sphere of permissibility $S^+$.

So, to review. Whenever a permission to $\varphi$ is issued, it's as though the initial command list had consisted of two commands:

first, one saying (precisely) *do not $\varphi$*.
second, a command that allows $\varphi$-ing,

Our job as sphere-redrawers is to throw out the *do not* $\varphi$ command and form the set of worlds allowed by the command that remains. This is nothing like an algorithm, because there is more than one way of choosing the command that remains. (There are many sets whose intersection with $|\sim\varphi|$ is S.) But it is instructive nevertheless.

One way it helps is by showing how to conceive the task diagrammatically. We are given the $|\varphi|$-region—that's the worlds where Slave takes Friday off, as he is permitted to do. We are given the $|\sim\varphi|$-region—that's the worlds where Slave works Friday, in accord with his pre-permission obligations. We are given the S-region—that's the set of initially permissible worlds where Slave works all week (Monday–Sunday). Our job is to extrapolate the S-region beyond the bounds imposed by the $|\sim\varphi|$-region, thus arriving at the set $|\psi|$ of worlds that are permissible after Master cancels the command to work Friday.

Three observations about this diagram. *First*, the diagram helps us to see what it means to say that $S^{+}$ "solves the equation" $S = |\sim\varphi| \cap S^{+}$. It means that S is the part of $S^{+}$ where the newly permitted behavior doesn't occur, or to run it the other way around, $S^{+}$ is the result of extending the S-region into the region where the newly permitted behavior does occur.

A *second* thing the diagram helps us to see is that the extrapolation approach is no panacea. There is not going to be just a single way of extending S into

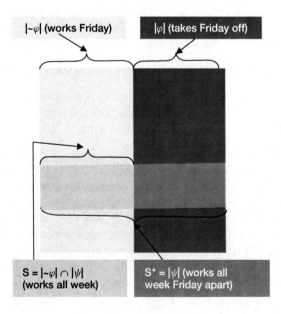

Fig. 11.1.

the $\varphi$-region, the region where Slave takes Friday off. One could in principle let $S^+$ suddenly triple in width as it crosses the $\varphi$-border, so that Slave is allowed to take the weekend off too. And various other improper extrapolations can be imagined.

A *third* thing that the diagram helps us to see, however, is that some ways of extrapolating are more natural than others. Extending S "directly" into the $\varphi$-region, ignoring the $\varphi/{\sim}\varphi$ boundary, is better than taking notice of that boundary. This is the geometrical upshot of our remarks above about clean cancellation. To the extent that an extrapolation takes account of the $\varphi/{\sim}\varphi$ boundary, the supposedly canceled prohibition on $\varphi$-ing is still exerting some influence from beyond the grave. Another way to put it is that we want our remainder command $\psi$, aka $S^+$, to be *free* of any taint of the canceled command ${\sim}\varphi$.

Our problem boils down to this: what could it mean for one proposition (in this case, $|\psi|$) to be "free" of another ($|{\sim}\varphi|$), in the sense of indifferent to whether that other proposition is true or false. The following answer looks plausible:

> *A is B-free* iff
> in worlds where A is true, it is true for reasons compatible with B's falsity, and in worlds where A is false, it is false for reasons compatible with B's truth.[12]

This notion of "true for the same reason" will have to be left at an intuitive level, but it basically means true with the same truth-maker—and here one wheels in an appropriate theory of truth-makers. The proposed update rule for permissions is this:

> (URi)
>
> Suppose that S is the present sphere of permissibility and that $\varphi$ holds in no S-worlds. $S^+ = S + i\varphi$ iff four conditions are met:
>
> *Difference*  $S^+ - S$ is non-empty
> *Equality*    $S = |{\sim}\varphi| \cap S^+$
> *Freedom*     $S^+$ is $|{\sim}\varphi|$-free
> *Goodness*    Other satisfiers of D, E, and F are "less good".

For our purposes today, the fourth condition is just to ensure that "$+ i\varphi$" is a function.[13] It is a non-trivial question what makes one otherwise qualified contender for the role of $S^+$ better than another; it could be a matter of relative naturalness, or logical strength, or something else again. That does not have to be decided here, however; all the work will be done by conditions D, E, and F.

Suppose that S, our initial sphere of possibility, is the proposition that Slave works all week, and $|{\sim}\varphi|$ is the proposition that Slave works on Friday. How

---

[12] Perhaps we should say, "in all not too remote worlds where A is true/false . . .".
[13] Albeit perhaps a partial function.

good a candidate is the proposition that Slave works Monday–Thursday and the weekend for the role of what's permitted after Slave is given Friday off?

Is the difference condition met? Yes—not all worlds where Slave works Monday–Thursday and the weekend are worlds where Slave works Monday thru Sunday.

Is the equality condition met? Yes, for the work-Monday-to-Sunday worlds are the intersection of the work-Monday-to-Thursday-and-the-weekend worlds with the work-Friday worlds.

Is the freedom condition met? In worlds where $S^+$ is true, it is made true by Slave's rock-carrying activities Monday–Thursday and the weekend. Those activities, whatever exactly they may be, are compatible with Slave taking Friday off. In worlds where $S^+$ is false, it is made false by Slave's non-rock-carrying activities on some day or days other than Friday. Those activities, whatever they may be, are compatible with Slave carrying rocks on Thursday. "Slave works Monday–Thursday and the weekend" is thus free of any taint of "Slave works Friday". That and the equality fact already mentioned are what makes "Slave works Monday–Thursday and the weekend" a good candidate for what is left over when we subtract Slave's working Friday from his working every day of the week.

Now let's consider some other hypotheses about what is ultimately required of Slave when we first command him to work Monday–Sunday and then relent, allowing him to take Friday off.

> *Harsh hypothesis*: Slave still has to work Monday–Sunday, exactly as before.
>
> *Lenient hypothesis*: Slave only has to work Monday–Thursday; after his Friday holiday he can stay off through the weekend.
>
> *Strange hypothesis*: Slave has to work Monday–Thursday, the weekend, and Master's birthday.

The harsh hypothesis—Slave still has to work every day—falls afoul of the Difference condition, which says permission to $\varphi$, issued in a context where $\varphi$ was previously impermissible, must result in the addition of at least one $\varphi$-world to the previous sphere. Obviously no Friday-off worlds have been added if $S^+$ is (like S) the set of work-Monday-to-Sunday worlds.

The lenient hypothesis—Slave only has to work Monday–Thursday—falls afoul of the Equality condition. The work-everyday worlds are not identical to but a proper subset of $S^+$ (the work-Monday-to-Thursday worlds) intersected with $|\sim\varphi|$ (the work-Friday worlds).

The strange hypothesis—Slave works Monday–Thursday, the weekend, *and* Master's birthday—falls afoul of the Freedom condition, by which I mean that it is not free of any taint of the canceled work-Friday command.

A is B-free, recall, iff A is true, in an A-world $w$, for reasons compatible with B's falsity, and false, in a $\sim$A-world $w$, for reasons compatible with B's truth. But consider a world *w* where Master's birthday falls on a Friday, and Slave works Monday–Thursday, the weekend, and Master's birthday, as the strange hypothesis requires him to. The hypothesis's truth-maker involves in part that Slave works Friday, given that Friday is Master's birthday. And this is not compatible with $\sim\varphi$ being false, in other words with Slave's taking Friday off. Alternatively consider worlds where Master's birthday falls on a Friday, and the strange hypothesis *doesn't* hold, because Slave takes Friday off. Is the falsity-maker here compatible with $\sim\varphi$'s truth, that is, with Slave's working Friday? Clearly not. So our update rule predicts that Slave is not required to work Monday–Thursday, the weekend, *and* Master's birthday, *even where that birthday is not on Friday*, because in some not-too-distant worlds the command *would* be obeyed by working on Friday, or disobeyed by taking Friday off; and what Slave does on Friday should not make him either obedient or disobedient, once he has been freed of all Friday-related obligations.

That is my first-pass story about how to understand the semantic effect of permissions. There are gaps in it, to be sure. One large gap traces back to how Lewis sets the problem up. Lewis assumes that permission to $\varphi$ "makes a difference" if, *but only if*, the sphere has to be enlarged for there to be permissible worlds in which $\varphi$. If there were any permissible $\varphi$-worlds beforehand, then the permission accomplishes exactly nothing.

This may seem only reasonable. The first day of camp, Counselor says: "It is forbidden to climb trees." The director then whispers something in her ear, and she adds, "except you may climb trees to rescue a kitten". Here "you may climb trees to rescue a kitten" deletes something from the list of what was ruled off limits by "It is forbidden to climb trees". It might seem at first that all permission statements are like that. What would be the point of allowing something which had never been forbidden in the first place?

And yet we do it all the time. I had Counselor first forbidding tree climbing and then relenting a bit: "It is OK to climb trees to rescue a kitten." But she might just as well have granted the permission first. There would be a clear point to doing this. If Counselor says nothing, then campers don't know if tree climbing is forbidden; perhaps she hasn't got around to announcing it yet. If she says tree climbing after kittens is OK, that tells them she is rejecting the opportunity to announce it.

There are also intermediate cases where a permission "softens" earlier commands, even though the earlier commands did not strictly rule out behavior of the kind now permitted. On day one, Counselor says, "You must never climb trees." On day two, she says, "You may do whatever you like on your birthday." Lewis would, it seems, have to say that the permission on day two leaves the command on day one entirely in place, since there are plenty of worlds where you never climb trees and still do whatever you like on your birthday, for instance, worlds where you have no desire to climb trees. Intuitively, though, the day one command is weakened. More on this in a moment.

Now I want to explore the epistemic analogue of Lewis's Master–Slave game. Here is how I understand the new game to work.

(1) The players this time are Teacher and Student, and the sphere of permissibility becomes the sphere of believability.

(2) The old game had Slave constantly adjusting his plans to fit with changes in what was permissible; the new one has Student constantly adjusting his theory to fit with changes in what is believable.

(3) It contracted the sphere of permissibility when Master said, "Do $\psi$"; the sphere expanded when Master said, "You may do $\varphi$". Likewise it contracts the sphere of believability when Teacher says "$\psi$ is so"; the sphere expands when Teacher says "$\varphi$ may be so".

(4) There was no great mystery about the *kind* of contraction brought on by "Do $\psi$"; one simply rejected as impermissible worlds where $\psi$ failed. Similarly there is no great mystery about the kind of contraction brought on by "$\psi$ is so"; worlds where $\psi$ fails are rejected as unbelievable.

(5) It was initially mysterious how "You may do $\varphi$" enlarged the sphere of permissibility. Similarly it is mysterious to begin with how "$\varphi$ may be so" enlarges the sphere of believability.

   Let's continue the pretense that "$\varphi$ may be so" has no effect on a sphere of believability that contains $\varphi$-worlds; it's only when all believable worlds are $\sim\varphi$ that we get an expansion. The question is, what expansion do we get? I propose that the update rule is pretty much as before.

   (UR$\Diamond$)

   Suppose that S is the present sphere of believability and that $\varphi$ holds in no S-worlds. $S^+$ is $S + \Diamond\varphi$ iff four conditions are met:
   *Difference*   $S^+ - S$ is non-empty
   *Equality*     $S = |\sim\varphi| \cap S^+$
   *Freedom*      $S^+$ is $|\sim\varphi|$-free
   *Goodness*     Other satisfiers of D, E, and F are "less good".

Once again, the point of the fourth condition is to ensure that "$+ \Diamond\varphi$" is a function.[14] I am not sure what makes one otherwise qualified contender for the role of $S^+$ better than another. Naturalness plays a role, presumably, and perhaps

---

[14] Albeit perhaps a partial function.

also logical strength. This does not have to be decided here, however; all the work will be done by conditions D, E, and F.

Imagine that Teacher starts by saying it will rain all week, meaning Monday–Sunday. She thereby banishes from the sphere of believability all worlds where this doesn't happen, where the rain lets up on one or more days. When Teacher learns that her evidence as regards Friday was shaky, she says, "Hold on, it might not rain Friday after all." Which worlds is Student to put back into the sphere of believability? Or to put it in more intuitive terms, what remains of Teacher's original prediction of rain all week, once she has conceded it might not rain Friday?

One hypothesis, the strong hypothesis call it, has Teacher still predicting that it rains every day. That is not allowed by our update rule, however, for it violates Difference. Difference says that new worlds *have* to be added to accommodate a previously unbelievable hypothesis. And it is clear from Equality that the added worlds have to be $\varphi$-worlds; for if a $\sim\varphi$-world $w$ is added, then S is a proper subset of $|\sim\varphi| \cap S^+$, not equal to it as required by Equality. Teacher's announcement that it might not rain Friday forces the addition of at least one dry-Friday world to the sphere of believability, so the strong hypothesis is mistaken.

A second hypothesis, the weak hypothesis call it, has Teacher now predicting only that it rains Monday–Thursday. That too is not allowed by our update rule. For suppose $S^+$ is the set of worlds where it rains Monday–Thursday. Then $S^+$ intersected with $|\sim\varphi|$ (the set of wet-Friday worlds) contains worlds where Saturday and Sunday are dry. There are no such worlds in S, however; before Teacher allows it might be dry Friday, all believable worlds have it raining Monday–Sunday. It follows that $S^+$ intersected with $|\sim\varphi|$ contains worlds outside of S, which is contrary to Equality. So the weak hypothesis about what remains of the Teacher's original prediction is mistaken too.

A third, intermediate, hypothesis has Teacher now predicting that it rains Monday–Thursday, the weekend, and on Teacher's birthday. The problem with this is that "It rains on Teacher's birthday" is not free of any taint of the canceled wet-Friday assertion; for in worlds where Teacher's birthday falls on Friday, either "It rains on Teacher's birthday" is true for reasons incompatible with the falsity of "It rains Friday", or it is false for reasons incompatible with the truth of "It rains Friday". Our update rule objects to "It will rain Monday–Thursday, the weekend, and Teacher's birthday," *even if her birthday is not on Friday*, because in some worlds it *is* on Friday. In those worlds the prediction *is* verified (falsified) by Friday's lack of rain; and Friday's lack of rain ought to be irrelevant given that Teacher freely admits there might be no rain on Friday.

I want to return now to a limitation of the Lewis game noted earlier. Lewis stipulates that permission to $\varphi$ has no impact unless $\varphi$ was antecedently forbidden. That makes nonsense both of out-of-the-blue, discourse-initial, permissions and permissions that weaken earlier commands that didn't strictly forbid the now-permitted behavior. The same points apply to our epistemic analogue of the Lewis game. We have been assuming that "might $\varphi$" has no impact unless $\varphi$ was antecedently denied. But then what is going on in this conversation?

> A: Where is Bob?
> B: Hmmm, don't know for sure, but he might be in his office.
> A: *I never said he wasn't!

Or this one?

> A: Bob will be at the office tomorrow.
> B: Not so fast, he might still have the flu tomorrow.
> A: *That's compatible!

Lewis confronts what might be considered the dual of this difficulty in "A Problem About Permission". Having laid it down that commands shrink the sphere of permissibility, he remarks that

One sort of commanding may seem to require special treatment: commanding the impermissible. Suppose that $|\varphi|$ contains no worlds that are. . . permissible. . . The Master may nevertheless wish to command. . . that $\varphi$ . . . . Having commanded at dawn that the Slave devote his energies all day to carrying rocks, the Master may decide at noon that it would be better to have the Slave spend the afternoon on some lighter or more urgent task. If the master simply commands. . . that $\varphi$, then no world. . . remains permissible; the Slave, through no fault of his own, has no way to play his part by trying to see to it that the world remains permissible. . . Should we therefore say that in this case the sphere evolves not by intersection but in some more complicated way? (2000, p. 27)

He notes a possible fix: whenever $\varphi$ is impermissible, "a command that $\varphi$ is deemed to be preceded by a tacit permission that $\varphi$, and the sphere of permissibility evolves accordingly" (2000, p. 27). Our present concern can be put in similar language:

One sort of permitting may seem to require special treatment: permitting the not impermissible. Suppose that the sphere of permissibility contains $\varphi$-worlds. The Master may nevertheless wish to permit that $\varphi$. Having at dawn permitted the Slave to take the day off, the Master may decide at noon that the Slave should be permitted to visit his mother this week. If the Master simply permits the Slave to visit his mother this week, then no additional worlds become permissible; for there are already permissible worlds where the Slave visits his mother, namely worlds where the Slave visits his mother today. Should we therefore say that in this case the sphere evolves not by the remainder rule but in some more complicated way?

I suggest we can avoid saying this by a maneuver similar to Lewis's: whenever $\varphi$ is already permissible, permission to $\varphi$ is deemed to be preceded by a tacit command not to $\varphi$, with the sphere of permissibility evolving accordingly.

Likewise whenever $\varphi$ is already believable, "it might be that $\varphi$" is imagined to be in response to the unspoken assertion that $\sim\varphi$.

How much justice does this kind of maneuver do to our feeling of still *conveying* something when we permit the not previously permissible, or suggest that things *might* be a way that no one had ever said they weren't?

The first thing to notice is that, just as permitting and then immediately commanding that $\varphi$ can (even by our existing rules) change the sphere of permissibility, forbidding and then permitting $\varphi$ can change the sphere of permissibility too. Mathematically speaking there is no reason whatever to expect that $S^{-+} = i\varphi$ ($!\sim\varphi(S)$) will just be S again. Indeed there is reason to expect it often won't. We know by Freedom that

$\quad$ $S^{-+}$ is $|\sim\varphi|$-free.

It follows that whenever S (which is arbitrary, recall) is *not* $|\sim\varphi|$-free, $S^{-+}$ is not S, which is just to say that the operation of forbidding and then permitting $\varphi$ will have non-trivial effects. Example: we saw above that |Slave works on Master's birthday| is not free of |Slave works on Friday|. So if we let S be the first of these and $\sim\varphi$ be the second (so $\varphi$ says that Slave takes Friday off), we should have a case where $S^{-+} \neq S$.

Let's try it. Master first says that Slave is to work on her (Master's) birthday. That gives us the desired S. Then Master further commands that Slave is to work on Friday. That gives us $S^{-} = !\sim\varphi(S) =$ the worlds where Slave works Friday and Master's birthday. Then Master permits Slave not to work on Friday. $S^{-+}$ can't be the worlds where Slave works on Master's birthday again, because that is not free of Slave's working on Friday, which he has just been permitted not to do. A better because more Friday-free candidate for $S^{-+}$ is the set of worlds where Slave works on Master's birthday unless Master's birthday falls on a Friday. So permitting Slave to take Friday off in a context where Slave was required only to work on Master's birthday has a non-trivial effect on the sphere of permissibility.

Like remarks apply to asserting that $\varphi$ and then immediately allowing it might be that $\sim\varphi$. Suppose I've asserted that it will rain on my birthday. Allowing it might not rain on Friday has the effect, I'm suggesting, of asserting it will rain on Friday and then taking it back. Once again this does not leave everything as it was. The prediction that remains is that it will rain on my birthday, provided that my birthday doesn't fall on a Friday.

I have argued that forbidding and then immediately permitting $\varphi$ can change the sphere of permissibility, and also that asserting $\varphi$ and then immediately allowing that maybe $\varphi$ is not the case can change the sphere of believability.

But there are also cases where permitting what I've just forbidden (admitting that a previous assertion might be wrong) leaves the sphere just as it was. An example might be this. Nothing has been said about Bob's location, but I know you want to find him. What is accomplished by saying, "He might be in his office," when no one has suggested otherwise? Likewise what is accomplished by announcing out of the blue that it is permitted to climb trees in order to rescue kittens?

It seems to me these things are not so mysterious, once we distinguish what *has* been forbidden, in the sense that the command has been given, and what *is* forbidden, in the sense that it's against the rules but Counselor may not have got around to announcing it yet. The children may know when the first permission is given that nothing *has been* forbidden, but they have no idea what might or might not *be* forbidden in the sense of being off limits or against the rules. When they hear that tree climbing after kittens is permitted, they learn an upper bound on what *is* forbidden, namely that it doesn't include tree climbing after kittens. This is not because Counselor has *said* climbing after kittens is not forbidden; she has the ability to forbid but not, as we're imagining the game, the ability to comment on the extent of the forbidden. What the counselor has done is "shown" that climbing after kittens is not forbidden by staging a confrontation with an imagined off-screen forbidder, and *canceling* that imagined person's decree.

Something similar is going on when I say to someone looking for Bob that he might be in his office. The distinction we need this time is between what has been asserted, and what is understood to be so even if no one has got around to announcing it yet. Before I spoke, my friend might have been wondering whether an assertion that Bob was not in his office was in the cards. I satisfy her curiosity not by *saying* that an assertion to that effect is not in the cards; my subject matter is Bob and his office, not assertions about them. I satisfy my friend's curiosity by *showing* that an assertion to that effect is not in the cards, by staging a confrontation with someone imagined to have made the assertion, and undoing what they are imagined to have done.

Let's return now to some of the problems raised at the outset, starting with problems for the standard semantics (SS). One problem was that SS gave "might $\varphi$" the wrong subject matter. "Bob might be in his office" seems intuitively to be about whatever "Bob is in his office" is about. Neither concerns the speaker or the extent of her knowledge. The present view construes "might $\varphi$" as a device for retracting or canceling an assertion of $\sim\varphi$. If $\varphi$ has the same subject matter negated as unnegated, and $\sim\varphi$ has the same subject matter retracted as asserted, then "might up" comes out with the same subject matter as $\varphi$.

A second worry was that the truth-conditions assigned by SS, in its Moorean form at least, were too weak. If "might $\varphi$" says only that *my* information doesn't rule $\varphi$ out, why do I accept correction by observers with information that I didn't possess?[15] It is indeed puzzling why I would accept correction, if that means agreeing I have misstated the epistemic facts. But suppose that "might

---

[15] See however the "Mastermind" example in von Fintel and Gillies (2008).

$\varphi$" is not a statement of fact. Suppose it is a "cancellation order", an attempt to undo or reverse the assertion that $\sim\varphi$, an insistence that $\sim\varphi$ not be part of the common ground. If *that* is what the observer is taking issue with, then her point can be understood as follows: however well intentioned, the cancellation order was unfortunate. Given that somebody knew that $\varphi$, it would have been better not to block $\varphi$'s addition to the common ground.

Now, as we discussed, the standard semanticist's response to the "too weak" objection is to make the truth-conditions stronger: $\varphi$ should be consistent not only with *my* information, but all *pertinent* information—where the test of pertinence must presumably be that the speaker concedes that if that information really does obtain, then he was in error. The third worry was that these revised truth-conditions are too strong. If "might $\varphi$" is false when $\varphi$ is ruled out by pertinent facts, then speakers should restrain themselves except when such facts are known not to obtain. I shouldn't say that Bob might be in his office, if there's a chance that Bob has unbeknownst to me been seen elsewhere. Clearly, though, speakers do *not* restrain themselves in this way. (If they did, "might"-claims would hardly ever get made.) What can the cancellation theory say about these sorts of cases? How much restraint to expect depends on what speakers are afraid of. If I am afraid that my claim might be *false*, then I should hold back until I have tracked down all pertinent facts. But what if I am concerned only that my claim will turn out to have been ill-advised, or counterproductive, given the purposes of the conversation? The claim is counterproductive just to the extent that it pre-empts or cancels better-informed assertions of $\sim\varphi$ by others. And I *do* restrain myself from saying "might $\varphi$" when there is a danger of this. If someone announces over the phone that they are looking at Bob right now, I am hardly likely to tell them that Bob might be in his office.

The fourth problem was that SS is too epistemic. It reckons "I might vote for Kucinich and I might not" false unless I am genuinely undecided how I am going to vote. The present theory can say that I am showing my audience, by example, as it were, that no assertion is to be expected on the topic of how I am going to vote; I do it by giving myself an opportunity to make that sort of assertion and visibly passing it up.

The fifth problem was that "Bob might be in his office" does not entail "Bob might be in his office or in an opium den," as SS would lead you to expect. "Bob might be in his office or in an opium den" seems to imply both that he might be in his office and that he might be in an opium den. The analogous phenomenon with permission is perhaps better known. Suppose you are hungry and I tell you: You may have a piece of cake or a piece of pie. You reach for the pie and I snatch it away. What gave you the idea that *that* was a permissible disjunct?

A "stronger statement" in the context of the cancellation theory is a statement that cancels more; so it is enough to show that whereas $\Diamond\varphi$ cancels only $\sim\varphi$, $\Diamond(\varphi$

or $\psi$) cancels $\sim\varphi$ and $\sim\psi$ both. Let S be a sphere of believability that implies $\sim\varphi$ and implies $\sim\psi$. The update rule for "might" tells us that $S + \Diamond(\varphi \vee \psi)$ is a superset $S^+$ of S that is free of $\sim(\varphi \vee \psi)$. By the definition of freedom, $S^+$ is free of $\sim(\varphi \vee \psi)$ only if

> (#) $S^+$ is false, when it is, for reasons compatible with the truth of $\sim(\varphi \vee \psi)$, that is, for reasons compatible with the combined falsity of $\varphi$ and $\psi$.

We have, then, that facts making $S^+$ false are compatible with the joint falsity of $\varphi$ and $\psi$. Facts making either $\varphi$ or $\psi$ true are not compatible with the joint falsity of $\varphi$ and $\psi$. So facts making either of $\varphi$ or $\psi$ true do not make $S^+$ false. If $S^+$ implied $\sim\varphi$, however, then facts making $\varphi$ true presumably *would* make $S^+$ false; and there would be a similar issue if $S^+$ implied $\sim\psi$.[16] Therefore $S^+$ does not imply $\sim\varphi$ and it does not imply $\sim\psi$; which, bearing in mind that S itself does imply $\sim\varphi$ and $\sim\psi$, means that the effect of $\Diamond(\varphi$ or $\psi)$ is to cancel $\sim\varphi$ and $\sim\psi$ both. This accounts for the feeling that "It might be that $\varphi$ or $\psi$" implies both "It might be that $\varphi$" and "It might be that $\psi$".

The sixth and final problem we raised for SS is that it has trouble explaining why "$\varphi$ & it might be that $\sim\varphi$" is not coherently supposable, e.g., in the antecedent of a conditional, when no such problem arises with "$\varphi$ & I/we don't know that $\varphi$". The problem with "$\varphi$ & it might be that $\sim\varphi$" is not that no *world* can answer both to the specification that $\varphi$ and the specification that $\Diamond\sim\varphi$; it's that no world-*specification* can both demand that $\varphi$ (as the first conjunct requires) and not demand that $\varphi$ (as the second conjunct requires).

Update semantics, we said, left it un- or under-explained why allowing that Ringo might not go to the party leaves intact the information that John, Paul, and George will be there. The present theory says that it is only prior assertions bound up with (= not free of) Ringo's being at the party that get canceled. "John, Paul, and George will attend" is free of "Ringo will attend" in that facts making the first true (false) do not conflict with facts making the second false (true). This is just one more instance of Lewis's problem of clean cancellation: prior assertions that entail the falsity of what we learned might be true are canceled, while prior assertions that do not entail the falsity of what we learned might be true are left in place.

Our second worry about update semantics was this. It tells us that $\Diamond\varphi$ uttered in information state S has no effect unless S and $\varphi$ are inconsistent. Suppose that $S = \{\sim\chi\}$ and $\varphi = \Diamond(\chi$ or $\psi)$. ($\chi$ or $\psi$) is consistent with $\sim\chi$, so $S + \varphi$ should be S again. But we know that $\Diamond(\chi$ or $\psi)$ generally entails $\Diamond\chi$ and $\Diamond\psi$. And to be told that it might be that $\chi$ presumably cancels any prior information we had to

---

[16] The inference here does not go through in every case. For $\varphi$'s truth-makers need not always be falsity-makers for each $\chi$ that implies $\sim\varphi$. Let $\chi$ = "There's a French king in my pocket" and $\varphi$ = "France has no king". $\varphi$ is false because France is a republic but $\chi$'s falsity is due to the fact that my pocket is empty.

the effect that $\sim\chi$. Here then is a case where $S + \varphi$ is a proper subset of S, even though $\varphi$ is consistent with S.

How does the cancellation theory deal with this case? $S + \Diamond\varphi$ is the $\sim\varphi$-free part of S. From the fact that $\varphi$ is consistent with S, that is, S does not *imply* $\sim\varphi$, we cannot infer that S is absolutely *free* of $\sim\varphi$. An example has just been mentioned: ($\chi$ or $\psi$) is consistent with $\sim\chi$ and $\sim\psi$—it does not imply $\chi$ or $\psi$—but a disjunction can hardly be considered free of its disjuncts. *Non-implication of* $\chi$ is a much weaker property than *freedom from* $\chi$.

This completes my explanation and defense of the cancellation theory. I am aware that many important topics have been left unaddressed: the Frege–Geach problem, for instance, and the problem of how deontic/epistemic *peers* discuss what to do/think.[17] I would like to take the opportunity in closing to cancel any would-be assertions to the effect that these topics will not be discussed in future work.

## APPENDIX

FACT: Any S defined by a reasonable command list $= |\sim\varphi| \cap |\psi|$ for some $\psi$.

PROOF: From (p3), which says that the right expansion should bring in at least one $\varphi$-world, we conclude that any package of commands each of whose members is consistent with $\varphi$ is unreasonable. Such a package fails to enlarge the sphere of permissibility, as it has to be enlarged to make room for $\varphi$-worlds. From (p2), which says that the right expansion should bring in *only* $\varphi$-worlds, we conclude that any package of commands none of whose members is consistent with $\varphi$ is unreasonable. The reason is that that kind of package expands the sphere of possibility to include *every* world, and we know by (p2) that permission to $\varphi$ should bring in only some worlds, only $\varphi$-worlds. So, any reasonable package of commands $< \psi_i >$ has members consistent with $\varphi$ and members inconsistent with $\varphi$. Let's use $\chi$ for the conjunction of all $\psi_i$s *inconsistent* with $\varphi$, and $\psi$ for the conjunction all $\psi_i$s individually *consistent* with $\varphi$. Then

---

[17] The games studied here are unrealistic in that one of the players is entirely in charge. A more realistic version of the Master–Slave game would have the players working out what to do together, with an eye to some shared goal. Each makes proposals about how to proceed which may or may not be accepted by the other. When a "let's do this" proposal is accepted, the sphere of permissibility shrinks; when a "let's allow ourselves not to do that" proposal is accepted, the sphere grows. A more realistic version of the Teacher–Student game would have two parties working out what to think, or assume, together. Assertions are proposed lower bounds on an evolving body of shared assumptions. If accepted, they shrink the sphere of believability, or at least stand in the way of certain imaginable expansions. Might-statements are proposed upper bounds on our shared assumptions; if accepted they expand the sphere, or else stand in the way of imaginable proposals to shrink it. The Master–Slave game thus modified brings in a degree of mind-to-world direction of fit, since certain proposals about what to do are objectively unwise given the players' goals. The Teacher–Student game thus modified has a world-to-mind element; the players are haggling, wikipedia-style, about what goes into the body of shared assumptions—what can be taken for present purposes as settled fact. (Thanks here to Sally Haslanger and Bob Hale.)

$S =$ the set of $(\chi \wedge \psi)$-worlds
$S^+ =$ the set of $\psi$-worlds
$S^+ - S =$ the set of $(\psi \wedge \sim\chi)$-worlds

Again, $< \psi_i >$ is reasonable only if

$\exists$  some worlds in $S^+ - S$ are $\varphi$-worlds (from (p3))
$\forall$  all worlds in $S^+ - S$ are $\varphi$-worlds (from (p2))

From $\exists$ it follows that $\psi$ is consistent with $\varphi$. For: suppose not. Then $S^+ =$ the set of $\psi$-worlds does not contain any $\varphi$-worlds. But $\exists$ implies that $S^+$ does contain $\varphi$-worlds, since $S^+ - S$ contains them. A more interesting result follows from $\forall$: for all $S^+$-worlds $w$, $\chi$ holds in $w$ iff $\varphi$ does not hold in $w$. The "only if" direction is easy since each of $\chi$'s conjuncts is by definition inconsistent with $\varphi$. For the "if" direction, suppose contrapositively that $\chi$ does not hold in $w$. $w$ cannot be an S-world because S-worlds have to satisfy all the $\psi_i$s. But then $w$ is in $S^+ - S$. And according to $\forall$, every world in that set satisfies $\varphi$. So, the implicit commands suitable to serve as backdrop to a permission to $\varphi$ must be divisible into two parts: first, $\chi \approx \sim\varphi =$ the part that forbids $\varphi$-ing, second, $\psi =$ the part that allows $\varphi$-ing. QED

# Response to Stephen Yablo

## David Efird

In 'Permission and (So-Called Epistemic) Possibility' (Chapter 11, above), Stephen Yablo presents a unified semantics of the deontic and the epistemic senses of 'may'. His strategy is first to propose a semantics for deontic modality which solves Lewis's (1979a) problem about permission and then to construct a parallel semantics for epistemic modality. In doing this, however, he does not consider the interaction between the deontic and the epistemic modalities, and this interaction seems to pose a difficulty for his semantics for deontic modality.

Consider the following set of sentences:

(1) You may go to the football match or ride the trains.

(2) Lewis may go to the football match or ride the trains, but I don't know which.

(3) You may go to the football match or ride the trains, but I don't know which.[1]

In sentence (1), the permissive sense of 'may' seems forced by the occurrence of 'you', while in sentence (2) the epistemic sense of 'may' seems forced by the occurrence of 'but I don't know which'. But what of sentence (3)? 'You' seems to force the deontic sense of 'may', but the occurrence of 'but I don't know which' seems to introduce an additional epistemic sense of 'may'. In effect, the deontic and the epistemic senses of 'may' seem to be interacting in this sentence. It is a consideration of the logical form of this sentence which leads into a discussion of a difficulty with Yablo's proposal.

## 1. THERE ARE IRREDUCIBLY DISJUNCTIVE PERMISSIONS

In this section I aim to show that there are irreducibly disjunctive permissions, that is, there are some disjunctive permissions which entail neither a disjunction nor a conjunction of permissions.

Thanks to Tom Stoneham and especially to Stephen Yablo for helpful comments on previous drafts of this paper.

[1] An example of this kind is discussed by Hans Kamp (1979), pp. 271–3.

Consider the following set of sentences:

(1) You may go to the football match or ride the trains.

(4) You may go to the football match.

(5) You may ride the trains.

(6) You may go to the football match and you may ride the trains.

(7) You may go to the football match or you may ride the trains.

It seems that there are two ways to read (1). On the first reading, (1) entails (4) and also (5) and so (6), but neither (4) nor (5) entails (1). So, on this reading a disjunctive permission entails a conjunction of permissions, but neither conjunct entails the disjunctive permission. On the second reading, the situation is reversed: both (4) and (5) entail (1), but (1) entails neither (4) nor (5). On this reading, then, (1) is read as (7). Now it is well known that combining the logical properties of these two readings results in disaster, for the permission operator then becomes tonk-like: from 'You may $\varphi$' one can infer 'You may $\psi$' for any $\varphi$ and $\psi$.[2] But there is an additional problem with combining the two readings, one that concerns the interaction of the deontic and the epistemic senses of 'may', which has yet to be explored

Consider what we would have if we appended 'but I don't know which' to the first reading, that is, (1) as entailing (6), which would, in effect, combine the two readings. We would then have:

(8) You may go to the football match and you may ride the trains, but I don't know which.

Now (9) is an instance of a pragmatic contradiction, that is, it is an instance of Seth Yalcin's (2007) version of Moore's paradox, '$\varphi$ and it might be that not-$\varphi$'. Formally, (9) is:

(8*) (PA & PB) & ($\Diamond\neg$PA & $\Diamond\neg$PB)

where 'P' denotes the deontic possibility operator, A and B are schematic letters standing for sentences, and '$\Diamond$' denotes the epistemic possibility operator, which is logically equivalent to a conjunction of two instances of the Moore–Yalcin paradox:

(8**) (PA & $\Diamond\neg$PA) & (PB & $\Diamond\neg$PB)

So (3) cannot be read as (8) on pain of paradox.

What of the second reading? The second reading is appropriate when one wishes to report that a certain permission amongst a set of permissions is in force

---

[2] See Prior (1960) for the introduction and elimination rules of the tonk operator.

but one does not know which permission it is. On this second reading of (1), then, 'but I don't know which' gets implicitly added to (1) to obtain (3). So, if we make this explicit, the second reading becomes:

(9) You may go to the football match or you may ride the trains, but I don't know which.

Formally, (9) is:

(9*) $(PA \vee PB)$ & $(\Diamond \neg PA$ & $\Diamond \neg PB)$

which entails

(9**) $[(PA$ & $\Diamond \neg PA) \vee (PB$ & $\Diamond \neg PA)]$ & $[(PB$ & $\Diamond \neg PB) \vee (PA$ & $\Diamond \neg PB)]$

where we have two instances of the Moore–Yalcin paradox appearing as the first disjunct of each conjunct. Now even if we eliminate these paradoxical disjuncts out of charity in interpretation, we would still have two further instances of the Moore–Yalcin paradox, that is, we would have what would be tantamount to (8**).

It seems then that (3) cannot be interpreted as either (8) or (9), that is, the disjunctive permission in (3) must be interpreted as irreducibly disjunctive, in the sense that it entails neither a conjunction nor a disjunction of permissions. Formally,

(10) $P(A \vee B)$ entails neither $(PA \vee PB)$ nor $(PB$ & $PB)$.

## 2. IRREDUCIBLY DISJUNCTIVE PERMISSIONS DO NOT OBEY FREEDOM

On Yablo's semantics, (1) entails (6), but, as we have found, it seems this entailment must be restricted when 'but I don't know which' is appended to (1), on pain of the Moore–Yalcin paradox. The problem is that Yablo's update rule for permissions seems to fail for cases like (3). In particular, the 'Freedom' clause does not seem to hold, which requires that $S^+$ is $\neg(A \vee B)$-free, in this case. Now for $S^+$ to be $\neg(A \vee B)$-free is for it to be $(\neg A$ & $\neg B)$-free. But this is just what one does not have in the case of irreducibly disjunctive permissions. For if $S^+$ were $(\neg A$ & $\neg B)$-free, then where $S^+$ is true it is so for reasons compatible with the falsity of $(\neg A$ & $\neg B)$. Now where $S^+$ is true is where $P(A \vee B)$ is true, and the reasons, in part, for its being true, in cases such as (3), is a certain indeterminacy, an indeterminacy which engenders incomplete, non-maximal worlds in the sphere of permissibility. This is what it is for a disjunctive permission to be irreducible in the sense defined above. So, the reasons for $S^+$ being true are not compatible with the falsity of ($\neg A$ & $\neg B$), that is, the truth of ($A \lor B$), since this requires a sort of determinacy which is precisely what is lacking in this case. This indeterminacy then results in $S^+$ not being ($\neg A$ & $\neg B$)-free. Consequently, Yablo's update rule for permission fails in the case of irreducibly disjunctive permissions.

# 12

# Possible Worlds and the Necessary *A Posteriori*

*Frank Jackson*

1

W. V. Quine's famous objection to essentialism has provoked two responses. The unfriendly response is that it conflates the *de re* and the *de dicto*. A valid point about *de dicto* modality is wrongly carried across to what is an issue about *de re* modal properties. The friendly response—suggested by Richard Cartwright, I take it—does not dispute the point about conflation but argues that, behind Quine's argument, lies an important epistemological problem for essentialism; indeed, it may be that that was what Quine really had in mind all along.[1]

I agree that there is an important epistemological problem for essentialism lying behind Quine's argument. However, I also think that we now know how to respond to it—by looking at the issue through the lens of possible worlds approaches to modal questions. With those glasses on, we can see how to settle questions about essential properties.

In this paper I start by filling out the above remarks as a preamble to addressing the corresponding issues for the necessary *a posteriori*. I think, in much company, that there is an important epistemological problem for the necessary *a posteriori*. Roughly, the problem is that if *S* is offered as a candidate necessary *a posteriori* truth, how could we *show* that it is necessary, in the face of the fact that it takes investigation to show that *S* is true, and so, in some sense, *S* might have turned out to be false? But I think that, as is the case with the corresponding issue for essentialism, the possible worlds approach to modal questions tells us how to answer the epistemological problem. I will be using, that is, the example of essentialism as a stalking horse for the claim about the necessary *a posteriori*.

I would like to be able to say that all this is pretty non-controversial. However, the way that the approach via possible worlds solves the epistemological problem for the necessary *a posteriori* implies that the necessary *a posteriori* is at bottom a linguistic phenomenon (or, maybe, that it is for all the standard examples),

[1] Cartwright (1968).

and many dispute this, including some who played a major role in developing the two-dimensional modal logic framework that, as we will see, lies behind the 'linguistic' treatment of the necessary *a posteriori*.[2]


## 2

First, the debate over essentialism. Quine—or anyway Quine as often portrayed—reasoned somewhat as follows:[3]

"They tell me that there are essential properties, that some things that have the property of being *F*, have that property essentially. But if *x* has *F* essentially, then *x* has it no matter how we refer to *x*. Being essentially *F* will be subject to Leibniz's law. But when I ask for examples of a thing and a property, such that the thing has the property essentially, all the examples I am offered violate Leibniz's law. I am told, for example, that

(a)  9 is essentially composite.

But

(b)  9 = the number of planets.

So, by Leibniz's law, we can derive

(c)  The number of planets is essentially composite.

But (c) is false. Therefore, as (b) is true without question, and the same goes for Leibniz's law, it follows that (a) is false. And once you've seen one you've seen them all. We have, as we might put it, a 'refutation recipe' for any proposal that some object has some property essentially."


## 3

The unfriendly response accuses this argument of a fallacy of equivocation. There are two ways of reading sentences of the form 'The *F* is essentially *G*'. On one, (c) is false, as Quine says, but on that reading, it does not follow from (a), (b), and Leibniz's law. On the other reading, (c) follows from (a), (b), and Leibniz's law, as Quine says, but, on that reading, (c) is true—or, better, it is not obviously false. Neither way do we have a *reductio* of (a). There is no uniform way of reading (c) that allows (a) to lead to a clearly false (c).

---

[2] e.g. Stalnaker (2004). The 'linguistic' treatment of the necessary *a posteriori* in the two-dimensional framework has a number of sources; I learnt it from Tichý (1983).

[3] Quine (1953).

What are the two readings, and where do things go wrong for Quine's argument on each? There are various ways of putting the two readings in symbols but I will say it in English—philosophical English, that is.

I will start with the reading on which (c) is false but on which (c) does not follow from (a) plus (b) and Leibniz's law. We can read sentences of the form 'The *F* is essentially *G*' as ascribing essential truth to something that is truth-valued—namely, that the *F* is *G*. We can label this the *de dicto* reading. On this reading, (c) is false. It is contingent that the number of planets is composite. There might have been seven planets, in which case it would have been true that the number of planets is prime. But on this reading of (c), it does not follow from (a), (b), and Leibniz's law. (a) is formulated using a name and not a definite description and is a claim about a property of something that lacks a truth value, namely, the number 9. In this sense, (a) is a *de re* claim, and not a *de dicto* claim. The trouble for Quine's argument on the *de re* reading of (a) is that there is no way of getting from (a) so read, via (b), and Leibniz's law, to (c) read *de dicto*; but that is the reading of (c) on which (c) is false.

We can, however, read sentences of the form 'The *F* is essentially *G*' as ascribing essential *G*-ness to something that is not truth-valued, namely, the *F*. We might force this reading by using a form of words like 'The thing which is *F*, that very thing, is such that it itself is essentially *G*'.[4] On this second, *de re*, way of reading sentences of the form 'The *F* is essentially *G*', (c) does follow from (a), (b), and Leibniz's law. But, on this reading, (c) is not obviously false. What is obviously false is a quite different contention, namely, the *de dicto* one that it is necessarily true that the number of planets is composite, as we have recently observed.

In sum, we can read (c) *de dicto* or *de re*. Read *de dicto*, the mistake in Quine's argument is that (c) so read does not follow from the premises; read *de re*, (c) does follow from the premises but is not obviously false.

4

It seems that Quine commits a basic fallacy, and so he does on the face of it. But the friendly response to Quine argues that we should not read his words too literally. In reality he was making an important epistemological objection to essential properties—or better an objection that one introduces via a bit of epistemology only to see that at bottom it isn't any such thing.

Let me explain these slightly gnomic remarks.

---

[4] This reading gives the definite description wide scope relative to the modal expression; the *de dicto* reading discussed earlier gives the description narrow scope.

Think of the examples that make it plausible that for pairs

> Had *P* been the case, then *Q* would have been the case
>
> Had *P* been the case, then ~*Q* would have been the case

it is not always the case that one or the other is true;[5] examples like

> Had Bizet and Verdi been compatriots, they would both have been French
>
> Had Bizet and Verdi been compatriots, they would both have been Italian, not French.

On plausible assumptions—and, more importantly, the kind of assumptions such that if they don't hold for this pair, clearly they do hold for other pairs—there is no choosing between these two. But although it is an epistemological fact that we cannot choose between them, the reason we cannot lies in the fact that, on the plausible assumptions, there is nothing to make a difference between them. There is nothing that might be a truth-maker for one over the other. The epistemology makes salient a feature of the situation that is not itself an epistemological feature, and is the feature—the symmetry of the situation—that has rightly convinced (most) philosophers that we should hold that both counterfactuals are false or that both lack a truth-value, and that the wrong way to go is to insist that one or the other must be true although we cannot say which.

The friendly reading of Quine's objection to essentialism says something similar. How are we supposed to adjudicate essentialist claims? What makes it plausible to hold that nine is essentially composite? The only answer would appear to be, Quine holds, that 'Nine is composite' is necessarily true. But in that case we could equally argue that nine is not essentially composite on the ground that 'The number of planets is composite' is not necessarily true. True, it is a fallacy to confuse a *de re* claim with a *de dicto* one. But, on the friendly reading, Quine wasn't doing that. He was asking after the epistemology of the relevant *de re* claim and arguing, first, that it could only lie in certain *de dicto* facts, and, second, that any argument taking off from plausible *de dicto* facts could be deployed both to support that view that nine is essentially composite, and to support the thesis that nine is not essentially composite.[6]

## 5

One way of sharpening the friendly reading of Quine's objection to essentialism is to take examples that involve objects that we understand better than numbers—tables, as it might be. Suppose that a certain table, *T*, is made of plastic.

---

[5] Goodman (1947).

[6] And, it seems to me, there is textual evidence for the friendly reading in the last page of Quine (1953).

Most supporters of essentialism hold that if $T$ is made of plastic, it is essentially made of plastic. How might one argue for this view? Does the table look or feel different because, in addition to being made of plastic, it is essentially made of plastic? Does the physics of tables go better if we ascribe being essentially made of plastic in addition to being made of plastic to tables made of plastic? Supporters of essentialism typically argue that it is *a posteriori* what a table's essential properties are. But if it is *a posteriori*, we should ask after the evidence, and the empirical evidence would seem to relate solely to the properties the table in fact has.

Quine's objection on the friendly reading is that the only way of responding to these questions is to appeal to *de dicto* modal facts, but they give us no reason to favour the position that a plastic table is essentially plastic over the alternative that it is contingently plastic. And the key point here is of course not an epistemological one. What we learn from asking after the epistemology, according to the friendly reading of Quine, is that there is nothing to make the difference between a table's being contingently plastic and its being essentially plastic.

6

I think that there is a lot to be said in favour of Quine's objection read in the friendly way. I also think, however, that once we see how to explain essential properties in terms of possible worlds, we can see that his objection fails. The possible worlds account of essential properties tells us how to reply to the epistemological challenge and tells us what makes the difference between, for example, a table's being contingently plastic and its being essentially plastic, all in terms of notions that we need elsewhere in philosophy. Essential properties turn out to hang off ideas that are required for work elsewhere.

On the possible worlds account, $x$'s being essentially $F$ is nothing more nor less than $x$'s being $F$ in every world in which it appears. A property is possessed essentially by something if and only if that something is $F$ in every world in which it appears. We mentioned earlier that 'The $F$ is essentially $G$' can be read two ways. On one, the *de dicto* reading, it ascribes necessary truth to the $F$'s being $G$; on the other, the *de re* reading, it ascribes being essentially $G$ to the $F$. On the *de re* reading, it is true if and only if a) the $F$ is $G$ in the actual world, and b) in every world $w$ in which the thing which is the $F$ in the actual world appears, it is $G$ in $w$, regardless of whether or not it is the $F$ in $w$.

The beauty of this account of essential properties is that it uses notions we need anyway, notions we understand, and notions on which there is a fair degree of non-collusive agreement sufficient to be the basis of principled discussions about which properties are and which properties are not essentially possessed. The idea that something's identity can survive certain changes but cannot survive other changes comes up in almost every episode of *Star Trek*. True, it comes up in this context for the special case of personal identity but whenever someone buys a car at auction on Monday for collection on Tuesday, they are aware of the distinction between getting the very car they bid for, albeit with some change in properties, versus getting a substituted car. Numerical identity through change is a folk notion.

Quine's objection, even on the friendly reading which puts the objection at its best, falls to the possible worlds explication of essential properties.

I am not saying that there are no difficult issues raised by the possible worlds explication. Should we treat the talk of identity across possible worlds literally or should we cash it out in counterpart terms à la David Lewis?[7] What anyway is identity across possible worlds for the majority who have little time for modal realism? But that's par for the course—and a lot of the fun—in philosophy.

7

Quine objected to property essentialism. Daughter of Quine objects to the necessary *a posteriori*.

Daughter of Quine reasons somewhat as follows.

"I am happy to accept essential properties. Father was wrong. My puzzle is over the claim that there are necessary *a posteriori* truths, a claim that, I am told, follows from acknowledging that there are essential properties, combined with its being *a posteriori*, in many cases, what a thing's essential properties are. Take the table in front of me as I write. It is made of plastic. Its being made of plastic is an essential property of it, for it could not remain the same table were its composition changed. A change in composition is necessarily a change in identity. But that principle is, in addition to being necessary, *a priori*. There is no example here of the necessary *a posteriori*. What then is supposed to be necessary *a posteriori*? It cannot be 'The table in front of me is made of plastic', as it is obviously contingent; there are possible worlds where it is false by virtue of some other, non-plastic table being the table in front of me. Equally, it cannot be 'The plastic table in front of me is made of plastic' as that is *a priori* (given that the table exists).

What convinced me that father was wrong was my apprehension of *a priori*—*a priori*—principles governing identity through change of properties. How then are we supposed to get *a posteriori* necessities out of essential properties?"

8

Again we have an unfriendly and a friendly way of reading this objection, this time by the daughter of Quine rather than Quine, and to the necessary *a posteriori* rather than essentialism.

---

[7] In e.g. (1986b), ch. 4.

The unfriendly way of reading this objection treats it as making a mistake like Quine's, namely, that of addressing a question other than the one on the table. Quine in effect addressed a *de dicto* question when it was a *de re* question that was on the table. Daughter of Quine is in effect addressing the modal status of the wrong 'dicto'. Those who believe in the necessary *a posteriori* do not affirm that, for example, 'The table in front of me is made of plastic' is necessarily true. Nor do they affirm that 'The plastic table in front of me is made of plastic' is *a posteriori* (given it exists). What they affirm is, for one example, that 'The *very* (in the sense of the actual) table in front of me is made of plastic' is necessarily true and *a posteriori*; a quite different *dicto*. Like father like daughter; they shoot down the wrong target.

9

The friendly way of reading the daughter of Quine's objection grants that, read literally, she shoots down the wrong target, but urges that she raises an important epistemological problem for the necessary *a posteriori*, and moreover an epistemological problem that serves to introduce a more fundamental truth-maker question about the necessary *a posteriori*.

There is an issue about how we could be entitled to hold that some claim is a necessary *a posteriori* truth. If it is *a posteriori*, there is some good sense in which it might, as the saying goes, turn out to be false. How then do we show that the 'possibility' of being false is not in fact a possibility? One might well worry about this at the same time as holding that there are for sure necessary *a posteriori* truths. The worry is about how, for some particular case, we could be rationally entitled to be sure that *it* is a case. Of course there are *a priori* truths whose status is obscure. Mathematics is full of examples. But in these cases, once we've seen that the truth is indeed a truth, we can see that it is *a priori*. That's what happens when we do the mathematical proof, but that is most definitely *not* what is supposed to happen with the famous examples of necessary *a posteriori* truths.

Consider the two sentences given above, in the case where the table in front of me is indeed made of plastic, with a bit of rewriting to avoid possible complications arising from the fact that the very table in front of me might not exist:

(d) Anything identical to the table in front of me is made of plastic

(e) Anything identical to the very table in front of me is made of plastic.

The point we are making is that, although it is a mistake to infer from the common ground position that (d) is contingent to the conclusion that (e) is contingent, this does not obviate the need to give a good account of how we are supposed to know that (e) is necessary. Moreover, it is not an answer to this question that we know that being made of plastic is an essential property of the table. If that answer were correct, we should, by parity of reasons, hold that (d) is necessary—and that would be a mistake. There are possible worlds where something identical to the table in front of me is not made of plastic because in those worlds the table in front of me (in those worlds) is not made of plastic. (We could write the previous sentence out to avoid scope ambiguities but readers will know the reading intended.)

## 10

The puzzle isn't merely how we might come to know that (e) is necessary. The puzzle is what might make it the case that, although (d) is contingent, (e) is necessary. If someone asks what makes it the case that I essentially have the origin I do but only contingently have a beard, we all know the answer. It lies in the fact that in every possible world I have the origin I do—or anyway that what's required for it to be the case that I have my origin essentially—whereas there are possible worlds where I lack a beard. But what is the corresponding answer to the 'making it the case' question for (e)?

We know what is required to make (d) true. There needs to be a single table in front of me which is plastic. If God arranges things in such a way that that's the case, She makes (d) true. But that of course is exactly what God needs to do to make (e) true. God does not need to do anything extra to make (e) true. After making (d) true, there is nothing more for her to do to make (e) true. A single table in front of me which is made of plastic is quite enough. What then makes the difference between (d)'s being only contingently true and (e)'s being necessarily true? That's the nub of the daughter of Quine's objection to the necessary *a posteriori*, on the friendly reading of her objection.

## 11

I think that, on the friendly reading, daughter of Quine has an objection we should take very seriously to the necessary *a posteriori*. Indeed, without the two-dimensional treatment of the necessary *a posteriori* I do not know how one might answer it. But with the two-dimensional treatment to hand, we can answer both the epistemological question and the making-true question for the necessary *a posteriori*. Here is the answer to the epistemological question; the question of how we might come to know that the very table in front of me is made of plastic is necessarily true despite its being *a posteriori* that the very table in front of me is made of plastic.

Consider the following premise set:

(f) If *x* is made of plastic in the actual world, then *x* is made of plastic in every world in which it exists

(g) The table in front of me is made of plastic

(h) If *x* is the table in front of me, then *x* is the very table in front of me

(i) If *x* is the very table in front of me in the actual world, then *x* is the very table in front of me in every world in which *x* exists.

The set (f) to (i) entail that it is necessarily true that anything identical to the very table in front of me is made of plastic, that in every world anything identical to the very table in front of me is made of plastic. The entailment is *a priori* and so poses no special epistemological problem—that is, no special problem beyond that posed by our access to the *a priori*. No small matter of course, but something we are taking for granted here. Equally there are no special epistemological problems posed by the premises. (f) is *a priori*. (g) is something empirically confirmable. (h) is *a priori*. (i) is *a priori*. We have, that is, a set of premises one member of which is a straightforward empirical fact, the rest of which are *a priori*, that lead *a priori* to the desired conclusion. And that's a pretty fair answer to the epistemological challenge posed by Quine's daughter, read in the friendly way.

12

But of course we have more than an answer to the epistemological question in the above. The set (f) to (i) are more than good evidence that it is necessarily true that anything identical to the very table in front of me is made of plastic. It would be wrongheaded to say something like 'I now see that it is *very probable* that it is necessarily true that anything identical to the very table in front of me is made of plastic.' What we have in the set (f) to (i) is what it takes for it to be the case that it is necessarily true that the very table in front of me is made of plastic. That is, if one wonders why God does not need to do more than make it the case that the table in front of me is made of plastic in order to make it the case that anything identical to the very table in front of me is made of plastic is necessarily true, the answer lies in the *a priori* truth of (f), (h), and (i), plus the fact that (f), (g), (h), and (i) together *a priori* entail that it is necessarily true that anything identical to the very table in front of me is made of plastic.

13

The final step is to observe that the account we have just given of how come it is necessarily true that the very table in front of me is made of plastic is the two-dimensional account of the necessary *a posteriori* as applied to this particular example.

A contingent *a posteriori* fact, that the table in front of me is made of plastic in the sense of there being exactly one table in front of me and its being made of plastic, leads *a priori* to how a world would have to be for the sentence to be false: it would have to be a world with something plastic not made of plastic, and we know *a priori* that there is no such world.

The condition on *worlds* is such that it is *a priori* that it cannot be satisfied. It is *a posteriori* and contingent that that is the condition imposed. That's the essence of the two-dimensional account of necessary *a posteriori* sentences.

# Response to Frank Jackson

*Penelope Mackie*

Frank Jackson holds that there is an important epistemological problem for the necessary *a posteriori*, a problem that can, however, be solved (he argues) by the two-dimensional account of necessary *a posteriori* truth. He also argues that the epistemological problem leads to an important 'making-true' problem for the necessary *a posteriori*, but that the solution to the epistemological problem provided by the two-dimensional account also solves the making-true problem. Although Jackson does not claim to have established that the two-dimensional account is the *only* one that can provide a solution to these problems, he does seem to suggest that without it we would be at a loss as to how to solve them.

Jackson suggests that the two problems about the necessary *a posteriori* can be seen as developments of Quine's scepticism about essential properties. In the first part of his paper, he argues that an account of essential properties in terms of possible worlds answers Quine's objections to essentialism, when those objections are interpreted in a friendly way, as based on legitimate concerns rather than on a confusion of the *de re* with the *de dicto*. I'm not so sure that Quine should capitulate quite as readily as Jackson suggests that he should. But because of shortage of time I won't comment on this part of the paper. Instead, I'll move straight on to the objection that is put into the mouth of the character that Jackson calls 'the daughter of Quine'.

## 1. THE EPISTEMOLOGICAL PROBLEM

The daughter of Quine, unlike her father, accepts essential properties, but she is nevertheless sceptical about the necessary *a posteriori*. She is puzzled about how we are supposed to get necessary *a posteriori* truths out of essentialism. And, according to Jackson, the daughter of Quine may be seen as raising an important epistemological problem for the necessary *a posteriori*, expressed in the following passage:

> There is an issue about how we could be entitled to hold that some claim is a necessary *a posteriori* truth. If it is *a posteriori*, there is some good sense in which it might, as the saying goes, turn out to be false. How then do we show that the 'possibility' of being false is not in fact a possibility? . . . The

worry is about how, for some particular case, we could be rationally entitled to be sure that *it* is a case. (p. 263)

This echoes Jackson's remark in the opening section of his paper:

I think . . . that there is an important epistemological problem for the necessary *a posteriori*. Roughly, the problem is that if *S* is offered as a candidate necessary *a posteriori* truth, how could we *show* that it is necessary, in the face of the fact that it takes investigation to show that *S* is true, and so, in some sense, *S* might have turned out to be false? (p. 257)

Daughter of Quine's objection is illustrated using the pair of sentences

(d) Anything identical to the table in front of me is made of plastic

and

(e) Anything identical to the very [i.e., the actual] table in front of me is made of plastic.

where (e) is the proposed candidate for a necessary *a posteriori* truth (in contrast to (d), which everyone agrees is contingent). Daughter of Quine is envisaged as accepting the essentialist principle that anything made of plastic is essentially made of plastic. Yet she is represented as still worrying about how we could know that (e) is a necessary truth.

The answer that Jackson proposes, to the daughter of Quine's epistemological worry, is that we could come to know that (e) is necessary by putting certain *a priori* premises together with a piece of *a posteriori* knowledge of a purely contingent truth, viz. that the table in front of me is made of plastic. For although this truth is contingent, we can see that it 'leads *a priori* to how a world would have to be for the sentence [(e), i.e., "Anything identical to the very table in front of me is made of plastic"—PM] to be false: it would have to be a world with something plastic not made of plastic, and we know *a priori* that there is no such world' (p. 266).

In more detail, this way in which we could come to know that (e) is a necessary truth is based on the following four premises, (f), (g), (h), and (i), of which (f), (h), and (i) are *a priori*, and (g) is both contingent and *a posteriori*.

(f) If $x$ is made of plastic in the actual world, then $x$ is made of plastic in every world in which it exists.

(g) The table in front of me is made of plastic.

(h) If $x$ is the table in front of me, then $x$ is the very table in front of me.

(i) If $x$ is the very table in front of me in the actual world, then $x$ is the very table in front of me in every world in which $x$ exists.

These four premises together lead *a priori* to the desired conclusion (that (e) is a necessary truth). However, this way of arriving at the conclusion crucially relies on a premise that is a purely contingent truth (i.e., premise (g)) together with an *a priori* connection between the non-rigid description 'the table in front of me' and the corresponding rigidified description 'the very table in front of me', as expressed in premise (h), which we might call 'the rigidification premise'. And, of course, as Jackson indicates, the reliance on such a combination is characteristic of a two-dimensional account of the necessary *a posteriori*.

My problem with this is that I do not see why these two features—the ones that are characteristic of the two-dimensional account—need to be invoked to answer the epistemological question posed by the daughter of Quine, at least as her question has been stated.

The daughter of Quine is supposed to be worried about how we could know that (e) is necessary (i.e., necessarily true), given that it is *a posteriori*. However, as far as I can see, she has the resources to answer *this* worry simply on the basis of her acceptance of the essentialist principle (f) and the premise (i)—the premise that says, in effect, that the expression 'the very table in front of me' is a rigid designator. Since she accepts (f) and (i), she should surely accept, on purely *a priori* grounds, that *if* (e) is true, it is necessarily true. In other words, she should accept, as an *a priori* truth, the following conditional:

(j) If (anything identical to) the very table in front of me is made of plastic [in the actual world], then, necessarily, anything identical to the very table in front of me is made of plastic.

But now: if daughter of Quine accepts that (j) is an *a priori* truth, why does she *still* worry about *how one could come to know* that

(e) Anything identical to the very table in front of me is made of plastic

is necessarily true? For once you have accepted that (j) is true, you should accept that in order to know that its consequent is true, all you need is to know that its antecedent is true. But (you can see *a priori* that) to accept that the consequent of (j) is true is to accept that (e) is a necessary truth.

If, given her acceptance of (j), daughter of Quine still worries about how she could know that (e) is a necessary truth, then it looks as if her worry must be about how she could come to know the *antecedent* of (j). But if this is her worry, then it seems easy to answer it. The way she can come to know that the very table in front of her is made of plastic is just the way that we usually find out what things are made of, by empirical investigation. But now that we have shown the daughter of Quine how she can come to know that (e) is true, and how she can come to know that if (e) is true, (e) is necessarily true, haven't we shown her how she can come to know that (e) is necessarily true? Yet *this* answer to the epistemological problem makes no appeal to the distinctive features of the two-dimensional account of the necessary *a posteriori*. In particular, the answer makes no appeal either to the fact that the rigid designator involved in this example of the necessary *a posteriori* is a rigidified version of a non-rigid description, or to the related fact that one can come to know that (e) is true via knowledge of the contingent truth (g) together with the 'rigidification premise' (h).

However, since the answer makes no such appeal, there is no obvious reason to think that it cannot be generalized to proposed cases of the necessary *a posteriori* that (unlike (e)) do *not* fit the two-dimensional account, and to which premises such as (g) and (h) are inapplicable. Suppose, for example, that the name 'Willard' is a rigid designator of the table in front of me, but one that is *not* presumed to be equivalent to a rigidified description such as 'the very table in front of me'. Then we may propose, as a candidate for a necessary *a posteriori* truth:

(eW)  Anything identical to Willard is made of plastic.

Suppose that the daughter of Quine is worried about how she could come to know that (eW) is a necessary truth, given that it is *a posteriori*. Why can't we answer her worry in the same way (*mutatis mutandis*[1]) that I have suggested that we should answer her worry about how she could come to know that (e) is a necessary truth? But if we can do so, then it seems that we can answer her worry *without* supposing that (eW) must resemble (e) in being capable of subsumption under the two-dimensional account of the necessary *a posteriori*.

Let me try a different tack. Perhaps the response I've given fails to do justice to the daughter of Quine's epistemological worry. For part of her worry, as expressed in the passage I quoted on pp. 267–8 (Jackson, p. 273), has to do with the fact that, since (e) is *a posteriori*, the falsity of (e) *appears* to be possible. It seems to follow that, if I am to be justified in claiming that (e) is necessary, I must also be justified in claiming that this apparent possibility is not a real possibility.

But now, *if* one accepts the conditional (j), one thereby accepts the principle that *if* (e) is true, the apparent possibility of (e)'s falsehood is not a real possibility. So although it may be true that, in order to be justified in thinking that (e) is necessarily true, I must be justified in thinking that the apparent possibility of its falsity is not a real possibility, it looks as if I *can* have such a justification—one that is derived from my (*a priori*) justification for thinking that (e) is, if true, necessarily true, together with whatever justification I have for thinking that (e) is true!

But, it may be said, this is uncharitable. Maybe the worry of the daughter of Quine is a worry of the following kind: although merely showing that *S* is

---

[1]  i.e., by appeal to the essentialist premise (f), together with an appropriately modified version of premise (i), viz.

(iW)  If *x* is Willard (in the actual world), then *x* is Willard in every world in which it exists

(where (iW) says, in effect, that 'Willard' is a rigid designator). From (f) and (iW) we derive the conditional (jW):

(jW)  If (anything identical to) Willard is made of plastic [in the actual world], then, necessarily, anything identical to Willard is made of plastic

from which it follows (*a priori*) that if (eW) is true, (eW) is necessarily true.

necessary may be enough to show *that* the falsity of *S* is not a real possibility, it might still leave it a mystery *how* it could fail to be a real possibility, given that it seems to be one. In other words, perhaps the daughter of Quine wants, not a reason for thinking *that* the illusion of possibility in this case *is* an illusion, but, rather, an explanation of *why*, in this case, the 'illusion of possibility' arises at all. And I agree that the two-dimensional account does offer such an explanation, for the case of a necessary *a posteriori* truth such as (e), by reference to a related genuine contingency (such as (g)).

Nevertheless, if what the daughter of Quine wants really is an *explanation* of the illusion of possibility, then I think that she has misstated her problem about the necessary *a posteriori*.[2] It seems to me, then, that if daughter of Quine's epistemological questions are taken literally to be the ones stated, then they can be answered without invoking the special features of the two-dimensional account, in which a crucial role is played by the connection between the contingent truth of (g) and the necessary truth of (e).

## 2. THE TRUTH-MAKER QUESTION

Jackson argues that his proposed answer to the epistemological problem also provides an answer to another (more fundamental) truth-maker (or 'making-true') question about the necessary *a posteriori*. However, the 'making-true' problem, as Jackson presents it, is, as far as I can see, one that can arise for a case of the necessary *a posteriori* only if the case is already assumed to be one for which the two-dimensional treatment is appropriate.

The 'making-true' question or problem is exemplified as follows. There is (supposedly) a puzzle about 'what might make it the case that, although (d) is contingent, (e) is necessary' (p. 264). The puzzle arises because:

> If God arranges things in such a way that [there is a single table in front of me which is plastic], She makes (d) true. But that of course is exactly what God needs to do to make (e) true. . . . After making (d) true, there is nothing more for her to do to make (e) true. A single table in front of me which is made of plastic is quite enough. What then makes the difference between (d)'s being only contingently true and (e)'s being necessarily true? (p. 264)

Now there is, it seems to me, something of a puzzle about what the puzzle here is supposed to be. Some of the remarks in the quoted passage suggest that what is supposed to be puzzling is that what is *sufficient* for the truth of a contingent

---

[2] I suppose someone might hold that one cannot be justified in holding that *S* is a necessary truth, when its falsity appears to be possible, unless one possesses an explanation of *why* the illusion of possibility occurs. However, I am not sure what the argument for this principle would be. And I suspect that I am a counterexample to the principle.

truth is also *sufficient* for the truth of a necessary truth. But, on the face of it, this is an odd thing to be puzzled about. On the face of it, this is just what one would expect: that anything that God does that is enough to make any contingent truth true will also be, trivially, *enough* to make any necessary truth true. If so, the fact that God needs to do no more to make a given necessary truth true than to make a given contingent truth true should be completely unpuzzling, and suggests no special problem about the relation between the contingent truth (d) and the necessary truth (e).

   If there is a 'making-true' puzzle concerning (d) and (e), then, perhaps it is not that God need do *no more*, in order to bring it about that (e) is true, than to bring it about that (d) is true, but, rather, that God *has* to bring it about that the contingent truth (d) is true in order to bring it about that the necessary truth (e) is true. That this (rather than the sufficiency claim) represents the 'making-true' problem is suggested by the portion of the passage quoted above that contains the words 'But that [i.e., what is needed to bring about the truth of (d)] of course is exactly what God *needs to do* to make (e) true' (my italics).

   Now, I agree that if this is so—if there is some contingent truth that God needs to make true in order to make true a necessary truth—it does indeed present a puzzle. How can a necessary truth depend for its truth on a contingency, and still be a necessary truth? For example, how can it be that, in order to make (e) true (something that is, since it is a necessary truth, true with respect to all possible worlds) God needs to make it the case that the actual world is a certain way—a way that other worlds are not? In other words, how can it be that, if some different possible world had been actual, (e) would not have been a necessary truth, although as a matter of fact it is?

   However, if this is the alleged puzzle, then the appropriate reaction is surely that *this* puzzle arises only because the particular case of the necessary *a posteriori* being considered is one for which the two-dimensional account is guaranteed to be appropriate. It is only because we believe that the rigidified description 'the very table in front of me' *would have (rigidly) designated a different object, had a different possible world been actual,* that we think that, had a different possible world been actual, (e) would have expressed a falsehood rather than a truth.[3]

   To conclude, then, I agree that the two-dimensional account does raise a 'making-true' problem for the necessary *a posteriori*, a problem to which the two-dimensional account also provides a solution. (They have first raised a

---

   [3] By contrast, in the absence of an argument that the rigid designator 'Willard' *must* be equivalent to some relevant rigidified description, there is no evident reason to suppose that there is *any* possible world such that, had that possible world been actual,

   (eW)  Anything identical to Willard is made of plastic

would have expressed a falsehood rather than a truth.

dust, and then boast that they can clear it?) But, obviously, although it is to the credit of the two-dimensional account that it can provide a solution to a puzzle that it generates, this fact does nothing to support the conclusion that the two-dimensional account should be adopted as an account of the nature of all cases of necessary *a posteriori* truth.

# 13

# Apriorism about Modality

*Scott Sturgeon*

## 1. THE ISSUE

Modal beliefs concern how things can or must be, and they arise in various ways. Sometimes they are based on reliable evidence, and sometimes they are not. Apriorism about modality is the view that modal beliefs based on apriori reflection are reliably based. As I shall put the point: it is the view that apriori reflection is a *mark* of modality.

In this paper, I argue that apriori reflection is at best a fallible guide to modality (both possibility and necessity). I also claim its usefulness as a guide turns on the "bounty" of modality: if possibility turns out to be plentiful—in a sense to be glossed—apriori reflection will be a good-but-fallible guide to it; if necessity turns out to be meagre—in a dual sense of that gloss—apriori reflection will not be a mark of possibility. Our take on bounty itself should turn on how best to systematize thought, so our take on apriorism about modality should turn on the deepest of philosophical concerns. Or so I will argue.

## 2. APRIORISM ABOUT POSSIBILITY

Three questions structure debate about apriori reflection and belief in possibility. The first is

*Question 1*: Is apriori coherence a guide to possibility?

I am grateful to many people for help with this paper. As best I can reckon they are David Chalmers, Dorothy Edgington, Kit Fine, Dominic Gregory, Bob Hale, John Hawthorne, Jen Hornsby, Frank Jackson, Carrie Jenkins, Barry Lee, Stephan Leuenberger, Jonathan Lowe, Fraser MacBride, Mike Martin, Michael McKinsey, Daniel Nolan, Gideon Rosen, Nick Shea, Susanna Siegel, Steve Yablo, Alan Weir, Tim Williamson, Crispin Wright, Dean Zimmerman, and Maja Spener most of all.

Those who say *yes* think an apriori feature of a claim is a mark of its possibility. Specifically, they think a claim's withstanding apriori reflection indicates it is possible. When a claim is not ruled out by such reflection, they say, that is a mark of its possibility.

This is not yet to say what kind of mark is in play, but a *yes* to Question 1 does entail that withstanding apriori reflection indicates possibility. Those who say *no*, therefore, are non-apriorists about possibility.[1] They deny apriori coherence is a mark of possibility, claiming instead that a view's withstanding apriori reflection is no modal indication at all. Hence they avoid

*Question 2*:  Is apriori coherence a fallible guide to possibility?

Those who say *yes* here think withstanding apriori reflection is a fallible mark of possibility. This goes some way toward saying what kind of mark is in play. It comes to the view, after all, that failing to be ruled out apriori is an imperfect mark of possibility. That is just what most philosophers think. They say withstanding apriori reflection is a good-but-fallible guide to possibility. They are modest in their apriorism. They are *apriori fallibilists about possibility.*[2]

Yet a growing number disagree. They answer Question 2 *no*, claiming that apriori coherence is an *in*fallible mark of possibility. On their view: when a claim withstands ideal apriori reflection, that guarantees it can be true. This is *apriori infallibilism about possibility*, a view which naturally prompts

*Question 3*:  What of aposteriori necessity?

And now we face a challenge. We are asked to reconcile infallibilism about possibility with intuitions which lead many to embrace aposteriori necessity. Most who attempt it do so by semantic means. As we will see in §5, they use *two-dimensional semantics* to argue that intuitions which drive Kripkean thoughts on necessity are consistent with infallibilism. They put forth a *semantic*-based reconciliation of infallibilism about possibility and the intuitions which prompt belief in aposteriori necessity. That is the dominant strategy amongst such infallibilists. Eventually we shall reject the position.[3]

---

[1]  Edgington (2004), Leeds (2001), Putnam (1990).

[2]  Kripke and Putnam have done most to promote apriori fallibilism about possibility. Kripke has been the dominant influence, so I describe Kripke- and Putnam-like considerations on the topic as "Kripkean". That makes for ease of expression and puts credit where it is mostly due. Also, I leave out the qualifications "apriori" and "about possibility" when context permits. See Kripke (1980) and Putnam (1975); and for related discussion see Levine (1998) and (2001), Papineau (2002), Robertson (1998), Salmon (1989), Sidelle (1989), Tichý (1983), and Yablo (1993) and (2002).

[3]  Two-dimensional semantics grew from Davies and Humberstone (1981), Evans (1979), Kaplan (1979) and (1989), Lewis (1979b), and Stalnaker (1979). It is in the work of Chalmers and Jackson that we find the most forceful use of it to defend apriori infallibilism. See Chalmers (1996), (1999), (2002), Jackson (1998), and Chalmers and Jackson (2001). I also think, somewhat hesitantly, that early time-slices of Lewis were infallibilist. His discussion of temporal bi-location in the preface of (1986c) looks to be, though later time-slices seem to have given up the view. See related discussion in (1994a) and (2009). I do not know what prompted the shift if it is there, although two reasons for

But notice: a much more direct line is available. One might respond to Kripkean intuitions by concocting a tougher apriori test of possibility. One might finesse putatively infallible apriori conditions, saying that they involve *more* than withstanding apriori reflection. Then one could deny that apriori coherence infallibly depicts possibility yet maintain finessed apriority does the job. One could put forth two claims at once: apriori coherence is a fallible guide to possibility; finessed apriority is an infallible guide to possibility. This would be an *epistemic*-based reconciliation of infallibilism about possibility and Kripkean intuition. §3 shows the view is easy to construct and demonstrably resistant to Kripkean counter-instance.

In this way Questions 1–3 induce a nice structure on the debate about apriori reflection and possibility:

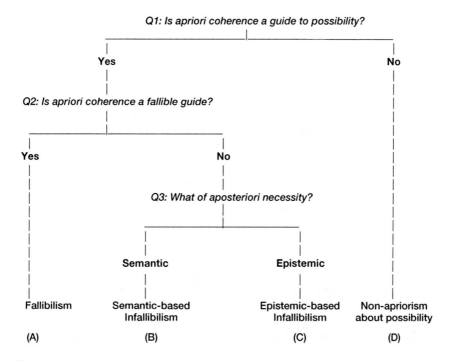

Fig. 13.1.

(A)–(C) are apriorist views of possibility. They say that withstanding apriori reflection is a mark of possibility: (A) claims it is a fallible mark, (B) and (C)

it can be found in §§7–8 of Sturgeon (2006). See also Balog (1999), Block and Stalnaker (2000), Hill and McLaughlin (1998), Loar (1999), Rosen (2006), and Yablo (2002).

claim it is an infallible one. (D) disagrees upstream when it denies that withstanding apriori reflection is a mark of possibility at all. (D) is a non-apriorist view.

In the next two sections I work up epistemic-based infallibilism. §4 then explains why it has no Kripke-style refutation, why the view can withstand Kripkean intuition about aposteriori necessity. That will show why rejecting infallibilism must rest on *more* than such intuition, on larger philosophical commitment, on deeper philosophical concern. §5 looks at two large-scale worries and uses them to reject epistemic-based infallibilism. §6 then explains how they cut against semantic-based infallibilism too (i.e. how they cut against two-dimensional semantics as a ground for modal epistemology). §§5–6 thus make for a general case against infallibilism about possibility. There are deep reasons to reject the view in both its epistemic and semantic guise. Reflecting on them makes clear how one should decide whether apriorism about possibility is true. That is explained in §§7–8.

## 3. MODALITY

Modal operators will stand for *genuine* modality throughout: $^\circ\blacklozenge\text{ø}^\circ$ will mean ø is genuinely possible; $^\circ\blacksquare\text{ø}^\circ$ will mean ø is genuinely necessary. This will be our label for what is sometimes called "metaphysical modality" and other times called "logical modality".[4] A new label is called for, in this context, for a simple reason. It is normally assumed that logical modality is shot through with apriority; and even metaphysical modality is often said to be "logical" when logic is "broadly construed". Later we will see why that is so, by the way; but for now we note merely that both of the standard labels are apt to bias the discussion. Both are liable to suggest that there is an internal link between modality and apriority. I must blanche the discussion of just that bias, so I use new terms. They are meant to leave open by fiat whether our target modality is shot through with apriority, whether it deserves the honorific "logical". By genuine modality I shall mean simply this: *the most absolute realistic modal space*. The idea can be glossed via possibility or necessity.

For instance: when ø is genuinely possible, it is a mind- and language-independent fact that ø can happen. That fact does not spring from how we

---

[4] By Kripke and Lewis respectively. The conception of genuine modality used in this paper is meant to capture the presently-relevant core aspects of modality common to Kripke and Lewis's otherwise very different approaches to the topic. We shall simply assume here—with the vast majority of philosophers, of course—that there is such a thing as genuine modality. Our prime concern will turn on its scope.

think or talk (even in the rational ideal). It can be individuated independently of mind- or language-related phenomena. Genuine possibility is like genuine actuality: it does not depend on us for its existence or its nature. It is a realistic domain. Realism is a component of genuine possibility; and so is weakness: whenever there is a realistic sense in which ø can happen, ø is genuinely possible. Such possibility is the weakest kind of realistic possibility, including every kind of realistic possibility. The "diamond face" of genuine modality is a two-part affair: it is the most inclusive realistic space of possibility.

Similarly: when ø is genuinely necessary, it is a mind- and language-independent fact that ø must happen. That fact does not spring from how we think or talk (even in the rational ideal). It too can be individuated independently of mind- or language-related phenomena. It too is like genuine actuality. Realism is a component of genuine necessity; and so is strength: when ø is genuinely necessary, it is necessary in any realistic sense. Genuine necessity is the strongest kind of realistic necessity, included in every realistic necessity. The "box face" of genuine modality is a two-part affair: it is the least inclusive realistic space of necessity.

Think of it this way: genuine possibility contains all realistic possibility. It contains, for instance, nomic possibility; so if there are counter-legal genuine possibilities—as is usually supposed—then nomic possibility nests within genuine possibility. In pictures:

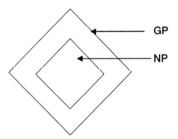

**Fig. 13.2.**

NP contains all nomically possible claims, GP contains all genuinely possible claims. Genuine possibility is the weakest realistic modal space, so all realistic diamonds nest within GP.

Similarly: genuine necessity is contained within all realistic necessity. It is contained, for instance, within nomic necessity; so if there are genuinely contingent nomic necessities—as is also usually supposed—then genuine necessity nests within nomic necessity. In pictures:

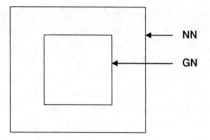

**Fig. 13.3.**

NN contains all nomically necessary claims, and GN contains all genuinely necessary claims. Genuine necessity is the strongest realistic necessity, so it nests within all realistic boxes.

In a nutshell: genuine modality is the most absolute realistic modality. It is logical and/or metaphysical modality cleansed of the *assumption* that such modality enjoys an internal link to apriority. With that in mind, we turn to apriorism about possibility.

## 4. THE EPISTEMIC-BASED VIEW

Let us say ø is *prima facie apriori coherent* when it is coherent after a bit of apriori reflection. The idea, roughly, is that ø does not get ruled out by what turns up during such reflection. Let us write $^\circ$pfac(ø)$^\circ$ to express that basic idea. In the event, super-naïve apriori infallibilism is the view that this schema has no counter-instance:

(p)  pfac(ø) ⊃ ◆ø.[5]

If that is so, then belief in ø's genuine possibility based on its prima facie apriori coherence is infallible. But the line is obviously not right. After all, apriori reflection can self-correct. When we see that not all clear concepts yield extension sets, or that not all infinite sets are equinumerous, for instance, apriori reflection self-corrects. Genuine *im*possibilities are often prima facie apriori coherent. Inferring ◆ø from pfac(ø) is at best a fallible affair.

So let us idealize and say ø is *limit coherent* when it is coherent at the limit of apriori reflection. The idea here is that ø remains coherent in light of all that is rational after ideal apriori reflection. We permit maximal time for thought,

---

[5] At this stage of discussion I shall understand the validity of schemata to consist in their lack of a counter-instance which is logically simple or the negation of such. That keeps things where they initially belong, on base-case bother. Later we'll drop this restriction when it is apt to do so.

concentration, memory, computational power, etc. We maximize smarts, as it were, along purely epistemic dimensions. When ø is not ruled out by what turns up, it is limit coherent. Let us write $°\lim(ø)°$ to express that basic idea. In the event, naïve apriori infallibilism is the view that this schema has no counter-instance:

(I)  $\lim(ø) \supset \blacklozenge ø.$

If that is so, then belief in ø's genuine possibility based on its limit coherence is infallible. The view here allows that everyday apriori coherence is a fallible guide to genuine possibility, but it insists that limit coherence is infallible.[6]

It is not obvious this is wrong. After all, refuting the view was a key move in Kripke's war to segregate limit coherence and genuine modality. Yet most think he won the war. They think he showed that limit case apriori reflection does not infallibly mark genuine possibility, that non-modal fact can rub out limit coherence. On their view, something coherent at the limit of apriori reflection can be genuinely *im*possible; and apriori reflection on non-modal fact can show it to be so.

For instance: let K be the claim that Mark Twain is Sam Clemens. Both K and ¬K are limit coherent. No amount of apriori reflection can show that Twain is Clemens, and no amount can show that he is not. The matter is not apriori. Twain *is* Clemens, as it happens; but that cannot be shown apriori. You have to look. Since they are one, though, they cannot help but be so. There is no way to pull them apart. Not only is K true, it is genuinely necessary. ¬K is genuinely impossible. Despite its limit coherence, ¬K fails to be genuinely possible. It is a counter-instance to (I). Or so it is said.

In essence, the line here plumps for the *existence* of counter-examples on purely apriori grounds. An instance of it runs thus:

|       | (1) | $K \vee \neg K$ | premise |
|-------|-----|-----------------|---------|
|       | (2) | $K \supset \neg\blacklozenge\neg(K)$ | premise |
|       | (3) | $\neg K \supset \neg\blacklozenge(K)$ | premise |
| so    | (4) | $\neg\blacklozenge\neg K \vee \neg\blacklozenge K$ | from (1)–(3) |
| but   | (5) | $\lim(K) \ \& \ \lim(\neg K)$ | premise |
| so    | (6) | $[\lim(K) \ \& \ \neg\blacklozenge K] \vee [\lim(\neg K) \ \& \ \neg\blacklozenge\neg K]$ | from (4)–(5) |
| so    | (7) | $(\exists ø) \lim(ø) \ \& \ \neg\blacklozenge ø.$ | from (6) |

---

[6] (I) uses idealizing assumptions which cannot, in fact, be satisfied by humans. This is common within epistemology but not without bother. After all: when idealizing assumptions become *too* extreme, epistemology has no purchase on real subjects. Yet idealizing assumptions are crucial to normative epistemology. So we are left with a good question: when does idealization go too far? We cannot hope to resolve that here. We must assume, for the sake of argument, that (I) and its ilk are not too idealized, that they can throw light on how we should reason. Divergent views on epistemic idealization can be found in Cherniak (1986), Christensen (2005), Kaplan (1996), Lewis (1988), Pollock (1989), Stalnaker (1991) and (1999a), Sturgeon (forthcoming), and Weirich (2005).

The premises are meant to be apriori obliged: (1) is got by appeal to propositional logic, (2) and (3) are got by appeal to our notion of strict identity, and (5) is said to spring from the philosophical insight that K is aposteriori. We are thus meant to be led apriori to the view that (1) is blemished, that it has a counter-instance. We cannot say apriori whether K or its negation is the rub, but we can say apriori that one of them must be. Naïve infallibilism is kaput, or so Kripkeans argue.[7]

Think of it this way. First, set aside claims involving 'here', 'now', 'I', 'actually', and so forth. Then set aside Kripke's metre-rod, Evans's zip-inventor, and suchlike. In a nutshell: set aside claims our grip on which comes by indexicality and/or stipulation. These are (what I shall call) *unusual* claims. They create wrinkles in our topic that need not concern us, so focus on usual claims. Our grip on them does not come by indexicality and/or stipulation.[8] Put them in a region and go through them one by one. Consider everything apriori to see whether each can be true (its logical form, conceptual content, relation to apriori obliged usual views, etc.). Assume a claim is possible unless shown otherwise. This yields an apriori partition:

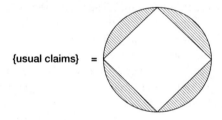

**Fig. 13.4.**

The shaded region contains limit *in*coherence. The inner diamond contains limit coherence.

It is tempting to equate this divide with that between genuine possibility and impossibility. Kripke's argument is then meant to show, in effect, that the latter divide nests within the unshaded region.[9] In pictures:

---

[7] Kripke (1980).

[8] Unusual claims have been used to argue for the contingent apriori. For relevant discussion see Donnellan (1979), Evans (1979), Kitcher (1980), Kripke (1980), Salmon (1987), and Sutton (2001).

[9] The "in effect" hedge is needed because this way of setting things up presupposes limit *in*coherence ensures genuine *im*possibility. It presupposes $\neg\text{lim}(\emptyset)$ is sufficient for $\neg\blacklozenge\emptyset$. We discuss that in §8.

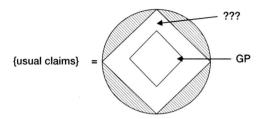

Fig. 13.5.

The inner diamond divides genuine possibility and impossibility. The outer diamond divides limit coherence and incoherence. The queried space is the *Kripke Zone*. It harbours usual claims, like ¬K, which are limit coherent yet genuinely impossible. It harbours counter-instances to (I), showing that limit coherence does not infallibly mark genuine possibility.

Kripke's strategy runs on claims which are

- about matters of actual fact;
- such that both they and their negation are limit coherent;

and

- such that it is apriori obliged that the matter they raise is non-contingent.[10]

Thus it is with K, the view that Twain is Clemens. Not only is it aposteriori whether K is true, one is apriori obliged to regard the matter as non-contingent. It is apriori obliged that if K is true, it is necessary; and likewise for ¬K. It is apriori that however things stand it could not have been otherwise, yet both K and ¬K are limit coherent; hence limit reflection does not infallibly mark genuine possibility. That was Kripke's line. How should we react?

Well, let us say *Kripke claims* are claims like K and ¬K: they are claims about matters of actual fact; both they and their negations are limit coherent; yet it is apriori obliged that the matter they raise is non-contingent. Then we define: ø is *Kripke coherent* when it is limit coherent in light of Kripke *truths*; and we write °kc(ø)° to express that. We set

---

[10] There is debate about which claims satisfy these conditions. In particular, there is debate about which claims about matters of actual fact truly underwrite apriori "bridge laws" like the necessity of identity and the necessity of distinctness. Kripke argues that certain claims about constitution and aetiology do so as well. We only make use of claims about identity here, assuming the necessity of identity and the necessity of distinctness are apriori obliged. See Kripke (1980), esp. n. 56, Robertson (1998), and references therein.

kc(ø) = lim(ø/**K**),

with **K** the set of true Kripke claims.[11]

The most conservative reaction to Kripke is then simple. It admits there are counter-instances to (l) but insists that Kripke coherence infallibly marks genuine possibility. It swaps (l) for

(k)  kc(ø) ⊃ ◆ø.

This is less-naïve infallibilism. The view admits the space of limit coherence exceeds that of genuine possibility. To reach the latter from the former, it says, one must shave down the space of limit coherence; but the view claims that one need *only* throw out false Kripke claims. If that is right, limit coherence marks genuine possibility unless Kripke truth rubs out the coherence.

What should we make of this? Should we accept that Kripke coherence infallibly marks genuine possibility? Should we embrace Kripke's argument in the most conservative way? Put in present terminology: should we say that the queried region of Figure 13.5 contains *only* false Kripke claims, i.e . only false claims about matters of actual fact such that both those claims and their negations are limit coherent despite its being apriori that the matter they raise is genuinely non-contingent?

No. There are Kripke coherent claims that are not genuinely possible. There are counter-examples to (k), and the argument for their existence directly echoes Kripke's line on (l). To see this, consider the view that Lewisian worlds are the possible worlds. The idea, basically, is that maximally fine-grained points in the space of genuine possibility are mereological sums of a certain sort; so the relevant claim here is at bottom one of identity: sums of that sort are identical to maximal genuine possibilities.[12] Call the view "L". Both L and ¬L are prima facie coherent, and they look limit coherent too. There may be aesthetic reasons to favour L or its negation in one's total theory, but neither gets definitively ruled out apriori. That is one lesson of Lewis's surprisingly robust defence of L in the repeated face of attempted refutation.[13] Neither L nor its negation is apriori obliged, of course, so a question is presently sharp: are there truths about matters of actual fact to rub out their coherence?

I doubt it. Both L and ¬L look Kripke coherent:

(8)  kc(L)

(9)  kc(¬L).

---

[11] Note false Kripke claims are not Kripke coherent. **K**'s negation, for instance, is not. After all, **K** is a Kripke truth; and it is apriori obliged the matter **K** raises is non-contingent; hence it is limit *in*coherent that ¬**K** is true in light of Kripke truth, for ¬**K** is ruled out by such truth. And the point holds in general: no Kripke falsehood is Kripke coherent. All such falsehood is ruled out by Kripke truth.

[12] See Lewis (1986c). For other counter-examples to (k) see Rosen (2006) and Sturgeon (2006).

[13] See e.g. Maudlin (1996) and Lewis (1999).

In English: it is Kripke coherent that maximal genuine possibilities are Lewisian mereological sums; and it is Kripke coherent they are not. Take apriori reflection to the limit, throw in Kripke truth, both L and ¬L stay coherent. Neither gets definitively ruled out.

This spells trouble for (**k**); for (8), (9), and (**k**) jointly yield

(10) $\blacklozenge$L

and

(11) $\blacklozenge$¬L.

But consider the view that Lewisian modal metaphysics is true but genuinely might not have been:

(12) L & $\blacklozenge$¬L.

This is genuinely impossible. Its first conjunct entails its second is true only if there is a Lewisian world at which there is no such world. (12)'s conjuncts cannot both be true, so we have

(13) $\blacksquare$(L ⊃ ¬$\blacklozenge$¬L).

Yet this and (10) yield

(14) $\blacksquare$L

which conflicts with (11), so (10) rules out (11). Similarly, consider the view that Lewisian modal metaphysics is false but genuinely might have been true:

(15) ¬L & $\blacklozenge$L.

This too is genuinely impossible, for its possibility implies that of its right-hand side, yet that leads back to (10). As we have just seen, though, (10) leads via (13) to (14); and (14) conflicts with (15)'s left-hand side.[14]

The moral is clear: whichever of L and ¬L turns out true, it is genuinely necessary as well. (10) and (11) cannot both be true, so at least one Kripke coherence is genuinely impossible. There are counter-instances to (**k**). Not surprisingly, the schema breaks down on the metaphysics of genuine modality. There are Kripke coherent claims about that metaphysics which genuinely cannot be true. Less-naïve infallibilism breeds conflict in modal metaphysics. One should not react, then, in the most conservative way to Kripke's efforts to segregate limit coherence and genuine modality. A more radical reaction is needed, but what should it be?

---

[14] The step from (13) to (14) leans on S5 for genuine modality. That is contentious of course: see Forbes (1985), Salmon (1989), and references therein. But note that L is an identity claim. The conclusion of the argument can also be got by appeal to the necessity of identity and that of distinctness. And that appeal entails nothing about the logic of genuine modality. I present the S5-argument because I think it best edifies L's modal status, because I accept its underlying logic. We will see in §8 how that might be epistemically grounded.

Well, K-style counter-examples to (l), and L-style counter-examples to (k), share two features emphasized by Kripke in his discussion of these issues:

($\kappa_1$)  both they and their negation are limit coherent;

and

($\kappa_2$)  it is apriori obliged that the matters they raise are non-contingent.

When a claim satisfies these principles it cannot be ruled out apriori, cannot be ruled in apriori, yet the claim and its negation concern a subject matter that can be seen apriori to be non-contingent. Hence we can see on purely apriori grounds that apriori reflection must be insensitive to impossibility somewhere. Either the claim or its negation is the rub. Either the first cannot be true despite remaining in play at the limit of apriori reflection, or its negation cannot be true despite remaining in play at that limit. Impossibility slips through the net of apriori reflection somewhere.

This means there will be further systematic misalignments between apriori coherence and genuine possibility. For instance, let R be any claim satisfying ($\kappa_1$) and ($\kappa_2$). Neither R nor its negation can be ruled out apriori, yet it is apriori that R is either necessary or impossible. Consider next any contingent claim C which is apriori independent of R and its negation. If R is necessary, (C&¬R) is limit coherent yet impossible. If R is impossible, (C&R) is limit coherent yet impossible. The phenomenon here occurs, of course, because claims which satisfy ($\kappa_1$) and ($\kappa_2$) *logically embed* to generate systematic apriori blind spots, places at which apriori coherence and genuine possibility misalign.

More generally, whenever R is a claim which satisfy ($\kappa_1$) and ($\kappa_2$) there will be a host of other claims with these two features:

($\kappa_1$)  both they and their negation are limit coherent;

and

($\kappa_3$)  it is apriori for at least one of them that it is non-contingent in light of the truth-value of some claim satisfying ($\kappa_1$) and ($\kappa_2$).

To see how this works, let R be any old chestnut satisfying ($\kappa_1$) and ($\kappa_2$), say the claim that Hesperus is Phosphorus. In the event, consider this claim about position:

P =  The claim that Hesperus is in one place while Phosphorus is in another.

Both P and its negation are limit coherent: neither can be ruled out by apriori reflection alone, not even ideal apriori reflection. It is apriori true, however, that *if* R is true then P *must* be false. It is apriori true, in other words, that if Hesperus is Phosphorus then it cannot be the case that Hesperus is in one place while

Phosphorus is in another. And since all this is apriori, as is the fact that R satisfies ($\kappa_1$) and ($\kappa_2$), it follows that P satisfies ($\kappa_3$). More generally for any feature F, it will be apriori—due to the apriority of Leibniz's Law, of course—that *if* R is true, then it cannot be the case that Hesperus has F while Phosphorus lacks F. And the same kind of thing will hold true apriori of any such claim that satisfies ($\kappa_3$). Claims of this form will have a modal status which is apriori linked to the truth-value of claims satisfying ($\kappa_1$) and ($\kappa_2$). In turn that will signal real danger of misalignment between apriori coherence and genuine possibility.

Claims which satisfy ($\kappa_1$) and ($\kappa_2$) are *apriori red flags*: both they and their negations are in play at the limit of apriori reflection, yet it can be seen apriori that their subject matter is non-contingent. Claims which satisfy ($\kappa_1$) and ($\kappa_3$) are *apriori yellow flags*: both they and their negation are in play at the limit of apriori reflection, yet it can be seen apriori for at least one of them that it is non-contingent in light of a red flag's truth.

By trading on ($\kappa_1$) and ($\kappa_2$) Kripke has argued for the existence of counter-examples to (I). By trading on ($\kappa_1$) and ($\kappa_2$) I have argued for the existence of counter-examples to (k). One can locate further potential modal blind spots by seeking claims which satisfy ($\kappa_1$) and ($\kappa_3$). Since a claim's satisfaction of ($\kappa_1$) and ($\kappa_2$) entails its satisfaction of ($\kappa_3$), it follows that an apriorist about modality can avoid this *entire* line of thought by constructing apriori conditions which rule out ($\kappa_3$).

So let us say ø is *apriori open*—or *open* for short—when two things happen

($\kappa_1$)  both ø and ¬ø are limit coherent;

but

¬($\kappa_3$)  it is *not* apriori for at least one of them that it is non-contingent in light of the truth-value of some claim satisfying ($\kappa_1$) and ($\kappa_2$).

And let us write $^\circ o(\text{ø})^\circ$ to express that. When ø is open, both ø and ¬ø are coherent at the limit of apriori reflection, but it is not apriori that at least one of them is non-contingent if some red flag turns up true. Condition ($\kappa_3$) fails. The thought is then to swap (k) for

(o)  $o(\text{ø}) \supset \blacklozenge\text{ø}$.

This is seasoned apriori infallibilism. It is the view that openness infallibly marks genuine possibility. If a claim and its negation are limit coherent, and it is not apriori that at least one of them is linked to a red flag, then both claims are genuinely possible. What should we make of the idea?

The first thing to note is this: there can be no purely philosophical counter-instance to (o), for such a claim would be an open apriori impossibility. Yet no claim can be open and apriori impossible, the latter precludes the former. If a claim is apriori impossible, it is apriori obliged that the matter it raises is non-contingent, so the claim is apriori ruled out. It thus satisfies neither clause in the definition of openness; and so that is why there can be no purely philosophical counter-instance to (o).

The second thing to note is this: Kripke-style arguments for the *existence* of counter-instances do not work against (o), for they turn on showing apriori of a claim or its negation that the non-contingency of their subject matter is linked to the truth of a red flag. But that is ruled out by $\neg(\kappa_3)$; and so neither K-style claims, nor L-style claims, nor P-style claims are open. None satisfy the antecedent of (o). It is apriori obliged that the non-contingency of their subject matter is linked to the truth of a red flag. That is why they can play spoiler in Kripkean discussion of naïve and less-naïve infallibilism. That is why they can be used apriori to plump for the existence of counter-instances to (l) and/or (k). But this very fact precludes their cutting against (o). Openness rules out the second condition used in the Kripkean line, so the strategy is inapplicable. It is impossible to argue in a Kripkean way against the validity of (o). The schema is immune to such an attack.

Having said that, there is an obvious problem with (o)'s scope; for the schema is too restricted. The definition of openness guarantees that it is closed under negation: ø is open just if its negation is too. (o) has no counter-instance, therefore, only if openness marks contingency. (o) is problem-free only if this schema is too:

(o)*  o(ø) ⊃ ø is contingent.

The problem is that there are non-contingent possibilities marked by apriori reflection: that everything is self-identical, for instance. Surely we mark this possibility with apriori reflection. (o) misses it altogether. The schema is suited to contingent possibilities if suited to anything. It skips non-contingent ones entirely and thus we need a condition designed for apriori necessity.

Let us say that ø is *apriori forced*—or *forced* for short—when three things are true:

(i)  ø is limit coherent,

(ii)  ¬ø is not limit coherent,

but

(iii)  it is apriori obliged that the matter they raise is non-contingent.

And let us write $^{\circ}f(ø)^{\circ}$ to express that. Then we say ø is *apriori apt*—or *apt* for short—when ø is open or forced, we write $^{\circ}apt(ø)^{\circ}$ to express that, and we swap (o) for

(a)  apt(ø) ⊃ ◆ø.

This is highly seasoned apriori infallibilism. It amounts to endorsing the validity of

(o) $o(\emptyset) \supset \blacklozenge\emptyset$

and

(f) $f(\emptyset) \supset \blacklozenge\emptyset$.

The view here is that aptness infallibly marks genuine possibility, and the putative mark is built from two conditions. One is designed for apriori necessity, the other for when there is no limit-case barrier to contingency. What should we make of the view?

Well, we have seen that there can be no apriori counter-instance to (o). There is such a counter-instance to (a), therefore, only if a claim can be forced and apriori impossible. Yet these too are incompatible: if you show something apriori to be impossible, it is apriori obliged the claim is false. That means the claim is apriori ruled out, so it is not limit coherent, so the claim is not forced. It fails condition (iii) above. Just as there can be no apriori counter-instance to (o), there can be none to (a). It too side-steps direct refutation.

Moreover, there is no way to press the Kripkean line against (a), for that would require locating claims so that

($\kappa_1$)  both they and their negation are limit coherent;

and

($\kappa_3$)  it is apriori for at least one of them that it is non-contingent in light of the truth-value of some claim satisfying ($\kappa_1$) and ($\kappa_2$).

Yet openness is defined expressly to preclude ($\kappa_3$); and forcedness is defined, at condition (iii), to preclude ($\kappa_1$). This means nothing remotely like Kripke's strategy is applicable to (a). Highly seasoned infallibilism is immune to Kripkean attack.[15]

## 5. CONTRA EPISTEMIC-BASED INFALLIBILISM

I reject the validity of (a). I have no direct counter-instance to offer, of course, as the schema does not permit one. Nor do I have a Kripke-inspired existence proof to cut against (a)'s validity, as the schema precludes that too. But I do have a pair of large-scale worries. One cuts against infallibilism *per se*, the other cuts against views which respect Kripkean intuition yet defend

[15] I became seriously interested in the topics of this paper when stumped by a student during an undergraduate lecture. After setting out various bits and pieces from *Naming and Necessity*, and arriving at our Fig. 13.5 complete with its Kripke Zone, a student raised her hand: 'Would you please specify exactly what goes into that space?', she asked. But I quickly found that I could not do so to my own satisfaction. And for a self-contained discussion about why that issue turns out to be very contentious, see the Appendix to this chapter.

some style of apriori infallibilism about possibility. I press the points here against epistemic-based infallibilism. I press them in the next section against its two-dimensional cousin.

1.   To begin, note humans tend to blur epistemic and metaphysical matters: credence with chance, certainty with truth, apriori tie with causal determination. We see this in our students all the time, and in ourselves more than we'd like. Call it the *ep-&-met tendency*. In my view, it explains why it is so natural to say that apriori reflection infallibly depicts genuine possibility. The temptation springs from our disposition to blur epistemic and metaphysical fact. Specifically, it springs from our tendency to blur apriori coherence, conceivability, and such with genuine possibility.

But temptation should be resisted, for genuine possibility is mind- and language-independent, a non-epistemic domain. This alone should ensure that purely epistemic procedures, like idealized apriori reflection, are *fallible* guides to genuine possibility. After all, that is how good epistemology and metaphysics fit together. When doing the former on mind- and language-independent fact, the result is humble pie, epistemology cleansed of magical error-free capacities to interrogate mind-independent reality. The result is fallibilism.

Think of it this way. Whether a claim is limit coherent is a purely epistemic fact about it, an idealized epistemic mark, one signalling that norms which govern apriori reckoning fail to rule out a claim. But whether a claim is genuinely possible is a purely metaphysical fact about it, a non-epistemic mark, one indicating that a region of modal reality—a set of genuinely possible worlds, say—is correctly described by a claim. There is two-way independence between the two marks. Limit coherence is not individuated by genuine possibility. Genuine possibility is not individuated by limit coherence. Fallibilism *should* characterize the link from the latter to the former. That is how epistemology and metaphysics fit.

For instance, visually based belief is an instructive case in point. The process takes visual experience as input and yields worldly belief as output. It fallibly targets non-epistemic fact and the same is true of other experience-to-belief procedures. They too fallibly target non-epistemic fact; so the moral I am pressing here is a familiar from epistemology: externally-directed belief based in "internal" evidence is fallible. That is true throughout non-modal epistemology and it should also be true of belief in genuine possibility based on (anything like) aptness.

Some will doubt the analogy:

> "Hang on!", they will say, "Belief in genuine modality based on (anything like) aptness is meant to be epistemically *ideal*. The proper analogy is with ideal visual belief; yet that kind of belief is based on veridical perception, not mere visual experience. That kind of belief *is* infallible. The proper analogy sees modal belief based on (anything like) aptness as modal belief based on *modal perception*. It too should be infallible."

But this cannot be right, for idealization works differently in the two cases. Believing a cat is before you, on the basis of seeing one, *is* an infallible process. Yet one cannot manage it alone. A cat must pitch in. Seeing a cat requires feline support, cat participation, and the point holds for perceptual belief in general. It leans on the world, obliging world-involvement. That is why it can be infallible yet non-magical at once. When one idealizes *from* belief based on hallucinatory experience *to* that based on veridical perception, one idealizes *toward* world-involvement, toward belief grounded in its truthmaker.

This has no echo in the modal case. In particular, idealization in that case does not involve reaching into modal reality. The idealization used by highly seasoned infallibilism, for instance, maximizes smarts along epistemic dimensions—time for thought, memory, computational capacity, and so on—but it does *not* make for genuine-modality-involvement. When ø is apt that does not consist in ø's genuine possibility, not even in part. The modal fact does not pitch in. Aptness springs from a certain kind of internal coherence in the epistemic limit, but it is non-modal-involving. The link from it to modality *should* be fallible. There is no scope here for talk of modal perception. The belief-forming process envisaged is infallible only if it is magic. Call this the *Objection from Magic*.

It is based, at bottom, on our best view of the fit between epistemology and metaphysics. That view cuts against apriori infallibilism about possibility. We thus face a choice: either the epistemology of genuine modality is special or infallibilism is wrong. We have no good reason to make an exception, so far as I can see, so we should not complicate theory. The simplest view should be ours. We do feel the tug of the ep-&-met tendency, of course, but that is no reason for us to complicate theory, since it is just our recognized tendency wrongly to blur epistemology and metaphysics.[16]

2.  My second point springs from an observation. As we have seen, the Kripkean line focuses on claims so that

$(\kappa_1)$ both they and their negation are limit coherent;

and

$(\kappa_2)$ it is apriori obliged that the matter they raise is non-contingent;

---

[16] A conceptual-role based approach to modal discourse could anchor a sensible-yet-non-magical version of modal infallibilism. To do so, however, the view would have to avoid perfectionism from the start. It would have to avoid the assumption—made by Peacocke (1999), for instance—that our modal-concept-investing tacit knowledge hits its target perfectly. After all, we know from work on the Principal Principle, Humean chance, and the latter's potential for undermining that perfectionism is not simply to be *assumed*. It must be earned by any conceptual-role-based approach to any topic; and it is earned, of course, by such a view's explanation of how and why it is that a given conceptual practice not only implicitly generates its target but manages to hit it perfectly. When it comes to a conceptual-role based approach to genuine modal concepts, no one has begun to explain how or why that could be true.

and the more general worry, which grows from the Kripkean line, focuses on claims that satisfy ($\kappa_1$) and

> ($\kappa_3$) it is apriori for at least one of them that it is non-contingent in light of the truth-value of some claim satisfying ($\kappa_1$) and ($\kappa_2$).

The epistemic strategy side-steps the line entirely by using apriori conditions which rule out ($\kappa_3$). It then claims the result is an infallible guide to genuine possibility. This presupposes limit reflection goes modally wrong *only* in cases that fall under ($\kappa_3$)'s purview. But that is extra magic. The idea, after all, is that limit coherence marks genuine possibility except when apriori red or yellow flags warn of modal mishap. The epistemic strategy presupposes this thought:

> (X) Limit-case apriori reflection infallibly depicts genuine possibility *unless when admitting a claim and its negation as coherent it also admits there is danger of their non-contingency.*

That is hard to believe.

To see why, suppose you had a pair of fallible glasses. Sometimes they serve-up veridical experience of your environment, sometimes delusive experience; but whenever they yield delusive experience they also produce a warning at the foot of your visual field. "Beware!" it says, "There is a good chance this experience is delusive". Suppose the glasses are *metaphysically guaranteed* to yield veridical experience unless such a worry is produced. The idea makes sense on its face, of course, but it is also an incredible one. The glasses cry out for explanation. We should accept that a given pair of glasses work this way only if we understand how they *could* do so, only if we understand (in some detail) how underlying mechanisms make it the case that the glasses work in the perfectly helpful way specified.

Highly-seasoned infallibilism sees limit coherence as a pair of magic glasses. It says such coherence stands to genuine possibility as the glasses stand to the world. Limit coherence is said to be almost delusion proof, to go wrong only if it serves-up a warning. This too is coherent on its face, of course; but it's also incredible. After all, the suggestion is that a purely epistemic procedure is perforce 100% reliable about non-epistemic fact save when it warns of bother. I take it commitment to this kind of view is why philosophers sometimes call metaphysical modality "logical" when logic is "broadly construed". The construal obviously leans on apriori red and yellow flags as emphasized in the text.

In my view, however, we should believe such a story only if we have a clue how it might work. But we have no idea how such exact reliability, such exact fine tuning might come to pass between limit coherence and genuine possibility. It would be little short of miraculous, after all, if limit coherence always had in-built corrections to hand. That would be like sensory belief being outright infallible except when one sensed that one suffered delusion. It seems to me that such a view tempts only when blinded by the ep-&-met tendency. Once that tendency is resisted, however, the view looks obviously wrong; and so it should be with views like highly-seasoned infallibilism, for they perfectly align two-way independent phenomena. Call this the *Objection from Extra-magic*.

The Objections from Magic and Extra-magic rule out epistemic-based infallibilism about possibility. As we are about to see, however, they also cut against semantic-based infallibilism. Reflecting on that makes clear how to determine whether apriorism about possibility is true.

## 6. THE SEMANTIC-BASED VIEW

It is common these days to see two-dimensional semantics pressed into service in order to reconcile modal infallibilism and Kripkean intuition. The approach begins with a simple thought: concepts like *Hesperus*, *Phosphorus*, *water*, and $H_2O$ have two readings (or functions-to-extension) associated with them. That is the view's main semantic claim. It then says one of the readings—which we will call reading 1—captures "pure apriori import"; and that builds a bridge from the view's main semantic claim to modal epistemology. In turn the bridge implies that claims of the form

X is Y

can be read (at least) four ways:

    (i) $X_1$ is $Y_1$
    (ii) $X_1$ is $Y_2$
    (iii) $X_2$ is $Y_1$
    (iv) $X_2$ is $Y_2$.

Subscripts mark when a concept is read in the apriori/non-apriori way. It is with readings like these that two-dimensionalism aims to reconcile modal infallibilism and Kripkean intuition.

Before getting to that, though, a remark is in order about the origin of the subscripted semantic dimensions. It turns out they can be motivated in various ways. Mostly it is done by appeal to one of two things: facts about reference fixation or those concerning the way that suppositional reasoning works. But we need not adjudicate the details of this debate within the two-dimensionalist framework; nor need we accept any particular two-dimensionalist semantics. All we need to do is postulate—for the sake of present argument—two semantic dimensions one of which captures apriori import. That permits the semantic-based reconciliation of modal infallibilism and Kripkean intuition no matter how the machinery is motivated.[17] The line runs as follows:

> Apriori reflection is an infallible guide to genuine possibility. Appearances to the contrary deceive. Specifically, they result from projecting the modal status of readings like (ii)–(iv) onto readings like (i). If a claim is apriori coherent when read in the purely apriori way—when read wholesale along the apriori dimension 1—that claim is genuinely possible. Or again: if a claim is apriori coherent when all its constituent concepts are read in the pure apriori way, that claim is genuinely possible. Apriori reflection secures possibility after all. To think otherwise is to mix-up semantic dimensions, wrongly to pair epistemic intuition about one dimension with modal intuition about another.

When apriori reflection and *im*possibility look to cohabit, says the view, that is because we "cross read" claims, hearing some concepts involved along the apriori dimension and others not in that way. Then we illegitimately link intuitions about apriority concerning one dimension with those about modality concerning another. The result is said to be illusion of apriori coherence without genuine possibility.[18]

This line is subject to the Objection from Magic, and its semantic dimensions yield extra-magic of their own. Let me explain why.

1.    Semantic-based infallibilism is like its naïve cousin; and the latter view, recall, says that limit coherence infallibly marks genuine possibility. The view is that this schema has no counter-instance:

(l)  lim(ø) ⊃ ◆ø.

The semantic view almost agrees, insisting that ø-concepts be read along the apriori semantic dimension. The view claims that limit reflection yields genuine possibility when run along that dimension.

Let us mark it with **bold-face** and *italics*. In the event, semantic-based infallibilism swaps (l) for

(*l*)  *lim(ø)* ⊃ ***◆ø***.

It is the view that (*l*) has no counter-instance; and if that is right, of course, belief in the genuine possibility of [ø-read-along-the-purely-apriori-semantic-dimension] based on that reading's limit coherence is infallible. The process is

---

[17] For reference-theoretic two-dimensionalism see Chalmers (1996), Jackson (1994) and (1998), Lewis (1994b), Stalnaker (1979), and Tichý (1983). For supposition-theoretic versions see Chalmers (2002) and (2004), Davies and Humberstone (1980), and Weatherson (2001).

[18] For a classic statement see Chalmers (2002).

said to move, without hiccup, from the purely epistemic to veridical belief in the purely metaphysical.

That is plain magic. After all, the semantic view—as thus presented any-way—simply *helps itself* to a semantic dimension limit reflection along which is said infallibly to mark genuine possibility. The view so far simply *assumes* that naïve infallibilism is true along the apriori semantic dimension. That conflicts with our best take on the fit between epistemology and metaphysics, for it yields an infallible link between two-way independent conditions: purely apriori limit coherence and genuine possibility. Why should we accept such a view? Doesn't it face the Objection from Magic squarely along its apriori semantic dimension?

It is a striking fact that semantic-based infallibilists provide almost *no* positive argument for their infallibilism. David Chalmers's classic work on the topic, for instance, consists almost exclusively of arguments against arguments against semantic-based infallibilism. (But nowhere does he consider *our* arguments against the view.) In fact, his only positive argument for the view turns on the idea that we should locate

the roots of our modal concepts in the rational domain. . . . when one looks at the purposes to which modality is put, it is striking that many of these purposes are tied closely to the rational and the psychological: analysing the contents of thoughts and the semantics of language, giving an account of counterfactual thought, analysing rational inference. It can be argued that for a concept of possibility and necessity to be truly useful in analysing these domains, it must be a *rational* modal concept, tied constitutively to consistency, rational inference, or conceivability.[19]

The quotation here is the full backbone of Chalmers's positive argument for semantic-based infallibilism. By my lights, the considerations within it are simply *outweighed* by those canvassed here, by our theoretical need to keep epistemology and metaphysics distinct, by our desire to be fully realistic about the world and our place within it.

Note well that the worry I am pressing here applies even if two-dimensional semantics is correct. We should reject semantic-based infallibilism about genuine possibility even if we *accept* its semantics. Even if concepts like *Hesperus*, *Phosphorus*, *water*, and $H_2O$ have two semantic dimensions, and even if one of those dimensions captures apriori import, there is *still* insufficient reason to think that best reflection along it *guarantees* genuine possibility. Modal infallibilism is bad epistemology even if two-dimensionalism is good semantics; it is bad epistemology no matter how it is semantically clothed.

2.    Recall that highly-seasoned infallibilism sees limit coherence as almost delusion proof; and it adds that such coherence goes wrong only if it warns of modal mishap. For this reason, the view sees limit coherence as a pair of magic

---

[19] Chalmers (2002), p. 193.

glasses: fallible about its target yet failsafe to warn of bother. Not only does
the view say finessed apriori conditions are magically infallible, it also says limit
reflection warns of its own fallibility whenever it must. But that too is magic,
extra magic.

Similarly, semantic-based infallibilism says limit coherence is fully delusion
proof along the apriori dimension of meaning. It adds that apriori reflection
reveals just where modal muddle is *apt* to occur, for the view says that one can
detect apriori when there is potential divergence across dimensions of meaning;
and it uses that divergence to diagnose apriori what is then said to be modal
mishap. Specifically, the semantic approach uses meaning divergence across
dimensions to account apriori for Kripkean intuition. A failure to recognize the
cross-dimensional nature of such intuition is said to lead people to misjudge
the contours of modality. Such misjudgement would not happen to an ideal
apriori reasoner. And hence the view in question here presupposes that one can
detect apriori when there is danger of modal muddle. But that too is magic,
extra magic. Once again we find the idea that apriority contains in-built alarms.
The semantic view says that whenever one is apt to fall prey to bogus Kripkean
intuition, further apriori reflection will unmask the temptation to muddle.

We should believe the story here only if we have a clue how it might work; but
we have no idea how such exact reliability, such exact fine tuning might come
to pass between limit coherence and genuine possibility. It would be little short
of miraculous if apriori reflection always had in-built corrections to hand. That
is true along one semantic dimension, to be sure; and it remains true along two
of them. The two-dimensional approach to modal infallibilism generates its own
Objection from Extra-magic.

The Objection from Magic applies squarely to semantic-based infallibilism's
story about reflection along the apriori semantic dimension. The Objection
from Extra-magic applies to its diagnosis of Kripkean intuition. The view is
unacceptable for the same basic reason its epistemic cousin is unacceptable: both
tell a bad story about the fit between epistemology and metaphysics, both accept
magic correlation between the two.


## 7. CHASING THE MORAL

Suppose, then, that modal infallibilism is false. No reading of

$$(\blacklozenge) \quad \neg\text{limit-reject}(\text{ø}) \supset \blacklozenge\text{ø}$$

is infallible. What difference does that make? What is the moral of infallibilism's demise?

It is tempting to say this:

(!) Limit coherence is obviously *some* kind of guide to genuine possibility.
The question is what kind. Infallibilism says it is an infallible guide, but

the truth is more modest. Limit coherence is a fallible guide to genuine possibility. When ø passes apriori muster, that is reason to think ø can genuinely happen; but the reason is fallible. It is a good question why that is so, but it is not a good question whether that is so. There is no question but that limit coherence fallibly marks genuine possibility. That fact is a cornerstone of our modal practice without which no practice remains.

I used to accept this line of thought, and I think many still do accept it; but it now strikes me that the line's plausibility is induced by the ep-&-met tendency I have been at pains to avoid.[20] Seeing why helps make clear whether apriorism about modality is true.

To begin, note the first sentence of (!) is just false. It is not obvious that passing apriori muster is a guide to genuine possibility. It is only obvious that doing so is a guide to possibility *full stop*. The bedrock datum is unqualified:

(BEDROCK) Limit coherence is some kind of guide to possibility.

This *is* a datum: failing to be ruled out apriori is obviously a mark of possibility; and hence we must find truth in (BEDROCK). But the principle's quotidian status has a key consequence, to wit, that its modal notion is *pre*-theoretic. (BEDROCK)'s status *as* a datum ensures that its modal notion is a quotidian notion, an everyday notion, a pre-theoretic notion. And therein lies the rub.

To see why, recall that there are objective, subjective, and purely mathematical notions of probability just as there are such notions of possibility.[21] Yet none of the probabilistic notions—credence, chance, Popper–Rényi function—are *pre*-theoretical. They are all highly theoretical successor notions, notions which jointly replace our haphazard pre-theoretic notion of probability and thereby correct practice. Successor notions allow unequivocal grip on problems which are distinct in nature but alike in structure. Our pre-theoretic notion of probability elides key non-structural differences between these problems. It thereby generates muddled thought and reasoning prone to confusion. Successor notions are literally tailor made to respect those non-structural differences. That is why replacing our pre-theoretic notion of probability with its successors is advance, why doing so corrects practice.

It is of first importance to realize that the clean-up job is obliged. Our pre-theoretic notion of probability—and the practice that goes with it—is enslaved by the ep-&-met tendency. It blends epistemic and metaphysical considerations beyond repair, resulting in fallacy-ridden cognition. That is why we must jettison the old notion and replace it with better ones. They should be cleansed of

---

[20] e.g. Hill (1997), Levine (1998), Sturgeon (2006), and Yablo (1993).

[21] This is to be expected, of course, as probability is a measure on a space of possibility. What makes for the objectivity or otherwise in a given kind of probability is the nature of things within its domain.

the ep-&-met tendency. They should answer to purely metaphysical, epistemic, mathematical fact. They should guard against probability-based fallacies induced by our intellectual inheritance, properly gripping tasks over which our pre-theoretic notion equivocates.[22]

Modality is no different. Our pre-theoretic modal notions—and the practice that goes with them—are enslaved by the ep-&-met tendency. They too blend epistemic and metaphysical matters beyond repair resulting in fallacy-ridden cognition. They too should be replaced. To the extent we are clear about that, however, the epistemology of modality becomes murky. Just think of (BEDROCK) cleaned up twice over via an epistemic and metaphysical reading:

> (E)  Limit coherence is a guide to conceivability.

> (M)  Limit coherence is a guide to genuine possibility.

(E) is perfectly obvious: passing apriori muster is trivially one way of *being* conceivable; so it's perfectly obvious that limit coherence is a guide to conceivability. It's perfectly obvious, in fact, that limit coherence is an infallible guide to that kind of conceivability. And in my view it is *that* fact which sources our taste for infallibilism about "possibility". Our taste for it grows from the trivial status of (E). We can easily find truth in (BEDROCK), then, but the point does nothing to secure (M).

Once it is clear that genuine possibility is in play—and neither a partial nor full epistemic analogue—it is intuitively *un*clear that passing apriori muster is a guide to the phenomenon. It is unclear that apriorism about genuine possibility is true, and the reason is just that the issue is not pre-theoretic. After all, the issue is whether failing to be ruled out apriori reliably indicates the most inclusive mind- and language-independent space of possibility. That is not something everyday commitment can resolve, nor is it something everyday intuition can resolve. The issue is not common-sense: only *theory* can say whether such failure is a guide to such possibility.

The same point applies to apriori reflection and genuine necessity. Consider the rule:

> (■)  limit-adopt(ø) $\supset$ ■ø.

The possibility rule (♦) is fallible just if a genuine impossibility is not ruled out apriori. We have seen at least one parade case: that Sam Clemens is not Mark Twain. The necessity rule (■) is fallible just if a genuine non-necessity is ruled in apriori. We have not seen a parade case of that. But we *have* seen reason to expect one; for everything mentioned of late about apriori reflection

---

[22] There is debate about which notions are needed to correct practice. There is no debate about whether successor notions are needed. See Carnap (1945), Glymour (1992), Howson and Urbach (1989), Lewis (1980), Pollock (1990), Roeper and Leblanc (1999).

and genuine possibility carries over, *mutatis mutandis*, to the relation between such reflection and genuine necessity. Whether a claim is ruled in apriori is a purely epistemic fact about it, an idealized epistemic mark signalling that norms which govern apriori reckoning oblige adopting a claim. But whether a claim is genuinely necessary is a purely metaphysical fact about it, a non-epistemic mark indicating that all of genuine modal reality is correctly described by a claim. Yet there is two-way independence between the two marks. Limit obligation is not individuated by genuine necessity. Genuine necessity is not individuated by limit obligation. Fallibilism *should* characterize the link from the latter to the former. That is how epistemically based belief in external fact is best understood. That is how apriori epistemology and metaphysics fit together.

This threatens cognitive discord. After all, fallibilism about genuine necessity requires a non-necessity to be apriori obliged, a conceptual obligation must turn out to be possibly false. At least one claim must be epistemically like the view that red things are coloured yet modally like the view that red things exist. This can *look* incoherent, for it can look "conceptually true" that conceptual obligations are necessary. And for this reason, it can look as if no such obligation can be false; but if that is right, fallibilism about genuine necessity is a conceptual non-starter.

But look again. The line just sketched leans on a muddled schema:

(BEDROCK)* If limit reflection rules in ø, then it must be ø.[23]

This *is* a datum: being ruled in apriori is obviously evidence of necessity. We must find truth in (BEDROCK)*; but here too the quotidian status of the principle guarantees that its modal notion is pre-theoretic. (BEDROCK)*'s status *as* a datum ensures its modal notion is an everyday notion, the kind of notion that blends epistemic and metaphysical matters. The datum can be heard two ways:

(E)* If limit reflection rules in ø, then it must be adopted ø.

(M)* If limit reflection rules in ø, then it is genuinely necessary ø.

(E)* is perfectly obvious: being ruled in apriori is the same thing as limit obligation, the same thing as one kind of "must". It is plausible that this fact sources our taste for the view that limit obligation brings "necessity" with it. That taste grows from the trivial status of (E)*. We can easily find truth in (BEDROCK)*, then, but the point does nothing to secure (M)*.

Once it is clear that genuine necessity is in play—and neither a partial nor full epistemic analogue—it is intuitively unclear that limit obligation is sufficient for genuine necessity. After all, the issue is whether limit obligation marks the least

---

[23] For instance: if limit reflection rules in that flounders snore, then it must be that flounders snore; if limit reflection rules in that red things are coloured, then it must be that red things are coloured; and so on.

inclusive realistic space of necessity. That is not something everyday commitment can resolve; nor is it something everyday intuition can resolve. Only *theory* can say whether it is so.

When it comes to apriori reflection and genuine modality, then, we face a double-barrel theoretical question. How do these schemata fare:

> (♦)  ¬limit-reject(ø) ⊃ ♦ø
>
> (■)  limit-adopt(ø) ⊃ ■ø?

Folk wisdom cannot answer this question for it is too theoretical. In the next section I propose how we should go about answering it.

## 8. THE CRUX

The first step is to note that (■) is equivalent to (♦)'s converse. To see this, contrapose (■):

> (i)  ¬■ø ⊃ ¬limit-adopt(ø).

Next turn the negated box into a possible negation:

> (ii)  ♦¬ø ⊃ ¬limit-adopt(ø).

Then note a sound schema holds for a claim just if it holds for its negation, so we can rewrite (ii):

> (iii)  ♦ø ⊃ ¬limit-adopt(¬ø).

Yet an ideal agent should reject a claim just if she adopts its negation, so we can rewrite (iii):

> (iv)  ♦ø ⊃ ¬limit-reject(ø).

Thus we find that (■) is equivalent to (♦)'s converse. Our two modal principles jointly entail

> (v)  ¬limit-reject(ø) ≡ ♦ø.

This affords progress.

After all, idealized apriori rejection aligns with *conceptual impossibility*, with impossibility grounded in conceptual content. This means the left-hand side of (v) aligns with conceptual possibility, with possibility ground in conceptual content. That is a murky notion, to be sure, but it helps to work with it; so let us write $^\circ\Diamond(ø)^\circ$ to express that ø is conceptually possible (and also to mark the murkiness of this notion). In the event, we have this by hypothesis:

> (vi)  ¬limit-reject(ø) ≡ ◇ø.

In the ideal case: a claim should fail to be ruled out apriori just if it is conceptually possible. Or again: a claim should be ruled out apriori just if it is conceptually impossible. This and (v) yield the key biconditional:

($\equiv$)   $\diamond\varnothing \equiv \blacklozenge\varnothing.$

Apriorism about genuine modality turns on two schemata: ($\blacklozenge$) and ($\blacksquare$). They lead directly to ($\equiv$). This means apriorism about genuine modality turns on the link between conceptual and genuine possibility, on the alignment between the two.[24]

Think of it this way. Put all usual claims in a region, mark out conceptual possibilities from the rest and paint their region yellow:

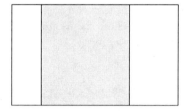

**Fig. 13.6.**

Now put all usual claims in a new region (organized as before), mark out genuine possibilities from the rest and paint their region blue:

**Fig. 13.7.**

---

[24] Equivalently it turns on the alignment between genuine necessity and limit obligation. To see this, note ($\blacklozenge$) can be rewritten: ¬limit-adopt(¬ø) ⊃ $\blacklozenge$ø. Now contrapose, turn the negated diamond into a necessary negation, and drop the double negation. Then you have: $\blacksquare$¬ø ⊃ limit-adopt(¬ø). The negations here do not work, so rewrite again: $\blacksquare$ø ⊃ limit-adopt(ø). This is the converse of ($\blacksquare$), so ($\blacklozenge$) and ($\blacksquare$) lead to this biconditional: apriori-adopt(ø) ≡ $\blacksquare$ø. Apriorism about genuine modality equally turns on the alignment between genuine necessity and limit obligation.

Next superimpose the Figures:

Fig. 13.8.

Apriorism about genuine modality turns on the extent to which green dwarfs yellow and blue in Figure 13.8. Yellow claims are conceptually possible but not genuinely possible, counter-examples to

(♦)    ¬limit-reject(ø) ⊃ ♦ø.

Blue claims are genuinely possible but not conceptually possible. Their negations are apriori obliged but not genuinely necessary, counter-examples to

(■)    limit-adopt(ø) ⊃ ■ø.

For this reason: apriorism about genuine modality turns on the extent to which conceptual and genuine possibility line up, the extent to which they marry into a "green light". The key question is thus how big a green light do we have? How well do conceptual and genuine possibility line up?

Here things become difficult. In §2 we pictured genuine and nomic possibility this way:

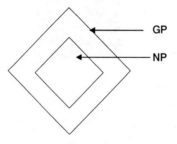

Fig. 13.2.

But we did so merely to echo a widespread-but-undefended *assumption*. Specifically, we drew inclusion relations to mimic the popular idea that genuine possibility outstrips nomic possibility, to allow for genuinely contingent nomic necessity. That assumption is neither obligatory nor obvious. It needs defence.[25]

That defence will turn on an issue beyond the scope of this paper. To see why, consider a famous passage from Lewis:

[Conceptual] space is a paradise for philosophers. We have only to believe in the vast realm of *possibilia*, and there we find what we need to advance our endeavours. We find the wherewithal to reduce the diversity of notions we must accept as primitive, and thereby to improve the unity and economy of the theory that is our professional concern—total theory, the whole of what we take to be true. What price paradise? If we want the theoretical benefits that talk of *possibilia* brings, the most straightforward way to gain honest title to them is to accept such talk as the literal truth. It is my view that the price is right. . . The benefits are worth their ontological costs.[26]

Two things happen in this passage (both central to Lewis's work on modality). One is that non-eliminativism about genuine possibility is defended. The other is that genuine possibility is aligned with conceptual possibility. Their conjunction is grounded in putative theoretical benefit brought on by its adoption, but it is important to emphasize that two views are in play. One is that genuine possibility is real. The other is that genuine possibility is conceptual possibility. The conjunction of these two views is said to make for best total theory.

I think Lewis must be partly right. After all, the practice and analysis of science, ordinary life, and philosophy itself turn on genuine possibility.[27] There must *be* such a thing as genuine possibility. The only question for our purposes is whether it aligns with conceptual possibility. Lewis thinks so and grounds that conviction in cost–benefit analysis, paying for ideological and explanatory economy in the coin of plentiful possibility. Lewis packs his ontology with countless nomically inert possibilities precisely because he thinks they best systematize total theory.

Trade-offs like that are notoriously disputable. One person's bargain is another's excess; yet there is no way to avoid the calculation when deciding whether genuine and conceptual possibility align. There is no way to avoid it when deciding, as I'll say, on the *bounty* of genuine possibility. One must discern costs and benefits of views about such bounty and see how they stack up. Cost–benefit analysis is simply obliged. To the extent that benefits of a view outweigh its costs, one should accept genuine possibility has the bounty in question. To the extent they do not, one should not. Take-home theory should mimic the best bottom line: one should believe in a plentiful bounty like conceptual possibility,

[25] Some write as if it is obvious that the space of genuine possibility outstrips that of nomic possibility. In my view that springs from the ep-&-met tendency, buying into leftover residue from pre-Kripkean days when apriority and modality were run together in thought. The view often taken as given might be true, of course; but it should not be taken as *given*. It is a theoretical view and there is nothing obvious about it.

[26] Lewis (1986b), p. 4.

[27] Just as the practice and analysis of science turn on objective probability. See Lewis (1980).

a meagre one like nomic possibility, or a middling bounty in accord with the best total picture.[28]

Constructing a total picture of the world is beyond the scope of this paper. Comparing total pictures is way beyond that scope. We must proceed from assumptions rather than conclusions about the bounty of genuine possibility. We must tailor our conclusions to those assumptions; and there is a spectrum of them available. On its plentiful end lies the view that genuine and conceptual possibility align. On its meagre end lies the view that genuine and nomic possibility align. The truth could be anywhere on the spectrum:

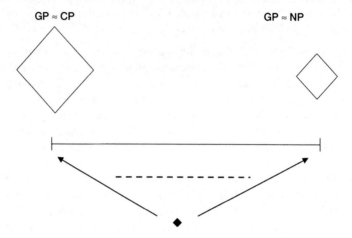

Fig. 13.9.

We cannot decide here where genuine possibility lies. That must await total theory. But we can link the issue with our primary concern, for we can say this:

> ✪ Apriori reflection is a guide to genuine modality to the extent that genuine possibility is plentiful—to the extent, that is, that it aligns

---

[28] This echoes a choice point in the theory of universals: are they abundant in number, sparse, or somewhere in-between? The choice should turn on best theory. See Armstrong (1978), Lewis (1983) and (1986b). In my view the same is true of the space of genuine possibility. But this is not to recommend a "best system" analysis of modal bounty. I do not say that bounty turns out as it does *because* bestness turns out a certain way. My claim is purely epistemic here: one's view of bounty should turn on bestness. Bounty itself most likely turns on nothing at all, since it's most likely a fundamental aspect of reality. This means modal reality might turn out to be cruel: best total theory might use a grossly mistaken view of modal bounty. In the event, total theory is best systematized by a drastically unreal modal ontology. See Lewis (1994a) for a "best system" analysis of single-case objective probability.

with conceptual possibility. If non-trivial alignment takes place: limit coherence will be a useful guide to genuine possibility, and limit obligation will be a useful guide to genuine necessity. If non-trivial alignment does not take place: apriori reflection will be useless as a mark of genuine modality. Limit coherence will not mark genuine possibility, and limit obligation will not mark genuine necessity.

As we have seen, there is good reason to think limit coherence does not infallibly mark genuine possibility. That reason turns on our best understanding of the fit between epistemology and metaphysics. Yet limit coherence might well fallibly mark genuine possibility. That will depend on the extent to which genuine and conceptual possibility align.

Similarly: there is good reason to think limit obligation does not infallibly mark genuine necessity, turning as well on the fit between epistemology and metaphysics. Yet limit obligation might well fallibly mark genuine necessity. That too will depend on the extent to which genuine and conceptual possibility align.

When it comes to alignment itself, however, our view should turn on how best to systematize thought. If postulation of plentiful genuine possibilities better systematizes total theory than not doing so, then, and for that reason, we should accept alignment between conceptual and genuine modality. In turn that will mean limit coherence is a good-but-fallible guide to genuine possibility, and limit obligation is such a guide to genuine necessity. We cannot say here whether alignment takes place. But we can say that apriorism about genuine modality turns on whether it does.


## APPENDIX: LIMNING THE KRIPKE ZONE

In what follows apriori reason will be ideal: 'accept(ø)' will mean that an ideal apriori reasoner accepts ø, 'rej(ø)' will mean that such a reasoner rejects ø. A claim will be said to be *unresolved*—'un(ø)' for short—exactly when two things are true:

$\neg rej(ø)$

and

$\neg rej(\neg ø).$

Intuitively put, unresolvedness occurs when a claim can be neither ruled out nor ruled in apriori.

Prior to Kripke and Putnam's work on aposteriori necessity, a natural thought would have been that unresolvedness was sufficient for genuine possibility. In other words, prior to that work a natural thought would have been that this schema is valid:

(un) $un(ø) \supset \blacklozenge ø.$

But let K be the claim that Mark Twain is identical to Jack Kennedy. Then ideal apriori reasoning will endorse three further claims:

$$K \lor \neg K$$
$$K \supset \neg\blacklozenge\neg K$$
$$\neg K \supset \neg\blacklozenge K.$$

From these it follows that

$$\neg\blacklozenge\neg K \lor \neg\blacklozenge K.$$

But it looks as if apriori reasoning also endorses

$$un(K) \ \& \ un(\neg K).$$

From these last two claims it follows that

$$[un(K) \ \& \ \neg\blacklozenge K] \lor [un(\neg K) \ \& \ \neg\blacklozenge\neg K].$$

And from this it follows that

$$(\exists\o)[un(\o) \ \& \ \neg\blacklozenge\o].$$

This looks to be an apriori existence proof of an aposteriori necessity.

The key insight driving it is that there are unresolved claims such that it is apriori that if they are false they cannot be true. In our terminology, the key insight is that there are claims ø so that:

$$un(\o)$$

and

$$accept[\neg\o \supset \neg\blacklozenge\o].$$

Let ø be a "KP-claim" when this happens (in honour of Kripke and Putnam)—'kp(ø)' for short. Note the conditional in its definition marks an intrinsic modal fact about ø, something salient to apriori reasoning about ø alone. The modal status of KP-claims is intrinsically worrisome to apriori reasoning.

So let a claim ø be *intrinsically clean*—written 'int(ø)'—exactly when two things happen:

$$un(\o)$$

and

$$\neg accept[\neg\o \supset \neg\blacklozenge\o].$$

Intuitively put, intrinsic cleanness occurs when a claim is unresolved but not intrinsically worrisome to apriori reasoning. Intrinsic cleanness is just unresolvedness minus the key feature noticed by Kripke and Putnam: namely, being a claim such that it is apriori that if the claim is false then it cannot be true.

A natural first reaction to the existence proof above is to admit that (**un**) is invalid but to insist that this schema is valid:

(**int**)  $int(\o) \supset \blacklozenge\o.$

Two problems jump out with the strategy right away:

*Case 1.* Let ø be a false KP-claim, something like the claim that Mark Twain is identical to Jack Kennedy. Then let ψ be an unresolved claim which is apriori independent of ø. In other words, let ψ be so that

> un(ψ)

and

> ¬accept [ø ⊃ ψ]

and

> ¬accept [ψ ⊃ ø].

Then we have

> un(ø& ψ)

and

> ¬accept [¬(ø& ψ) ⊃ ¬♦(ø& ψ)].

Hence we have located a counter-example to (**int**), for we have both

> int(ø& ψ)

and

> ¬♦(ø& ψ).

*Case 2.* Let ø be the claim that Hesperus has a feature lacked by Phosphorus. Then

> un(ø)

and

> ¬accept [¬ø ⊃ ¬♦ø].

Yet ø is impossible, so it too is counter-example to (**int**).

Both Cases turn on a KP-claim so that it's apriori that if the claim is true, then the relevant counter-example to (**int**) is not possible. In Case A the relevant KP-claim is ¬K. In Case B it is K. This suggests we say that a claim is *fully clean*—written 'clean(ø)'—exactly when two things happen:

> un(ø)

and

> ¬(∃ψ){kp(ψ) & accept[ψ ⊃ ¬♦ø]}.

Intuitively put, full cleanness occurs when a claim is unresolved but there is no KP-claim such that it is apriori that if that KP-claim is true, then the original claim in question is not genuinely possible. Full cleanness is just unresolvedness minus the existence of a trouble-making KP-claim.

A natural first reaction to the Cases above is to admit that **(int)** is invalid but to insist that this schema is valid:

**(clean)** clean(ø) ⊃ ◆ø.

And it would be natural to sum up the proceedings with the following diagnostic *spiel*: being unresolved is insufficient for genuine possibility—and being intrinsically clean is too—but being fully clean is sufficient for genuine possibility; and *that* is the take-home message of Kripke and Putnam's work on aposteriori necessity. Intuitively put: if one starts with the set of unresolved claims and wishes to shave down that space to reach the set of genuine possibilities, one must throw out exactly the unclean claims with which one starts. One must throw out exactly the unresolved claims for which there is a KP-claim such that it is apriori that if that KP-claim is true, then the unresolved claim in question is not genuinely possible.

Would that it were so simple.

Take any unresolved claim ø and let X be the claim that ø is not genuinely possible. Suppose it can be shown apriori—as seems likely—that some claims are unresolved yet not genuinely possible. Then apriori reasoning cannot rule out that ø is one of them. This means X is itself unresolved, for we have both

¬rej(X) = ¬rej(¬◆ø)

and

¬rej(¬X) = ¬rej(◆ø).

But it is trivial that

accept[X ⊃ ¬◆ø],

as X is the claim that ø is not genuinely possible. If X is a KP-claim, therefore, it follows that ø is itself *not* fully clean; for X will be an unresolved claim which bears witness to the quantifier in our definition of cleanness for ø. So ask yourself this: *is* X a KP-claim?

Well, we've seen that Kripke and Putnam's work likely renders X unresolved. X is a KP-claim, therefore, if the following is true as well:

accept[¬X ⊃ ¬◆X].

But this is equivalent to

accept[◆ø ⊃ ¬◆¬◆ø],

which is equivalent to

accept[◆ø ⊃ ■◆ø].

And this last conditional is the characteristic formula of S5. If it is apriori that S5 is the right logic for genuine possibility, therefore, X will turn out to be a KP-claim and ø will turn out *not* to be fully clean. So we have this result:

> If the apriori nature of our existence proof renders claims like X unresolved, and if it is apriori that the logic of genuine possibility is S5, then *no* unresolved claim is fully clean.

The satisfaction of these antecedent conditions would render the schema (**clean**) useless for limning the contours of the Kripke Zone. That is why the exact scope of that Zone turns on a philosophically charged issue. That is why it turns on which kind of modal logic is apriori apt for genuine modality.

# Response to Scott Sturgeon

## C. S. Jenkins

These comments fall into two sections. The first section is a mixed bag; in this section I shall pick up on a number of interesting issues and ideas raised in Sturgeon's paper, making some brief remarks on each. In the second, I turn to what struck me as the main focal point of the paper, the objections (from 'Magic' and 'Extra Magic') to infallibilist apriorism about modal knowledge. I shall offer a more sustained discussion of these objections. Most importantly, I shall attempt to locate them as part of a long-standing debate over a priori knowledge.

## 1. A FEW REMARKS

The first infallibilist apriorist view put up for discussion is the view that the following schema has no counter-instance:

(p)  pfac(ø) ⊃ ◆ø

In words: the prima facie a priori coherence of ø materially implies the possibility of ø. Most of the later, more sophisticated, proposals also take the form of claims of one-way material implication.

But all instances of a schema like (p) would come out true provided it were the case that no ø met the condition described in the antecedent. It seems to me that no interesting form of infallibilist apriorism will amount to a view that could be rendered true by the mere fact that nothing is a priori coherent in the relevant sense (or the fact that everything is possible). The infallibilist apriorist believes in an epistemologically significant connection between a priori coherence and possibility. This is not well captured by a material conditional, since for all it says there may be no epistemologically interesting link at all between a priori coherence and possibility.

At first blush, it might look as though the material biconditional version of infallibilism mentioned in the paper, which appears much later (see p. 301), avoids this sort of worry. This is the claim that ø is genuinely possible iff it is conceptually possible. A scenario where nothing is conceptually possible is not one where this biconditional comes out true (at least, assuming that some things are still genuinely possible in that scenario).

However, the problem also affects the use of material biconditionals to try and capture the thesis that a priori reflection can be a good epistemic guide to the modal facts (i.e. a way of acquiring knowledge of those facts). To see this, consider the following analogy. Gullible (an infinitely long-lived individual) goes to study with the Modality Guru (another infinitely long-lived individual). Gullible believes that Guru will, over an infinite amount of time, utter all and only things that are possible. Gullible blindly accepts as possible everything Guru says, even though Gullible has no good reason to trust Guru. As it happens, Guru does in fact utter all and only the possible things. Now consider the schema:

(g)  guru(ø) ≡ ♦ø

In words: Guru's uttering ø materially implies the possibility of ø and vice versa. Clearly, this is true in the envisaged situation. Equally clearly, asserting its truth is not a way of defending the claim that blindly trusting Guru is a good epistemic guide to the modal facts (i.e. a way of acquiring knowledge of those facts). In the envisaged situation, blindly trusting Guru is *not* a good epistemic guide to the modal facts, even though that material biconditional is true.

The crux of my point is that using a material biconditional to capture an epistemological thesis, as Sturgeon does, is tantamount to assuming a very crude form of reliabilism, susceptible to counterexample in the way described above. Sturgeon's emphasis on mere *alignment* between conceptual possibility and genuine possibility, in his closing passages, is another symptom of the same malady.

My second observation concerns the purported difference between Sturgeon's (k) (for which see p. 284) and his (o) (see p. 287). (k) claims that 'Kripke coherence' materially implies possibility Kripke coherence is limit coherence 'in the light of' Kripke truths. A Kripke truth is a true claim which is non-modal, is such that it and its negation are limit coherent, and is such that it is a priori obliged that the matter it raises is non-contingent. Something's being limit coherent 'in the light of' Kripke truths is a matter of its being limit coherent *with* the Kripke truths. (See footnote 11, where a claim ¬K's being ruled out by a Kripke truth is taken as showing that ¬K is not Kripke coherent.)

Sturgeon then argues that there are Kripke coherent claims which are not genuinely possible, and hence counterexamples to (k). His example is L: the claim that Lewisian worlds truthmake claims of genuine modality. He goes on to argue that at least one of L and ¬L is not genuinely possible (an argument which I shall comment on in a moment). He also claims that both L and ¬L are Kripke coherent. Here is his argument (which appears on p. 285): 'Take apriori reflection to the limit, throw in Kripke truth, both L and ¬L stay coherent'.

Evidently, then, Sturgeon does not think that one of L and ¬L is itself a Kripke truth. But why? They both seem to be Kripke claims by Sturgeon's lights, and since Sturgeon assumes the Law of Excluded Middle at various points during the paper, he should think that one of them is true. Why do I say they are Kripke claims by Sturgeon's lights? Because Sturgeon should think that they meet all the conditions he has given for being a Kripke claim. First, they are non-modal. (They are *about* modal metaphysics, of course, but they are not claims to the effect that something is possible or necessary.[1]) Secondly, they are (by Sturgeon's lights) both limit coherent (after all, he thinks they are limit coherent with the Kripke truths, which is stronger). And thirdly, Sturgeon gives an argument on pp. 284–5 which attempts to show, on purely a priori grounds, that 'whichever of L and ¬L turns out to be true, it is genuinely necessary as well'. Indeed, he explicitly says that it is a priori obliged that the matter they raise is non-contingent (see p. 286, where he says that property ($\kappa_2$) is had by L-style claims).

Sturgeon's further examples (on p. 286) of 'systematic misalignments between apriori coherence and genuine possibility' seem to be offered as further counterexamples to (**k**), and further motivation for the move to (**o**). But again, Sturgeon does not establish that these are counterexamples to (**k**). Take Sturgeon's example of (C&R) and (C&¬R), where R is such that both it and its negation are limit coherent but it is a priori obliged that the matter it raises is non-contingent, and C is some contingent claim which is independent of R and its negation. Suppose R and ¬R are Kripke claims. Then by Sturgeon's lights one of them is a Kripke truth. If ¬R is a Kripke truth, then even if, as Sturgeon says, (C&¬R) is limit coherent, it is not Kripke coherent. It is ruled out by a Kripke truth, namely R. Similarly, if ¬R is the Kripke truth, then (C&R) is not Kripke coherent, even if it is limit coherent. To find counterexamples to (**k**) in this vicinity, Sturgeon would need to show that there are claims meeting the conditions on R which are not Kripke claims.

The conditions on R are two of the three necessary and sufficient conditions on being a Kripke truth, so the only option here is to show that some claims meet the conditions on R but fail that final condition on Kripke claims, i.e. are modal. An obvious kind of modal claim which meets the conditions on R is a modalized version of an identity claim, such as: Possibly, Mark Twain is Sam Clemens. Let's take this as our R, and for ease of expression, let's use 'P' to stand for the unmodalized claim, Mark Twain is Sam Clemens. The trouble is that taking a claim like this as our R will not help us establish that there are counterexamples to (**k**) along the lines Sturgeon envisages. For then, even if (C&R) and (C&¬R) are both limit coherent, one of them (whichever one is genuinely impossible) is not Kripke coherent. For one of P and ¬P is a Kripke truth. If it is P, then ¬R is

---

[1] Clearly, the Kripke truths will include several claims which are about modal metaphysics, so Sturgeon cannot have in mind that no claim which is about modal metaphysics counts as a Kripke claim. For instance, let 'Universe' be a name for the actual universe around us, and let 'World' be a name whose referent Lewisians attempt to fix as the actual Lewisian truthmaker. Then the claim that Universe is World ought to count as a Kripke claim (at least, Lewisians will think it is one). It is very closely analogous to Sturgeon's paradigm Kripke claim, the claim that Mark Twain is Sam Clemens.

genuinely impossible and so is (C&¬R). But in this case ¬R is incoherent with (ruled out, by a priori means, by) a Kripke truth, namely P, and hence ¬R is not Kripke coherent. So (C&¬R) is not Kripke coherent either. If it is ¬P that is the Kripke truth, then R is genuinely impossible and so is (C&R). But now R is incoherent with a Kripke truth, namely ¬P, and hence R is not Kripke coherent. So (C&R) is not Kripke coherent either.

So we cannot establish by these means that one of (C&R) and (C&¬R) is Kripke coherent yet genuinely impossible.

The third issue I would like to turn to is the discussion of Lewisian modal metaphysics at pp. 284–5. My point here is much less significant than the preceding two, since it is specific to the particular example Sturgeon uses. Nevertheless, I think it is interesting enough to be worth noting.

'L' is the claim that Lewisian worlds truthmake claims of genuine modality. Sturgeon argues that it is impossible that

(12) L & ◆¬L.

The reason he cites is that '[i]ts first conjunct entails its second is true only if there is a Lewisian world at which there is no such world' (p. 285). But in fact the first conjunct at most entails that there is a Lewisian world at which that world is not a truthmaker for any modal claims.

In fact, it doesn't even seem to entail as much as that. In order for L to entail anything of the kind Sturgeon has in mind, L must be the claim that Lewisian worlds truthmake all claims of genuine modality. So one way for ¬L to be true is if Lewisian worlds truthmake some but not all claims of genuine modality. Now, for all Sturgeon has argued, at this world all modal claims are truthmade by Lewisian worlds, so L is true, but there is a world w where some but not all modal claims are truthmade by Lewisian worlds, and where w itself does truthmake some modal claims.

My fourth comment in this section concerns Sturgeon's interpretation of Lewis at p. 303. Sturgeon cites Lewis (1986b, p. 4), claiming that in this passage Lewis is aligning conceptual possibility with genuine possibility. Here is the passage, as quoted by Sturgeon:

[Conceptual] space is a paradise for philosophers. We have only to believe in the vast realm of *possibilia*, and there we find what we need to advance our endeavours. We find the wherewithal to reduce the diversity of notions we must accept as primitive, and thereby to improve the unity and economy of the theory that is our professional concern—total theory, the whole of what we take to be true. What price paradise? If we want the theoretical benefits that talk of possibilia brings, the most straightforward way to gain honest title to them is to accept such talk as the literal truth. It is my view that the price is right . . . The benefits are worth their ontological costs.

I do not think this passage supports Sturgeon's reading. As far as I can tell, here and in the surrounding sections, Lewis is merely arguing that the ontological costs of believing in possible worlds are justified by the theoretical benefits of such a belief. Conceptual modality in Sturgeon's sense doesn't seem to come into it, let alone the relationship between conceptual modality and genuine modality. Lewis himself does not use the word 'conceptual' at the beginning of the passage. He says 'logical'. And Sturgeon argues earlier in his footnote 4 that Lewis means by 'logical' modality what he (Sturgeon) means by 'genuine' modality.

Fifthly, and finally for this section, let me make a quick remark about Sturgeon's closing claim (p. 304) that '[a]priori reflection is a guide to genuine modality to the extent that genuine possibility is plentiful—to the extent, that is, to which it aligns with conceptual possibility'. It seems that Sturgeon is assuming here that genuine modality cannot be *too* plentiful to align well with conceptual possibility. But nothing Sturgeon has said rules that out. And there are some examples which could be taken as showing that genuine possibility outstrips conceptual possibility. For instance, non-Euclidean geometry understood as a theory of physical space, and certain results in quantum mechanics, might with some justification be said to be conceptually incoherent and yet not only genuinely possible, but actually true.

## 2. THE OBJECTIONS FROM MAGIC AND EXTRA MAGIC

I begin this section with a few words about realist epistemology. I will use these as a framework within which to recast what I see as the principal concerns raised in Sturgeon's paper, in what I hope is an illuminating fashion. Then I shall suggest that the deep issues in the vicinity of these worries are not, *contra* Sturgeon, worries about the *infallibility* of the conceivability method of coming to know modal truths. I shall also claim that these deep issues are old ones to which a variety of responses are already on the market.

By a 'realistically construed subject matter', I shall mean a subject matter about which we are inclined to be mind-independence realists (in the sense of my 2005). Satisfying accounts of how we know facts about some realistically construed subject matter seem to fit a three-step pattern. First there is worldly input of some kind into our mental processes. Then, at least typically, some kind of mental processing takes place. And finally, we arrive at a belief.

Take, for example, the visual story which we tell to account for much of our knowledge of the physical world around us. First, the physical world impacts causally upon our eyes, and the eyes carry signals to the brain. This constitutes the worldly input into our mental processes. Then various sorts of mental processing of that input take place. And the upshot is that we arrive at a belief about what the physical world around us is like which is responsibly based upon the information received. Of course there is a great deal of detail to be filled in around this bare-bones outline, but (except in sceptical moods) most of us are confident that some story of this general kind can be told to account for visually based knowledge in the good cases.

There is widespread disquiet as to how such a method as attempting to conceive of a proposition's being true—even when this method is made more sophisticated by sensitivity to 'red flags' and 'yellow flags', and to what is a priori forced (see the 'highly seasoned apriori infallibilism' of p. 288)—can help us understand a priori knowledge. In my opinion, the correct diagnosis of this disquiet is that knowledge to be had merely by attempting to conceive of something does not appear to fit the pattern for realist epistemology. The second two steps seem fine (or rather, although they are not fully worked out, they are at least not obviously problematic): the mental processing in this case is some sort of introspective investigation of what one can conceive of (whatever we take that to amount to), and at the end of this process a belief is arrived at. But what of the initial step, the input step?

Sturgeon's 'Magic' and 'Extra Magic' worries are both cast as worries about infallibility for an idealized conceivability method, i.e. worries for those who accept the following material conditional:

IC: (Modal belief B is arrived at through the idealized conceivability method) ⊃ (Modal belief B is true).

(This is intended as equivalent to Sturgeon's (a) on p. 288). Sturgeon is not similarly troubled by the corresponding claim for idealized *vision*, namely:

IV: (Belief B is arrived at through idealized vision) ⊃ (Belief B is true).

The reason Sturgeon is not troubled by IV is (if I understand correctly the gist of his comments at p. 291) that the kind of idealization relevant to idealized vision has partly to do with conditions on the input step: idealized vision is veridical. By contrast, the kind of idealization relevant to idealized conceivability has nothing to do with any input step; the idealization is all on the processing side.[2] So how could a guarantee of truth sneak in? Realism about the subject matter makes this sort of guarantee bewildering. Epistemology and realist metaphysics, as Sturgeon stresses on p. 290, just don't fit together like that.

While I agree with Sturgeon that there is an important issue in this vicinity that is in need of philosophical attention, I think his emphasis on infallibility is a red herring. My point here will be an analogue of the point one often makes to students who think that Hume's worries about induction may show that we aren't *guaranteed* to get true beliefs by inductive methods, but they do not undermine the thought that such beliefs are *likely* to be true.

---

[2] Sturgeon calls this kind of idealization 'epistemic', but that may not be the best name. 'Epistemic' means having to do with knowledge, and knowledge, being factive, is world-involving in the way Sturgeon wants to avoid here.

For exactly the same reasons Sturgeon thinks we should be worried about IC, namely because epistemology and realist metaphysics just don't fit together like that, we should also be worried about the claim that it's even likely that the application of a conceivability method idealized only along processing dimensions should lead to a true belief. Epistemology and realist metaphysics don't fit together like *that* either: absent further explanation, you don't get reliable ways of finding out about the independent world just by looking inside your head. It's not just that you don't get infallible ways; you don't even get mostly-successful ways.

So infallibility is not needed to generate the kind of worry Sturgeon is interested in (as, indeed, Sturgeon himself seems to acknowledge on p. 297, when he diagnoses the plausibility of (!) as due to the same 'ep-and-met tendency' as he thinks motivates infallibilism). In fact, it's not sufficient either. If we could include a satisfactory input step into our conceivability method, and then include idealization of that step as part of idealization of the conceivability method, then Sturgeon's worries will be dissolved. For this would set up an analogy with the vision case, where (by Sturgeon's lights) there is no problem.

I recommend that we leave infallibility to one side and focus on the real issue in this area. If we are mind-independence realists about modality, we expect a realist-type epistemology for modal truths. But the conceivability method as normally construed, even when idealized, involves no input step, and hence it cannot fill this role.

Now this problem is a *very* good one, but it's an instance of a very general problem, namely that of saying how we can have a priori knowledge—which seemingly requires no input from the mind-independent world—of facts which belong to some mind-independent domain. And this is also a very old problem, to which there are many purported answers available already. For instance, rationalists might claim that rational intuition somehow provides input into the conceivability method (see e.g. Bealer 2000, BonJour 1998). Others would argue that the lack of any plausible input step is a reason to reject mind-independence realism about modal truth; they may adopt instead some form of Ayerian or Carnapian anti-realism (see e.g. Ayer 1936, Carnap 1950a). Still others would say that the conceivability method cannot be our method of coming to know the (mind-independent) modal truths, since it involves no input step. Rather, they will argue that we must be using ordinary empirical methods (see e.g. Mill 1891, Quine 1951). I have a horse in this race myself: I believe that the conceivability method involves an empirical input step. I believe that empirical input renders our concepts good guides to the world, so that we can recover information about the world from those concepts, through the practice of attempting to conceive of various scenarios. (See e.g. Jenkins 2008.)

If Sturgeon wants to press his worry in a *new* way, he owes us an account of what is wrong with the various extant positions which exist in response to it. Otherwise he is, when it comes down to it, simply reminding us that a priori knowledge of realistically-construed subject matters is a philosophical puzzle.

# 14

# Conceivability and Apparent Possibility

*Dominic Gregory*

## 1. INTRODUCTION

Certain sorts of mental states tend to lead us to certain sorts of beliefs. Thus what we seem to see and hear affects our beliefs about the external world, and what we seem to remember affects our beliefs about the past. Here are two questions which we can ask in such cases. First, whether we *ought* to form the relevant beliefs—does our having been in the previous mental states really justify them? And, second, why it *is* that we form them—what are the features of the previous mental states that lead us to the subsequent beliefs?

We often base ascriptions of possibility upon our conceivings. So we can pose versions of the above two questions about those beliefs. Ought we to base beliefs about possibility upon what we conceive, then? And why do we pass so readily from conceivings to ascriptions of possibility? My focus in this paper will primarily be on an approach to that second descriptive question, although I'll consider how answers to it might be relevant to the task of justifying conclusions about possibility.

## 2. MORE PREPARATORY MATERIAL

There are various things which we may mean when we state that something is 'conceivable'. For instance, as Yablo (1993) observes, one who states that $P$ is 'conceivable' may mean merely that $P$ is believable, or merely that $P$'s possibility is believable. But the only types of conceivings which are relevant to what follows

Many thanks to Bob Hale, Rob Hopkins, Rosanna Keefe, Jonathan Webber, and two anonymous readers for OUP, for lots of very helpful comments on earlier versions of this material. Many thanks also to Ross Cameron, for his thought-provoking comments on this paper at the Arché Modality conference in 2006, and to the audience at that talk for their very helpful questions. The final version of this paper was prepared during a period of research leave funded by the Arts and Humanities Research Council, for whose support I am very grateful.

are those which count as uses of our *imaginations*. That restriction partly serves
a practical function, by narrowing the field of investigation. But it also reflects
an important fact, namely that the fundamental instances of inferences from
'conceivability to possibility' start from exercises of our imaginative powers.[1]

I'll also concentrate upon certain sorts of imaginings. I'll often be considering
what are commonly known, following Yablo (1993), as *objectual* imaginings.[2]
Objectual imaginings are imaginings of objects, where the imagined objects may
of course be imagined to have properties and to stand in relations to other
things, as when one imagines a man wrestling with a crocodile. As Yablo (1993)
points out, propositional imaginings—imaginings *that* such-and-such—often
ride piggyback on objectual imaginings.[3] For instance, I can imagine that there
is a cow with fangs by imagining a fanged cow.

I'll also discuss examples of *perceptual* imaginings and *sensory* ones. Those are
experiences which are imagined 'from the inside', like when one imagines what
it feels like to have a sore throat and an itchy nose. I'll assume that 'perceptions'
feature veridical sensory appearances,[4] ones which correspond to how things
really are. So I'll take 'perceptual imaginings' to feature imaginings of sensory
appearances which are imagined to be veridical—that is, which are imagined to
capture what things are like in the imagined situation in which the appearances
are enjoyed. Objectual imaginings often ride piggyback on perceptual ones,
just as propositional imaginings often ride piggyback on objectual ones: we
commonly imagine an *F* by imagining a perceptual encounter with an *F*. (We
can, for example, imagine a heron by imagining seeing—in the factive sense—a
heron sitting on a cow's back.)

When I speak of 'sensory imaginings', by contrast, I will be talking about
imaginings which don't decide whether any imagined sensory appearances
featuring in the imagining are veridical or not. (We can imagine having visual
sensations which match those which one might have if, for instance, one were to
see a heron sitting on a cow's back, without thereby either imagining a heron or
imagining that a heron isn't present.) Similarly, when I talk about our capacity to
have 'sensations' of various sorts, I'll merely be speaking of our capacity to enjoy
sensings involving certain sorts of sensory appearances, whether those appearances
are veridical or not, or to enjoy sensings which don't involve appearances at all.

While I take it that perceptual and sensory imaginings are naturally regarded
as 'imagistic'—as imaginings whose contents derive entirely from the sensory

---

[1] Thus the search in Yablo (1993) for an account of 'philosophical conceivability' arrives at an
imaginative notion of conceivability (see pp. 25–30).

[2] See Yablo (1993), p. 27.      [3] Yablo (1993), p. 27.

[4] As far as I know, there's nothing in this paper which essentially depends upon any contentious
views about the natures of sensory appearances or appearances of other kinds. For instance, I'll
typically speak as though there are certain things, sensory appearances, which often feature in our
sensations. But that can be treated as a picturesque way of capturing the idea that, in the course of
sensory episodes, things often appear to us to be the case.

imagery at their hearts—the relations in the other direction aren't immediately clear. For example, we often imagine objects using visualization. Some philosophers claim that, in those cases, we imagine seeing the visualized items.[5] A weaker view states that visualizings may involve the use of distinctively visual imagery to imaginatively represent objects without our thereby imagining those objects *as seen*. I think that the weaker of those two views is correct, and that there are consequently imagistic imaginings which are neither sensory nor perceptual, but none of the arguments below will trade on that assumption.[6]

The next section will isolate a strategy which one might hope to use to answer the descriptive question why we tend to ascribe possibility to what we imagine. I'll then briefly discuss how one might hope to fit that strategy into an answer to the justificatory question whether imaginatively-based ascriptions of possibility are justified, before attempting to assess, over the course of Sections 5–7, whether the described strategy can really be applied to various sorts of imaginings.

## 3. AN ANALOGY WITH SOME OTHER MENTAL STATES

There are especially intimate links between sensory appearances and many of our beliefs about the outside world. Indeed, the links are so intimate that some philosophers have identified sensory appearances with beliefs, or with the acquisition of beliefs.[7] That identification is too strong—the appearances persist when we've not got any inclination to trust them—but there is something right about it: part of what it is for sensory appearances to be *appearances* is that they can be accurate or inaccurate in just the way that beliefs can be. As Heck puts it, 'both [sensory appearances and beliefs] . . . have assertoric force'.[8]

If we are seeking to explain the links between sensory appearances and the beliefs about the external world which we form in direct response to them—our *perceptual* beliefs, for short—we therefore don't have to look far beyond those appearances themselves. For instance, suppose that I seem to see a cat sitting on a wall, and assume that I trust what my senses are telling me to be the case. Then I will form the belief that a cat is sitting on a wall.

To take another example, there are equally strong connections between our apparent first-personal memories and our beliefs about the past. If someone

---

[5] See the discussion in Martin (2002), for instance, from p. 404. See also Peacocke (1985), p. 21.

[6] Thanks to Rob Hopkins for pointing out to me that earlier versions of this paper didn't attend carefully enough to questions about the relationships between imagistic imaginings and perceptual plus sensory ones.

[7] See Armstrong (1968), pp. 216–26 and Pitcher (1971), pp. 64–96.

[8] Heck (2000), p. 508. For similar claims, see e.g. Burge (2003), p. 542; Martin (2002), pp. 386–92; Pendlebury (1986), p. 95; Yablo (1993), p. 5. One should be wary of overstating the assertoric force of our sensations, however. So consider the after-imageish visual effects which occur, among other times, when one is in the dark; it's far from clear that those sensations purport to present us with how things are.

has an apparent first-personal memory, it thereby appears to the person that a certain event once occurred; and those appearances amount to more than mere beliefs or mere inclinations to form beliefs. Part of what it is for apparent first-personal memories to involve appearances of pastness is for the former to feature states which have the same assertoric force as belong to *beliefs* to the effect that something once happened. Again, the matching force of the appearances figuring in apparent first-personal memories and beliefs about the past means that we can easily explain our tendency to base the latter upon the former.

Perhaps the connections between conceivings and beliefs about possibility are as close as those holding between sensory appearances and our perceptual beliefs, and between apparent first-personal memories and beliefs about our own pasts. As Yablo points out,[9] that idea is suggested by one reading of Hume's articulation of 'an establish'd maxim in metaphysics, *That whatever the mind clearly conceives, includes the idea of possible existence*'. And Yablo himself endorses it in the following passage:

> Just as [for it to appear sensorily to one] that *p* is to be in a state that (i) is veridical only if *p*, . . . to find *p* conceivable is to be in a state which (i) is veridical only if possibly *p* . . .[10]

How, in more detail, is the position supposed to run? Its central component, as I'll understand the view, is the thesis that one who imagines a thing, sensation or perception thereby enjoys the appearance that an item of the imagined kind is possible.[11] But if that's right, then imaginings, involving as they do appearances of possibility, have the same assertoric force as beliefs about possibility. Our tendency to move from the conceiving of a thing of some type to a belief that such items are possible may then be explained as arising from our inclination to take our conceivings straight; that is, as a product of our inclination to ascribe possibility to what our conceivings tell us is possible. More generally, I'll say that an explanation of our tendency to ascribe possibility to the objects of a

---

[9] Yablo (1993), pp. 4–5. The proposed reading of Hume's comment (which is also employed in the editors' introduction to Gendler and Hawthorne (2002), on p. 17) is, in some respects, slightly strained. A more natural construal, briefly discussed below, takes Hume's remark to state that imagining an *F* involves imagining a possible *F*.

[10] Yablo (1993), p. 7. Although Yablo is there concerned with propositional conceiving, he eventually explains propositional conceiving in terms of objectual conceiving (p. 29), and claims that 'to imagine an *X* is *thereby* to enjoy the appearance that an *X* could exist' (p. 30).

[11] When one imagines something, what one imagines will generally fall under various categories, and one will be unaware of its falling under some of them. So strictly speaking, for example, when I talk below about imaginings producing the appearance that there can be things of 'the' sort that one has imagined, I should instead talk about something like 'the appearance that there can be things of each of the types which one has explicitly imagined being exemplified'. I've ignored such complications, however, below. In the case of sensory imaginings, an important point to note is that each of the sorts which one imagines to be instantiated (whether knowingly or not) meets the following condition: one's having a sensation of that sort doesn't entail that one has a perception. (For recall that any sensory appearances which one imagines having when one engages in a sensory imagining aren't imagined to be veridical.)

range of imaginings is an *appearance-based* explanation just in case it assumes that imaginings in the relevant range produce the appearance that there could be things of the sort that have been imagined.

Of course, if appearance-based accounts are to have any explanatory power at all, the notion of someone's enjoying an appearance that a thing of some kind is possible must come to something other than the person's simply being inclined to form the belief that such items are possible. The relevant appearances must be, in that sense, *nondoxastic*. But that isn't a problem. The general notion of a nondoxastic appearance evidently cries out for further philosophical examination, but we've already seen that sensations and apparent memories generate distinctive ranges of such appearances, so it is unclear why there should be any immediate objections of principle to the view that imaginings do so too.[12]

Some additional clarificatory remarks are now in order. We can easily explain our propensity to ascribe possibility to what appears to us to be the case through the workings of our senses. For instance, suppose that it looks to us as though a magpie is sitting on a roof. The veridicality of that appearance very obviously requires that a magpie *can* sit on a roof. So if we trust the appearance, we will profess that a magpie can sit on a roof.

The power of that explanatory strategy depends crucially upon the fact that we find it very obvious that actuality implies possibility. If that weren't transparently clear to us all, the previous explanatory mechanism wouldn't account for the way in which it is immediately obvious to everyone that accurate sensory appearances correspond to possibilities. For example, if we could only see that actuality implies possibility through the formulation of an esoteric argument, the readiness with which everyone ascribes possibility to what their sensations present to them as factual would be unexplained.

Because it's so obvious to us that actuality implies possibility, it makes good sense to allow that—in a slightly extended sense—sensory appearances provide us with 'appearances of possibility', although those latter appearances are mediated by more fundamental appearances of actuality. I'll therefore allow that imaginings may produce appearances of possibility even if they only do so in the sort of mediated fashion just described; that is, by the production of some appearance whose accuracy seems to everyone very obviously to require the possibility of the type of thing which has been imagined.[13]

---

[12] 'Small children can imagine things, but it's ridiculous to suppose that they enjoy anything as sophisticated as appearances of possibility!' I've got some sympathy with this objection when it is aimed at the idea that imaginings invariably produce appearances of possibility in an unmediated manner (see the next paragraph in the main text for an explanation of what means), but we'll see shortly that there are other ways of developing the idea that imaginings produce appearances of possibility.

[13] The relevant notion of 'seeming very obviously to everyone to require' clearly needs further elucidation, but it's meant to mark the sort of obviousness which is present in traditional examples of analytically valid inferences. Someone might claim that imaginings evidently produce mediated appearances of possibility, using the following argument: first, one who imagines an object, sensation

Appearance-based explanations of our inclination to ascribe possibility to what we imagine contrast with numerous other explanations which don't assume that imaginative states somehow present things as being a certain way. For example, it might be claimed that we tend to move from conceivability to possibility merely because we were taught to do so as children. Or it might be said that the tendency is owed to our having remarked a correlation between imaginability and possibility in the past.[14]

Appearance-based positions may get some specious plausibility from their conflation with a quite different view, one that is also suggested by Hume's remark that 'whatever the mind clearly conceives, includes the idea of possible existence'. For example, suppose that somebody asks you to imagine a furry desk. Would your response to that request have differed in any substantial way from your response to the request to imagine a *possible* furry desk? Surely not. So, making the obvious extrapolation from that case, it may seem that our imaginings carry a commitment to the possibility of their objects, as appearance-based views claim.

That there's something wrong with the previous argument becomes obvious when one reflects on analogous cases. So, one who imagines an $F$ doesn't need to alter his imagining to comply with the request to imagine an existing $F$. But our imaginings don't typically carry a commitment to the existence of their objects; one who imagines an $F$ doesn't usually thereby enjoy the appearance that an $F$ exists.[15] Why should we think that the relationships between imagined possible existence and appearances of possibility are any different? In summary, Hume's claim about imaginings and possible existence is perhaps clearly true when construed as stating that possible existence is invariably among the imagined properties of imagined objects.[16] But that doesn't establish that imaginings always impart appearances of possibility.

---

or perception thereby enjoys the appearance that he's imagined what he's imagined; but, second, imaginability seems very obviously to imply possibility. If the arguments in Section 5 below are sound, though, it is wrong to claim that imaginings always produce mediated appearances of possibility in the manner just described; the error presumably arises because imaginability doesn't always seem very obviously to imply possibility.

[14] Noordhof (2002), p. 453 briefly suggests an inductive account of 'the legitimacy of appealing to imagination to establish that something is possible', which would obviously dovetail nicely with the above associative explanation of why we make those appeals. Also, somebody might claim that imaginings present their objects as being a certain way, even though those appearances can't then be used to explain why we tend to ascribe possibility to what we imagine. For instance, Sartre claims that imaginings posit their objects as absent in a certain sense (Sartre [1940] 2004, pp. 11–14), and it is unclear how to get appearances of possibility from appearances of absence.

[15] The qualifications are present because there may be 'reflexive' cases in which one who imagines an $F$ does thereby enjoy the appearance that an $F$ exists; consider someone who imagines an imaginer, for instance. A similar point arises below, in the discussion of supposition-like elements of nonimagistic imaginings.

[16] If Hume's claim *is* true on that reading, that raises the question why it is true. One might suggest that the imagined features of an imagined object are, for us, partly determined by the

Sections 5–7 of this paper will examine the core of appearance-based theories, the idea that classes of imaginings yield appearances of possibility. But before considering whether any imaginings in fact produce such appearances, it will be helpful to consider how appearance-based views might fit within attempts to justify ascriptions of possibility. And the obvious place to look is at justificatory strategies which are, like appearance-based explanations themselves, inspired by the relationships between our sensations and our perceptual beliefs.

## 4. APPEARANCES OF POSSIBILITY AND THE JUSTIFICATORY TASK

Here is a crude reliabilist account of why our perceptual beliefs are (prima facie) justified.[17] First, some beliefs are justified if they are the product of a belief-forming process that reliably produces true beliefs when employed within the environments in which the believer is typically placed. Second, the sensory processes which lead us to perceptual beliefs do work reliably in the situations in which we ordinarily find ourselves. Hence, third, our perceptual beliefs are justified.

That account may, for all I know, correctly identify one of the sources of the justification which attaches to the beliefs which it discusses. But it is hard to believe that it tells the whole story. For instance, suppose that somebody is inclined to form beliefs about the weather in Timbuktu whenever she feels an itch on her left calf.[18] And suppose that the beliefs which the person thereby forms tend to be true. Then, regardless of whether or not the beliefs which the

---

a priori obvious consequences of the features which we explicitly imagine the thing to have. (So, for example, we cannot imagine a nonmale bachelor because it is a priori obvious to us that all bachelors are men.) The inevitable inclusion of possible existence among the imagined features of the things which we imagine would then merely manifest the a priori obviousness of entailments of the form 'an $F$ is $G$' to 'it is possible that an $F$ exists'. That approach has the nice feature that it doesn't require that conceptually unsophisticated imaginers like small children and animals should have to explicitly ascribe possible existence to the things which they imagine. But it needs further development. For instance, assume that $P$'s entailing $Q$ amounts to the impossibility of $P$ and not-$Q$. Then the a priori obviousness to us of an entailment from 'an $F$ is $G$' to 'it is possible that an $F$ exists' amounts to its being a priori obvious that it cannot be both that an $F$ is $G$ yet it is impossible for an $F$ to exist. But why should that affect our assessment of our imagining of an $F$ which is $G$ unless we have already specified that we are imagining a *possible* $F$ which is $G$?

[17] Some writers, like Burge, preserve talk of 'justification' for 'warrant by reason that is conceptually accessible on reflection to the warranted individual' (Burge 2003, p. 505). I'm not following that practice; in Burge's terms, I'm classifying beliefs to which we have an 'entitlement' as justified (alternatively, I'm identifying the class of justified beliefs with the class of 'warranted' ones).

[18] The following sort of case often features in critical discussions of reliabilist theories of knowledge. I'm not interested in the issue whether the people figuring in such cases end up with knowledge, however. My interest is rather in the very obvious contrast between such cases and what happens when we form perceptual beliefs.

foregoing process produces are warranted, it seems odd to assimilate perceptual beliefs to the beliefs figuring in that example. For that move completely ignores one of the central features of our sensations—that in having sensations we often enjoy nondoxastic appearances.

But why, someone might now ask, should that phenomenological fact about our sensations be relevant to an account of why our perceptual beliefs are justified? Isn't the phenomenology merely relevant to that small part of the beliefs' etiology which occurs in our consciousnesses, and entirely incidental to whether or not the beliefs are justified? That might turn out to be so. But if one is seeking to explain why our perceptual beliefs are justified, it is at least natural to suspect that sensory appearances will play a major role. It is therefore also natural to suspect that the simple reliabilist position described at the start of this section is missing something important.

How might sensory appearances pull their weight in an account of why perceptual beliefs are justified? A simple thought is that the appearances just do the justifying. To quote Pryor:

> In my view, it's not the irresistibility of our perceptual beliefs, nor the nature of our concepts, which explains why our experiences give us the immediate justification they do. Rather, it's the peculiar "phenomenal force" or way our experiences have of presenting propositions to us. Our experiences represent propositions in such a way that it "feels as if" we could tell that those propositions are true—and that we're perceiving them to be true—just by virtue of having them so represented. . . . It is difficult to explain what this "phenomenal force" amounts to, but I think that it is an important notion, and that it needs to be part of the story about why our experiences give us the justification they do.[19]

It would clearly be a major job to demonstrate the view endorsed by Pryor, and it's not one that I'm about to undertake. But let's suppose that the position is a workable one. Let's assume, that is, the following: if we form a perceptual belief that *p* by trusting a sensory appearance that *p*, the very way in which our senses have presented *p* to us as obtaining means that our belief is justified (unless we have grounds for distrusting our senses on that occasion[20]). Then can advocates of appearance-based explanations use related ideas in arguing that some of our beliefs about possibility are justified?

That depends upon why it is that we are entitled to accept as being the case what our senses tell us to be the case. If what's doing the work there is the peculiarly *sensory* nature of the appearances, the previous strategy won't be adaptable to the imaginative case. But if what's working is the simple fact that sensory appearances are *appearances*, it will be adaptable. More precisely, suppose that we are entitled to accept whatever is presented as obtaining by some nondoxastic seeming. Then appearance-based views look set to do some justifying.

---

[19] Pryor (2000), p. 547 n. 37.          [20] I'll make this qualification tacit from now on.

The idea that we are always entitled to accept nondoxastic appearances is suggested by one of the many a priori principles of entitlement which Burge identifies, namely the Acceptance Principle:

> *A person is apriori entitled to accept a proposition that is presented as true and that is intelligible to him, unless there are stronger reasons not to do so, because it is prima facie preserved (received) from a rational source, or resource for reason; reliance on rational sources—or resources for reason—is, other things being equal, necessary to the function of reason.*[21]

It is also a theme in the work of some of the authors who have recently marched under the rationalist banner. So, for instance, Bealer distinguishes sensory and non-sensory seemings, labelling the latter 'intuitions'. And, he claims, just as sensory seemings may provide us with prima facie justification so too do intuitions.[22]

Here is one way of incorporating appearance-based approaches to the imagination within a scheme for the justification of ascriptions of possibility. Begin with the idea that we are entitled to accept whatever is presented as being the case by some nondoxastic seeming. Next, take some occasion on which you imagine an *F*, with something's thereby appearing to you to be the case, where the accuracy of the foregoing appearance seems very obviously to imply the possibility of *F*s. Then (and assuming that you're entitled to assume that the previous implication holds) you are entitled to accept that *F*s are possible. Hence your belief was in fact justified by your initial imagining.

I don't know whether the fundamental assumption of that justificatory schema, that we are entitled to trust nondoxastic seemings, is correct. The schema is merely meant to illustrate one fairly natural, and not obviously wrong, way of linking the descriptive claims featuring in appearance-based accounts to the problem of justifying beliefs about possibility. But suppose that the schema's fundamental assumption is correct. That will only enable us to justify some beliefs about possibility if imaginings sometimes produce appearances of possibility. Do they?

---

[21] Burge (1993), p. 469.

[22] Bealer (2002), pp. 73–4. Bealer is rather hostile to the idea that that conceivability can provide evidence for possibility (see pp. 75–7). He claims that the notion of conceivability is rather obscure and argues that modal intuitions are anyway the proper justificatory basis for modal claims. The first worry can be circumvented by fixing on particular notions of conceivability; in particular, imaginings are no more obscure than Bealer's intuitions. And the second one will be compatible with our assigning an important place to the imagination in modal epistemology, if some imaginings are themselves modal intuitions. Bealer recognizes the option of holding that imaginings produce appearances of possibility, but he thinks that attempts to justify beliefs about possibility using that view take us 'right back to relying upon modal intuitions' (p. 76 n. 4). (The point of that last remark is perhaps that the justificatory force of imaginings will then be entirely inherited from the evidential force of nondoxastic seemings more generally, and so we should be concentrating on the latter.)

The obvious way of tackling that question is to look and see—to examine the introspective evidence. Perhaps it is naïve to think that such a direct approach could work, but I don't know of any reasons for thinking that it is doomed to utter failure. So that's the method I'll use.[23]


## 5. UNIVERSAL APPEARANCES OF POSSIBILITY?

The *simplest appearance-based view* states that imaginings always generate appearances of possibility. If that is right, and if the justificatory schema described in the previous section holds water, we will always be entitled to infer that what we imagine is possible. It will be helpful to have some examples in front of us before we start evaluating the simplest appearance-based position:

> [A] Imagine merely having auditory sensations of the type which you might have if you were to hear a nearby car (that is, without imagining that any of the auditory appearances which you've imagined having either are or aren't veridical).

One who follows that command—who performs an *[A]-imagining*, as I'll say—performs a sensory imagining. The next command is very different:

> [B] Imagine a universe which contains infinitely many stars.

For, I take it, one who performs a [B]-imagining performs a nonimagistic imagining: one whose content isn't fixed by the content of the sensory imagery at its centre.

The simplest appearance-based view implies that anyone who obeys one of commands [A] and [B] will thereby enjoy the appearance that what she has imagined is possible. And [A]-imaginings do seem to impart something which we might be tempted to regard as appearances of possibility. So, for instance, perform an [A]-imagining. If you're anything like me, the sort of sensation which you've imagined will clearly seem like something which could be enjoyed, and enjoyed by you. And it's not just that you happen to form the belief that you could hear a suitable series of sounds. Rather, the felt nature of your [A]-imagining makes the claim that there couldn't be a hearing of the imagined sort seem mistaken.

How do those phenomena arise? In particular, do the putative appearances meet the demands which I earlier made of appearances of possibility, having at least arisen in the mediated manner described in Section 3? I'll answer those questions in the next section. For the moment, though, it will be useful to bear

---

[23] Introspection certainly makes a compelling enough case for the view that, say, memories provide us with appearances of pastness but hopes don't. The perplexities arising in Section 7 suggest that additional resources may be needed, though.

[A]-imaginings in mind, as providing a benchmark against which we can measure the plausibility of assigning appearances of possibility to other imaginings.

Now reconsider command [B]. We are, I think, perfectly capable of performing [B]-imaginings. Do [B]-imaginings produce appearances of possibility? Perform a [B]-imagining. Your imagining probably inclines you towards a belief that is incompatible with the claim that there cannot be universes with infinitely many stars. But is that because your imagining produces some appearance, where the accuracy of the produced appearance seems flatly incompatible with the claim that each universe must have only finitely many stars?

Reconsider, first, our [A]-imaginings. If we were to accept that we cannot have sensations of the type specified in [A], we would view our [A]-imaginings as having misinformed us about our sensory capacities; in that respect, our imaginations would have generated illusions. But if we were to accept that universes can only have finitely many stars, we wouldn't similarly regard our [B]-imaginings as misinforming us about what's possible—our [B]-imaginings wouldn't themselves have had an illusory character. For a [B]-imagining has the force of a simple supposition to the effect that there is a universe with infinitely many stars.[24] And our making the supposition that there is such a universe hardly makes it seem to us that there could be one, not even in the mediated sense introduced earlier.

Anscombe makes a related point in her discussion of Hume's argument that it is possible for something to come into existence without a cause. She writes:

> But what am I to imagine if I imagine a rabbit coming into being without a cause? Well, I just imagine a rabbit coming into being. That this *is* the imagination of a rabbit coming into being without a cause is nothing but, as it were, the *title* of the picture. Indeed I can form an image and give my picture that title. But from my being able to do *that*, nothing whatever follows about what is possible to suppose "without contradiction or absurdity" as holding in reality.[25]

Anscombe perhaps overplays her hand in the final sentence of that quotation, as the possibility of a rabbit's just springing into existence may in fact be implied by the imaginative feat which she describes. But what I take to be her central point is a good one.

An imagining of a rabbit which just pops into existence involves the imaginative imposition of certain conditions which transcend those which are derivable from the imagining's imagistic aspects. Indeed, that holds quite generally of

---

[24] Peacocke says that the differences between distinct imaginings with a shared imagistic core arise through 'differences in which conditions are S-*imagined* to hold', where ' "S" is for "suppose" ' (1985, p. 25). He distinguishes S-imagining from supposing, but says that 'it shares with supposition the property that what is S-imagined is not determined by the subject's images, his imagined experiences'. If the claims in the text are correct, Peacocke's label is apposite for more than the reason which he mentions—S-imaginings also have a merely suppositional force.

[25] Anscombe (1974), p. 150. Many thanks to Jonathan Webber for pointing me towards Anscombe's paper.

nonimagistic imaginings. But our enforcing of such conditions is achieved through something like[26] our merely supposing that, say, an imagined rabbit has come into being without a cause. Or, to put the point in Anscombe's manner, the conditions are enforced through something like our simply labelling an imagined rabbit as 'a rabbit that came into being without a cause'.

In particular, our imaginative imposition of nonimagistic constraints is like mere supposition and mere labelling in the following respect: our having imposed the constraints doesn't generally make their satisfaction appear possible, no more than mere suppositions and mere labellings typically produce appearances of possibility.[27] In that sense, nothing generally 'follows from' a nonimagistic imagining concerning the possibility of its objects. The simplest appearance-based view is therefore wrong, and wrong for a very wide range of our imaginings.[28]

It has sometimes been assumed, though, that there will be a constant account of how imaginings connect to appearances of possibility. Yablo's final description of the relationships between imaginings and apparent possibility, for example, explicitly uses the principle that 'to imagine an $X$ is *thereby* to enjoy the appearance that an $X$ could exist'.[29] That assumption of constancy has little to recommend it besides its explanatory virtues, however.

---

[26] This qualification is important. The range of things which we are capable of supposing outruns the range of things which we are typically happy to regard as imaginable. For instance, we can suppose that explicit contradictions hold, but most people deny being able to imagine explicit contradictions. I have no idea why this discrepancy exists.

[27] The qualifications are needed because there may be cases in which our imposition of the constraints does make their satisfaction appear possible. So, to continue the analogy with suppositions, although one's supposing something doesn't standardly make the content of the supposition seem possible, it may sometimes have that result—consider suppositions to the effect that someone is supposing something, for instance.

[28] Note that, even if that last comment is correct, we may still be convinced that very much of what we nonimagistically imagine is possible; it's just that appearances of possibility arising from those imaginings won't typically be what produces those convictions. Nonimagistically imagine a hundred-sided polygon, for instance. Then you're probably certain that what you've imagined is possible; but that isn't because your imagining makes the imagined shape seem possible. (Perhaps, for example, your knowledge that certain polygons are possible combines with your implicit acceptance of a recombinatory principle for possibilities to make it look obvious to you that the sort of shape that you've imagined is possible.) Many thanks to an anonymous referee for pressing me on these issues.

[29] Yablo (1993), p. 30. (I should mention that, in a footnote attached to the quoted passage, Yablo proposes converting the previous claim into a stipulation concerning the range of imaginings with which he is concerned. The problem with this move is that, if the arguments in this section and Section 7 are correct, it isn't clear how much will be contained in the resulting class of imaginings.) This may be the place to mention some slightly puzzling features of Yablo's position. His account of 'philosophical conceivability' on p. 29 states that a proposition is conceivable if one can imagine a world which one takes to verify the proposition. In the discussion that leads to that statement, Yablo seems to identify worlds with *possible* worlds. And, one might think, the presumed possibility of those worlds is meant to play a role in explaining why imaginings provide appearances of possibility. If that were right, Yablo would be heading for an implausible position on which imaginings provide appearances of possibility by presenting their objects—namely, possible worlds of various sorts—as existent. But the assumed possibility of the imagined worlds seems in fact to be unnecessary for

## 6. MORE ON SENSORY IMAGININGS

We saw earlier that our [A]-imaginings somehow conflict with the claim that there could be no sensations of the sort which you imagined in response to command [A]. But do [A]-imaginings produce appearances of possibility in the sense articulated earlier? That is, do [A]-imaginings make something appear to be the case, where that thing's obtaining seems evidently to require that there could be sensations of the imagined sort? They do, and their doing so can moreover be traced back to some of the peculiarities of sensory imaginings.

There is a clear way in which imagined auditory sensations are like real ones.[30] And those phenomenological relationships are the source of the stark clash between an [A]-imagining and the claim that sensations of the sort specified in [A] are impossible. So perform an [A]-imagining. Then it seems very obvious that you would have sensations of the imagined type if things were to be a certain way for you auditorily, a way which you identify with your 'inner ear'. But, and taking the experience of performing an [A]-imagining unquestioningly, how could it be impossible for you to hear *those sounds*? Accordingly, it seems very obvious that you could have a sensation of the sort which [A] specifies.

More fully, take some sensory imagining; a [C]-imagining, for example:

[C] Imagine merely having visual sensations of the sort which you might have if you were to see a single pink crow against a cloudless blue sky.

It seems clear that we would have a sensation of the type specified in [C] if things were to be a certain way for us sensorily; and our sensory imaginations present the relevant way for things to be for us in a mysteriously sensory manner.

We can put things more sharply by referring to the phenomenal character of our imagined sensation using what I'll term *quasi-perceptual* demonstratives—we can say that it seems very obvious to us that we would have a sensation of the imagined type if things were to be like *that* for us.[31] But the phenomenological

---

Yablo's purposes, because he is committed to holding that one who imagines a world of some sort (no mention of possibility needed) thereby enjoys the appearance that there could be a world of the relevant sort. The most likely explanation of what's going on is perhaps that Yablo's earlier apparent identification of worlds with possible worlds is trading on the later principle just quoted in the main text, which implies that, in imaginings, worlds always get presented as possible.

[30] Hume thought that imaginings and perceivings differ with regard to their 'vivacity' ('force', 'liveliness', and 'strength'). The idea that imagined sensations are less 'vivacious' versions of the real thing provides a nice way of marking the way in which imagined sensations and real ones are similar yet different, but it doesn't provide a good theory of the differences between real sensations and imagined ones.

[31] I'm tempted to think that sensory imaginings (and perceptual ones) always license the use of quasi-perceptual demonstratives, and the rest of this paper assumes that thesis for simplicity's sake.

similarities between our imaginative grip on feeling like *that* and the real thing means that our sensory imagining produces the appearance that we could indeed feel like *that*. And this appearance is a nondoxastic one. For the remarked phenomenological similarities would be there even if we weren't inclined to believe that we could have sensations of the sort described in [C].

Our sensory imagining therefore produces a mediated appearance of possibility. For, first, the imagining produces the nondoxastic appearance that things could be like *that* for us. But, second, it seems obvious that if things were to be like *that* for us, we would have a sensation of the imagined type. And so, third, the accuracy of the initial appearance produced by our sensory imagining seems evidently to require that we could have a sensation of the imagined kind.

There is, of course, a lot that is very puzzling here. How can the similarities between real and imagined sensations lead to imagined sensations making real sensations seem possible, for instance, when there are other respects in which imagined sensations and real ones are very different? And what does it mean to say that a particular sensory imagining makes it appear that we would have sensations of the imagined variety if things were to be like *that* for us? Doesn't the relevant demonstrative need to single out a real instance of a type of sensations, rather than a merely imaginary sensation? How, then, can the special way in which imagined sensations are presented to us in sensory imaginings amount to anything at all, let alone enough to ensure that sensations of the relevant kind appear to be ones which we could have?

Those are good questions and I've not got answers to them. A fully comprehensive explanation of how sensory imaginings produce appearances of sensory possibilities would doubtless involve mention of facts about the relationships between the neural systems which underlie both imagined and real sensations.[32] But the queries just raised don't undermine the claim that sensory imaginings produce appearances of possibility; they merely underscore how hard it is to provide a philosophically adequate description of what's going on when imaginings produce such appearances.

The previous line of thought, concerning how sensory imaginings produce appearances of possibility, can be further supported by considering other sorts of cases in which sensations are presented to us in the oddly sensory way in which we encounter imagined sensations in sensory imaginings. For appearances of possibility are produced in those cases too, and through the very pathways just described.

---

But there may be exceptions to that claim. If there are exceptions to it, I'm happy to allow that the relevant sensory imaginings may also fail to make the imagined sensations seem like ones which can be had.

[32] There is a lot of data showing that imagined sensings and real ones activate related parts of the brain. So, to take the case of imagined proprioception, Decety (2002) reports that there are important relationships between the neurological activity which occurs 'during motor imagery, motor preparation, and actual motor performance' (p. 301).

So obey command [D]:

> [D] Recall some sensations which you've enjoyed, where those sensations are instances of some merely sensory type (that is, some type of sensations whose instances don't have to be perceptions).

Now suppose that your apparent [D]-memory is mistaken, and that you never had the sensation which you seem to remember. Your apparently recalled sensation is nonetheless presented to you in the special way that imagined sensations are presented to us in sensory imaginings—for instance, it seems obvious that you would have a sensation of the apparently remembered variety if things were like *that* for you.

It may be thought that one way in which apparent memories produce appearances of possibility is as follows: apparent memories present their objects as more than simply things that once happened—they present them as things which we witnessed; but it is obvious that if we underwent a sensation of some kind, a sensation of that type is possible; so the accuracy of the appearance of pastness produced by your apparent [D]-memory seems very clearly to require that you could have the sort of sensation that you appear to have recalled. Your supposition that your apparent [D]-memory is mistaken means that you've got no reason to trust any appearances of possibility which are produced in that manner, however.

But, I take it, your supposition about the veracity of your apparent [D]-memory doesn't call into question the apparent information about your sensory capacities that the apparent memory provides. Why so? Well, apparent [D]-memories have the same sort of peculiarly sensory nature as sensory imaginings: for example, you can use quasi-perceptual demonstratives to characterize conditions under which you would have a sensation of the apparently remembered category. And, as we saw above when considering sensory imaginings, our apparent [D]-memories' being like that is *itself* enough to mean that they will produce mediated appearances of possibility, regardless of whether those apparent memories are accurate or not.[33]

---

[33] Someone might suggest that the appearances of possibility resulting from sensory imaginings are owed to the intimate relationships between recalled sensations and sensory imagery. In particular, it might be held that our sensory imaginations work by suitably recombining components of sensory memories, and that the apparent pastness of those memories is somehow responsible for the appearances of sensory possibility produced by sensory imaginings. The points in the text suggest that that view is mistaken, however. For assume that the apparent pastness of the elements combined in a sensory imagining is what makes the imagined sensation seem like one which we could have. Then suitable suppositions about the accuracy of our recall of the combined components should remove our grounds for trusting the relevant appearances of sensory possibility. But the suppositions don't actually have that effect. There are additional reasons for denying that the relationships between recalled sensations and sensory imagery are what's responsible for the apparent possibility of imagined sensations. For instance, there could perhaps be human-like beings who have the capacity for, say, visualizing but who lack working visual systems; they might have lost the capacity to see as a result of evolution. Their visual imaginings would make the imagined sensations seem

The considerations rehearsed over the last couple of pages help to shed light on some further interesting features of sensory imaginings. Certain conceivings have traditionally been assigned an especially powerful role as proofs of possibility—namely, 'clear and distinct' ones. So, for instance, consider the following passage by Descartes:

the rule 'whatever we can conceive of can exist' is my own, [but] it is true only so long as we are dealing with a conception which is clear and distinct, a conception which embraces the possibility of the thing in question, since God can bring about whatever we clearly perceive to be possible.[34]

(According to Descartes, a conceiving is 'clear and distinct' if 'it is present and accessible to the attentive mind [. . . and . . .] it is so sharply separated from all other perceptions that it contains within itself only what is clear'.[35])

Although Descartes's attitude towards imagistic imaginings was rather dismissive, the idea that sensory imaginings can be rated with regard to their clarity is an appealing one, as is the idea that those variations feed into the relationships between sensory imaginings and our assessments of what's possible. For instance, compare your [C]-imaginings ('Imagine merely having visual sensations of the sort which you might have if you were to see a single pink crow against a cloudless blue sky') with your [E]-imaginings:

[E] Imagine merely having visual sensations of the sort which you might have if you were to see more than twenty but fewer than thirty pink crows against a cloudless blue sky.

[C]-imaginings are typically more clear than [E]-imaginings, in various ways.

For instance, the overall imagined sensory content of [C]-imaginings is usually more definite than that of [E]-imaginings. What [C]-imaginings tell us about what it might be like to have real visual sensations is therefore more clear than the information with which we are provided by [E]-imaginings. Also, the imagined sensory details figuring in [C]-imaginings tend to provide us with our basis for classifying those imaginings as [C]-imaginings. But our categorizations of imaginings as [E]-imaginings are less likely to stick so closely to imagined sensory details. So, our response to command [E] may well result in an imagining whose imagined sensory details don't really differ from our response to command [F]:[36]

---

to them like the sort of thing which they could experience, but those appearances of possibility obviously wouldn't be owed to their memories of visual sensations.

[34] I've taken this quotation from Gendler and Hawthorne (2002), p. 18—it is originally from Descartes's *Comments on a Certain Broadsheet*.

[35] Again, see Gendler and Hawthorne (2002), p. 18 n. 39 for the source of the quotation (which is from Descartes's *Principles of Philosophy*).

[36] The context in which command [E] figures perhaps makes this less likely than it would otherwise be. When presented by [E] in isolation, we try to perform an imagining whose classification as an [E]-imagining is based more fully upon the imagined sensory details than it would be if we were to try to perform an [E]-imagining when reading a novel, for example.

[F] Imagine merely having visual sensations of the sort which you might have if you were to see at least thirty pink crows against a cloudless blue sky.[37]

Again, then, the information which our [C]-imaginings provide us with is clearer than that with which our [E]-imaginings provide us.

As we've seen, sensory imaginings provide us with a very direct form of information about what it might be like to undergo sensings, and they thereby yield appearances relating to our sensory powers. But the variations in imaginative clarity just described arose precisely from differences in how clearly imaginings speak to us about what sensations might be like. One would accordingly expect such variations to be reflected by differences in the clarity of the appearances of possibility produced by the imaginings. And they are.

For instance, [C]-imaginings are generally very clear, in that their overall sensory content is relatively definite. And they also inform us that we are capable of enjoying fairly finely individuated sensory states. But [E]-imaginings provide us with a less firm grasp on what a real visual sensation might be like. The appearances of possibility associated with [E]-imaginings are correspondingly less clear, in a sense; what we learn about our sensory powers is much rougher.

This section has explored the particular means by which sensory imaginings generate appearances of sensory possibilities, and some of the complexities to which those means give rise. The next section looks at whether similar mechanisms can give us appearances of possibility which reach out into the world itself.


## 7. PERCEPTUAL IMAGININGS

We often use perceptual imaginings when exploring modal matters. For instance, suppose that someone asks whether there could be a single pink crow against a cloudless blue sky. Then most of us will reply that there could be. And one fact which we would take to support that response is that we are capable of performing a [G]-imagining:

[G] Imagine seeing a single pink crow against a cloudless blue sky.

In that case, and in many others, we take a perceptual imagining to support a claim about how the external world might have been.

---

[37] Descartes famously makes this sort of point in his discussion of our imaginings of chiliagons, at the start of the *Sixth Meditation*. Peacocke remarks that '[t]he images which serve in the fulfilment of a request to imagine a chiliagon (a thousand-sided figure) and in the fulfilment of a request to imagine a 999-sided figure may match: for an experience produced by a chiliagon and an experience produced by a 999-sided figure are not, for us, discriminably different' (Peacocke 1985, p. 24). But the images involved in [E]-imaginings and [F]-imaginings might be the same even though we

We've seen that sensory imaginings produce appearances of possibility: the sensations which we imagine having when engaging in sensory imaginings seem to be the kind of sensations that we could have. And we've seen that nonimagistic imaginings don't make their objects seem possible. But do perceptual imaginings make the imagined perceptions seem like ones which we could have?

One model of the perceptual imagination adapts a well-known picture of the relationship between genuine perceptions and mere sensations. According to the relevant 'highest common factor' picture of perception, one who sees a pink crow against a cloudless blue sky is in the same sensory state as one who suffers from a corresponding hallucination, a hallucination that seems the same from the inside. The difference between them lies merely in the relationships which their common sensory states have to the outside world. It might be suspected, then, that [G]-imaginings, for instance, work in a similarly bipartite way: we imagine enjoying a certain range of visual appearances and, in addition, we suppose the relevant visual appearances to be veridical.[38]

If that's right, it's natural to think that perceptual imaginings won't make the imagined perceptions seem like ones which we could have. For the nonsensory suppositional elements which that view ascribes to perceptual imaginings look very similar to the constraints which, as we saw earlier, figure in nonimagistic imaginings. And, as we also saw, the purely suppositional force of the latter conditions means that our imposition of them won't typically make their satisfaction seem possible, with the result that nonimagistic imaginings won't usually produce appearances of possibility.

Someone might object to that line of argument, however. When we perform [G]-imaginings, don't we just imagine having a certain perception, namely seeing a sole pink crow against a cloudless blue sky?[39] Do perceptual imaginings really have to tack veridicality suppositions onto imagined sensory appearances? The

surely could discriminate real versions of those imagined sensations. Our being prepared to use a single image in imagining types of sensations which we could discriminate illustrates that the use of a single image in imaginative acts with distinct objects doesn't always correspond to our inability to discriminate the objects of the relevant imaginings; it sometimes results from our just not expending the effort required to fill in the details of the images in suitably different ways.

[38] More than mere veridicality suppositions may be required here; for instance, perhaps we also need to suppose that there are suitable causal connections between the appearances and items in the imagined situation. The veridicality bit is the only relevant factor for my purposes, however, so I'll speak as though veridicality suppositions are the only ones needed. Peacocke (1985), p. 25 takes the sort of line currently being considered. He points out that the same imagery may be involved in 'imagining being at the helm of a yacht; imagining from the inside an experience as of being at the helm of a yacht; and imagining from the inside what it would be like if a brain surgeon were causing you to have an experience as of being at the helm of a yacht' (p. 18). He states that the differences between those imaginings 'result from different conditions which the imagined experience is imagined to fulfil. In one case it is imagined that the experience is perceptual; in the second it is left open; in the third, it is imagined that it is produced by an intervening brain surgeon' (p. 25).

[39] I'm here bracketing questions about the precise contents of perceptual appearances. So someone might deny that I could see a pink crow as opposed to, say, a pink bird-like thing that's at

simpler view of perceptual imaginings suggested by those questions fits nicely with another philosophical picture of the connections between perceptions and mere sensations. The relevant 'disjunctivist' view states that perceptions and other sorts of corresponding sensations don't have a common sensory state at their core, that there isn't a highest common factor which is shared by perceptions, corresponding hallucinations and the rest.[40]

Let's assume, for the moment, that perceptual imaginings indeed involve the imaginative enjoyment of sensations which, by their very nature, present us with facts. Then won't perceptual imaginings produce appearances pertaining to what we can perceive, for precisely the same sort of reasons that sensory imaginings produce appearances of sensory possibilities? For example, perform a [G]-imagining. Then your imagining surely produces the appearance that things could be like *that* for you! And it seems very obvious that you would have a perception of the imagined kind if things were like *that* for you. So it seems very clear that the accuracy of the appearance produced by your [G]-imagining requires the possibility of the sort of perception specified in command [G].

Perceptual imaginings don't exhaust the range of imaginings of which we are capable. There may even be, as remarked earlier, imagistic nonsensory imaginings which also aren't perceptual. But if perceptual imaginings were to generate appearances of possibility in the way just articulated, we could use that fact to account for a vast swathe of the inferences from imaginability to possibility which we in fact make. Even if appearance-based explanations of inferences from imaginings to ascriptions of possibility cannot be universally applied, their coverage would then nonetheless be impressive.

Alas, the line of reasoning rehearsed in the penultimate paragraph goes too quickly. It's true that [G]-imaginings make it seem possible that things should be a certain way for us. But that doesn't settle the crucial question concerning the reach of those appearances of possibility—whether they really involve *perceptions* of the sort described in [G] or merely states which, in phenomenological terms, match perceptions of that sort. To put the point another way, suppose that the unitary conception of imagined perceptions is right. Then the accuracy of the appearances produced by perceptual imaginings like [G] might nonetheless only

some distance from me; and similar claims might be made about what we can, in the strictest sense, perceptually imagine.

[40] This is a pretty rough characterization of disjunctivism but it's sharp enough for my current purposes. Someone might naturally wonder how we could be capable of sensory imaginings if the highest common factor view of imagined perceptions is incorrect. To adapt some remarks which Martin makes concerning imagined hallucinations (Martin 2002, pp. 416–17), perhaps sensory imaginings themselves have the sort of complex structure which the first reply ascribes to perceptual ones. So maybe, for instance, [D]-imaginings build on our ability to perform [G]-imaginings: to perform a [D]-imagining, we perform a [G]-imagining; and then we imagine a situation which we cannot sensorily discriminate from the one which we imagined when performing our [G]-imagining, but which may not in fact be as it appears to be.

*Dominic Gregory*

require that we can occupy disjunctive states like 'either seeing or merely seeming to see a single pink crow against a cloudless blue sky'.[41]

Anyhow, we can try to directly address the question of the moment. That is, consider those quasi-perceptually ostendible elements of perceptual imaginings which provide us with appearances relating to our sensory capacities. Do they make perceptions appear possible? Here is a fairly plausible series of considerations leading to the conclusion that they don't.

Perform a perceptual imagining. Then a certain range of sensations seem to be ones which you could enjoy: things could be, visually or whatever, like *that* for you. But there could surely be circumstances in which things were like *that* for you even though the sensation which you've imagined having featured nonveridical sensory appearances. That is, for instance, one imaginative source of the force belonging to certain sceptical strategies: we run through sensory scenarios in our heads; and, as we do so, we acknowledge that things could be like *that* even if all of the imagined sensations were to be illusions. More generally, perceptual imaginings make us seem capable of experiencing a certain range of ostendible stuff, but that stuff doesn't ensure the veridicality of the imagined sensory appearances.[42]

If that's correct, perceptual imaginings don't make perceptions of the imagined type appear possible in the way that sensory imaginings make sensations of the imagined type seem possible. That doesn't imply that perceptual imaginings don't make perceptions of the imagined kind appear possible, of course. But, it's natural to wonder, how else is a perceptual imagining meant to make the imagined perception seem possible, if not in the mediated manner just considered? There are, then, pretty good reasons for thinking that perceptual imaginings don't make the imagined perceptions seem possible. But there are also reasons why one might be troubled by the argument just run.

Consider the following argument, which is at least superficially analogous to the one concerning perceptual imaginings run over the last two paragraphs: an apparently remembered sensation merely makes it seem like things were once like

---

[41] Disjunctivists typically claim that perceptions have certain sorts of priority over subjectively indistinguishable nonperceptual states. If some such view is correct, perhaps the possibility of a disjunctive state like the one mentioned in the text implies the possibility of the corresponding and more fundamental perceptual state. And so, it might be claimed, if perceptual imaginings make disjunctive states seem possible, then those imaginings also produce mediated appearances of possibility, ones whereby the imagined perceptions seem like ones which we could have. That reasoning is flawed, however. Mediated appearances of possibility arise in the following manner: an imagining of an *F* makes it seem that something holds, where that thing's holding *seems very obviously* to imply that Fs are possible. But it is very far from obvious to us that the possibility of the disjunctive states requires the possibility of the corresponding perceptions, even if it actually does.

[42] Note that it's no objection to the remarks in the last paragraph that there also happens to be a perfectly acceptable use of the demonstrative 'that' on which, when I perform a [G]-imagining, things being like *that* for me requires that I am actually seeing a pink crow. For that is beside the point: if the remarks in the text are right, the stronger understanding of the demonstrative isn't associated with an appearance of possibility in the way that the weaker construal is.

*that* for one; but, as shown for example by the force of familiar sceptical attacks, things could be like *that* for one even if any sensory appearances forming part of the sensation were nonveridical; hence the apparent memory doesn't make a perception proper seem like something which one underwent; but how else is an apparently remembered sensation meant to make a perception seem like something which one underwent . . . ?

That argument leads to the conclusion that one who seems to recall a sensation won't ever thereby enjoy the appearance that he perceived something. But one might well think that, if someone were apparently to recall a *perception*, he would thereby enjoy the appearance of having perceived something. So that most recent argument leads to the bizarre conclusion that nobody who ever seems to recall a sensation ever also seems to remember perceiving anything. Now there may be relevant ways in which the argument in the previous paragraph is unlike the earlier argument concerning perceptual imaginings. But breaking the analogies isn't easy.

This section must therefore end in aporia. On the one hand, it's hard to see how perceptual imaginings could make their objects seem possible, unless through a version of the process by means of which sensory imaginings produce appearances of possibility. But introspection suggests that perceptual imaginings won't produce appearances of possibility through a version of that process. On the other hand, the preceding considerations threaten to generalize disastrously.

## 8. CONCLUSION

The heterogeneity of our imaginings, with their various relations to our sensory powers, is reflected by differences in how they relate to appearances of possibility: a sensory imagining makes sensations of the imagined kind seem possible, but nonimagistic imaginings don't generally make objects of the imagined variety seem possible. And although the status of perceptual imaginings is unclear, the previous point is enough to raise the question why we are quite so prone to ascribe possibility to what we imagine. For our propensity to do so rides rough-shod over the distinction between those imaginings which produce appearances of possibility and those which don't.

Before making some concluding remarks on that topic, I should note that the miscellaneous nature of our imaginings may have important consequences for the epistemological status of inferences from imaginability to possibility. For instance, it will do so if it implies that some of our imaginings, but not others, fit into the sort of justificatory schema outlined in Section 4. And, more generally, it will do so if the production of nondoxastic appearances of possibility by imaginings of certain kinds is somehow relevant to the justification of any ascriptions of possibility based upon them.

Discussions of inferences from conceivability to possibility have nonetheless tended to handle our imaginings as if they form a homogeneous clump. Thus none of the discussions of justificatory issues in Chalmers (2002), Gregory (2004), and Yablo (1993) acknowledges that the differences between imagistic imaginings and nonimagistic ones might be relevant to the justification of modal beliefs.[43] Regardless of the different relationships to appearances of possibility noted here, it's surprising that modal epistemologists have paid so little attention to the fine structure of our imaginings.

To return to the question raised at the start of this section, if imaginings don't generally present their objects as possible, why are we so susceptible to ascribe possibility to what we can imagine? It would be good to have an account of why we ascribe possibility to the objects of our imaginings which makes sense of our very general propensity to reason in that way; an account which provides a charitable explanation of why, in a suitably wide range of cases, the conclusions which we thereby draw seem to us like evidently sensible ones.

The simplest appearance-based model holds out the hope of a theory which will meet that demand by assimilating the relevant inferences to those which underwrite many of our perceptual beliefs; and what could seem more reasonable than those? But if one endorses what this paper has suggested, that the appearance-based approach cannot generally be applied to nonimagistic imaginings and can't clearly be applied to perceptual ones, one might fear that no decent theory is to be had which has the attractive property just mentioned.

For instance, sensory imaginings produce appearances of possibility, so it's to be expected that we will ascribe possibility to the sort of sensations that figure in our sensory imaginings. Someone might therefore suggest that what produces the very general tendency remarked above is this: we just ignore the distinctions between sensory and nonsensory imaginings, and end up ascribing possibility on the basis of the lot of them. But that view makes our inclination to ascribe possibility to what we imagine seem rather foolish.

Or suppose that the appearance-based approach doesn't just break down for nonimagistic imaginings, but for perceptual ones as well. Then while imaginings of those types may in fact reliably correlate with facts about possibility, there is nothing in our very experience of them which leads us to think that their objects are possible. And so, somebody might conclude, although inferences from imaginings to beliefs about possibility seem to us to be patently reasonable ones even in the perceptual and nonimagistic cases, that is probably because they are inferences which we are simply used to making. But, again, that is a rather uncharitable explanation of why we ascribe possibility to what we imagine.

---

[43] Peacocke thinks that the differences are relevant, however: see the discussion of 'W-imagining' on pp. 31–2 of Peacocke (1985).

Finally, McGinn suggests that 'modal beliefs are best seen as based on inferences to the best explanation with respect to acts of imagination'.[44] Now, the ascriptions of possibility which we base upon imaginings may turn out to be abductively justifiable. But it seems wrong to claim that the beliefs in fact seem to us like reasonable ones because they've resulted from our performance of inferences to the best explanation. For that doesn't do justice to how obviously right such ascriptions of possibility seem to us to be. I typically find the modal inferences utterly compelling, for instance, but I can't envisage any remotely plausible abductive reconstruction of them.

Whatever the proper response to the issues just considered, the descriptive question why we tend to infer possibility from our imaginings is both important and wide open. The wider ramifications of answers to that question—for example with regard to the justificatory issues concerning our modal beliefs which have tended to preoccupy philosophers—are also unclear. And it is surely a measure of the currently primitive nature of modal epistemology that it is a question on which the most well-developed accounts of modality are entirely silent.

[44] McGinn (2004), p. 138. He states that 'modal belief relates to imagination in very much the way that ordinary knowledge relates to perception' (McGinn 2004, pp. 138–9), thereby claiming that our perceptual beliefs are also produced using abductive inferences. That seems hugely implausible to me, and the worry briefly raised in the text for McGinn's views about our modal beliefs can evidently be transformed into a problem for his views about our perceptual beliefs.

# Response to Dominic Gregory

*Ross P. Cameron*

First question: suppose everything Gregory tells us is correct—why should we care? George Bealer remarks that modal intuitions are the proper basis for a modal epistemology, not conceivings. He says that attempts to justify modal beliefs by an appeal to conceivability considerations will just take us "right back to relying upon modal intuitions".[1] Why does he think this?

Here is an attempt to bring out Bealer's worry. Suppose I am concerned with the justificatory basis for our modal beliefs and I consider the claim that conceivability is a guide to possibility. I am only justified in believing this claim, one might think, if I am justified in believing that we can't in general conceive of impossible situations, or at least that there is something peculiar about the cases when we conceive of the impossible—something that we can come to be aware of, and so disregard the 'illusions of possibility' we get in those situations. If I am not justified in believing either of these claims then I have no reason to think that the move from 'x is conceivable' to 'x is possible' is even close to reliable, and so I am not justified in appealing to conceivability considerations as the justificatory basis of my modal knowledge.

So it looks as though I need some way of checking the modal status of the situations that I can conceive of. But how do I check this? Not by relying on their conceivability and inferring their possibility, obviously, since the move from conceivability to possibility is what is under question. I need some independent method of checking the modal status of the conceived situations then: perhaps modal intuition. But if such a method is available, why am I bothering with conceivability at all? Isn't it whatever method I use as the independent check that is the proper justificatory basis for our modal knowledge?

How serious is this Bealer-esque[2] worry? Consider a parallel worry in the case of our beliefs concerning the external world. I am concerned with the justificatory basis for such beliefs and I consider the claim that what is perceived[3] is, by and large, a guide to what there is. This claim is pretty widely accepted: perception goes wrong in some circumstances, of course; but I have a pretty good idea of

---

[1] Bealer (2002), p. 74 n. 4.

[2] I should say that I have no idea whether this is what Bealer is actually concerned about.

[3] Or what is apparently perceived, if you think that I can't perceive there to be a tiger unless there is a tiger.

when it goes wrong, and so I can disregard the illusions of reality I get in those circumstances. But wait a minute!—how do I know perception is not leading me astray systematically? Surely to be justified in believing that perception is a guide to reality I need to check that the situations my senses reveal to me are ones that are really out there. I can't check this by relying on the link from perception to reality, since that is what is up for question, so I need some independent method to check this: perhaps reality intuition. But if I have reality intuition, why am I bothering with perception? Reality intuition is the *real* justificatory basis for my beliefs about the external world.

I imagine you're not convinced to abandon perception as the justificatory basis for (many of) our beliefs concerning the external world? But why, what is wrong with the above challenge? It seems to me it is this. It is not that we are simply faced with the conjecture that what is perceived is, by and large, real, and then face the task of justifying this conjecture. Rather, when we have a perception we enjoy the appearance of reality. It simply seems to us, when we perceive that p, that p; we don't *infer* p from 'I am perceiving things to be p' and 'perception is a guide to reality'. There is still a justificatory question of course, but it is not a question of justifying the claim that perception is a guide to reality; it is, rather, a question of whether or not we are justified in trusting the appearance of reality that is enjoyed as an immediate result of having a perception. That question isn't trivial; but it is clear that we can make an attempt at answering it without either presupposing that perception is a guide to reality or relying on some independent route to knowledge of the external world.

Gregory claims that the conceivability/possibility case is analogous, at least in some cases, to the perception/reality case. When we conceive that p (at least, when we have a certain type of conceiving that p) we thereby enjoy the appearance of possibility. We do not *infer* the possibility of p from our having the conceiving and the conjecture that conceivability is a guide to possibility: if we did, we would face the task of justifying the conjecture, which would lead to circularity or obviating the need for conceivability, but instead we face only the less threatening task of saying why we are entitled to accept as veridical the appearance of possibility that is enjoyed as a direct result of our conceivings. So if Gregory is right, we can avoid the Bealer-esque objection.

That is the major benefit of Gregory's approach, I think. But I have a couple of concerns. First, there is the 'revenge of Bealer' threat. Gregory does not think that *all* of our beliefs of the form 'p is possible' are justified by an appearance of possibility gained from conceivings. That is wise, for such a claim is hopeless. Consider, for example, the sceptical possibility that you are a brain in a vat. I don't learn that that situation could obtain by imagining things seeming a certain way, because the situation in question is precisely that things are radically different from how they seem. Or consider the claim that there is a possible world exactly like the actual world from the year 2000 on, but which contains no history before that: i.e. a world which comes into existence with things exactly as they actually were at the turn of the second millennium, and which proceeds from there as the actual world proceeded from the year 2000. If I am justified in believing this claim, and I think I am, it is not as a result of conceiving things seeming a certain way. I can conceive of things seeming to be the way they actually seem to be from the year 2000 on, of course; and we can grant that this allows me to infer the possibility of things being as they actually are from the year 2000 on; but that is a world away (literally!) from what I need. The possibility of things being as they actually are from the year 2000 on is represented by the *actual* world. But that is not the possibility in question: the possibility in question is things being as they actually are from the year 2000 on *and not being any way before that*. But it is no part of the content of my conceiving that nothing happened before the events that account for the way I am conceiving things to be, so this conceiving cannot be the justificatory basis for my knowledge of that possibility.

So how do we know that these situations are possible? The threat is that we're going to need to appeal to something like modal intuition here, in which case why not simply appeal to modal intuition in every case—why worry about conceivability at all?

My second worry is this: it is not entirely obvious to me that we *do* enjoy an immediate appearance of possibility in many of the cases Gregory thinks we do. It seems to me likely that in many of the cases Gregory thinks we enjoy an immediate appearance of possibility we are in fact relying (albeit tacitly) on some kind of recombination principle. Suppose I have heard a bunch of notes and I imagine hearing them in an order I have never heard before, thus composing a musical piece. I have the belief that it is possible to hear the notes in that order, and I think this is a case where Gregory would say that I enjoy the appearance of possibility immediately as a result of conceiving the notes heard in that order. But it seems to me plausible that in this case, and in many similar cases, I *infer* the possibility in question from the belief that, for each of the notes, it is possible to hear that note, together with an application of a recombination principle which takes us from the various individual possibilities to the possibility of the notes being arranged in a certain order.

To illustrate this, consider a character who composes a musical piece in his head but believes that the composed piece *couldn't* possibly be heard for the following reason: (1) it's terrible—the conceived musical piece would sound really bad, and (2) necessarily, there exists an aesthetic God who would prevent any process whereby really bad musical pieces would be heard. This character's beliefs are nuts, of course (in particular, (2) is falsified by most contemporary music), but that is not the point. The point is this—what seems more plausible: (i) that this character differs internally from us in that we have an immediate appearance of possibility that he lacks, (ii) that this character is in some kind of internal tension, denying the appearance of possibility he enjoys, or (iii) that this character does not differ from us in any relevant internal respect, but that he doesn't form the same modal beliefs as us because his strange religious views commit him to the denial of recombination? I find the third hypothesis the most plausible: this character is *just like us* in the data he receives from his acts of conceiving, but he refuses to *infer* what we infer from that data, since he (thinks he) has reason to believe that recombination is false. And if I'm right about the role of recombination here then I suspect it may be recombination, and not conceivability, that is the real justificatory basis for much of our modal knowledge.

# Bibliography

Adams, R. M. (1981) 'Actualism and Thisness', *Synthese* 49, pp. 3–41.

Anscombe, G. E. M. (1974) '"Whatever Has a Beginning of Existence Must Have a Cause": Hume's Argument Exposed', *Analysis* 34, pp. 145–51.

Armstrong, D. M. (1968) *A Materialist Theory of the Mind* (London: Routledge).

—— (1978) *Universals and Scientific Realism* (Cambridge: Cambridge University Press).

—— (1989) *A Combinatorial Theory of Possibility* (Cambridge: Cambridge University Press).

—— (1997) *A World of States of Affairs* (Cambridge: Cambridge University Press).

Audi, P. (2007) 'Beyond Causal Theories of Mind', unpublished dissertation, Princeton University.

Ayer, A. J. (1936) *Language, Truth and Logic* (London: Penguin).

Balog, K. (1999) 'New Conceivability Arguments or Revenge of the Zombies', *Philosophical Review* 108.

Bealer, G. (2000) 'A Theory of the A Priori', *Pacific Philosophical Quarterly* 81, pp. 1–30.

—— (2002) 'Modal Epistemology and the Rationalist Renaissance', in Gendler and Hawthorne (2002), pp. 71–125.

Benacerraf, P. (1973) 'Mathematical Truth', *Journal of Philosophy* 70, pp. 661–80.

Blackburn, S. (1984) *Spreading the Word* (Oxford: Clarendon Press).

—— (1986) 'Morals and Modals', in G. MacDonald and C. Wright (eds.), *Fact, Science, and Value: Essays in Honour of A. J. Ayer's Language, Truth, and Logic* (Oxford: Blackwell), pp. 119–42, repr. in Blackburn (1993).

—— (1993) *Essays in Quasi-Realism* (New York: Oxford University Press).

—— (1998) *Ruling Passions: A Theory of Practical Reasoning* (Oxford: Clarendon Press).

—— (1999) 'Morals and Modals', in Jaegwon Kim and Ernest Sosa (eds.), *Metaphysics: An Anthology* (Oxford: Blackwell), pp. 634–48.

Block, N., and Stalnaker, R. (2000) 'Conceptual Analysis, Dualism and the Explanatory Gap', *Philosophical Review* 108, pp. 1–46.

BonJour, L. (1998) *In Defence of Pure Reason: A Rationalist Account of A Priori Justification* (Cambridge: Cambridge University Press).

Bostock, D. (1988) 'Necessary Truth and A Priori Truth', *Mind* 97, pp. 343–79.

Bueno, O., and Shalkowski, S. A. (2004) 'Modal Realism and Modal Epistemology: A Huge Gap', in Erik Weber and Tim De Mey (eds.), *Modal Epistemology* (Brussels: Koninklijke Vlaamse Academie van Belgie / Royal Flemish Academy of Belgium), pp. 93–106.

Burge, T. (1993) 'Content Preservation', *Philosophical Review* 102, pp. 457–88.

—— (2003) 'Perceptual Entitlement', *Philosophy and Phenomenological Research* 67, pp. 503–48.

Burgess, J., and Rosen, G. (1997) *A Subject with No Object: Strategies of Nominalistic Interpretation of Mathematics* (Oxford: Clarendon Press).

Cameron, R. (forthcoming) 'What's Metaphysical About Metaphysical Necessity?', *Philosophy and Phenomenological Research* 77/3 (2008).

Carnap, R. (1945) 'Two Concepts of Probability', *Philosophy and Phenomenological Research* 5, pp. 513–32.

—— (1950a) 'Empiricism, Semantics, and Ontology', *Revue internationale de philosophie* 4, pp. 20–40; repr. in H. Feigl, W. Sellars, and K. Lehrer (eds.), *New Readings in Philosophical Analysis* (New York: Appleton-Century-Crofts 1972), pp. 585–96.

—— (1950b) *Logical Foundations of Probability* (Chicago: University of Chicago Press).

Cartwright, R. L. (1968) 'Some Remarks on Essentialism', *Journal of Philosophy* 65, pp. 615–26.

—— (1997) 'Singular Propositions', *Canadian Journal of Philosophy*, suppl. vol. 23, pp. 67–84.

Chalmers, D. (1996) *The Conscious Mind* (Oxford: Oxford University Press).

—— (1999) 'Materialism and the Metaphysics of Modality', *Philosophy and Phenomenological Research* 59/2, pp. 473–96.

—— (2002) 'Does Conceivability Entail Possibility?', in Gendler and Hawthorne (2002), pp. 145–200.

—— (2004) 'The Foundations of Two-Dimensional Semantics', *European Review of Philosophy*.

Chalmers, D. and Jackson, F. (2001) 'Conceptual Analysis and Reductive Explanation', *Philosophical Review* 110/3, pp. 315–60.

Cherniak, C. (1986) *Minimal Rationality* (Cambridge, Mass.: MIT Press).

Chihara, C. S. (1998) *The Worlds of Possibility* (Oxford: Clarendon Press).

Christensen, D. (2005) *Putting Logic in its Place* (Oxford: Oxford University Press).

Craig, E. J. (1975) 'The Problem of Necessary Truth', in S. Blackburn (ed.), *Meaning, Reference, and Necessity* (Cambridge: Cambridge University Press), pp. 1–31.

—— (1985) 'Arithmetic and Fact', in I. Hacking (ed.), *Exercises in Analysis: Essays by Students of Casimir Lewy* (Cambridge: Cambridge University Press), pp. 89–112.

Davidson, D. (1984) *Inquiries into Truth and Interpretation* (Oxford: Clarendon Press).

Davies, M. K. (2004) 'Reference, Contingency, and the Two-Dimensional Framework', *Philosophical Studies* 118, pp. 83–131.

Davies, M. K., and Humberstone, I. L. (1980) 'Two Notions of Necessity', *Philosophical Studies* 38, pp. 1–30.

Decety, J. (2002) 'Is There Such a Thing as Functional Equivalence between Imagined, Observed, and Executed Action?', in Meltzoff and Prinz (2002), pp. 291–310.

Dennett, D. (1981) 'Three Kinds of Intentional Psychology', in R. Healey (ed.), *Reduction, Time, and Reality* (Cambridge: Cambridge University Press), pp. 37–61.

DeRose, K. (1991) 'Epistemic Possibilities', *Philosophical Review* 100/4, pp. 581–605.

Descartes, R. (1641) *Discourse on Method and The Meditations* (1968 edn.) trans. F. E. Sutcliffe (Harmondsworth: Penguin).

Divers, J. (1999a) 'A Genuine Realist Theory of Advanced Modalizing', *Mind* 108, pp. 217–39.

—— (1999b) 'Kant's Criteria of the A Priori', *Pacific Philosophical Quarterly* 80, pp. 17–45.

—— (2004) 'Agnosticism About Other Worlds: A New Antirealist Programme in Modality', *Philosophy and Phenomenological Research* 69, pp. 660–85.

—— (2006) 'Possible-Worlds Semantics Without Possible Worlds: The Agnostic Approach', *Mind* 115, pp. 187–225.

Divers, J., and Melia, J. (2002) 'The Analytic Limit of Genuine Modal Realism', *Mind* 111, pp. 15–36.

—— —— (2006) 'Genuine Modal Realism: Still Limited', *Mind* 115, pp. 731–40.

Donnellan, K. (1979) 'The Contingent Apriori and Rigid Designators', in P. A. French et al. (eds.), *Contemporary Perspectives in the Philosophy of Language* (Minneapolis: University of Minnesota Press).

Dorr, C. (2005) 'What We Disagree about when We Disagree about Ontology', in M. E. Kalderon (ed.), *Fictionalism in Metaphysics* (Oxford: Clarendon Press).

Dummett, M. A. E. (1959), 'Wittgenstein's Philosophy of Mathematics', *Philosophical Review* 68, pp. 324–48; repr. in Dummett's *Truth and Other Enigmas* (London: Duckworth, 1978), pp. 166–85.

—— (1976), 'What Is a Theory of Meaning? Part II', in Evans and McDowell (1976).

—— (1981) *Frege: Philosophy of Language*, 2nd edn. (London: Duckworth).

—— (1993) 'Could There Be Unicorns?' in his *The Seas of Language* (Oxford: Clarendon Press), pp. 328–48.

Edgington, D. M. D. (2004) 'Two Kinds of Possibility', *Proceedings of the Aristotelian Society* 78/1, pp. 1–22.

Egan, A. (2007), 'Epistemic Modals, Relativism and Assertion', *Philosophical Studies* 133, pp. 1–22.

Egan, A., Hawthorne, J., and Weatherson, B. (2005) 'Epistemic Modals in Context', in Gerhard Preyer and Georg Peter (eds.), *Contextualism in Philosophy: Knowledge, Meaning, and Truth* (Oxford: Clarendon).

Evans, G. (1979), 'Reference and contingency', *The Monist* 62, pp. 161–89; page refs. are to the reprint in Evans (1985), pp. 178–213.

—— (1985) *Collected Papers* (Oxford: Clarendon Press).

—— (2004) 'Comments on "Two Notions of Necessity"', *Philosophical Studies* 118, pp. 11–16.

Evans, G., and McDowell, J. (1976) (eds.), *Truth and Meaning: Essays in Semantics* (Oxford: Clarendon Press).

Field, H. (1980) *Science Without Numbers* (Oxford: Blackwell).

—— (1989) *Realism, Mathematics, and Modality* (Oxford: Blackwell).

Fine, K. (1970) 'Propositional Quantifiers in Modal Logic', *Theoria* 36, pp. 336–46.

—— (1977) 'Postscript' to A. N. Prior and K. Fine, *Worlds, Times, and Selves* (London: Duckworth).

—— (1981) 'First-Order Modal Theories I—Sets', *Noûs* 15, pp. 177–205.

—— (1985) 'Plantinga on the Reduction of Possibilist Discourse', in J. Tomberlin and P. van Inwagen (eds.), *Alvin Plantinga* (Dordrecht: D. Reidel), pp. 145–86.

—— (1994) 'Essence and Modality', in J. Tomberlin (ed.), *Philosophical Perspectives*, 8. *Logic and Language* (Atascadero: Ridgeview), pp. 1–16; repr. in P. Grim (ed.), *The Philosopher's Annual for 1994*, vol. 17 (Atascadero: Ridgeview).

—— (1995) 'The Logic of Essence', *Journal of Philosophical Logic* 24, pp. 241–73.

—— (2000) 'Semantics for the Logic of Essence', *Journal of Philosophical Logic* 29, pp. 543–84.

—— (2002) 'The Varieties of Necessity', in Gendler and Hawthorne (2002), pp. 253–82.

—— (2007a) *Semantic Relationism* (Oxford: Blackwell).

—— (2007b) 'Response to Alan Weir', *Dialectica* 61/1, pp. 117–25.

Fodor, J. A. (1987) *Psychosemantics* (Cambridge, Mass.: MIT Press).

Føllesdal, D. (2004) 'Quine on Modality', in R. Gibson (ed.), *The Cambridge Companion to Quine* (Cambridge: Cambridge University Press), pp. 200–13.

Forbes, G. (1985) *The Metaphysics of Modality* (Oxford: Clarendon).

Foster, J. (1976) 'Meaning and Truth Theory', in Evans and McDowell (1976), pp. 1–32.

Foster, J. and Robinson, H. (1985) (eds.), *Essays on Berkeley* (Oxford: Clarendon Press).

Frege, G. (1893) *Grundgesetze der Arithmetik*, vol. i (Jena: Hermann Pohle).

——(1904) 'What Is a Function?' in his *Collected Papers on Mathematics, Logic and Philosophy*, trans. M. Black, V. Dudman, P. Geach, H. Kaal, E.-H. W. Kluge, B. McGuinness, and R. H. Stoothoff (New York: Basil Blackwell, 1984).

——(1915) 'My Basic Logical Insights', trans. by P. Long and R. White, in M. Beaney (ed.), *The Frege Reader* (Oxford: Blackwell).

Fuhrmann, A. (1996) *An Essay on Contraction* (Chicago: University of Chicago Press).

——(1999) 'When Hyperpropositions Meet', *Journal of Philosophical Logic* 28, pp. 559–74.

Gendler, T. S., and Hawthorne, J. (2002) (eds.), *Conceivability and Possibility* (Oxford: Oxford University Press).

Gillies, A. S. (2004) 'New Foundations for Epistemic Change', *Synthese* 138/1, pp. 1–48.

Glymour, C. (1992) *Bayes or Bust?* (Cambridge, Mass.: MIT Press).

Goodman, N. (1947) 'The Problem of Counterfactual Conditionals', *Journal of Philosophy* 44, pp. 113–28.

Gregory, D. (2004) 'Imagining Possibilities', *Philosophy and Phenomenological Research* 69, pp. 327–48.

Hacking, I. (1967) 'Possibility', *Philosophical Review* 76, pp. 143–68.

Hale, B. (1989) 'Necessity, Caution, and Scepticism', *Proceedings of the Aristotelian Society*, suppl. vol. 63, pp. 175–202.

——(1999) 'On Some Arguments for the Necessity of Necessity', *Mind* 108/429, pp. 23–52.

——(2002) 'The Source of Necessity', in J. Tomberlin (ed.), *Philosophical Perspectives*, 16. *Language and Mind* (Oxford, Blackwell), pp. 299–319.

——(2003) 'Knowledge of Possibility and Necessity', *Proceedings of the Aristotelian Society* 103, pp. 1–20.

Hale, B., and Wright, C. (2003) *The Reason's Proper Study* (Oxford: Clarendon Press).

Hart, H. L. A. (1961) *The Concept of Law* (Oxford: Clarendon Press).

Hart, W. D. (1989) 'The Price of Possibility', *Pacific Philosophical Quarterly* 70, pp. 225–39.

Heck, R. G. Jr. (2000) 'Nonconceptual Content and the "Space of Reasons"', *Philosophical Review* 109, pp. 483–523.

Hill, C. (1997) 'Imaginability, Conceivability, Possibility and the Mind–Body Problem', *Philosophical Studies* 87, pp. 61–85.

——(2006) 'Modality, Modal Epistemology, and the Metaphysics of Consciousness', in S. Nichols (ed.), *The Architecture of the Imagination: New Essays on Pretense, Possibility, and Fiction* (Oxford: Oxford University Press), 205–36.

Hill, C., and McLaughlin, B. (1998) 'There Are Fewer Things in Reality than are Dreamt of in Chalmers's Philosophy', *Philosophy and Phenomenological Research* 59, pp. 445–54.

Hookway, C. (1988) *Quine: Language, Experience, and Reality* (Cambridge: Polity Press).

Howson, C., and Urbach, P. (1989) *Scientific Reasoning* (Chicago: Open Court Publishing).

Hudson, J. L. (1975) 'Logical Subtraction', *Analysis* 35, pp. 130–5.

Hughes, G., and Cresswell, M. (1996) *A New Introduction to Modal Logic* (London: Routledge).

Humberstone, I. L. (1981) 'From Worlds to Possibilities', *Journal of Philosophical Logic* 10, pp. 313–39.

—— (2000) 'Parts and Partitions', *Theoria* 66/1, pp. 41–82.

Hume, D. (1739) *A Treatise of Human Nature*, ed. L. Selby-Bigge, rev. P. H. Nidditch, 2nd edn. (Oxford: Clarendon Press, 1978).

Jackson, F. (1994) 'Metaphysics by Possible Cases', *The Monist* 77, pp. 93–110.

—— (1998) *From Metaphysics to Ethics: A Defence of Conceptual Analysis* (Oxford: Oxford University Press).

Jaeger, R. A. (1973) 'Action and Subtraction', *Philosophical Review* 82, pp. 320–9.

Jenkins, C. (2005) 'Realism and Independence', *American Philosophical Quarterly* 42/3, pp. 199–209.

—— (2008) *Grounding Concepts* (Oxford: Oxford University Press).

Johnston, M. (1992) 'How to Speak of the Colors', *Philosophical Studies* 68/3, pp. 221–63.

—— (2004) 'The Obscure Object of Hallucination', *Philosophical Studies* 120, pp. 113–83.

Kamp, H. (1973) 'Free Choice Permission', *Proceedings of the Aristotelian Society* 74, pp. 57–74.

—— (1979) 'Semantics versus Pragmatics', in F. Guenthner and S. J. Schmidt (eds.), *Formal Semantics and Pragmatics for Natural Languages* (Dordrecht: Reidel), pp. 255–88.

Kant, I. (1781) *Critique of Pure Reason*, trans. N. Kemp Smith (London: Macmillan, 1929 edn.).

Kaplan, D. (1970) 'S5 with Quantifiable Propositional Variables', *Journal of Symbolic Logic* 35, p. 355.

—— (1979) 'Dthat', in P. Cole (ed.), *Syntax and Semantics* (New York: Academic Press).

—— (1989) 'Demonstratives', in J. Almog, J. Perry, and H. Wettstein (eds.), *Themes from Kaplan* (New York: Oxford University Press).

—— (1996) *Decision Theory as Philosophy* (Cambridge: Cambridge University Press).

King, J. C. (2007) *The Nature and Structure of Content* (Oxford: Oxford University Press).

Kitcher, P. (1980) 'Apriority and Necessity', *Australasian Journal of Philosophy* 58, pp. 89–101.

Kment, B. (2006) 'Counterfactuals and the Analysis of Necessity', *Philosophical Perspectives* 20, pp. 237–302.

Kneale, W., and Kneale, M. (1962) *The Development of Logic* (Oxford: Clarendon Press).

Kratzer, A. (1981) 'The Notional Category of Modality', in H. Eikmeyer and H. Rieser (eds.), *Words, Worlds, and Contexts: New Approaches in Word Semantics* (Berlin: de Gruyter), pp. 38–74.

Kripke, S. A. (1963) 'Semantical Considerations on Modal Logic', *Acta Philosophica Fennica* 16, pp. 83–94.

—— (1972) *Naming and Necessity*, rev. and enlarged (1980) edn. (Oxford: Blackwell).

—— (1982) *Wittgenstein on Rules and Private Language* (Cambridge, Mass.: Harvard University Press).

Leeds, S. (2001) 'Possibility: Physical and Metaphysical', in Carl Gillett and Barry Loewer (eds.), *Physicalism and Its Discontents* (Cambridge: Cambridge University Press).

Lehrer, K. (1990) *Theory of Knowledge* (Boulder, Colo.: Westview Press).

Lepore, E., and Ludwig, K. (2005) *Meaning, Truth, Language, and Reality* (Oxford: Clarendon Press).

Levine, J. (1998) 'Conceivability and the Metaphysics of Mind', *Noûs* 32, pp. 449–80.

—— (2001) *Purple Haze* (Oxford: Oxford University Press).

Lewis, D. K. (1973a) 'Counterfactuals and Comparative Possibility', *Journal of Philosophical Logic* 2, pp. 418–46; repr. in Lewis (1986b), to which page numbers refer.

—— (1973b) *Counterfactuals* (Oxford: Blackwell).

—— (1979a) 'A Problem about Permission'; as reprinted in Lewis (2000), pp. 20–33.

—— (1979b) 'Attitudes *de dicto* and *de se*', *Philosophical Review* 88, pp. 513–43.

—— (1980) 'A Subjectivist Guide to Objective Chance', in Richard Jeffrey (ed.), *Studies in Inductive Logic and Probability II* (Berkeley and Los Angeles: University of California Press); repr. in Lewis (1986b).

—— (1983) 'New Work for a Theory of Universals', *Australasian Journal of Philosophy* 61, pp. 343–77.

—— (1986a) *Counterfactuals*, rev. edn. (Oxford: Blackwell).

—— (1986b) *On the Plurality of Worlds* (Oxford: Blackwell).

—— (1986c) *Philosophical Papers II* (Oxford: Oxford University Press).

—— (1988) 'Desire as Belief', *Mind* 97, pp. 323–32.

—— (1994a) 'Humean Supervenience Debugged', *Mind* 103, pp. 473–90.

—— (1994b) 'Reduction of Mind', in Sam Guttenplan (ed.), *A Companion to Philosophy of Mind* (Oxford: Blackwell Press).

—— (1999) 'Maudlin and Modal Mystery', in his *Papers in Metaphysics and Epistemology* (Cambridge: Cambridge University Press).

—— (2000) *Papers in Ethics and Social Philosophy* (Cambridge: Cambridge University Press).

—— (2009) 'Ramseyan Humility', in David Braddon-Mitchell and Robert Nola (eds.), *The Canberra Plan* (Cambridge, Mass.: MIT Press), pp. 203–22.

Linsky, B., and Zalta, E. (1994) 'In Defense of the Simplest Quantified Modal Logic', in J. Tomberlin (ed.), *Philosophical Perspectives*, 8. *Logic and Language* (Atascadero: Ridgeview), pp. 431–58.

———— (1996) 'In Defense of the Contingently Nonconcrete', *Philosophical Studies* 84, pp. 283–94.

Lipton, P. (2004) *Inference to the Best Explanation*, 2nd edn. (London: Routledge).

Loar, B. (1999) 'David Chalmers's *The Conscious Mind*', *Philosophy and Phenomenological Research* 59, pp. 465–72.

Locke, J. (1690) *Essay on the Nature of Human Understanding* (many edns.).

Lowe, E. J. (1998) *The Possibility of Metaphysics: Substance, Identity and Time* (Oxford: Oxford University Press).

MacBride, F. (2006) (ed.) *Identity and Modality* (Oxford: Oxford University Press).

McDowell, J. (1976) 'Truth-Conditions, Bivalence, and Verificationism', in Evans and McDowell (1976), pp. 42–66.

—— (1977) 'On the Sense and Reference of a Proper Name', *Mind* 86, pp. 159–85; repr. in M. Platts (ed.), *Reference, Truth, and Reality* (London: Routledge and Kegan

Paul, 1980), pp. 141–66; also in A. W. Moore (ed.), *Meaning and Reference* (Oxford: Clarendon Press, 1993), pp. 111–36.

MacFarlane, J. (2003) 'Epistemic Modalities and Relative Truth', MS, University of Berkeley.

—— (2005) 'Making Sense of Relative Truth', *Proceedings of the Aristotelian Society* 105/1, pp. 321–39.

—— (2008, MS) Epistemic Modals are Assessment-Sensitive <http://sophos.berkeley.edu/macfarlane/epistmod.pdf>.

—— (forthcoming) 'Epistemic Modals are Assessment-Sensitive', in Brian Weatherson and Andy Egan (eds.), *Epistemic Modality* (Oxford: Oxford University Press).

McFetridge, I. G. (1990a) 'Explicating "x knows a priori that p"', in McFetridge (1990c), pp. 213–32.

—— (1990b) 'Logical Necessity: Some Issues' in McFetridge (1990c), pp. 135–54.

—— (1990c) *Logical Necessity and Other Essays*, ed. J. Haldane and R. Scruton (London: Aristotelian Society Monograph Series, 11).

McGinn, C. (1989) 'Can We Solve the Mind–Body Problem?', *Mind* 98, pp. 349–66.

—— (2004) *Mindsight: Image, Dream, Meaning* (Cambridge, Mass.: Harvard University Press).

Mackie, J. L. (1977) *Ethics: Inventing Right and Wrong* (Harmondsworth: Penguin).

Martin, M. G. F. (2002) 'The Transparency of Experience', *Mind and Language* 17, pp. 376–425.

Maudlin, T. (1996) 'On the Impossibility of Lewis's Modal Realism', *Australasian Journal of Philosophy* 74, pp. 671–82.

Meltzoff, A. N., and Prinz, W. (2002) (eds.) *The Imitative Mind: Development, Evolution, and Brain Bases* (Cambridge: Cambridge University Press).

Menzies, P. (1998) 'Possibility and Conceivability: A Response-Dependent Account of their Connections', *European Review of Philosophy*, pp. 255–77.

Mill, J. S. (1891) A System of Logic, 8th edn. (London: Longmans).

Moore, G. E. (1912) *Ethics* (London: Williams & Norgate).

—— (1922) *Philosophical Studies* (London: Routledge and Kegan Paul).

—— (1962) *Commonplace Book 1919–1953* (London: George, Allen, and Unwin).

Nolan, D. (1997) 'Impossible Worlds: A Modest Approach', *Notre Dame Journal for Formal Logic* 38, pp. 535–72.

Noordhof, P. (2002) 'Imagining Objects and Imaginings Experiences', *Mind and Language* 17, pp. 426–55.

O'Leary-Hawthorne, J. (1996) 'The Epistemology of Possible Worlds: A Guided Tour', *Philosophical Studies* 84, pp. 183–202

Papineau, D. (2002) *Thinking about Consciousness* (Oxford: Oxford University Press).

Peacocke, C. A. B. (1978) 'Necessity and Truth Theories', *Journal of Philosophical Logic* 7, pp. 473–500.

—— (1985) 'Imagination, Experience, and Possibility: A Berkleian View Defended', in Foster and Robinson (1985), pp. 19–35.

—— (1999) *Being Known* (Oxford: Oxford University Press).

Pendlebury, M. (1986) 'Perceptual Representation', *Proceedings of the Aristotelian Society* 87, pp. 91–106.

Piaget, J. (1987), *Possibility and Necessity* (2 vols.), trans. H. Feider (Minneapolis: University of Minnesota Press) (originally published 1981, 1983).

Pitcher, G. (1971) *A Theory of Perception* (Princeton: Princeton University Press).

Plantinga, A. (1974) *The Nature of Necessity* (Oxford: Clarendon).

—— (1983) 'On Existentialism', *Philosophical Studies* 44, pp. 1–20; repr. in Plantinga *Essays in the Metaphysics of Modality* (Oxford: Oxford University Press, 2003), pp. 158–75.

—— (1985) 'Reply to Kit Fine', in Tomberlin and van Inwagen (1985).

—— (1987) 'Two Concepts of Modality: Modal Realism and Modal Reductionism', in J. Tomberlin (ed.), *Philosophical Perspectives*, 1. *Metaphysics* (Atascadero: Ridgeview Publishing Company).

Pollock, J. (1989) *How to Build a Person* (Cambridge, Mass.: MIT Press).

—— (1990) *Nomic Probability and the Foundations of Induction* (Oxford: Oxford University Press).

Priest, G. (2005) *Towards Non-Being: The Logic and Metaphysics of Intentionality* (Oxford: Oxford University Press).

Prior, A. N. (1957) *Time and Modality* (Oxford: Clarendon Press).

—— (1960) 'The Runabout Inference-Ticket', *Analysis* 21, pp. 38–9.

—— (1967) *Past, Present, and Future* (Oxford: Clarendon Press).

Prior, E., Pargetter, R., and Jackson, F. (1982), 'Three Theses About Dispositions', *American Philosophical Quarterly* 19, pp. 251–7.

Pryor, J. (2000) 'The Skeptic and the Dogmatist', *Noûs* 34, pp. 517–49.

Putnam, H. (1975) 'The Meaning of "Meaning"', in *Mind, Language and Reality* (Cambridge: Cambridge University Press).

—— (1990) 'Is Water Necessarily H$_2$O?', in *Realism with a Human Face* (Cambridge, Mass.: Harvard University Press).

Quine, W. V. O. (1951) 'Two Dogmas of Empiricism', *Philosophical Review* 60; repr. in his *From a Logical Point of View: Nine Logico-Philosophical Essays* (1953; Cambridge, Mass.: Harvard University Press, 1980), pp. 20–46.

—— (1953) 'Three Grades of Modal Involvement', in Quine, *The Ways of Paradox and Other Essays* (New York: Random House, 1966), 156–74.

—— (1961) *From a Logical Point of View*, 2nd edn. (Cambridge, Mass.: Harvard University Press).

—— (1976) *The Ways of Paradox and Other Essays*, rev. edn. (Cambridge, Mass.: Harvard University Press).

—— (1981) *Theories and Things* (Cambridge, Mass.: Harvard University Press).

—— (1982) *Methods of Logic*, 4th edn. (Cambridge, Mass.: Harvard University Press).

Raz, J. (1979), *The Authority of Law* (Oxford: Clarendon Press).

Restall, G. (1996) 'Truthmakers, Entailment and Necessity', *Australasian Journal of Philosophy* 74, pp. 331–40.

Robertson, T. (1998) 'Possibilities and the Arguments for Origin Essentialism', *Mind* 107, pp. 729–50.

Roeper, P., and Leblanc, H. (1999) *Probability Theory and Probability Logic* (Toronto, University of Toronto Press).

Rosen, G. (1990) 'Modal Fictionalism', *Mind* 99, pp. 327–54.

—— (2006) 'The Limits of Contingency', in MacBride (2006).

—— (forthcoming) 'The Limits of Contingency', in Fraser MacBride (ed.), *Being Committed* (Oxford: Oxford University Press).

—— (MS), 'Numbers and Reality'.

Rosen, G., and Smith, N. J. J. (2004) 'Worldly Indeterminacy: A Rough Guide', *Australasian Journal of Philosophy* (Special Issue in Honor of D. K. Lewis) 82, pp. 185–98.

Rosen, G., and Yablo, S. (MS), 'Solving the Caesar Problem—with Metaphysics'.

Ross, W. D. (1930) *The Right and the Good* (Oxford: Clarendon Press).

Rumfitt, I. (2001) 'Semantic Theory and Necessary Truth', *Synthèse* 126, pp. 283–324.

—— (2003) 'Contingent Existents', *Philosophy* 78, pp. 461–81.

—— (2008) 'Knowledge by Deduction', *Grazer Philosophische Studien* 77, pp. 39–62.

—— (2009) 'What Is Logic?', in Zsolt Novák and András Simonyi (eds.), *Truth, Reference, and Realism* (Budapest: Central European University Press).

Russell, B. (1918) 'The Philosophy of Logical Atomism', in his *Logic and Knowledge*, ed. R. C. Marsh (London: Allen & Unwin, 1956).

—— (1919) *Introduction to Mathematical Philosophy* (London: Allen and Unwin).

Salmon, N. (1981), *Reference and Essence* (Princeton: Princeton University Press).

—— (1987) 'How to Measure the Standard Metre', *Proceedings of the Aristotelian Society* 88, pp. 193–217.

—— (1989) 'The Logic of What Might Have Been', *Philosophical Review* 98, pp. 3–34.

—— (1993) 'This Side of Paradox', *Philosophical Topics* 21, pp. 187–97.

Sartre, J. -P. ([1940], 2004) *The Imaginary*, trans. Jonathan Webber (London: Routledge).

Sidelle, A. (1989) *Necessity, Essence and Individuation*, (Ithaca, N.Y.: Cornell University Press).

Sider, T. (2003) 'Reductive Theories of Modality', in Michael Loux and Dean Zimmerman (eds.), *The Oxford Handbook of Metaphysics* (Oxford: Oxford University Press), pp. 180–208.

Sidgwick, H. (1907) *Methods of Ethics*, 7th edn. (London: Macmillan and Co.).

Smiley, T. J. (1995) 'A Tale of Two Tortoises', *Mind* 104, pp. 725–36.

Soames, S. (2003) *Philosophical Analysis in the Twentieth Century*, 2 vols. (Princeton: Princeton University Press).

Spinoza, B. (1677) *The Ethics*, in J. Curley (ed. and tr.) *A Spinoza Reader* (Princeton: Princeton University Press, 1994).

Stalnaker, R. (1968) 'A Theory of Conditionals', in *American Philosophical Quarterly Monographs* 2 (Studies in Logical Theory), pp. 98–112.

—— (1976) 'Possible Worlds', *Noûs* 10, pp. 65–75; rev. version published as ch. 3 of Stalnaker, *Inquiry* (Cambridge, Mass.: MIT Press, 1984); and in Stalnaker, *Ways a World Might Be: Metaphysical and Anti-Metaphysical Essays* (Oxford: Oxford University Press, 2003).

—— (1979) 'Assertion', in Peter Cole (ed.), *Syntax and Semantics* (New York: Academic Press); repr. in Stalnaker (1999b).

—— (1991) 'The Problem of Logical Omniscience, I', *Synthese* 89, pp. 425–40.

—— (1999a) 'The Problem of Logical Omniscience, II', in Stalnaker (1999b).

—— (1999b) *Context and Content* (Oxford: Oxford University Press).

—— (2004) 'Assertion Revisited: On the Interpretation of Two-Dimensional Modal Semantics', *Philosophical Studies* 118, pp. 299–322.

Stanley, J. (2005) 'Fallibilism and Concessive Knowledge Attributions', *Analysis* 65/2, pp. 126–31.

Sturgeon, S. (2006) 'Modal Infallibilism and Basic Truth', in MacBride (2006).

—— (forthcoming) *Epistemic Norms* (Oxford: Oxford University Press).

Sutton, J. (2001) 'The Contingent Apriori and Implicit Knowledge', *Philosophy and Phenomenological Research* 63/2, pp. 251–77.

Teller, P. (1972) 'Epistemic Possibility', *Philosophia* 2, pp. 303–20.

Thomson, J., and Byrne, A. (2006) *Content and Modality: Themes from the Philosophy of Robert Stalnaker* (Oxford: Clarendon Press).

Tichý, P. (1983) 'Kripke on Necessity A Posteriori', *Philosophical Studies* 43, pp. 225–41.

Tomberlin, J., and van Inwagen, P. (1985) (eds.) *Alvin Plantinga* (Dordrecht: D. Reidel).

van Fraassen, B. (1980) *The Scientific Image* (Oxford: Clarendon).

Veltman, F. (1996) 'Defaults in Update Semantics', *Journal of Philosophical Logic* 25/3, pp. 221–61.

von Fintel, K. and Gillies, A. S. (2008) 'CIA Leaks', *Philosophical Review* 117/1, p. 77.

——— (MS) Epistemic Modality for Dummies <http://mit.edu/fintel/www/fintel-Gillies-ose2.Pdf>.

Wallace, J. (1978) 'Logical Form, Meaning, Translation', in M. Guethener-Reutter (ed.), *Meaning and Translation* (London: Duckworth).

Weatherson, B. (2001) 'Indicative and Subjunctive Conditionals', *Philosophical Quarterly* 51, pp. 200–16.

Weirich, P. (2005) *Realistic Decision Theory* (Oxford: Oxford University Press).

Wiggins, D. R. P. (1976) 'The De Re "Must": A Note on the Logical Form of Essentialist Claims', in Evans and McDowell (1976).

—— (1993) 'Putnam's Doctrine of Natural Kind Words and Frege's Doctrines of Sense, Reference, and Extension: Can They Cohere?', in A.W. Moore (ed.), *Meaning and Reference* (Oxford: Oxford University Press), pp. 192–207.

—— (2001) *Sameness and Substance Renewed* (Cambridge: Cambridge University Press).

—— (2003) 'Existence and Contingency: A Note', *Philosophy* 78, pp. 483–94.

Williamson, T. (1990a) 'Necessary Identity and Necessary Existence', in R. Haller and J. Brandl (eds.), *Wittgenstein—Towards a Re-evaluation: Proceedings of the 14th International Wittgenstein Symposium*, vol. i (Vienna: Holder–Pichler–Tempsky).

—— (1990b) *Identity and Discrimination* (Oxford: Blackwell).

—— (1998) 'Bare Possibilia', *Erkenntnis* 48/2–3, pp. 257–73.

—— (1999) 'Truthmakers and the Converse Barcan Formula', *Dialectica* 53, pp. 253–70.

—— (2000a) 'Existence and Contingency', *Proceedings of the Aristotelian Society* 100, pp. 117–39.

—— (2000b) *Knowledge and its Limits* (Oxford: Oxford University Press).

—— (2002) 'Necessary Existents', in A. O'Hear (ed.), *Logic, Thought, and Language* (Cambridge: Cambridge University Press), pp. 233–51.

—— (2005) 'Armchair Philosophy, Metaphysical Modality, and Counterfactual Thinking', *Proceedings of the Aristotelian Society* 105, pp. 1–23.

—— (2006a) 'Indicative Versus Subjunctive Conditionals, Congruential Versus Non-Hyperintensional Contexts', in E. Sosa and E. Villanueva (eds.), *Philosophical Issues* 16. *Philosophy of Language* (Oxford: Blackwell), pp. 310–33.

—— (2006b) 'Must Do Better', in P. Greenough and M. Lynch (eds.), *Truth and Realism* (Oxford: Oxford University Press).

—— (2007a) 'Philosophical Knowledge and Knowledge of Counterfactuals', in C. Beyer and A. Burri (eds.), *Grazer Philosophische Studien*, 74. *Philosophical Knowledge* (Amsterdam: Rodopi), pp. 89–123.

—— (2007b) *The Philosophy of Philosophy* (Oxford: Blackwell).

Wittgenstein, L. (1964) *Remarks on the Foundations of Mathematics*, trans. G. E. M. Anscombe (Oxford: Blackwell).

Wright, C. (1980) *Wittgenstein on the Foundations of Mathematics* (London: Duckworth).

—— (1983) *Frege's Conception of Numbers as Objects* (Aberdeen: Scotts Philosophical Monographs).

—— (1986) 'Inventing Logical Necessity', in J. Butterfield (ed.), *Language, Mind, and Logic* (Cambridge: Cambridge University Press), pp. 187–209.

—— (1989) 'Necessity, Caution, and Scepticism', *Proceedings of the Aristotelian Society*, suppl. vol. 63, pp. 203–38.

—— (1992) *Truth and Objectivity* (Cambridge, Mass.: Harvard University Press).

Yablo, S. (1993) 'Is Conceivability a Guide to Possibility?', *Philosophy and Phenomenological Research* 53, pp. 1–42.

—— (1999) 'Concepts and Consciousness', *Philosophy and Phenomenological Research* 59, pp. 455–63.

—— (2000) 'Textbook Kripkeanism and the Open Texture of Language', *Pacific Philosophical Quarterly* 81/1, pp. 98–122.

—— (2002) 'Coulda, Woulda, Shoulda', in Gendler and Hawthorne (2002).

Yablo, S. (2006) 'Non-Catastrophic Presupposition Failure', in Thomson and Byrne (2006), pp. 164–90.

Yalcin, S. (2007) 'Epistemic Modals', *Mind*, 116/464, pp. 983–1026.

Zimmermann, T. E. (2000) 'Free Choice Disjunction and Epistemic Possibility', *Natural Language Semantics*, 8/4, pp. 255–90.

# Index

Lightning Source UK Ltd.
Milton Keynes UK
UKOW050955181212

203795UK00001B/1/P